Tourism in Southeast Asia

Tourism in Southeast Asia

Challenges and New Directions

Edited by

Michael Hitchcock, Victor T. King and Michael Parnwell

University of Hawai'i Press
Honolulu

Published in North America by
University of Hawai'i Press
2840 Kolowalu Street
Honolulu, Hawai'i 96822
www.uhpress.hawaii.edu

First published in Europe by
NIAS Press
Nordic Institute of Asian Studies
Leifsgade 33
2300 Copenhagen S, Denmark

Library of Congress Cataloging-in-Publication Data

Tourism in Southeast Asia : challenges and new directions / edited by
Michael Hitchcock, Victor T. King, and Michael Parnwell.
    p. cm.
  Includes bibliographical references and index.
  ISBN 978-0-8248-3250-6 (hardcover : alk. paper) – ISBN 978-0-8248-
3299-5 (pbk. : alk. paper)
  1. Tourism–Southeast Asia. I. Hitchcock, Michael. II. King, Victor T. III.
Parnwell, Mike.
  G155.A743T685 2008
  338.4'79159--dc22
2008004001

Printed in Malaysia

Contents

Tables

Figures

Contributors

Kathleen Adams, PhD, is Professor of Anthropology in the Department of Anthropology at Loyola University, Chicago. Her research interests include inter-ethnic relations, nationalism, and conceptions of heritage, tourism and the arts. She has published extensively on issues of cultural tourism and heritage among the Toraja of Indonesia. She has also conducted research in Alor, Indonesia and San Juan Capistrano, Southern California.

Jonathan Bennett, PhD, completed his doctoral studies on tourism business development in Vietnam at the Centre for South-East Asian Studies, University of Hull. A fluent Vietnamese speaker, he spent a period with the British Council in Istanbul, and is presently teaching English in Hanoi.

Henning Borchers, MA, undertook research on Komodo National Park as part of his MA in Development Studies at the University of Auckland, New Zealand, and continued following up on developments in the park for some years thereafter. His research interests range from tourism and resource management to human rights and conflict. He currently works with Peace Brigades International in Indonesia.

Janet Cochrane, PhD, is Senior Research Fellow in the Tourism, Hospitality and Events School at Leeds Metropolitan University. She has extensive research experience in nature-based tourism in developing countries in Asia and Africa. She has worked as a consultant for WWF, UNEP, The Nature Conservancy, and Conservation International. She has published widely in the field of ecotourism in Indonesia.

Heidi Dahles, PhD, is Professor of Organizational Anthropology in the Department of Culture, Organization and Management at the Vrije Universiteit Amsterdam. Her research interests include the anthropology of tourism and small-scale entrepreneurship in Indonesia, as well as transnational business organization, particularly among the Southeast Asian Chinese. She has published widely in these fields and especially on tour guides, entrepreneurship and gender relations in Java and Bali.

Mark Hampton, PhD, is Senior Lecturer in Tourism Management at Kent Business School, University of Kent. His research interests are within the broad field of tourism and economic development in less developed countries, and specifically island and backpacker tourism. He has also undertaken research on the development of island states, coastal areas and small states, as well as the political economy of offshore financial centres and tax havens. He is widely known for his published work on backpacker and island tourism and on global finance and tax havens.

Joanna Hampton is an ecologist specializing in coastal and marine habitats. She has worked in both nature reserve management and environmental education. Most recently, amid a career break to care for a young family, she remains involved in environmental campaigning with local faith-based communities. She has experience in the UK, the Mediterranean and in Southeast Asia.

David Harrison, PhD, is Professor of Tourism, Culture and Development at London Metropolitan University. He has written extensively on tourism in developing societies, and has carried out research on tourism as a development tool in Southeast Asia, the Caribbean, Eastern Europe and Southern Africa.

Michael Hitchcock, DPhil, is Professor and Director in the International Institute for Culture, Tourism and Development at London Metropolitan University. His research interests include tourism, development, material culture and business culture. He has worked on research and development projects in Indonesia and Vietnam.

Victor King, PhD, is Professor of South East Asian Studies and Executive Director of the White Rose East Asia Centre (Leeds/Sheffield) at the Department of East Asian Studies in the University of Leeds. He has published widely in the field of Southeast Asian social and cultural anthropology, sociology and development, and has recently written a general sociology of Southeast Asia and co-authored an introduction to the modern anthropology of Southeast Asia.

Michael Parnwell, PhD, is Reader in South East Asian Geography in the Department of East Asian Studies at the University of Leeds. He has researched and published widely on a variety of aspects of the development process in Southeast Asia, including migration, rural industrialization, urbanization, deforestation, sustainable development, localism, social capital and Buddhism, and has undertaken primary field-work in Thailand, Malaysia, Indonesia and Vietnam, as well as China.

Michel Picard, PhD, is a Research Fellow at the French National Centre of Scientific Research (CNRS) and a member of the Centre for Southeast Asian Studies (*Centre Asie du Sud-Est*) in Paris. He has published widely in the field of tourism as well as of Balinese studies. He is currently working on the dialogic construction of a Balinese identity, focusing on the relationship between religion, tradition and culture.

I Nyoman Darma Putra, PhD, is a Postdoctoral Research Fellow at the University of Queensland and is a Lecturer in the Faculty of Letters at Udayana University, Bali. His research interests include tourism, the media and Indonesian literature. He has published widely on Indonesia, especially Bali.

Linda Richter, PhD, is Professor of Political Science at Kansas State University. Her research interests include public administration, public policy, tourism, gender and agrarian reform. She has undertaken research in the Philippines, Pakistan and India and is widely known for her published work on public policy in the Philippines and on the politics of tourism in Asia.

Steven Schipani is a senior adviser to the Lao National Tourism Administration who has lived and worked in the Lao PDR since 1999, focusing on the development of pro-poor tourism, protected area management and cultural heritage protection. He has worked extensively in the Greater Mekong Subregion as the Regional Ecotourism Adviser for the UNESCO Bangkok Office and as a consultant to the Asian Development Bank on tourism planning and development that benefits the poor.

Shinji Yamashita, PhD, is Professor of Cultural Anthropology at the University of Tokyo and has also been one time President of the Japanese Ethnological Society. He has undertaken detailed anthropological research on tourism in Indonesia, specifically among the Balinese and Toraja, and has published widely on the anthropology of tourism. He has also worked recently on tourism issues in Sabah, Malaysia, and has published on the history and development of Japanese anthropology.

Yuk Wah Chan, PhD, is Visiting Assistant Professor in the Department of Asian and International Studies at the City University of Hong Kong. She has recently undertaken anthropological research and completed her doctoral thesis on Chinese–Vietnamese relations in the borderlands of northern Vietnam and southern China. Her research interests include regional studies in mainland Southeast Asia, transnationalism, tourism, gender and development, as well as outbound Chinese tourists in Asia.

1

Introduction: 'Tourism in Southeast Asia' Revisited

Michael Hitchcock, Victor King and Michael Parnwell

Preamble

Since the publication of our co-edited *Tourism in South-East Asia* (1993) over a decade ago there has been a rapidly growing scholarly and popular interest in tourism activities and development within Southeast Asia and the wider Asia Pacific region. We consider that the time is ripe to take stock and evaluate what has been happening in tourism studies since the publication of our first book, and, as a necessary next step, begin to chart the future direction of research in the region. We began our excursion into the subject of Southeast Asian tourism in the early 1990s by remarking on the then boom in both foreign and domestic tourism, particularly in the newly industrializing capitalist countries of the region – Singapore, Malaysia, Indonesia, Thailand and the Philippines. There were also signs of increasing interest in the economic developmental potential of tourism in Cambodia, Laos, Vietnam and Myanmar (Burma). The reasons for this expanding tourist interest in the Far East were obvious: rising levels of affluence in the visitor source countries; the falling costs of international travel and its increasing availability; the more effective organization of tourism both domestically and internationally in terms of infrastructural support, packaging and promotion and the move towards regional promotional strategies in the ASEAN countries; the positive policy support given by governments to tourism development and its importance in national development plans; and the search on the part of tour companies and tourists for new, alternative, more exciting and exotic destinations away from the overcrowded, overdeveloped resorts of Europe and North America (Teo and Chang, 1998: 120).

At the time that we were in the process of producing the first general book on Southeast Asian tourism there was an urgent need to understand and analyse the dynamics of its development in the region using a combination of different disciplinary perspectives and to expand the store of case-study material and deploy it in comparative studies. Our edited volume was explicitly multidisciplinary and comparative in orientation and organization, drawing on the skills and expertise of historians, economists, political scientists, geographers, anthropologists and sociologists, as well as on empirical material from across the region. It focused on several key emerging themes at that time, the main ones among them being the changing conceptualizations of culture and ethnicity, given that one of the major foci of tourism interest in Southeast Asia has been cultural and ethnic tourism and the ways in which local communities are represented and portrayed (historically and in the current media, and in promotional and travel literature); the consequences of tourism for and the nature of its impacts on Southeast Asian economies, societies and cultures, particularly issues to do with whether or not tourism is having positive or negative developmental effects; the sustainability or otherwise of tourism activities, and the phenomena of alternative tourism, heritage tourism, ecotourism, educational tourism, and special interest tourism; and the policy and practical dimensions of tourism development. Finally, we emphasized the importance of addressing the main variables which bear upon the socio-economic, cultural and political effects of tourism, including changes through time, which require us to capture the dynamics of tourism development and attempt to address the limitations of snapshot, time-bounded studies; the character of the ethnic group, social class, community, or region involved in tourist activities; the kinds of tourism in operation and the ways in which they are organized; the scale of tourist activity, its duration, concentration or dispersal; the origins, character, socio-economic background and motivations of tourists; the ways in which destinations and populations are touristically portrayed; the nature of the interactions between 'hosts' and 'guests', though we recognized the problematical nature of these categories; the interrelationship between tourism and other processes of change, and the implications of the increasing 'touristification' of certain communities and their deliberate traditionalization or retraditionalization in the interests of responding to the needs and objectives of the tourist market.

In the early 1990s we also indicated which directions tourism research on Southeast Asia might profitably take in the next decade or so. We were very aware that our book was a first but important step in raising important conceptual issues and presenting more detailed empirical material on such matters as ecotourism and national parks, handicrafts and regional development, cultural tourism, performance, and sex tourism; above all we recognized the need to continue to gather much more detailed and reliable data on tourism activities (including statistical data on the economic benefits and costs of tourism). We referred to the importance of undertaking more detailed research on the images and symbolic representations of peoples, cultures and environments selected for tourism promotion, the ways in which these images change through time, and the similarities and differences in image production between the different media (postcards, posters, brochures, tourist guides, photographs, film, television and travel books) which portray Southeast Asian peoples and environments. In other words, we pressed for the need to consider multiple discourses on such issues as identity and cultural otherness. We drew attention to the need to examine in much more detail than hitherto local perspectives and views on tourism and leisure and the interrelationships between images held by 'hosts' on the one hand and 'guests' on the other, and the relations between the symbolic and the behavioural. In this regard we pointed to the crucial role of intermediaries in these encounters – the tour agents, guides and leaders who act as social and cultural brokers. We also emphasized the importance of studying the relations between national identity, political image-building and tourism and the contested nature of identity constructions at the national level, as well as locally-generated contestations and conflicts over tourism development and the images it creates. We pointed to the importance of more detailed research into the whole field of policy-making with regard to tourism (covering such areas as environmental conservation, spatial planning, employment regulations and infrastructural development) and the effectiveness or otherwise of its implementation. Finally, we recognized the value of comparative research and the importance of examining sets of related case studies in order to arrive at a more informed and sophisticated understanding of the different processes involved in and the consequences of different kinds of tourism evaluated from different disciplinary perspectives. In short, this was a very substantial agenda which we devised for ourselves and others in the further study of Southeast Asian tourism.

It is important to make a further introductory point, that *Tourism in South-East Asia*, although a regionally-based text, contained chapters by several researchers who have made major contributions to the more general study of tourism development. We should note that the analysis of the character and development of Southeast Asian tourism has provided the occasion and the inspiration for more general conceptual and theoretical contributions to the comparative understanding of tourism by such authors as Erik Cohen, Michel Picard, Linda Richter and Robert Wood. Nevertheless, we are re-producing a regionally framed text and we need briefly to contextualize this project.

The Regional Study of Tourism

At the outset it is worth noting that the term 'Southeast Asia' is a somewhat artificial, externally imposed catch-all, created primarily during World War II to impose some sort of conceptual, geographical and strategic order on a medley of territories lying to the east of India and south of China (see, for example, Chou and Houben, 2006; Kratoska et al., 2005; and also King, 2005). Divided by distinctive traditions and languages and colonial intervention from five European powers, and latterly the United States, it was not until the birth of the Association of Southeast Asian Nations (ASEAN) in 1967 and its subsequent expansion to include all the countries of the region, with the current exception of Timor Leste, that Southeast Asia assumed some kind of geo-political reality. In view of these observations it would thus not be unreasonable to ask what a regionally focused collection of chapters on tourism has to offer.

The first and most obvious point to make is that in terms of tourism there is an officially recognized tourism region known as 'Southeast Asia', which is technically a sub-region of the zone covered by the Pacific Asia Tourism Association (PATA). There is also the firm regional identity promoted by ASEAN, which, since the 1980s, has taken a keen interest in a co-ordinated approach to tourism development among its members. One of the regional body's most visible public faces is the ASEAN Tourism Forum, which comprises a trade fair and conference forum for businesspeople and public officials: academics rarely attend. ASEAN is also conscious of the need to widen its remit, and at the ASEAN Tourism Forum in Yogyakarta in 2002 there was talk of 'ASEAN Plus Two' – the 'plus two' being China and Korea, and the suggestion was that the region should co-operate with its neighbours to the north in the exchange of tourists and the co-promotion of tourism. The then President of Indonesia, Megawati Sukarnoputri, opened the forum and spoke about the regional need for co-operation on security, which was ironic given that the Bali bombers struck several months later (see Chapters 4 and 5 in this volume).

Aside from these political and economic considerations there are two sound cultural reasons for using the region as a subject of analysis. First, there are some major ethnolinguistic barriers, albeit porous ones, dividing Southeast Asia from India and China, as well as a less easily demarcated one with the Papuans and Polynesians (Hill and Hitchcock, 1996: 13–15). Polynesians and many coastal Papuans belong to the same language family as the peoples of the Philippines and Indonesia, but there appears to be a divide between these people and the upland Papuans. Likewise the border with China is not easily marked because, although the Chinese or Han speak dialects that belong to the Sino-Tibetan language family, so do the Burmese people of Myanmar and various upland groups elsewhere in Southeast Asia. Interestingly, the Vietnamese, who were subjected to a millennium of Chinese influence, speak an Austro-Asiatic language, one of the Southeast Asian language families, though their language is peppered with Chinese words. There are pockets of Southeast Asian people in India, but by and large the Indians belong to the Indo-European language family in the north with some upland Tibeto-Burman peoples and the Dravidian family in the south.

Second, the Southeast Asians may be divided internally between several language families – Austronesian, Austro-Asiatic, Tai-Kadai and Sino-Tibetan – but they share some important cultural features. Some have an ancient origin in the region's pre-classical period, but more particularly many communities were influenced by the religions of India at some point in their history, though the Vietnamese remain a special case due to their intense experience of Confucianism and Chinese culture more broadly (see, for example, Wolters, 1999; and King and Wilder, 2003: 1–24). Such is the debt to India in terms of literature, material culture and political organization that specialists often describe the civilizations of Southeast Asia as 'Indic'. Different societies were touched to different degrees by this Indic civilization with some being on the very fringes of it, but it creates important linkages between these disparate peoples. Islam later provided another strand, largely in the maritime parts of Southeast Asia, but this often occurred in societies that were already Indic. Since much of the debate about tourism has taken place in the cultural and ethnic domain, a regional focus can assist us in making internal comparisons that lead to substantiated generalizations. In the long term it will be useful to compare the various regional studies of tourism since much has been written about parts of the world from a regional perspective, notably Europe and the Caribbean.

There is also another good reason to look at tourism in a Southeast Asian area studies perspective, namely the role played by colonialism at the outset. In all but one case, the industry had colonial origins and, while similar observations can be made about India, tourism has yet to achieve the significance there that it has in Southeast Asia. In many respects the development of tourism in Southeast Asia has much in common with that of the Pacific and there is already sufficient literature on this (see, for example, Harrison, 2003) to facilitate meaningful comparison. Parallels can also be drawn with the colonial societies of East Africa and South Africa, especially when one compares how tourism developed with more general propositions such as Butler's oft cited 'tourism area cycle'. In Butler's scheme tourism often starts small-scale with international capital entering later in the cycle. In Southeast Asia international capital was often present at the outset with local businesses entering later, leading to a mix of local and international ownership (see Darma Putra and Hitchcock, 2007). We shall return to the theme of cross-national and region-wide comparative studies later in this introduction and in the concluding chapter (and see Chapter 2 in this volume).

Globalization and the Origins of Tourism in Southeast Asia

The subject of tourism in Southeast Asia is intimately caught up with the wider ongoing debates about the cultural and environmental ramifications of globalization. In common with the rest of the world Southeast Asia is being subjected to a variety of globalizing forces: the world capital markets, the international labour system, the interaction of nation states and the international military order, and tourism is part of these processes (see, for example, Teo, Chang and Ho, 2001a; 2001b). There is of course a huge literature on globalization which would be impossible to do justice to here, but it is worth reiterating the main points because they tell us something about the reasons behind the character and growth of tourism in this region.

The most generally agreed point is that globalization encompasses an intensification of social relations across the world, linking distant localities so that experiences in one location are affected by events taking place far away in another and vice versa (Giddens, 1991: 64). In relation to Southeast Asia this phenomenon was most vividly illustrated by the international outpouring of empathy and humanitarian aid in the wake of the tsunami of 26 December 2004. The immediacy of the suffering and the extensive news coverage helped to mobilise people to donate and to encourage others to do so. This empathy may be linked to the heightened awareness of people in the countries that supply Southeast Asia with most of their tourists: Europe, Japan and Australia. Many of those who were caught up in the experience had friends or family on holiday or working abroad in the countries affected by the tsunami, and thus were drawn intimately into the tragedy. Others had first hand experience of the places and people struck by the tsunami, and had a feeling of solidarity as a result of visiting the region. Thus it can be said that tourism is a part of globalization, albeit a rather special variant.

Different analysts trace the advent of globalization to two different periods, both of which have a connection with tourism. Wallerstein (1979), for example, traces it back to the sixteenth century when inter-continental trade, much of it seaborne, linked the far corners of the world for the first time. Anderson (1991 [1983]) has described the psychological impact on Europeans at this time of encounters with elaborate and ancient cultures, especially those of Asia that had developed independently of Europe, challenging the hitherto assumed centrality of Christian culture (but see Said, 1978). It is in these reactions that we can see the origins of some of the myths that later found their way into tourism, becoming virtually global tropes. One of the most prevailing of these is the exotic and beautiful maiden, whose association with Southeast Asia may be traced in part to an incident that allegedly took place in Bali when the Dutch captain, Cornelis de Houtman, landed there in 1597. His record of his visit to the island left an enduring impression on Western consciousness, partly because two of his crew vanished, entered the service of the local ruler and took Balinese wives (Hanna, 1976: 11–12). Western writers made much of this incident in the centuries that followed, though the real reason the men deserted remains unclear (Boon, 1977: 10; Picard, 1996: 18). Significantly, the myth of the 'beautiful women of Bali' makes a re-appearance in 1920 with the publication of Krause's photographs, which Picard describes as 'the first step in the touristic promotion of the island' (1996: 28). Variants of the myth live on and it is almost impossible to find an official piece of tourism promotional material that does not feature a beautiful young woman, the most famous of all being 'Singapore Girl', the young woman in her *sarung-kebaya* who graces Singapore Airlines promotional material. It would appear that a little bit of Bali pervades much of what the tourism industry refers to as Southeast Asia's 'tourism product'.

For other analysts, notably Giddens, the first truly global experience is linked to the twentieth century when technological advances from transport to information technology intensified our interconnectedness. If one looks at Southeast Asia, however, globalization might be regarded as a continuum, since the region was gradually drawn into the European orbit from the sixteenth century onwards, a process that was consolidated in the twentieth. It may be helpful to link the onset of truly global social relations in the region to the period of 'high colonialism', roughly 1870 to 1940 (Scholte, 1997: 24) when, significantly, tourism made its first appearance here. Improved communications and security in the areas under colonial control paved the way for up-market travellers, the forerunners of international tourism, and this is especially the case with British Burma, Malaya and the Straits Settlements and the Dutch East Indies (Indonesia).

What is striking about tourism in these territories is how quickly the industry was introduced once the area was pacified. Hardly had the Third Anglo–Burmese War been decided in favour of the British, with their famous flotilla of steamboats up the Irrawaddy in November 1885, than up-scale transport made an appearance. By 1890 The Irrawaddy Flotilla Company Limited had fitted out a steamer, known as the Beloo, with a saloon and other luxuries, to enable Prince Edward to travel up the same river used by the conquerors (Bird, 1897: 113). This is not so different from what happened in Bali where, after a protracted struggle lasting from 1847 to 1908, the Dutch quickly set about promoting tourism. This was a realistic strategy since Bali lacked lands suitable for colonial plantations and produced few export commodities. By 1914 Bali was being described as the 'Gem of the Lesser Sunda Isles' in official brochures, and when the first tourists came they were allowed to stay in the rest houses originally introduced to accommodate Dutch officials on their periodic rounds of the island (Picard, 1996: 23–24; and see Howe, 2005: 18–37). Similar arrangements were adopted in Malaya where early travellers passed through a network of personal contacts and introductions, sometimes staying at a Government House or Residency or taking out temporary membership of a club (Stockwell, 1993: 260). Such was the state of orderliness before World War I that J. H. M. Robson was able to advise motorists that, although carrying a revolver was not necessary, there was 'no harm' in carrying one. By the early 1920s he was pointing out that 'a revolver is not necessary' (1911: 212; 1923: 215).

With the exception of Thailand, which was never colonized, and whose tourism industry has different origins, the globalizing force of tourism was introduced via colonialism. The Philippines was under American control in this period, but it too facilitated the introduction of tourism and was an important stopping off point for cruise liners. It would appear that only Portuguese Timor was to be left out of the race. Interestingly, hardly had East Timor gained its independence when it decided to develop tourism: 'We have tremendous potential in tourism and fisheries, but one of the greatest challenges is to educate our people, to have a pool of trained people, and for that we are investing more than 30 per cent of our annual budget on education' (Jose Ramos Horta, 22.09.02, United Nations).

The Importance of Tourism in Southeast Asia

Tourism is a long established economic activity in Southeast Asia, dating back to the turn of the nineteenth and twentieth centuries, though mass tourism is a relatively recent phenomenon that largely began in the 1970s. The industry grew slowly for decades, but by the 1980s East Asia, Southeast Asia and the Pacific were experiencing the most rapid growth in regional tourism arrivals in the world, averaging 9.2 per cent per annum. Such was the success of the Visit Thailand Year campaign of 1987 that the various ASEAN government tourism boards agreed to combine forces to promote each successive country in turn, culminating in Visit ASEAN in 1992. By the early 1990s tourist arrivals were predicted to rise at 7 per cent annually until the end of the decade, as compared with a global average of around 4.5 per cent (World Tourism Organization, 1990). Such was the growth in countries like Singapore that local analysts worried that the labour requirements for the hotel, wholesale and retail sectors would not be met and would need to be replenished by migrant workers.

By the 1990s tourism had become one of Southeast Asia's foremost industries and, though the region was receiving less than 11 per cent of the world's international tourists, it was experiencing a boom (Hitchcock, King and Parnwell, 1993: 1). In Thailand it was the leading source of foreign exchange and in the Philippines it was the second largest industry. In Singapore tourism had become the third largest source of foreign exchange. Growth was fuelled by international arrivals, but there was also growing domestic demand. Despite this strong growth trajectory, there have been crises that have impacted on tourist arrivals. The First Gulf War of 1991, for example, coincided with Visit Indonesia Year and dented visitor numbers, though there was a recovery later in the year (Hitchcock, King and Parnwell, 1993: 1) and it looked for a while as if nothing could stop this upward trend.

The monetary crisis, however, that followed the flotation of the Thai baht on 2 July 1997 dashed the optimism of the region's tourism industry. Among the countries affected, Indonesia's economic malaise was the most acute, with a contraction of GDP of -15.9 per cent in 1998, as compared with Malaysia's -5.5 per cent (*The Economist*, 1998). The recession continued into 1999, though there was improvement towards the end of the year with growth in Indonesia rising to 0.5 per cent, and Malaysia bouncing back to 4.1 per cent (*The Economist*, 26.11.1999; see also Prideaux, 1999; Lew, 1999). The economic turmoil had an immediate and catastrophic effect on visitor arrivals, which in turn altered the character of the tourism industry in both countries. Generous supplies of capital had fuelled a hotel building boom and, though the effects were most visible in Jakarta, Kuala Lumpur and Surabaya, there had also been an upsurge in resort development. The downturn in demand had an impact on hotel trade worldwide as Asian owners responded to the crisis by selling assets in the peaking markets of North America, Europe and Australia. Political instability combined with the spread of the financial crisis to Korea and Japan – important sources of in-bound tourists – brought about a sharp decline in visitor arrivals.

Indonesia's international tourism receipts fell by 24 per cent in the first half of 1998, and continued to decline the following year (Travel and Tourism Intelligence, 1998: 90). Year-on-year growth in income from tourism in Thailand declined from 31.4 per cent in 1995 and 15 per cent in 1996 to just 0.6 per cent in 1997, even though tourist numbers increased from 7.19 to 7.22 million from 1996 to 1997, such was the impact of the devaluation of the baht and the level of discounting to maintain tourist flows (Mingsarn, 2002). So severe was the recession that Malaysian Airlines, along with Philippine Airways and Thai Airways, deferred deliveries of aircraft, mostly the long haul 747–400s and 777s that provide a lifeline for the region's tourism industry. Interestingly, the onset of the Asian financial crisis reinforced the need to see the region in its own terms since the cost-cutting led to job losses and the phasing out of expatriate employees, particularly senior managers earning dollar-based salaries, and the increasing localization of its management. Thailand resorted to crisis marketing to persuade visitors to return and to earn foreign currency to help alleviate the crisis (Henderson, 1999).

The financial crisis was the first of a series of shocks that Southeast Asia's tourism industry was to experience around the turn of the millennium. The first signs of stress became visible when terrorists linked to the Abu Sayyaf Group based in the southern Philippines attacked three exclusive tourist resorts in Malaysia and the Philippines: the Sipadan Resort on Pandanan Island in East Malaysia, where three tourists were taken hostage in September 2000; the Dos Palmas resort on the island of Palawan in the Philippines, where a group of 20 American and Filipino tourists and resort workers were kidnapped on May 27 2001, two Americans later being killed; and the Pearl Farm resort on Samal Island in the southern Philippines where two resort workers were killed, also in May 2001. These were followed by the terrorist attacks in New York and Washington on 11 September 2001, and the images of aircraft crashing into the World Trade Center led to a dramatic and devastating reduction in international travel which had significant implications for the tourism industry. People felt insecure about flying, although the greatest impact was felt in travel to and from the USA. The Bali bombings on 12 October 2002 and 1 October 2005 had a further impact on the image of Southeast Asia, and Indonesia in particular, as a 'safe' tourism destination (see chapters 4 and 5 in this volume).

Health epidemics have rarely had a pronounced impact on the tourism industry as a whole, principally because there have not been any which have had a global reach since the industrialization of tourism commenced in the 1970s. The SARS crisis in early 2003 was the first such epidemic (perhaps the first of many: the current avian influenza scare in Southeast Asia, particularly Vietnam and Thailand, whilst having a negligible impact on tourism at present, has the scope to become one of the world's most destructive epidemics), and its impact was momentarily severe. The World Travel and Tourism Council estimated that some three million people in the tourism industry lost their jobs in China, Hong Kong, Vietnam and Singapore (cited in McKercher and Chon, 2004: 716), and the Asian Development Bank anticipated a loss to the economies of China, Hong Kong, South Korea and Taiwan of $20 billion, and to Asia as a whole of $28 billion (cited in Mason et al., 2005: 14). SARS cost Asia's tourism industry about $11 billion during April and May 2003 (*China Daily*, 15.7.2003). Singapore lost 74 per cent of its tourism business during the peak of the SARS crisis in late April 2003, and passenger traffic through Changi Airport halved (Henderson and Ng, 2004: 413). Hotel occupancy rates in the second quarter of 2003 were around 21 per cent, compared with a seasonal norm of 75 per cent (Henderson and Ng, 2004: 414). Even countries which were only very lightly affected by the SARS outbreak were severely impacted, such as Thailand whose tourism business fell by 70 per cent (Henderson and Ng, 2004: 414), and Malaysia and Indonesia which recorded 34.6 per cent and 15.6 per cent year-on-year declines respectively in April 2003 (Australian Tourism Export Council, 2003). International tourist arrivals in the Asia–Pacific region as a whole fell by 6.6 million in the first five months of 2003.

According to McKercher and Chon (2004: 717) and Mason et al. (2005: 15), the tourism industry became falsely drawn into the crisis by sensationalist and alarmist media reports that attributed the spread of the disease to the oscillatory movements of international tourist vectors. The media view, in turn, was informed by a travel advisory from the World Health Organization (WHO, 2003) which, in retrospect, over-egged the cake in terms of its view on the contagiousness of the disease. Travel bans and quarantine periods were imposed on would-be tourists travelling from SARS-affected countries, and a whiff of hysteria swept across the region.

As already mentioned, the massive earthquake and tsunami that inundated coastal zones in the Indian Ocean on 26 December 2004 had a quite literally devastating impact on the region's tourism industry. Although Indonesia was most severely affected by the tsunami in terms of loss of life and damage to coastal communities, Aceh Province was not an important area for tourism and thus the country's tourism sector was not particularly badly affected by people cancelling holidays or choosing alternative destinations. It was noted (WTO, 2005) that, in contrast to the SARS scare, 'the tsunami did not insert a generalised uncertainty in the markets, undermining travel confidence. Travellers [understood] that the tsunami was a unique one-time event', and thus they were not scared away in large numbers: they did not refrain from travel, but instead found alternative destinations in the same country or region. Nonetheless, tourist arrivals in Bali dropped off dramatically in January 2005, falling 39.7 per cent compared with the same month the previous year, having just increased by 33.3 per cent year-on-year in December 2004 as the industry consolidated its recovery after the SARS scare and the Bali bombing (WTO, 2005).

Meanwhile, although Thailand was far less severely affected by the tsunami, its tourism sector in the vicinity of the Andaman Sea was damaged by this natural disaster. Tourist arrivals in Thailand as a whole fell by 18 per cent year-on-year in January 2005, wiping out the 18 per cent growth it had attained between 2003 and 2004 (WTO, 2005). This was expected to translate into a reduction of $1.2 billion in the contribution of tourism to GDP, and the loss of 94,780 jobs. In Phuket, hotel occupancy rates in the early part of 2005 were below 20 per cent, when they are normally above 80 per cent during what is the peak visitor season. The absence of tourists was referred to as the 'second wave'. The tsunami also led to a wave of sympathy and solidarity, but created a dilemma in tourists' minds whether to stay away while local communities grieved for their lost ones, or to return in order to help speed up the recovery process. A year or so on it would appear that much of the tourist infrastructure on Phuket has been fully rehabilitated and tourist flows are more or less back to normal levels. A much less optimistic picture emerges from the more remote island resorts, such as Khao Lak.

Putting all of the above shocks and disasters into relative perspective, the World Travel and Tourism Council (2005a) calculated, in its travel and tourism forecast for 2005, that the impact of the 9/11 terrorist attack in the USA was 37.5 times larger in monetary terms than the tsunami, and 2.8 times greater in terms of employment. The impact of SARS in Hong Kong equalled 40 per cent of the impact of the tsunami in monetary terms, and 10 per cent in terms of employment. The Bali bombing accounted for 20 per cent of the tsunami impact in monetary terms, but was 1.8 times larger in terms of the impact on employment.

Tourism eventually recovered from all of the above shocks and disasters, often remarkably quickly. Indeed, the prognoses for an industry that remains integral to Southeast Asia's economic health are very strong indeed. According to the World Travel and Tourism Council (2005a), travel and tourism is expected to contribute $43.2 billion to the region's GDP and be directly responsible for 6.96 million jobs in 2005, rising to $88.3 billion and 8.5 million jobs (2.8 per cent of total employment) by 2015. Demand was expected to have increased by 6.3 per cent in 2005, and by an average of 6.2 per cent per annum in real terms between 2006 and 2015 (World Travel and Tourism Council, 2005a).

It is not just Southeast Asia that is expected to experience strong tourist demand, but Asia in general, and the annual growth predictions between 1995 and 2020 are estimated at 6.2 per cent (South Asia) and 6.5 per cent (East Asia/Pacific) by the World Travel and Tourism Council (2005b). The market share of East Asia and the Pacific is expected to rise from 14.4 per cent in 1995 to 25.4 per cent in 2020. South Asia's share is more modest at a 0.7 per cent in 1995 and 1.2 per cent in 2020. This surge in visitors has already pushed China ahead of Italy in the top ten tourism destinations and if the current trajectory continues China will soon surge past the USA to take the third position behind France and Spain. China may dwarf the countries of Southeast Asia, but despite the tough competition the region contains very determined and well organized tourism authorities. Thailand, for example, has long been in the top twenty and has every intention of edging past some of the less successful Europeans to make it into the top ten.

Contributions to the Study of Southeast Asian Tourism Post-1993

A New Direction?

Having provided some introductory empirical material and some specific remarks on the importance of tourism in Southeast Asia, its scale and character, on regional perspectives in the study of tourism, and on the course of its historical development, we now turn to a commentary on some of the important work that has been undertaken since the publication of our *Tourism in South-East Asia* to determine whether or not our anticipated research agenda or elements of it have been adopted and to address some of the new, unanticipated research themes which have emerged recently. Our consideration of emerging research themes and the agenda for future research will be taken up again in our concluding chapter.

First, we shall need to draw attention to some of the more general contributions to the study of Southeast Asian, and in certain cases wider Asian or Pacific Asian, tourism. More specific country- and disciplinary-based studies and those which pursue a particular theme in the study of Southeast Asian tourism will be addressed in the later chapters in this book. We start with K. S. Chon's *Tourism in Southeast Asia: A New Direction* (2000) because its title suggests precisely that it is addressing new issues and material on tourism in the region and charts a way forward in tourism research, and that it might take forward the agenda which we had set out in the early 1990s. Unfortunately the book does not live up to its title. Certainly there is new empirical material on offer, but very little that suggests that Chon and his contributors are treading new conceptual ground or that they embrace our proposed multidisciplinary and comparative perspectives. It is in effect a book for tourism planners, or perhaps more accurately hospitality industry planners. Most of the contributors are involved in lecturing and training in tourism administration, and recreational, leisure and transport studies, and, as the editor states, in his preface, the 'new direction' is for tourism development, marketing and management (Chon, 2000: xiii).

The text presents relatively broad, sometimes country-based and empirical overviews of major areas of tourism development, policy, marketing, potential and constraints, organization and infrastructure in the region, and discusses in a relatively straightforward way the concerns of managers of tourism: sustainability, conservation, preservation, manageable scale and local participation through such activities as ecotourism, including coastal tourism; cross-border tourism planning through regional associations and sub-regional growth triangles and the obstacles to these initiatives; the management of crises which impact upon tourism and the problems of addressing vulnerability and risk; simple impact analyses of tourism in terms of benefits and costs or advantages and disadvantages; flows of tourists from source to destination countries, specifically from Australia to the ASEAN countries; the growth and development of the cruise line industry. Although lip-service is paid to multidisciplinary perspectives, the absence of any real engagement with conceptual and analytical issues makes it difficult to address the question of the advantages and disadvantages of multidisciplinarity, although the book makes the claim that it does adopt a multidisciplinary approach and that it fills a major gap because there is very little published on the area. We would challenge these claims, although we would concur that less attention was paid to the specifically management and planning dimensions of tourism development in the 1990s (and see Bhopal and Hitchcock, 2002).

Tourism and Ethnicity: The Construction of Identity and Culture

A theoretically exciting and important volume is Michel Picard's and Robert Wood's *Tourism, Ethnicity and the State in Asian and Pacific Societies* (1997). Both Picard and Wood were contributors to our 1993 book and Picard also reappears in our current revisitation. Of the eight chapters of their book the majority address Southeast Asian material and issues: Leong's study of ethnic tourism in Singapore; Kahn's piece on culturalization processes in contemporary Malaysia with specific reference to George Town, Penang; Michaud's chapter on cultural resistance and 'hill-tribe trekking' tourism among the Hmong of northern Thailand; Adams's examination of Indonesian national tourism policy and its effects on ethnic and cultural relations among the Toraja of Sulawesi; Picard's ongoing work on Balinese identity in the context of nation-building and the creation of regional cultures in Indonesia. All but one of the contributors are anthropologists and sociologists.

Picard's and Wood's collection concentrates on a theme which has become a major preoccupation in tourism studies during the past decade and which surfaced in our 1993 book and continues to loom large in our current volume. This is the issue of 'representation' or 'identity', or more precisely the politics of identity construction and transformation, the role of the state and national tourism development policies in cultural and ethnic processes, and the actions and reactions of local communities to these. The editors head their Preface with an appropriate though brief quotation from Marie-Francoise Lanfant, one of the doyennes of tourism studies, that 'the theme of identity is omnipresent within discourse about tourism' (1995b: 30). It is useful for our purposes to provide her elaboration of this statement, with which we concur, to reinforce the overwhelming importance of this focus in tourism policy, practice and research. She explains more fully that identity 'figures in the discourse of the international organizations which have been preaching the development of tourism; in that of the marketing people who have fashioned the product; in that of the states which have orchestrated promotional campaigns on behalf of tourism in their own countries; and in that of regions which have aspired to assume their proper place in tourism development. It is a theme which is dear to the hearts of those who work in the planning of tourism; and it is discovered equally in the writing of numerous sociologists and anthropologists. Identity is on the lips even of the tourists themselves' (Picard and Wood, 1997: 30–31).

The main focus of Picard's and Wood's volume is to establish or at least reaffirm the importance of the relationships between tourism and identity, and indeed to propose that 'tourism provides a way of understanding what has happened to ethnicity' (1997: viii). More specifically the editors are concerned with the ways in which identities have been commoditized and objectified, and even more specifically the ways in which the state or state policies and resources, which quite naturally are preoccupied with the national or supra-local dimension of identity and representation as well as with national responses to the forces of globalization, interact with or more accurately contest and challenge local level identities. The salience of these issues is particularly compelling in Asia and the Pacific because of the considerable ethnic diversity and the fluidity of identities there and the fact that, for political elites, diversity and indeed cultural otherness and difference, which offer the major attractions for tourists and have to be addressed in tourism development policies, present problems when the state's interests are also centred on national integration, unity, homogeneity and boundedness.

The two demands of diversity and unity, and of difference and homogeneity, in the arena of ethnic and cultural politics pull in opposite directions, and it is the exploration of this tension or contradiction, and of the ways in which it plays out, which is of considerable interest in tourism studies. Clearly state action can shape, sanction, objectify, define, marginalize and organize constituent ethnicities, and it does this not merely to promote tourism but also to press forward the more general state project. Nevertheless, at the same time, local responses to these constraints may not only express themselves in forms of resistance but they may also take advantage of opportunities presented in the promotion of their culture for tourism purposes. In other words, local communities work within the spaces which state-directed initiatives have failed to fill, as well as within those generated by processes of globalization, over which, in turn, the state may only have a loose hold. Much of this discussion demonstrates just how fluid identities are, and how significant such interventions as tourism can be in changing representations and images in a globalizing, interconnected, constantly interacting world.

In the introductory chapter of *Tourism, Ethnicity and the State* Robert Wood examines the implications or consequences of state action for ethnic identity formation and change, and, in turn, the importance of these cultural processes for political elites and the state. Just as Michel Picard, in his enormously important work on tourism and the Balinese, has argued for the internalization of tourism in Balinese culture and its 'touristification' (see, in particular, 1993; 1995; 1996), so that tourism is no longer seen as an external force impacting on the Balinese, Wood argues rather more generally for the increasing interpenetration of tourism and ethnicity (and see Howe, 2005). He proposes that 'tourism has to be seen as one element of the global phenomenon of ethnicity, not something appended to it', and perhaps most importantly tourism itself both comprises and provides an arena for inter- and indeed intra-ethnic relations (Wood, 1997: 4). In this connection, we are having to confront the growing phenomenon, of which Bali is perhaps the paradigm, of 'touristic cultures' and of the ways in which tourism and its demands and interests become incorporated into local definitions and expressions of ethnicity and into claims for cultural authenticity. Much of the discussion on identity is also bound up with the problematical notion of authenticity, and whether or not one's identity is genuine and can be demonstrated by recourse to tradition, history and the legitimation of others. In addition, Wood points to the open-endedness and unpredictability of the interaction between, in Robertson's words, 'people and the state' (1984) in that 'the state's political interest in tourism is potentially fraught with contradictions and unintended consequences' (Wood, 1997: 6). There are also obviously variations in the degree and kind of involvement of political elites in issues of ethnicity so that in some cases 'ethnic labels, ethnic cultural display, and tourist access are all tightly regulated by the state' and there is an overt public definition and official sanctioning of specific ethnic categorizations, whilst in others 'state intervention is fairly minimal and tends to be overshadowed by market dynamics' (Wood, 1997: 11).

In our 1993 volume Wood had already addressed the issue of the construction and reconstruction of tradition, and by implication ethnicity (1993: 48–70). He returns to this theme in the later book and re-emphasizes the point that 'ethnic identity is not something fixed and bequeathed from the past, but rather is something constantly reinvented – or reimagined, if we adopt Benedict Anderson's felicitous term – symbolically constructed, and often contested' (Wood, 1997: 18; and see Picard, 1995: 44–47). This entails not only local, national and tourist preoccupations with cultural boundary definition and, on occasion, boundary crossing, but also with the cultural composition of ethnic identity and its objectification in discourse, performance and display (or, more popularly in the tourism literature, 'staging'). This focus on cultural production and display also serves to generate, as Picard has argued in the case of the Balinese, an increasing consciousness or realization among local communities involved in tourism encounters of the importance of their culture as a resource. The acceptance of the fluidity and variability of culture and ethnicity also entails an examination of the multiple discourses involved in identity construction and cultural change and the often competing and conflicting modes of representation involved. These interrelated concerns, so ably captured by Wood in his discussion of ethnicity and tourism, surface with predictable regularity in other publications on tourism in the Asian region. They are also summarized in a very direct and apt way by Grant Evans, who, with reference to Balinese material, proposes that 'what looks like the persistence of "tradition" in the face of a massive tourist onslaught is in reality a transformed culture' (Evans, 1993: 373). In addition Hobart, Ramseyer and Leemann point to the dangers inherent in the assumption, at least with regard to Bali, that 'tourism impinges upon a static, receptive, closed society and culture, and is the most important trigger (although not the only reason) for change, which is judged to be negative, above all in the cultural sphere' (Hobart et al., 2001: 216; and see Howe, 2005).

Another edited volume which appeared at the same time as that of Picard and Wood, and which was also primarily directed to anthropological concerns, addresses this theme of cultural production and ethnic identity. Shinji Yamashita's, Kadir H. Din's and J. S. Eades's book *Tourism and Cultural Development in Asia and Oceania* (1997) considers how 'local cultures develop during the dynamic process of making use of tourism to re-define their own identities'. The examination of the relationships between tourism and culture, which the editors consider to be 'an extremely challenging field of study within the anthropology of culture' (Yamashita et al., 1997: 13), again requires the various contributors to come to terms with such processes as commoditization, deterritorialization, fragmentation, packaging, hybridization, invention and recreation. These processes might, in turn, be embraced by Lanfant's notion of 'global integration' in that 'those people who previously remained behind their frontiers are now invited to consider themselves part of great multi-cultural units' (1995a: 4). Again, as with the volume by Picard and Wood, the scope of the volume goes beyond Southeast Asia, and only five of the eleven chapters were focused primarily or exclusively on the region: they included Shinji Yamashita's analysis of the manipulation, re-making, staging and consumption of ethnic tradition in the case of the Toraja of Sulawesi and with reference to a central tourist attraction, the dramatic Torajan funeral rituals as well as Kadir Din's on the complex interrelationships between tourism and cultural development in Malaysia.

The editors also give us an important reminder, as others have before them (see, for example, Smith, 1989c: 1–17), that we must beware of imputing too much to tourism in our examination of social and cultural change because it is 'just one of the ways in which the contemporary world system brings about change in the societies within it' (Yamashita, 1997: 15). In addition, there are changes in identities and the creation of new identities 'which emerge naturally from the working of societies' (Lanfant, 1995: 4).

The themes of social and cultural change and tourism and identity are also pursued in Yamashita's recent sole-authored compilation of material on *Bali and Beyond*, in which he explores not only Balinese tourism, but also tourism-related changes and issues in Sulawesi, New Guinea and Japan (2003a). Again the book reinforces the significant contribution which anthropology has made to the study of tourism. *Bali and Beyond* raises the immediate question 'Where would the anthropology of tourism, let alone the study of South-East Asian tourism, be without Bali?' Indeed where would Balinese culture be without tourism, given that tourism has provided the main impetus for its invention, transformation and support? Ever since the publication of Gregor Krause's *Insel Bali* in 1920, with its extraordinarily seductive photographs of beautiful bare-breasted women in the 'last paradise' and its celebration of the more exotic and unusual aspects of Balinese culture, and then Miguel Covarrubias's popular and enticing description of culture and landscapes in the *Island of Bali* which appeared in 1937, foreign scholars have been entranced by Bali. During the inter-war years the Dutch and various foreign visitors and sojourners, particularly the talented German artist and aesthete, Walter Spies, helped to create the image of Bali as a rural idyll. Hitchcock's and Norris's book (1995) on the photographic archive of Walter Spies and Beryl de Zoete demonstrates both in the narrative and visually how Spies in particular became the 'impresario for cultural tourism', played a role in the modification and transformation of Balinese culture, art and performance, and then presented these images, in what he saw as a more comprehensible form, to a non-Asian audience. Then came scholars and researchers, including 'the newly wed anthropologists Margaret Mead and Gregory Bateson', who contributed to the presentation of a traditional image of Bali and lent scholarly authority to it as a 'living' or an 'imaginary museum' (Hitchcock and Norris, 1995: 4).

Yamashita studied the relationships between the Balinese and tourism between 1988 and 1996, and provides us with a succinct and thoughtful description and analysis of the development and character of Bali's 'touristic culture' and a more general evaluation of the relevant anthropological literature. His findings complement very well the work of Michel Picard, as do those of Howe (2005). What is especially valuable about the book is that it presents for the first time in English translation Yamashita's important text, which was originally published in Japanese in 1999, and which in turn comprised a collection of edited papers previously published from 1992 to 1998. Yamashita also makes frequent reference to the work of other Japanese scholars, and, for those of us who do not read Japanese, the consideration of Japanese perspectives on culture, tourism and Bali is particularly welcome. Yamashita also provides a Japanese dimension to Balinese tourism, specifically in his consideration of the encounter of Japanese tourists with Bali and the experiences of young Japanese 'brides heading for the Island of the Gods'. Yamashita also pursues the themes of Japanese tourism in, and perspectives on, Southeast Asia in a later chapter in our book (and see Mackie, 1992).

However, Yamashita's book is not only concerned with Bali, although it is given the most attention; the 'beyond' of the title refers to Torajaland in Central Sulawesi (where Yamashita conducted field research in 1976–1978 and 1983–1986), the Sepik River of Papua New Guinea and Tino in northern Japan. Yamashita skilfully uses comparative ethnography to reinforce certain observations about the relationship between culture and tourism. His central analytical ideas are not new ones and are drawn from the concepts of 'invention of tradition' and the contested and constructed character of culture – themes which have already surfaced in other research on the region in the 1990s and which we engaged with in the early 1990s. In Bali what appears to be 'traditional' and what is claimed as 'traditional' by the local people is in fact a recent creation, focused increasingly on Hindu doctrine and practice and its standardization. Balinese culture is being continuously created and recreated through artistic training in such areas as dance and performance and in cultural competitions in the context of Indonesian government policy directed to the construction of a national culture. The focus then is on image creation and pastiche, the relations between image and reality, the 'staging' of culture, and cultural manipulation, construction and consumption. The context of this process is that of globalization in which cultures are deterritorialized, translocalized, hybridized and essentialized. To capture this process of cultural production and transformation Yamashita coins the term 'narratives of emergence'. In other words he counters notions of cultural loss, the pollution, devaluation and undermining of pure or authentic traditional cultures, as well as perspectives which argue for homogenization, Disneyfication and McDonaldization. Instead he proposes that culture is dynamic and 'emerging'. In response to tourism development and the demands of cultural tourism, hosts, whether in Bali or beyond, invent, manipulate and stage tradition and become conscious of their culture as 'capital', and as a resource which can be deployed in the arena of the politics of identity.

Importantly, Yamashita places tourism at the heart of the study of culture and cultural change and demonstrates through a range of comparative studies that no modern anthropology can ignore tourism and its effects. He echoes Lanfant's position, but from a rather different perspective that '[t]ourism and anthropology are difficult to dissociate' (1995a: 21). Yamashita also captures the spirit and intention of the book when he concludes that '[t]ourism, rather than being an eccentric object of study for anthropologists is, on the contrary, essential if anthropologists are to restructure the objects of their research' (2003a: 151). And, one might add, resolve 'their own problem of identity' in that 'the boundaries between anthropology and tourism have become clouded' (Lanfant, 1995a: 21).

In this connection a major question which Crick raises elsewhere is 'What is the difference between an ethnologist and a tourist' when '[a]nthropologists and tourists are travellers and collectors – both literally and metaphorically – in the space of the "other"?' (1995: 207; and see Evans, 1993: 369–371). But whilst Crick tends to merge anthropologist and tourist, Bruner, in the same volume, prefers to see them as distant relatives (1995: 232–239). This theme re-emerges in King's chapter on anthropology and tourism (Chapter 2 in this volume), and although the dilemma is acute in anthropology it is by no means confined to it, and it raises the more general issue of the relationship between Western social scientists who study 'others' and their tourist counterparts who certainly visit and sporadically also study 'others'.

Finally, we should also draw attention to the special issue of *Anthropologie et Sociétés* (2001) edited by Jean Michaud and Michel Picard which focuses in part on Southeast Asian tourism and, from an anthropological perspective, again addresses the preoccupying issues of the representation, constitution and transformation of ethnic identities in the context of 'touristic transactions' (for more detail see Chapter 2). In their introductory remarks Picard and Michaud emphasize and reaffirm the importance of the phenomenon of tourism as a legitimate research focus within anthropological discourse (2001: 5–13). The centrality of the theme of representation and identity presented in this special issue is one to which we return later in our volume.

From the Specific to the General

No review of the study of tourism in Southeast Asia would be complete without some reference to the work of Erik Cohen, who also contributed to our 1993 book. His compilation of papers on Thai tourism (2001a) which he published over almost two decades from the early 1980s – although he had been publishing more generally on the sociology of tourism during the 1970s – deserves an appreciative comment. Cohen provides us with an overview of the work which he had undertaken first on hill tribe tourism and trekking tours in northern Thailand from the late 1970s, then on vacationing, beach-resort tourism on the islands of southern Thailand, particularly Phuket and Koh Samui, from 1979, and finally on sex tourism in Bangkok from the early 1980s. Although his gaze is fixed firmly on Thailand, he does make some especially appropriate remarks which have relevance for the processes of tourism development in Southeast Asia more generally, and it is worth summarizing these here in our overview of the literature. Cohen presents Thai tourism in terms of a duality and opposition: 'exoticism' and 'eroticism', or more popularly 'temples' and 'brothels' (2000b: 2–3). From the 1970s Cohen identifies four major themes in the development and transformation of Thai tourism, which provide a convenient means of comparing and contrasting the experiences of other Southeast Asian countries. These are 'massification' or the rapid expansion of both international and domestic tourism and the accompanying infrastructure with the end result that an initial personalized tourism becomes more depersonalized and commercialized; 'expansion' with the move from a centralized tourist industry concentrated in greater Bangkok to a more dispersed industry linked to the north with Chiang Mai and to the south with Phuket, and, on the eastern seaboard, Pattaya; 'heterogeneization' with an increase in the diversity of overseas tourists and a diversification of the facilities and amenities to cater for them; and 'regionalization' with the increasing cross-border linkages between Thailand and the neighbouring countries of Myanmar, southern China, Cambodia, Laos and Vietnam. We believe that Cohen's remarks and observations about these developmental processes do have a more general resonance in Southeast Asia, despite their particular relevance to tourism in Thailand, and can also be applied to rapidly developing tourist destinations like Malaysia and Indonesia.

With regard to his three major areas of research Cohen addresses several of the themes which we have already raised in this introduction: the whole issue of commoditization and cultural authenticity in relation to the increase in tourist traffic to the hill tribe areas and in the integration of minority groups into mainstream, national Thai society; the commercialization of the beach resorts and the diversification and specialization of their amenities; and the changes in sex tourism with the 'growing awareness and fear of AIDS' (Cohen, 2000b: 21), and a move from the 'playful, ambiguous and open-ended character' of pre-AIDS prostitution to a more 'guarded', risk-averse, 'more business-like' enterprise (Cohen, 2000b: 22). Overall Cohen relates the growth of tourism to a more general process of economic development. He also concludes that 'the impact of tourism on mainstream Thai culture has had some creative as well as debasing consequences', although 'its impact on the way of life of some small and vulnerable ethnic groups . . . can be seriously detrimental' (Cohen, 2000b: 26–27). Tourism in Thailand, as with tourism in the Southeast Asian region more generally, is 'a highly diversified, complex, and changing phenomenon, the impact and consequences of which have to be gauged within the wider process of economic development and social change' (Cohen, 2000b: 28). Interestingly, he presents a very ambivalent view of the social and cultural effects of tourism on local communities; in some cases they are generative (or 'emerging' in Yamashita's terms), and in other cases negative and destructive.

A Wider Asian Perspective?

There are very few informative reference works on tourism more generally in Asia, though these have been increasing in number during the past decade, and C. Michael Hall's *Tourism in the Pacific Rim: Developments, Impacts and Markets* (1997a), Hall's and Stephen J. Page's *Tourism in the Pacific: Issues and Cases* (1997b), and F. Go's and C. Jenkins's *Tourism and Economic Development in Asia and Australasia* (1997) are probably among the most relevant to our concerns. However, to our mind, one of the most useful edited volumes on wider Asian tourism, which raises issues of cultural change and host–guest interactions, but also other issues, which have not been covered in any detail elsewhere, is C. Michael Hall's and Stephen J. Page's edited *Tourism in South and Southeast Asia* (2000a). It provides us with an extremely valuable overview of tourism development in Asia, including historical coverage, written by specialists in tourism studies, commerce, business and marketing, geography and area studies. The collection is directed primarily to an undergraduate student market, addressing general issues in tourism research as well as presenting country case studies. It is also proposed in the promotional blurb that the text will have 'a specific appeal to tourism institutions in the region'. The volume, unlike our 1993 book, is not explicitly multidisciplinary and does not consider the different disciplinary contributions to tourism studies, and only six out of twenty chapters are devoted to Southeast Asia. The book is pitched at a relatively basic level in that the country case studies provide a substantial amount of empirical information on tourism. These studies are not designed to be analytical and at the time of publication much of the statistical data were already considerably out of date.

In our view, it also makes more sense to consider the relationships between East and Southeast Asia in tourist terms, and particularly the increasing flows of Chinese, Japanese, Taiwanese and Korean tourists to the region, rather than the connection with South Asia, although we also recognize the growing importance of tourist flows between the Indian sub-continent and Southeast Asia. Yamashita's contribution to our present book, for example, examines the Japanese tourism encounter with Southeast Asia, and a research student of Sidney Cheung, Yuk Wah Chan, considers in Chapter 10 Chinese–Vietnamese tourism interaction in the northern regions of Vietnam. Cheung was also the co-editor of a volume on *Tourism, Anthropology and China*, along with Tan Chee-Beng and Yang Hui (2001). That volume addressed the familiar themes in the anthropology of tourism of representation and the response of local Asian communities to state policies on tourism and minorities. The main foci in that book are those which Wood has already raised and which revolve around the creation of tourist cultures; the objectification, classification and signifying of ethnicity by the state; the ways in which global messages and images are interpreted in local settings; and the reaction of minority and marginal populations to national forces and global requirements.

Returning to Hall's and Page's text, the first section of the book examines general matters, placing tourism in South and Southeast Asia in a regional context, and examining the historical dimensions of tourism, social and cultural issues, transport and infrastructure, politics, political instability and policy, environmental problems and policies, and planning and development. Given the background and interests of several of the contributors, there is considerable emphasis on marketing, promotion strategies and integrated planning, and, in this sense, there are important connections with the interests and approach of Chon and his contributors in *Tourism in Southeast Asia: a New Direction*.

The authors are correct in pointing out that too often government efforts to increase tourist revenue are not matched by improvements in the facilities and infrastructure to support increased numbers of visitors and to facilitate sustainable tourism. The effects of uncontrolled expansion are plain to see in such Southeast Asian resorts as Pattaya. The importance of studying domestic as against long-haul tourism is also indicated, as are the issues of intra-regional business and leisure travel and that of regional cooperation in tourism development. Sofield also warns against too much reliance on analyses which are 'based on Western perceptions of Western tourists impacting upon Asian societies' (2000: 45) and he points to the significance of the diversity of the categories 'tourists' and 'hosts', the variations in tourist experiences and encounters, and the interconnectedness between tourism-generated changes and other processes of change. The general chapters by the Douglases on the history of tourism development, Sofield's on socio-cultural themes, and Page's on the neglected topic of the relationships between transport infrastructure and tourism development are particularly valuable contributions.

The remaining two sections of the text present country studies, predictably one on Southeast Asia and the other on South Asia. Most of the countries of Southeast Asia are covered with the exception of Brunei and the Philippines. One would not expect anything startlingly new in this compilation. The descriptive country chapters are designed as distillations of and commentaries on the published literature, supported by the presentation of a range of facts and figures, including government data on visitor figures and revenue, as well as government reports, available web materials, and newspaper and magazine articles (though the editors also note the relative paucity of 'reliable, up-to-date and meaningful tourism data', 2000b: 287). What is especially valuable in the case studies is the attention to the immediate consequences of the Asian economic crisis of 1997 as well as the drawing out of similarities and contrasts between the experiences of various of the Asian countries in planning for tourism – from the deliberate 'invention' of tourist assets and the vigorous promotion of niche markets in the modern city-state of Singapore, to Thailand's 'regional tourism hub' campaign and its mass tourism strategy, to the rather more subdued and commonplace promotional images of ethnic and cultural diversity in Malaysia, to the crisis-ridden uncertainty of Indonesian tourism development, to the more strictly government-controlled approaches of Vietnam and Myanmar. These comparative insights are of concern to us in our volume in that we shall also draw out the similarities and differences between the tourism experiences of several Southeast Asian countries (and see Chapter 2).

It is not entirely clear why South and Southeast Asia are brought together in Hall's and Page's volume rather than East and Southeast Asia and the western Pacific Rim, and there seems to be a lack of any convincing argument to explain why this has been done. There is a chapter on China, given its increasing importance as a source of tourists into Southeast Asia and the counterflow of ASEAN visitors to mainland China. The close tourist integration between Japan, China, South Korea, and Taiwan and the Southeast Asian countries might well have merited greater attention, and this is a theme which we have addressed in our present volume. But despite the increasing interest in tourism in Asia as an academic field of study and the fast increasing literature on tourism development in the region, there is room for a teaching text of this kind, packed as it is with information, maps, illustrations and statistical data, although some of the data and the pronouncements based upon them are rather dated, in that they only take us up to 1997–1998. Our text takes a rather different direction and is both conceptual and empirical and attempts to capture the 'state-of-the-art' in Southeast Asian tourism studies. However, we also think that Hall's and Page's book and our present volume complement one another in several important respects.

Interconnectedness and Globalization

We now turn to the theme of interconnectedness and globalization which has become increasingly important in the last decade or so in the study of Southeast Asian tourism, and to which we did not pay sufficient attention in our 1993 book. We have already drawn attention to its importance in a historical context earlier in this introductory chapter. The volume edited by Peggy Teo, T. C. Chang and K. C. Ho (2001b) explores precisely this rather new focus in research on the region, in particular the interlinkages between tourism companies, between the state and the private sector and between the countries of the Association of Southeast Asian Nations (ASEAN). It in turn relates to a research focus which has commanded increasing attention during the past decade – the interconnected concepts and processes of globalization and localization (and see Hitchcock and Wiendu Nuryanti, 2000). These concerns were flagged and prefigured in an earlier publication, and perhaps are particularly urgent and relevant from a Singapore perspective (Teo and Chang, 1998: 122–124). The 2001 book by Teo, Chang and Ho also contains sections, predictably, on reinventing tradition, as well as on the emerging phenomenon of ecotourism, but the main focus is on globalization and regionalization and there is also an emphasis on practical and policy issues. There is no specific attention paid to different disciplinary perspectives in the study of tourism.

To be more specific the editors propose that to date there has been little attention paid to 'the interconnections between economies, societies, individuals, corporations, city-states, countries and even whole regions' in the era of globalization and 'post-Fordist tourism' (Teo, Chang and Ho, 2001b: vii). An important, though by no means original conclusion, is that despite the powerful influence of globalizing forces, the increasing relationships across borders, as well as regional and sub-regional co-operation, nation-states are still important players and territoriality a key organizing principle in planning, generating, directing and locating economic activities and the operation of capital. In particular, the development of such innovations as growth triangles and sub-regional cross-border tourism resources has resulted so far in interdependent rather than integrated 'borderlands'. In addition, '[w]hat was once far is now near and what was once unfamiliar has become familiar. Since boundaries and frontiers have become more permeable, economies and cultures are now literally thrown into contact with one another' (Teo and Chang, 1998: 123).

The book emerged from a conference hosted by the National University of Singapore and the Singapore Tourism Board in September 1999 at which some 48 papers were delivered, 18 of which are published here. The Geography Department at the University clearly played a pre-eminent role. As one might expect from such a large endeavour the volume is something of a mixed bag; there are some strong papers and some not so strong; there are contributors well known to researchers on tourism (Kathleen Adams, Erik Cohen, Michael Hall, Stephen Page, Douglas Pearce, Geoffrey Wall, P. P Wong) and some newcomers. The succinct editorial introduction presents tourism as a significant embedded element in processes of globalization and argues that it is a force for both homogenization and differentiation in which states and other actors both shape and are shaped by international tourism and leisure activities. In other words, such generalized processes as Disneyfication and McDonaldization, underpinned by the penetration of international capital, technologies and business organizations as well as Western cultural forms, interact with 'local' agencies in generating the cultural diversities on which tourism thrives. There is nothing which would surprise the ardent student of globalization and post-modernism in this conclusion.

The book is divided into five sections. In the first section Michael Hall and Douglas Pearce separately provide a regional political and policy framework for understanding tourism development, expanding on the overarching themes introduced by the editors. Hall reminds us how closely tourism is implicated in nation-building enterprises or political 'showcasing' (Singapore and Indonesia provide apt examples) and in human rights issues (Myanmar being a case in point), whilst Pearce gives us a more directly practical and policy view on the development of regionally networked tourism activities; his chapter is full of planning-speak but he helpfully elaborates on key concepts in the applied tourism literature (nodal functions, visitor source areas, destination types, gateways, hubs, attributional and linkage-based strategies, scale and hierarchy of functions), and then relates these empirically to his own work on tourism planning in Sarawak and Sabah.

In section two, Singapore geographers (T. C. Chang, K. Raguraman, Carl Grundy-Warr and Martin Perry) dominate the exploration of 'deterritorialization and the development of new regionalisms', concentrating especially on Singapore as both a regional 'tourism and business capital' and as a hub for regional co-operation and, of course, competition. The Indonesia–Malaysia–Singapore (IMS) growth triangle features in this section, and an interesting observation, which merits more detailed future attention, is the role which Singapore plays in generating tourism ideas and concepts, and in exporting its tourism services to other countries in the region. Stephen Page then fleshes out Pearce's overview by concentrating on regional transport hubs and gateways, particularly with regard to air travel and airport development.

The third section, which we think carries the most interest, though it is a familiar focus in tourism studies, explores cultural processes, and global–local interactions. It examines the ways in which tourism resources are 'imaged' and 'themed', and traditions invented or reinvented and appropriated for political purposes. Trevor Sofield, whilst not telling us anything startlingly new, presents a useful overview of the relations between globalization, tourism and culture, especially in terms of postmodern interpretations of cultural identity and ethnicity (with reference to Indonesia and Singapore). Heather Black's and Geoffrey Wall's comparison of three UNESCO World Cultural Heritage Sites (Ayutthaya, Borobudur and Prambanan) reveals that local people usually attach values to a heritage site which are different from those of art historians, archaeologists, government officials, conservationists and heritage planners. A similar theme of global versus local interests in the development of Southeast Asian theme parks and cultural villages is pursued by Peggy Teo and Brenda Yeoh. Erik Cohen traces a ubiquitous process of transition from natural attractions to contrived ones and the authentication and appropriation of constructed cultural resources with reference to Thailand. Can-Seng Ooi, in a finely grained analysis of the policies and exhibitions of the National Museum of Singapore, shows how history, time and space are structured in the process of creating national and regional identities. And finally, Carolyn Cartier examines how the historically significant port and sultanate of Melaka is imaged in a Malay–Muslim-dominated multi-ethnic and modernizing Malaysia. She has strong views, potently expressed. This section complements the main interests expressed in our special issue of *Indonesia and the Malay World* on tourism and heritage in Southeast Asia to which we refer below (Hitchcock and King, 2003a).

Section four, entitled rather obscurely 'Acting as One in Ecotourism', seems to be rather amorphous. Kevin Markwell's examination of the representation of nature in Borneo promotional literature covers some well-trodden ground, and fixes on the wild–domestic duality. P. P. Wong, in another overview-type paper, focuses on the regional dimensions of environmental tourism. Michael Parnwell, in a wide-ranging piece, looks at the Greater Mekong Subregion (GMS) and the regulatory actions and functions of the participating states in developing niche ecotourism and adventure tourism. There seems to be some room for qualified optimism in the prospects for regulating tourism development in the GMS.

Finally, there is a reflexive 'potentials and problems' section on the challenges posed for Southeast Asia as a region by global interconnectedness and post-modern tourism development, though it seems to be a rather miscellaneous collection. There is an intriguing contribution by Kathleen Adams on the minority tourism interest of what she calls 'danger-zone tourism', or deliberate travel to areas of political instability and military conflict in search of adventure, risk and excitement. For obvious reasons Cambodia and Myanmar feature prominently (and see Parnwell on globalization and critical theory, 1998). What is also of interest is the influence which this kind of tourism has on local perceptions of identity and culture. Peter Burns considers domestic tourism development in Nghe An province, Vietnam in the context of relationships between the national tourism promotion body and the local People's Committee. Wiendu Nuryanti looks at the role of Bali as a tourism gateway in the Indonesian government's regional development policies. Finally, Geoffrey Wall comes full circle and presents some thoughts on trends in tourism development in Southeast Asia and yet again the interaction between local and global processes and forces.

The volume risks some repetition and there is not much to surprise us, though the collection is packed with information. There is some interesting and solid case material; some useful overviews of the field; sensible and practical advice for policy-makers; and a few rather more conceptual contributions which provide particular food for thought. But, overall, what the book helpfully does is to bring to the fore the importance of examining tourism as part of a more general process of globalization, the increasing interconnections between tourist destinations and between national governments involved in tourism policy-making and the ways in which 'the global' is localized or indigenized.

Tourism and Heritage

To conclude this 'taking stock' section it might be appropriate to refer to a special issue of *Indonesia and the Malay World* which also addresses Southeast Asia-wide themes and considers a recent emerging focus of interest (Hitchcock and King, 2003a; and see Harrison and Hitchcock, 2005). We came to the conclusion in early 2001 that there was a considerable amount of research under way on heritage tourism in Southeast Asia, and we convened a panel in London in September 2001 as part of the Third EUROSEAS Conference, to examine some of this research. Two especially strong unifying themes which emerged in the course of our discussions were, firstly, the flexible use and multivalent character of the concept of heritage, embracing tangible and concrete elements of the past such as historical sites, monuments and buildings, 'natural' landscapes and habitats, and archaeological finds, as well as culture and identity in their broadest senses, including ideas, values, beliefs, behaviour and performance; secondly, the political uses of heritage and more specifically the deliberate appropriation, manipulation, transformation and creation of heritage for political purposes by the representatives of the state.

The issue came out in 2003 as 'Tourism and Heritage in Southeast Asia' and contained papers on a range of issues and cases: the contested nature of archaeology in post-colonial states and the deliberate creation and development of discourses of the past to legitimize and strengthen the position of the state (Ian Glover); national identity and heritage tourism in Malaysia and the creation of a Malay-based national identity using Melaka as a symbol of nationhood in its early connections with Islam and Malayness (Nigel Worden); heritage and tourism development in George Town, Penang, where interestingly it is cultural diversity which is represented, as well as the juxtaposition of modernity and tradition, with the playing down of the specifically European colonial dimensions of the city (Gwynn Jenkins and Victor King); the clash of 'cultures' surrounding the UNESCO World Heritage Site of Angkor (one global, imaginary and computer-generated by the international film industry; and the other, in part domestic, and preoccupied with the conservation and restoration of high culture and serious cultural tourism) (Tim Winter); the ambiguities of Taiwan's heritage, as displayed in museums, in its connections with both East and Southeast Asia and with both the Han Chinese and an aboriginal Southeast Asian heritage (Michael Hitchcock); the competing and contradictory relationships between identities and tourism in relation to museum displays and cultural and historical representations in Singapore museums, given the city-state's position as a majority Chinese polity located in the heart of a non-Chinese Southeast Asia (Can-Seng Ooi); the national creation and portrayal of Balinese culture in regional terms and the problems of developing and controlling this regionalization in the context of the Indonesian government's post-1998 devolution of planning and financial responsibilities to the sub-provincial level (Michel Picard); the appropriation and construction of nature in the form of national parks and issues of 'natural' authenticity in Malaysia (Norman Backhaus); and finally, four papers by anthropologists on the perceptions, manipulation, deployment and contestation of cultural heritage at the local or community level, including the authentication of a Torajan village and its associated living cultural environment as a representation of traditional Torajan culture (Kathleen Adams); the creation and authentication of a Manggarai cultural village (Catherine Allerton); the disembedding and deterritorialization of Manggarai culture and identity (Maribeth Erb); and the conflicting local and touristic perceptions of megalithic stone structures among the Ngadha (Stroma Cole) on the eastern Indonesian island of Flores.

We consider heritage tourism and the politics of identity to be vitally important and increasingly salient issues in Southeast Asia. In our original planning for the current volume we included four chapters specifically on heritage, addressing, among other things, World Heritage Sites and urban conservation. Subsequently we decided that we should develop the theme of heritage in a separate companion volume, and bring these chapters together with several specially commissioned papers. Therefore, a second volume entitled *Heritage Tourism in Southeast Asia* is currently in preparation (Hitchcock, Parnwell and King, forthcoming).

THIS INTRODUCTORY REVIEW HAS indicated that there have been important general contributions to the study of Southeast Asian and Asian tourism during the past decade. But much remains to be done. From a specifically anthropological perspective Evans remarked in the early 1990s that there was 'little' research on Asian tourism within Asia, that is domestic tourism, available at that time, and the situation, though it has improved since then, is still unsatisfactory (1993: 376). We have noted various of the subjects and themes which have been covered in more detail in tourism research, particularly the creation, transformation and maintenance of ethnic identity and culture more broadly. However, very much more needs to be done in the fields of domestic tourism, crises and their effects on tourism (see, for example, Hitchcock, 2001; Hitchcock and I Nyoman Darma Putra, 2005; and see Chapter 4 in this volume), tourism policy-making, and cross-national integration and interconnections. Although we talk a great deal about globalization these days, and, of course, tourism is one of the dimensions of globalization par excellence, we also do not have many studies of Southeast Asian tourism which specifically address globalization issues in political, economic and cultural terms.

Continuity and Change

The aim of the present volume is not simply to produce an up-dated version of our 1993 publication, but to evaluate the development and direction of the region's tourism sector and academic analyses of Southeast Asian tourism as they stand a dozen or so years down the line. Our literature survey has highlighted a number of recurring themes and perspectives that have tended to map out the field of tourism studies on Southeast Asia, as elsewhere, during this period. These include globalization, identity, image-making, representation, tradition, commodification, massification, promotion and policy-making. These were prefigured to a greater or lesser extent in our 1993 volume, and most remain relevant today, of course, but the region's tourism industry, and both the world and region within which it is placed, have changed quite significantly in the last decade. Tourism analysis has to reflect these changes.

In 2004, Bryan Farrell and Louise Twining-Ward produced a challenging article entitled 'Reconceptualizing Tourism'. Their argument was that the study of tourism is theoretically quite barren territory and a quite isolated field *vis à vis* the main academic disciplines, and has a tendency to rely on orthodox, linear and deterministic modes of analysis. Debates about the industry's impact and sustainability, and actions that follow on from these debates, are constrained by a silo-like separation of strands and components, disciplines and discourses; the analytical fragmentation, particularization and reductionism of complex, dynamic, interdependent systems and processes. Farrell and Twining-Ward claim (2004: 276) that tourism is thus 'managed with remarkably incomplete knowledge'. They suggest that tourism is cloaked in uncertainty and contingency, rather than a sense of predictability and certitude, and that researchers and tourism industry stakeholders need to awaken to this fact. Unexpected processes and events – such as the myriad of crises that the region's tourism sector has experienced since our book was published – are a normal, not exceptional, part of the historical evolutionary process (see also McKercher, 1999; Faulkner and Russell, 1997). Thus 'tourism researchers schooled in a tradition of linear, specialized, predictable, deterministic, cause-and-effect science, are working in an area of study that is largely nonlinear, integrative, generally unpredictable, qualitative, and characterized by causes giving rise to multiple outcomes, quite out of proportion to initial input' (Farrell and Twining-Ward, 2004: 277).

We will return in Chapter 16 to the holistic and flexible approach that is recommended by Farrell and Twining-Ward (2004: 278), as we attempt a synthesis of the multidisciplinary perspectives that are presented in this volume. In the meantime, it may be valuable to reflect on the criticisms that Farrell and Twining-Ward level against tourism studies, and the implications of dynamism, contingency, complexity and unpredictability for our understanding of the nature and impact of tourism in Southeast Asia, and to use this to frame some research questions which may usefully guide the ensuing analysis and discussion.

According to Mason et al., 'Since the late 1980s, global tourism has grown fairly constantly. Events in the early twenty-first century, however, appear to have changed this and led to a reconsideration that growth is the norm' (2005: 12). As has been mentioned in the previous sections, Southeast Asian tourism has experienced a series of crises, shocks and disasters since the late 1990s which no-one realistically predicted and which have profoundly affected the region's tourism sector. Taking a couple of recent examples: a siege of an international school in Siem Reap, Cambodia, on Thursday 16 June 2005, and the subsequent murder of a three-year-old Canadian pupil, momentarily figured prominently in the global media, amid concern about its implications for tourism to one of the world's greatest heritage sites, Angkor, and the likely impact on a Cambodian economy that depends heavily on international tourism (tourism contributed $576 million, or 20 per cent of GDP, in 2002 and has since taken on greater importance as a result of faltering growth in the country's garment sector:

www.asiapacificms.com). Some 27 per cent of international tourists to Cambodia fly direct to Siem Reap airport (www.mot.gov.kh, 2005), almost certainly for the sole purpose of visiting the temple complex, and a good proportion of those who fly in to Phnom Penh airport (28 per cent) or arrive overland (32 per cent) also visit the UNESCO World Heritage Site at Angkor. Visitors from the emerging markets of Asia accounted for 52 per cent of all visitors to the country in 2003 (88,000 from Japan, 62,000 from South Korea), and these visitors, according to the WTO (2005), are more likely to refrain from travel during times of perceived insecurity than travellers from more mature markets. Thus the potential impact of even a small and ephemeral episode, magnified manifold by intense media reporting, on tourism and its economic contribution, can be huge, and frequently exceeds the magnitude of the event itself. More recently, on 1 October 2005 Bali suffered a second round of bombings when cafes along Jimbaran Bay and Kuta were targeted, leaving 23 dead (including three suicide bombers), most of whom were Indonesian citizens. They killed fewer people than in 2002, but the bombs were more sophisticated as they contained ball bearings, some of which were found in the bodies of injured victims. The attacks led to a second major slump in visitor arrivals, thought to rival the downturn that followed the 2002 bombings. Southeast Asian tourism has shown itself time and again to be highly sensitive, fickle and volatile at the demand end of the spectrum when there is a whiff of risk and (political, environmental, health) danger in the air(waves).

Having established that a series of shockwaves has been responsible for severe oscillations in tourist arrivals in Southeast Asia – particularly in individual countries – over the last decade or so, we nonetheless have to concede that the general trend appears to be one of inexorable growth. Each shock has been followed by a strong recovery, and then continued aggregate growth. As such, the region's tourism industry appears to be remarkably resilient despite its clearly evident periodic precariousness. Does this mean that Farrell and Twining-Ward are wrong to criticize so strongly the sub-discipline's alleged reliance on linear, predictable and deterministic modes of analysis? Despite everything that terrorists, nature and economics have thrown at it, tourism continues to out-perform virtually every other economic sector in most countries of Southeast Asia, and as we saw earlier the future prognosis is for much more of the same. Why should this be the case, and what are the social and economic implications of the industry's apparent resilience dynamics?

Although we lack data on precisely who is staying away or going elsewhere and who is returning or travelling afresh, the notion of a 'tourism iceberg' helps partly to explain the industry's apparent recoverability. In spite of some of the most severe shocks and disasters, in a matter of months people are refilling the void created by alarm and uncertainty. Similarly, in spite of gloomy predictions (made in our 1993 volume, as elsewhere) of the industry's unsustainability – of people 'voting with their feet' by moving on to touristic pastures new as established and mature destinations in the region become tarnished, transformed or *passé* – hordes of people seem quite willing to take their places in the region's hot-spots and beyond. A number of factors underpin the 'tourism iceberg' idea. Firstly, there is a vast array of hitherto untapped source markets globally, regionally and domestically (a point to which we will return shortly) which are gradually being mobilized to support the industry's continued growth dynamics. Secondly, and not unconnected to this, more countries and social groups are enjoying the levels of affluence and the expansion of leisure-mindedness and leisure-freedom that have driven the industry's expansion in the past, and this may be expected to continue, certainly in regional and domestic terms. China is presently the most strongly growing out-bound market, forecast to reach 100 million out-bound tourists by 2020 by which time it will be the world's fourth largest source market, and India is soon expected to become a major source of out-bound tourists (WTO, 1999b).

Thirdly, more and more tourism destinations and resources are being mobilized, more supporting infrastructure is being built, and more flair and imagination is being used to extend and diversify the range of tourism products on offer in order to attract and absorb growing tourist numbers and a more varied clientele. Finally, mixed in with the above is a diverse range of aspirations, expectations, behaviours and (price, image, promotion, perception) responsivities which buttress the heterogeneity of present, future and latent forms of tourism activity, and which may determine (future challenges and uncertainties notwithstanding) that there will be plenty of ice beneath the surface for some time to come.

Perhaps this paints too optimistic a picture of the region's tourism future. The numbers game of sustainability, as described above, which appears to be the principal preoccupation of the industry's main actors (e.g. WTO, PATA, national tourism boards, airlines, tour companies, other industry stakeholders), masks very real and pressing concerns about the environmental, social and cultural impacts of tourism with which academic analysis has been principally concerned over the last two to three decades – concerns which are leading to a steady evolution of tourism modalities and forms (ecotourism, special interest tourism, solidarity tourism, etc). Also, recovery and growth are not automatic processes, as the paragraphs above intimate, but require considerable efforts in promotion, incentives, facilitation, marketing, image-making and security enhancement.

An interesting question that emerges from the series of shocks experienced by Southeast Asia's tourism sector is not only how the industry has managed to recover from these crises but what changes, if any, have taken place during the crisis and recovery periods. Has the industry more or less reassembled itself in its pre-crisis shape and form, as the linear evolution hypothesis suggests, or have subtle or profound changes taken place which may alter its future direction, character and impact, and thus support Farrell and Twining-Ward's thesis?

The SARS crisis in Singapore had a profound impact on the Republic's travel and tourism sector, as we have seen, with the hotel industry being particularly badly affected. The larger, corporate segment of the market was able to ride out the storm by laying off contract staff, reducing salaries, introducing multi-tasking, staff taking unpaid leave and entire floors being taken out of service (Henderson and Ng, 2004: 414). Many were even able to turn the crisis into an opportunity by undertaking major renovation programmes while demand was at rock-bottom levels, or by taking advantage of the government's assistance package (the SARS Relief Tourism Training Assistance Programme) to up-grade their human resources (Henderson and Ng, 2004), both of which stood the firms in good stead when the crisis receded in mid-2003. Hotels also intensified their advertising campaigns, and entered into promotional link-ups with airlines, travel agencies and the Singapore Tourism Board – measures which continued in the post-SARS period and which have also yielded benefits in the longer term: occupancy rates in the larger hotels had increased to 73.2 per cent by the last quarter of 2003 (Henderson and Ng, 2004: 415). Thus, not only did the corporate sector manage to maintain its dominant position within the hotel industry, it also had the means and support to enable it quickly to resume a business-as-usual situation. The status quo had reassembled itself after a brief interlude, aided and abetted by the firms, agencies, actors and agendas that had underpinned the status quo in the first place.

Although it is still too early to assess the impact of post-tsunami reconstruction work on tourism in Thailand (the Southeast Asian tourism destination that was most badly affected), the early signs are that opportunities are also not being grasped to make a fresh start with regard to important social, environmental and distributional aspects of modern tourism. Indeed, the status quo also appears to be rapidly re-assembling itself here, suggesting that few lessons have been learned from more than two decades of critique of tourism's growth characteristics and impacts.

Before the tsunami Thailand had a reputation for poorly regulated tourism development. All of the resorts and locations in southern Thailand that faced the full force of the tsunami on 26 December 2004 had seen a phenomenal and only weakly controlled expansion in tourism infrastructure and activity over the last ten or so years. Phuket led the way, with a fifteen-fold increase in international tourist arrivals between 1986 and 2001 (Kontogeorgopoulos, 2004), during which time it metamorphosed from a destination for backpackers and Thai tourists into a resort dominated by major international hotel corporations, although there are also many smaller-scale bungalows and unlicensed guesthouses (Shepherd, 2002a: 309). More recently, destinations such as Khao Lak and the Phi Phi islands soon followed as booming tourism centres, with mostly small-scale and informal forms of infrastructure. Kontogeorgopoulos (2005: 5) describes Phuket as 'a typical mass tourism resort destination [which] features the crowded beaches, pollution, high-rise hotels, and water shortages associated with many other resort spots in the tropical world' and comments that there is a wide perception that the island is becoming 'ruined' through the unchecked growth of the tourism industry. Similar sentiments have been expressed about Khao Lak:

> On my first visit in January 2002 I didn't see any construction. When I went back 10 months later several areas resembled building sites. I was quite devastated but in Thailand the only consideration is money and not much thought is given to the environment. This was a lovely, green field a few months ago. Very soon it will be a mass of concrete. The natural beauty of Khao Lak is being wrecked but this doesn't matter to the people who are making a fast buck.
>
> (members.virtualtorist.com/m/34658/163697/)

Khao Lak was sadly devastated by the Boxing Day tsunami, and the greatest loss of life occurred in this burgeoning resort, partly because most of the accommodation consisted of low-rise bungalows. Tragic and traumatic though this natural disaster was, and it seems invidious to say this, the devastation in several locations across Thailand's Andaman coast gave planners and industry stakeholders the opportunity to make a fresh start, and to address long-standing environmental concerns. A UNEP report (2005: 53) expressed the concern that 'There is a risk that a fast track recovery of the tourism industry may lead to a rapid rebuilding of the infrastructure that existed before the disaster. Such an approach would pre-empt an integrated coastal zone management plan which is now absolutely essential to reduce human vulnerability to natural disasters and ensure long-term sustainability.'

Caroline Ashley (2005) also suggested that the reconstruction process might have been used to create employment and livelihood opportunities for the poor, vulnerable and marginal people who had been severely affected by the tsunami disaster, and, thereafter, to promote pro-poor forms of tourism which would continue to benefit the same groups of people. The large-scale, corporate segment of the industry could effectively look after itself, Ashley argued, with insurance payments, ready access to further investment capital and an ability to work proactively to woo back wary international tourists. Those at the smaller, more informal end of the tourism spectrum, who lost most and have the least means to recover and rebuild their livelihoods, need the greatest amount of support, a greater say and the fullest participation in the rebuilding process. Ashley (2005: 1) argues that 'What is needed is not just the restoration of tourism, but integration of pro-poor tourism strategies into reconstruction', but she was not optimistic that this would eventualize. The government, business and donor driven scramble to restore tourism infrastructure as quickly as possible in order to recommence the inflow of tourist dollars and resume returns on capital investment has largely eliminated the opportunity to reflect on the kinds of tourism development that would be most appropriate for a sustainable and equitable future which maximizes local benefits and minimizes local costs.

The above discussion is not entirely out of step with Farrell and Twining-Ward's challenge to linear and deterministic models of tourism development, in that the described facsimile-like recovery and reassembly of the tourism industry after shocks and crises may well be part of the problem rather than indicating the negation of risk, uncertainty and the threat of unsustainability. Farrell and Twining-Ward take a longer term view than the transient turbulence with which we have been concerned, and point to the need for the industry to undergo a 'sustainability transition'. To achieve this there is a need to overcome the 'powerful counter-forces in the form of firmly held social and cultural values, government economic policy, the insulating properties of social systems, persistent use of partial solutions, and problems of human adversity [sic] to grasping concepts of scale and uncertainty' (Farrell and Twining-Ward, 2004: 288). Gratifyingly in the context of the present volume, they point (Farrell and Twining-Ward, 2004: 287) to the essential need for transdisciplinarity and interdisciplinarity as a means of helping to build bridges between the industry's and the academy's silo-like structures. It is our hope that *Tourism in Southeast Asia* will be able to contribute to an integrated, holistic and multifaceted understanding of the drivers, character, impact, implications and future directions of tourism in the region.

Summary of the Chapters

The volume covers a wide territory both thematically and locationally, and aims to re-examine a number of the issues that were first raised in our 1993 volume *Tourism in South-East Asia*.

Victor King gets the journey under way with a wide-ranging survey of recent anthropological (and sociological) work on tourism in Southeast Asia in which he identifies the discipline's principal fields of investigation and specialization and assesses its contribution to our understanding of tourism and its various social and cultural manifestations and impacts. He examines at length the contributions of key anthropological writers on tourism in the region (mainly Indonesia, Thailand, Malaysia and Singapore), especially those of Erik Cohen in the context of Thailand and Michel Picard in Bali, but bemoans an overall lack of genuinely comparative studies of what are highly differentiated and complex tourism processes. He urges anthropologists to look beyond the local and the particular in order to construct a more holistic and comparative perspective on the interrelationship of tourism, globalization, modernization and socio-cultural change. He also emphasizes the importance of focusing on agency, particularly local actors, and the multiple discourses which agents engage in so that we can better capture processes of differentiation and variation in and between tourism activities and sites.

Kathleen Adams follows up a theme that was developed in our 1993 volume (Parnwell, 1993) in exploring some of the ways in which another manifestation of traditional culture – the arts and handicrafts of Southeast Asia – have been influenced by the growth in tourism and the exponential growth in demand for souvenirs and trinkets. Rather than dismissing so-called 'airport art' as an unwanted and uncompromising agent in the erosion of traditional material culture, Adams argues that we can learn a great deal about the forces that are being brought to bear on the traditional arts and crafts of the region – such as globalization, modernization, commoditization, territorial integration and cultural articulation – from the way that purchasers (tourists) and producers (entrepreneurs) are influencing the expression and manifestations of material culture. Adams focuses particularly on processes of 'deterritorialization' whereby handicrafts and souvenirs are increasingly being produced outside the locations and cultural zones to which they relate: she uses the example of Torajan crafts which are being manufactured in Makassar by Makassarese or Buginese, or on Java by Javanese, to capitalize on the growing local and international demand for Torajan crafts; and 'hybridization' whereby modifications are made to traditional material culture by borrowing iconic styles from other cultural groups; the most striking example Adams uses is of design elements of Peruvian 'worry dolls', derived from internet searches, being incorporated into Torajan replica *tau-tau* effigies for sale to tourists as souvenirs. Rather than condemning the 'bastardization' of traditional material culture, Adams shows how tourism has given artists and craftspeople new opportunities, avenues and material for self-expression, in the process creating 'mini-monuments of modernity'.

There follow two chapters that look at the Bali bombings of 12 October 2002 and 1 October 2005 and their aftermath. I Nyoman Darma Putra and Michael Hitchcock set the bombings within the wider context of tourism and terrorism, and show how the tourism industry is a soft target for groups who wish to promote their political agendas by violent means. They also demonstrate how sensitive tourists are to even the slightest threat of insecurity and instability, linked in no small measure to intense media attention and the issuance of travel advisories by foreign embassies. The tourism industry in Indonesia, and Bali in particular, was decimated by the bombings, bringing economic hardship to Muslims and Hindus alike. The chapter also looks at the backgrounds and motivations of the bombers, and finds an assorted mix of reasons for the terrorist attacks, ranging from intense anti-American feeling (and a misguided expectation that Americans and not Australians would be the principal target), to Bali's symbolic position as the epitome of international tourism and globalization and the wide publicity that the bombers' 'cause' would thereby receive, to the hedonistic behaviour of western tourists in Bali.

Michel Picard uses the local reaction to the bombings as a means of exploring wider issues of Balinese identity and the meaning of 'Balineseness'. The Kuta bomb in October 2002 brought to a violent and dramatic end an era of peace and prosperity on Bali – an island that hitherto had been remarkably resilient in the face of several crises that had befallen Indonesia during the previous decade or so. This forced a period of intensive reflection and introspection, and a number of opinion leaders suggested that too much of the cultural essence of Bali had been allowed to slip away in pursuit of the tourist dollar and as the doors had been flung open to the outside world. Here again the issues of agency and multiple discourses emerge. The Balinese felt under siege, not only through the impact of the terrorist outrage but also through the way that 'outsiders' – non-Balinese – had moved in and started to monopolize the island's tourism infrastructure, and also the development agenda that underlay it. Islamization and the politicization of Islam had also placed the island's religion, Balinese Hinduism, under perceived threat. The reaction in some influential quarters was to 'retreat to the local' in the face of this global (or at least external) assault. Ajeg Bali – a strong and everlasting Bali – became a slogan intended to revitalize, or at least preserve, Balinese culture, religion and tradition. A better balance between tourism and the non-tourist economy – especially agriculture – was advocated, as was a greater degree of 'special autonomy' for the Balinese in making decisions about the appropriate direction for cultural tourism, and about ownership of the resources and revenues of tourism. Discriminatory measures against non-Balinese were advocated, and indeed are already being promoted, and the localist revivalism of religion, culture and tradition are being actively pursued. Picard is quite critical of the conservative, static, homogeneous and romaniticized vision of Balinese culture upon which the post-Bali bomb Ajeg Bali campaign is built.

The volume now moves on to a series of chapters that have an economic and policy-making focus. Linda Richter presents an overview of policy-making issues in Southeast Asian tourism – a difficult task given the great complexity of political, geographical, historical and socio-cultural contexts. The main part of the chapter deals with 'what governments do', and takes us through a brief history of state inter-vention in the promotion and management of tourism in individual Southeast Asian countries, set against a back-drop of their prevailing political regimes and associated agendas. Formal planning of tourism started around the beginning of the 1970s, and in general gave greater priority to international over domestic tourism, Western over Asian tourists, and up-market over low-spending clientele. The singlemost important objective was 'more tourism', although efforts were increasingly made to spread the economic benefits of tourism to peripheral and marginal areas and social groups, although 'enclave tourism', as a means of controlling the socio-cultural effects of tourism, was the preferred model in several instances. Richter then considers the flip-side of policy-making – 'what governments don't do': how and why certain issues do not figure prominently on the policy agenda. She uses the example of sex tourism and paedophilia to show how governments have turned a blind eye to pressing social issues for fear of the way that a heavy-handed approach might affect tourism growth. Finally, Richter turns to look at Southeast Asian tourism in the twenty-first century, and identifies a number of sustainability issues, including the threat of future natural disasters like the Boxing Day tsunami; the need for regional co-operation to solve the haze crisis in maritime Southeast Asia; the persisting problem of the trafficking of women and children into the sex tourism sector; and growing public health issues exemplified by the SARS and avian flu crises. Richter finishes with a cautiously hopeful forecast for the future of tourism in the region.

The regulation of tourism by the state is also the focus of Jonathan Bennett's insightful study of the development of tourism businesses in post-Doi Moi Vietnam. Using qualitative material from in-depth local field research, Bennett shows how the state's efforts to control the development of tourism in this transitional economy are systematically thwarted by everyday corrupt practices whereby tourism enterprises are more or less obliged to provide kick-backs to officials if they are to introduce, sustain or expand their tourism businesses. Local-level officials are able to take advantage of the vague wording of state resolutions to allow considerable discretion to interpret the regulatory environment in a manner that ultimately gains them considerable personal leverage and financial benefit. Stifling bureaucracy also affords officials the opportunity to gain personally by 'oiling the wheels' for tourism businesses which might otherwise wither and die in a forest of paperwork. Officials thus become key conduits through which tourism entrepreneurs must operate if they are to negotiate the complex regulatory environment. Bennett shows how taxation revenue is lost to the state through personal negotiations between tourism businesses and tax officials. Using case material from Hanoi, Hue and Ho Chi Minh City, the chapter also highlights the importance of social capital (*quan he*) – often again spanning the business–government interface – in the development of tourism enterprises in Vietnam and in helping certain tourism businesses to manage to survive in the face of intensifying competition in the country's tourism sector.

David Harrison and Steven Schipani present a much more hopeful picture of tourism development in another transitional economy, the Lao PDR. A relative late-starter in regional terms, Laos has the advantage of being able to learn from its neighbours' errors in terms of mitigating some of the harmful effects of poorly-regulated tourism development, whilst at the same time steering the growth of tourism to achieve clear development objectives such as poverty alleviation and local capacity-building. Laos has been fortunate in being able to draw on substantial investment and support from the Asian Development Bank, the United Nations, bilateral development agencies and non-governmental organizations, which collectively have sought to operationalize theoretical models of pro-poor tourism, community-based ecotourism and other forms of 'appropriate tourism' in the Lao context. In general they have succeeded in laying the foundation for future tourism development, although hitherto tourism numbers have failed to match and deliver a reasonable financial return from the considerable investment that the agencies have made in developing community-level tourism infrastructure. There are also doubts about the appropriateness of international agencies and non-governmental organizations taking on a role that is more efficiently played by the private sector, and indeed there is anecdotal evidence in the chapter that 'conventional tourism' in the hands of small family-run businesses is making a larger contribution to local and national development than many of the ideologically-driven community-based tourism initiatives.

Two chapters follow which look specifically at East Asian tourists in the Southeast Asian setting. Shinji Yamashita looks at Southeast Asian tourism from the perspective of Japan and Japanese tourists. He first traces the historical roots and evolution of Japanese tourist connections with the 'southern seas' before exploring Japanese views of the region, which historically involved creating a civilized image of Japan by emphasizing the backwardness of the 'southern seas', and a process of 'orientalizing Southeast Asia' as a way of 'de-orientalizing Japan'. Past practice has had a strong influence on how Southeast Asia is viewed in the popular opinion of would-be tourists from Japan, which is seen as having an ambiguous cultural distance which is simultaneously far (different) and near (similar). The chapter emphasizes this by means of three short case studies of Japanese tourist encounters with Southeast Asia. Yamashita describes the growth of 'healing tourism' in the 'last paradise' of Bali, where young women in particular seek to escape the 'battlefield of the workplace' and find spiritual healing in the familiar and nostalgic cultural Balinese landscape – a Japanese 'spiritual homeland'. Nature tourism in Sabah is presented as a means of expressing the Japanese belief in the one-ness of human existence and nature, using the model of *sato-yama* (village-mountain) as a symbol of human–nature co-existence which is revitalized in the context of modern niche tourism, whilst conveniently glossing over the extent to which Japanese resource exploitation is threatening the very eco-niches upon which nature tourism in Southeast Asia depends. Finally, the phenomenon of 'lifestyle tourism', where increasing numbers of Japanese travel to Thailand to enjoy the Thai way of life, is discussed as a new form of non-labour migration, creating a growing phenomenon of 'lifestyle migrants', which suggests useful conceptual terrain at the nexus of tourism and migration.

Yuk Wah Chan presents the fascinatingly insightful findings of in-depth local research in the borderlands between China and Vietnam, focusing especially on the gender dimensions of sex tourism and the 'sexualizing and sensualizing of the border'. Cross-border trade and tourism in the border between Hekou (China) and Lao Cai (Vietnam) has boomed since the border was re-opened in 1991. An emerging transborder political economy has not only led to an economic boom but has also created a new social space for interaction between the Chinese and Vietnamese. Yuk Wah focuses on the gendered dimensions of this social interaction, in which large numbers of Chinese men visit the border towns for sexual purposes – *zhao xiaojie* ('looking for misses') – and young Vietnamese women seek financial reward and material benefit, and their own 'dream of modernity', through providing sexual services to cross-border tourists. Vietnamese tour guides and travel assistants also engage in sexual games and various forms of flirtatious behaviour with their relatively wealthy Chinese visitors as a way of increasing the tips they receive and of building acquaintances with Chinese tourists which may in the longer-term yield material or even marital benefits. Far from being characterized as a 'typical' situation of male dominance and female sub-ordination, as the literature tends to suggest, Yuk Wah Chan shows how the emerging cross-border sex politics is consciously used by Vietnamese women to escape the bitterness of their socially constructed role as self-sacrificing and faithful wives in a male-dominated society, and to pursue their private dreams for an independent and prosperous life, and their yearnings for true love and 'accesible modernity'.

Heidi Dahles adds further insight to the phenomenon of sex tourism, but adds a fresh angle. A great deal of earlier work on the connection between tourism and the sex industry in Southeast Asia has focused on Western (and Japanese) male tourist encounters with female prostitutes, bar girls, karaoke hostesses and so on and the myriad of social, economic and health consequences it has given rise to. Dahles' chapter looks at the phenomenon of 'romance tourism' undertaken by women who look for romantic and sexual encounters with young male 'gigolos', mainly in the Indonesian beach resorts and other tourism hot-spots. Dahles draws attention to the different ways in which both the providers and purveyors of sexual and 'friendship' services are perceived, both within the context of local socio-cultural norms and in the literature on sex tourism. Using a case study of Yogyakarta, she also places the gigolos – who she calls 'romantic entrepreneurs' – within the framework of both livelihood and lifestyle, showing how casual 'guides' struggle for income-earning opportunities within a swollen tourism informal sector, and how sexual encounters with (predominantly western) female tourists allows them the opportunity not only to increase their earnings potential but also gain in social standing in much the same way as with the so-called 'Kuta boys' on Bali. Dahles' chapter also outlines a future research agenda which must come to terms, both analytically and empirically, with a rapidly diversifying 'sex tourism' phenomenon in Southeast Asia.

Finally, there is a small cluster of chapters which looks at the environmental impact of tourism and some of the more recent policy responses. In an empirically-informed conceptual discussion, Michael Parnwell uses a political ecology framework to look at the structures of power within the Southeast Asian tourism sector and suggests directions for change if sustainable tourism is to become a realistic prospect. He shows how, at the macro level, international development organizations and, at the grassroots level, non-governmental organizations have helped to shift the regional tourism agenda from one of 'growth at any cost' to a much more democratic and participatory model where communities are increasingly given both a say and a stake in tourism developments that directly affect them. Competitive barriers between the various sets of stakeholders are gradually being dismantled, and are being replaced by more co-operative and collaborative efforts to build public–private partnerships, promote corporate social responsibility and to foster pro-poor, fair trade and community-based tourism development. This fairly optimistic chapter provides a range of examples of where constructive action has taken place in the countries of mainland Southeast Asia, including the use of tourism as a positive force in the conservation of threatened ecosystems and the promotion of development in marginal communities. However, much more work needs to be done in getting tourists to act as ethical consumers and to exert greater pressure on the industry's other stakeholders to move further and faster in the direction of sustainable tourism.

Janet Cochrane takes this discussion forward by looking at recent developments in the eco-tourism sub-sector in Indonesia. Indonesia has immense ecotourism resource potential, but has only recently started to establish an institutional environment that may be conducive to mobilizing these resources in a manner which will satisfy both conservation and development needs and objectives. Conservation measures in Indonesia, such as the establishment of national parks, were initially very eco-centric in nature, which meant that local people were often excluded from protected areas and their livelihood potential and the economic means of supporting conservation efforts – such as ecotourism – were largely overlooked. Bureaucratic inefficiency, corruption, power politics and institutional inertia were also substantially responsible for weaknesses in the implementation of conservation policy. Since the 1990s there has been a change in the approach to environmental management, with the co-management of natural resources – a multi-stakeholder approach which draws on the respective strengths of the public, private and non-governmental sectors, and which gives local communities a greater say in their developmental destiny – now being promoted as the preferred means of combining conservation and development objectives, such as in the form of Integrated Conservation and Development Projects (ICDP). Ecotourism is increasingly being incorporated into the co-management projects, although Cochrane draws a dinstinction between 'pure ecotourism', in which tourists are both environmentally aware and appropriately behaved, and forms of 'mass ecotourism' where copious coats of 'greenwash' are applied to the conventional forms of tourism which have been responsible for considerable ecological damage in the past.

Henning Borchers looks critically at a co-management scheme to improve the conservation of one of Indonesia's most important biodiversity resources, the Komodo National Park, which was the focus of a study by Michael Hitchcock in our 1993 volume. A joint venture between the US-based environmental organization, The Nature Conservancy, and an Indonesian tourism operator is intended to halt resource degradation within the National Park by supporting a self-financing, 25-year programme of environmental management which tries to strike a balance between ecological preservation and the economic development that is needed to finance conservation efforts. Borchers describes the allocation of a concession for environmental management and tourism development to a business firm as 'the privatization of Indonesia's natural heritage', and is very critical of the way that the resultant programme has followed an ecocentric bias which has systematically excluded local communities from access to the natural resources upon which their livelihoods have traditionally depended, whilst outsiders (particularly from neighbouring Sumbawa) have been able to compete for the same resources with relative impunity. Local residents have also largely been excluded from decision-making and the actualization of ecotourism development in the National Park, which is intended to provide alternative sources of livelihood to those which utilize under-pressure marine and terrestrial resources. Thus poverty and marginalization have persisted despite the promotion of a co-management plan which has been conceived and implemented in an era when biodiversity conservation and socio-economic development are supposed to go hand-in-hand and to be mutually sustainable. Poaching, cyanide fishing and other illegal and destructive practices thus continue, principally because local communities have been excluded from a series of largely eco-centric conservation measures. Following Hitchcock's conclusion in 1993, tourism continues to be a mixed blessing for Komodo Island and the Komodo islanders.

Finally, Mark and Joanna Hampton, respectively a tourism specialist and a marine biologist, examine some of the impacts of backpacker tourism on the fragile small-island marine environment of Gili Trawangan in Lombok, Indonesia. The first half of the chapter looks at the increasingly destructive impact of tourism on the terrestrial environment, in terms of pollution, garbage disposal, water demand and so on, and finds tourism numbers already to be at their maximum sustainable level, partly because the environmental impact of backpackers tends to be more limited than for other forms of mass tourism. And yet efforts are currently under way to upgrade tourism infrastructure on the island in order to attract and accommodate more tourists from the high-spending, luxury end of the tourism market, which, because of their consumption and life-style preferences, the authors feel will significantly tip the balance of tourism development beyond environmentally sustainable levels unless significant attention is given to management and mitigation measures. The second part of the chapter takes a close look at the coral reefs which fringe Gili Trawangan, and reveals significant damage from snorkeling and Scuba diving, from the boats which regularly bring tourists to the island, and from the exploitation of marine resources in support of tourism consumption and infrastructure. The Hamptons conclude that there is a need for much tighter environmental regulation, and a greater degree of local participation in environmental management, if future tourism development on Gili Trawangan is to be sustainable as the island moves from the vanguard of tourism development, dominated by adventurous and flexible backpackers, to more conventional forms of mass and organized tourism.

We finish with a short conclusion which reflects on some of the ways in which Southeast Asian tourism, and the academic study of the phenomenon, has changed since our 1993 volume was published. The growing differentiation and diversification of the tourism experience, the industry's increasing unpredictability, the conflation of tourism with many other social processes, the 'Asianization' of Southeast Asian tourism, and the emergence of new sets of actors at all levels who are influencing the agenda for the industry's future development, determine that researchers need to sharpen their analytical tools, and both listen to and reflect a multitude of voices, if we are to get fully to grips with new and future developments and their social, cultural, economic, political and environmental implications.

2

Anthropology and Tourism in Southeast Asia: Comparative Studies, Cultural Differentiation and Agency

Victor King

Introductory Remarks

This chapter provides a critical commentary on anthropological and some closely related sociological research on tourism in Southeast Asia. The crucial concerns for anthropology since the mid-1970s have been the social and cultural interactions between tourists, the agents and intermediaries (including tour companies, guides, entrepreneurs, bureaucrats, policy-makers and service providers), and the communities which they encounter; the organizational forms of tourism activities; the character, socio-economic backgrounds and motivations of tourists and their experiences of place and people in relation to different kinds of tourism; the images and representations of tourist destinations, local residents and tourists; the socio-cultural consequences of tourism for local communities; and the responses of those who are subject to, in Urry's terms, the 'tourist gaze' (Urry, 1990; Burns, 1999; Crick, 1989; Graburn, 1983a; Nash, 1981; 1984; 1996; Lett, 1989; Nash and Smith, 1991, Nuñez, 1989/1977). Tourism has excited increasing anthropological attention because of its 'inexorable links with culture' (Burns, 1999: 33) and 'cultural production' (Yamashita, 2003a: 3), and its constant and recurring encounter with cultural 'otherness' and 'difference' (Yamashita, Kadir Din and Eades, 1997: 14; Harkin, 1995: 650–670). The anthropology of tourism has also successfully inserted, or, in some cases, re-inserted considerations of culture into debates about modernization and development, and about the nature of the encounters between the developed and the developing world (see, for example, Wood, 1993: 50–54; King, 1999: 183–213).

After earlier attempts during the 1970s and 1980s to categorize tourists and types of tourism, conceptualize tourism as a dynamic process, understand its socio-cultural consequences or 'impacts', and examine tourist images of people and place, since the 1990s a major preoccupation in the literature has been the relationships between the state and its citizens in the appropriation, construction and transformation of ethnic identities, given that tourism plays a vital role in the creation and presentation of cultural images – images of the nation-state, local communities, places and environments, and 'heritage' (Picard and Wood, 1997a; Wood, 1997: 1–34; and see Adams, 1997a: 155–180; Crick, 1989: 307–344; Hitchcock, 1999: 17–32; Hitchcock and King, 2003a; 2003b; Kahn, 1997; 1998; King and Wilder, 2003: 219–227; Leong, 1997a: 513–534; MacCannell, 1984: 375–391; Selwyn, 1993: 117–137; Wiendu Nuryanti, 1996: 249–260). Governments can and do create or construct 'races', 'regional cultures', 'tribes' and 'minorities', in the course of processes of definition, rationalization, and domestication of those populations they govern. This entails in turn a reaction on the part of those who are subject to classification and control and '[b]oth ethnic and national identities will continue to be contested . . . and tourism will continue to be an important arena in which this contestation is played out' (Wood, 1997: 24; and see Adams, 2006). Hitchcock presents several examples from Southeast Asia of the ways in which tourism 'unleashes' or unlocks 'latent' identities or creates new ones and the active role of local populations in this process (1999: 23ff).

Anthropologists have also been involved rather more recently in comparing the dynamic social and cultural effects of tourism on different communities and in examining the changes which tourism activities generate within more general processes of modernization and globalization (see, for example, Sofield, 2000; 2001). This reference to changing themes or emphases in the anthropology of tourism has resulted in considerable discussion about what should be the proper subjects of investigation (Lett, 1989: 276; and for sociology see Cohen, 1979b; Dann and Cohen, 1991). Acknowledging this diversity in approaches and interests, my summary above of the main areas of anthropological research needs to be qualified by the perceptive remark of Wilson that 'definitions, concepts and research priorities [in the anthropology of tourism] have changed rapidly' (1993: 32–35). The range of themes which has emerged in the anthropology of tourism is also more diverse than Lett's (1989: 276) broad categorization of anthropological research into that which explores 'culturally defined meanings' in the experience of tourists and local communities (following Dennison Nash; see also de Kadt, 1979) and that which assesses 'the range of empirical effects that tourism has upon the sociocultural systems of host societies' (following Nelson Graburn).

Nevertheless, despite an increasing interest in the study of tourism among social and cultural anthropologists during the past two decades, there are still significant gaps in our knowledge. Tourism as a subject of study is still relatively under-represented in anthropological circles generally and also within the anthropology of Southeast Asia. We still know very little about tourism and its consequences in large parts of the region. In addition, the character and consequences of the rapid expansion of domestic tourism is still a largely uncharted field and the emphasis has been on foreign tourists and cross-national encounters (but see Hughes-Freeland, 1993; Adams, 1997b; Teo and Leong, 2006; Peleggi, 1996). After all it is said that tourism research only became a legitimate and respectable field of study in American anthropology following the publication of Valene Smith's *Hosts and Guests: The Anthropology of Tourism* in 1977 (Smith, 1989a; 1989b, second edition), although the major theoretical work on the 'leisure class' by Dean MacCannell (1976), Philip McKean's study of tourism in Bali (1973; 1976) and Nelson Graburn's edited book on ethnic and tourist arts (1976) also served to excite interest at that time among social scientists. Indeed, it has been claimed that MacCannell's study is 'widely seen as inaugurating contemporary tourism studies in the social sciences' (Picard and Wood, 1997b: vii).

Tourism research took even longer to gain respectability in European anthropological circles, where its effects were confronted usually accidentally by researchers pursuing some other scholarly objective. Even into the 1980s there was only a handful of European anthropologists/sociologists working on tourism in the region (these included Erik Cohen [2001], and an important French-speaking contingent, Gerard Francillon [1979; 1989], Jean Luc Maurer [1979; 1988] and Michel Picard [1996]), and only small numbers of local scholars (though see Kadir Din, 1982; 1988; 1989 and Thanh-Dam Truong, 1983; 1990). The major advances were being undertaken by American-based scholars, and the two studies of Southeast Asian communities in *Hosts and Guests* by McKean on the Balinese and Crystal on the Toraja served to set and stimulate the research agenda on Indonesian tourism from the 1980s, as did Wood's more general work on tourism and socio-cultural change (1979; 1980).

Despite this situation there have been some notable contributions to the anthropology (and sociology) of tourism in Southeast Asia. In this chapter I adopt what is a major methodological strength in anthropology and examine its contribution in a regionally comparative way, highlighting some common themes (see, for example, Wood, 1979; 1984; 1993; 1997). I also focus on issues which have had a special resonance in relation to particular countries, culture areas or communities. I have selected studies which, in my view, have made an important contribution to our understanding of the character and dynamics of Southeast Asian tourism, and those which have made a more general impact on tourism studies beyond the region.

Key Issues

Comparative Studies

Erik Cohen commented in the late 1970s, in his study of hill tribe tourism in northern Thailand, that at that time the academic literature on the social and cultural 'impacts' of tourism had failed 'to discuss systematic differences between types of tourists or types of communities' (1979a/2001a:115). What was lacking was 'the middle range of systematic comparative studies which are specifically designed to examine the differential impact of given types of tourism under different sets of conditions' (ibid.:115). He attempted to address this failure by examining the differential effects of 'tribal village tours' and 'jungle tours' on five communities drawn from three different ethnic groups (the Meo [Hmong], Lisu and Akha). He used three variables – the place of tourism within the local socio-economic environment, the character and organization of the tourism enterprise, and the nature of tourist–villager interactions (ibid.: 118–119). His main proposition was that tourism should be understood in terms of interrelated processes and not as 'an isolated event' and that it generates consequences for the host communities which are foreseen or intended, as well as 'unexpected and often not desired' (ibid.: 113). Based on this comparative study, Cohen concluded that 'although some of the villages may have been "spoilt" by tourism, and hence are no longer as "authentic" as they used to be in the past, intensive penetration of tourism has not had a markedly disruptive impact on the economic and social life of the villagers' (ibid.: 140).

Even though some comparative research has been undertaken in Southeast Asia since Cohen's study, there has not been a great deal of country-wide let alone region-wide comparison. Cohen remains an exception in his wide-ranging and systematic studies of the different dimensions of tourism in Thailand (2001a), although there have been several edited collections which have drawn attention to some of the similarities and differences in tourism experiences both within and across countries in Southeast Asia (see, for example, Hall and Page, 2000a; Picard and Wood, 1997a; Teo, Chang and Ho, 2001c; Hitchcock, King and Parnwell, 1993; Hitchcock and King, 2003a). Yamashita too has undertaken comparative work on tourism in Bali and Tana Toraja in his examination of 'sites in which cultural innovation takes place' (2003; and Eades, 2003: xiv), Hitchcock has drawn out comparative themes in his consideration of ethnicity and tourism entrepreneurship in Java and Bali (2000), and Dahles and Bras have compared the experiences and life-chances of young self-employed males in the informal sex or 'romance' tourism sector between Yogyakarta (Java) and Lombok, the different circumstances of tour guiding more generally, and small-scale female entrepreneurship (Dahles, 1998b; 1999; 2001; 2002; Dahles and Bras, 1999a; Bras, 2000; Bras and Dahles, 1998).

Impacts, Authenticity and Journeys of Discovery

I have chosen Cohen's comparative study and his related papers on hill tribe tourism (1989/2001a; 1983/2001a; 1982/2001a; 1992/2001a) by way of introduction not only because they were pioneering, but also because they address themes which continue to play a vital role in anthropological/sociological studies of tourism. A major concern is, in Cohen's terms, the 'impacts' of tourism on local communities. This has become a central preoccupation of anthropologists, although the ways in which tourist–local interactions and their consequences have been conceptualized have changed since Cohen undertook his studies, particularly the notion of tourism as an external force 'impacting' on local communities (see, for example, Wood, 1993; Picard, 1996). Rather than seeing the social effects of tourism on local communities as 'destructive', 'negative', or 'inimical' on the one hand or 'negligible', 'moderate', 'more beneficent' or 'positive' on the other (Cohen, 1979a/2001a: 113–121; 140–144), researchers have more recently moved beyond this 'naturalistic', 'organic', 'objective', 'normative' framework in understanding cultural change to one which conceptualizes 'culture' and 'tradition' in symbolic terms, as a 'hybrid entity', and as 'constructed' and 'reconstructed', 'invented', 'improvised', 'manipulated', 'relational', 'historically unfinished' and 'consumed', and local people as 'cultural strategists' (see especially Wood, 1993: 58–60; 64–66; and Adams, 2006: 19–23, 132–135, 210–211; Erb, 2000: 709–736; Hitchcock, 1999: 17–32; Picard, 1996: 190–200; Yamashita, 2003a: 4).

This is not to say that Cohen's earlier work on 'impacts' was not very carefully qualified in its attempts to assess the costs and benefits of tourism in different local contexts in northern Thailand, but he had not yet embraced fully the notion of 'traditions' as symbolically represented and attributed, though this perspective was prefigured in his rethinking of the sociology of tourism (1979b). Even after the re-conceptualization of 'culture' and 'cultural change' in the 1980s, we find, in the second edition of Smith's *Hosts and Guests* (1989), that the editor keeps to a concept of change as 'impact' or, in cost–benefit terms, as positive or 'damaging', as do certain of the contributors, and the preoccupation is with the encounter between 'domestic hosts' and 'foreign guests' (1989: 6–17; and see Crystal, 1989: 148–151; and McKean, 1989/1977b: 130–138; see also Hitchcock on the limited analytical value of the categories 'host' and 'guest' in 'a complex industry involving a plurality of relationships' [1999: 18] and Bruner [1991]).

Following his earlier empirical work on hill tribe tourism, Cohen addressed the problematical notion of 'authenticity' in evaluating the cultural effects of tourism. He argued more decisively in a post-normative way that conceptions of what is 'genuine' and what is 'invented' or 'false' are 'socially constructed' (1988a). He reconsidered MacCannell's concept of 'authenticity' and the view that tourists were in search of genuine, accurate, original 'social' experiences, and in this quest, beyond their everyday, fragmented, alienated, 'inauthentic' lives, they discover or rediscover their real selves; they recover a sense of personal and social wholeness and structure by re-creating something perceived as real and representative of a lost pre-modern state (1973; 1976). In his theoretical discourse on 'the structure of modern consciousness' (Cohen, 1989/2001a: 32) MacCannell also developed the related notion of 'staged authenticity' in which tourist hosts, entrepreneurs and representatives of the state, in promoting and enhancing the attractiveness of their tourist assets, contrive to construct seemingly authentic experiences to seduce their guests (1973: 602–603). In other words, the tourist becomes ensnared in an artificially created 'tourist space' which presents or 'stages' 'unchanging native traditions', 'pristine cultures', 'the last paradise' or 'exotic communities'. 'Staging' can also be of two main kinds, although these can be interrelated and complementary: 'substantive staging' where an attraction is altered or created anew, and 'communicative staging' where authenticity is either presented in tourist promotional literature without necessarily interfering with the attraction or site thus advertised, or where the attraction is interpreted as authentic by tour guides and intermediaries (Cohen, 1989/2001a: 33–35).

The preoccupation with the 'authentic' and the 'inauthentic' and the notion that 'tourism' and 'culture' are separable elements were given very firm attention in the planning of tourism development in Bali in the early 1970s. Tourism was thought to 'impact' on authentic cultural expressions and, through the need to 'stage', 'package' and 'sell' culture, render it inauthentic. Therefore, Balinese culture had to be given a measure of protection from this tourist influx, and partially segregated from the main sites of tourist accommodation. However, Shepherd, in his evaluation of the consequences of the Suharto government's plans for tourism development in Bali in the 1970s proposes, following Picard (1993; 1996), that 'tourism has neither destroyed authentic Balinese culture nor spurred its rebirth. Rather it has made local residents self-conscious about a thing they possess called culture' (2002b: 94). Perceptions of authenticity are relative and changing and tourism can itself become so enmeshed in cultural change and creativity that it becomes neither meaningful to separate the two nor appropriate to talk in simple terms about tourism destroying or regenerating culture.

In his exploration of authenticity, Cohen also addressed Graburn's proposition that tourism is 'a sacred journey' akin to a pilgrimage in which tourists experience a passage from the profane, mundane, compulsory round of work and existence ('stay-at-home') to the sacred, unfamiliar, voluntary world of 'awayness' (the 'touristic'), in which the escapers are re-created, refreshed and renewed in specifically 'ritualized breaks in routine that define and relieve the ordinary', and which are preferably authentic (1989: 23, 28; 1983). In other words, in the conceptualizations of MacCannell and Graburn 'imaginative pleasure-seeking' and travel for leisure and enjoyment in the encounter with the 'other' and the 'unfamiliar' are translated into journeys of self-discovery, the quest for fulfilment, social status and mental and physical health.

Cohen, however, argued for a much more diverse set of motivations and purposes for tourists, and for a concept of authenticity of which the criteria vary depending on the views, perceptions and evaluations of the tourist or observer (1988a: 378; and see Kontogeorgopoulos, 2003b). Authenticity is therefore negotiable and fluid, and this explains why 'a cultural product, or trait thereof, which is at one point generally judged as contrived or inauthentic may, in the course of time, become generally recognized as authentic' (ibid.: 379). Authenticity, like culture and ethnicity, is also a focus of debate and contestation among local hosts, and as Erb suggests, this arises partly from different readings of what authenticity might mean (2003: 131–132; and see Allerton, 2003: 124–126).

Recent debates on the concept of authenticity and the differences of interpretation between 'objectivists', 'constructivists' and 'post-modernists' do not seem to have advanced our understanding significantly. However, there appears to be a more general agreement that we should abandon attempts to determine 'objective authenticity' and address the diverse and personal nature of tourists' experiences, and that, for certain tourists, we accept that they can undergo an 'inauthentic authentic' experience and that we are dealing with intra- and inter-personal states connected to 'existential authenticity' (Reisinger and Steiner [2006] and Wang [1999]). In my view, therefore, we do not abandon the concept of authenticity; rather we personalize it, address its socially constructed nature, and recognize that tourists can perceive authenticity to their satisfaction even when it is staged. This perspective must also embrace those such as tour guides who have to articulate and mediate the contested images of tourist sites, including official and government, and decide whether or not they present something which they themselves perceive as culturally authentic or as something which plays to the demands of the market (Dahles, 2001: 3).

Cohen constructed a scheme in relation to tourist motivations with regard to authenticity, arguing for a range of tourist types, from 'authenticity-seekers' to 'recreational' tourists seeking not the authentic but the pleasurable, and to 'diversionary' tourists 'who seek mere diversion and oblivion . . . unconcerned with the problem of the authenticity of their experiences' (1988a: 377; 1979c). In other words for Cohen, 'not all tourists seem to seek authenticity, or to pursue it to the same degree of intensity' (1989/2001a: 32). Recreational tourists, for example, tend to 'exhibit a rather playful attitude to the authenticity of the visited attractions' and they 'willingly . . . cooperate in the game of touristic make-believe' (ibid.: 32). This 'make-believe' was dissected by Cohen when he examined the promotional literature provided by tour guides and companies on hill tribe trekking tourism in northern Thailand (ibid.). His assessment of the increasing 'gap' between 'image' and 'reality' provides a poignant reminder of what 'staging' entails in the incorporation and display of ethnic minorities (1992/2001a); 'As tribes are gradually deprived of their habitat in which their culture flourished and become socially and economically marginal, decultured [sic] appendages of the national society, the glorified hill tribe image presented to the tourists becomes an ironic reversal of their pathetic predicament' (ibid.: 147).

Here Cohen takes account of the consumerist dimensions of tourism and the provision or production of tourist experiences and resources as consumables or commodities to be displayed, sold and appropriated (and see Selwyn, 1993: 119–120; Urry, 1995; Watson and Kopachevsky, 1994). These considerations must be placed in a post-modern, globalized context within which culture and society become increasingly fragmented, pluralized, contested, imagined and commoditized and 'distinctions between "real" versus "fake" and "natural" versus "unnatural" [are pushed] beyond recognition' (Burns, 1999: 62; Sofield, 2000: 49–50; 2001: 106–108; Urry, 1990: 85; 156; Wood, 1993: 64–66). Debates about the nature of culture and identity and about whether or not these are, or elements of them are, 'authentic' are therefore 'complicated by the abrasive power of globalization, which is strong, visible and increasingly pervasive, especially with the rapid advancement in satellite-based information technology and mass media, together with the invasive dominance of multinational corporations' (Yamashita, Eades and Kadir Din, 1997: 30; and see Sofield, 2001: 103–120). Culture then is 'trans-localized' and 'de-territorialized' and one finds in, for example, items of material culture and 'tourist arts' the embodiment of a range of meanings which defy simple categorization as genuine handicrafts or 'airport art' (Yamashita, 2003a: 5; Adams, 2006). A classic example of this relationship and tension, expressed in material artefacts, between globalization and localization, the 'modern' and the 'traditional', the 'commodity' and the 'sacred' or 'symbolic', and between vulgarization and cultural creativity is Indonesian batik, one of the primary signifiers of Indonesian identity and yet something which has also become subject to innovation and trans-localization (Hitchcock and Wiendu Nuryanti, 2000).

Tourism as a Differentiated and Embedded Subject

One of Cohen's major conclusions in his work on northern Thailand is that there are considerable variations in the effects of tourism on local communities and the kinds of tourist and tourism activity there (1979a/2001a: 118–120). Sofield too, in his consideration of the contradictory tendencies in processes of globalization argues that 'in many instances, tourism strives to highlight difference, creates or even re-creates difference, aggressively re-imaging, re-constituting and appropriating heritage, culture and place, pursuing localization in marked contrast to its globalising influence' (2001: 104). This, in turn, entails the recognition that tourism is a complex, dynamic, unbounded and variegated phenomenon which is not amenable to one-dimensional explanations, single theory frameworks or 'universal generalizations' (see, for example, Cohen, 1979b; 1988b; Dann and Cohen, 1991; Sofield, 2000: 45; 49; Wood, 1993: 55). As Wilson warned some time ago: 'We must be wary of allowing ourselves to become entrapped by any one conceptual framework' (1993: 35; and see Echtner and Jamal, 1997; Tribe, 1997; Walle, 1997).

A difficulty in this recognition of diversity is the tendency in empirical research to concentrate on one or a small number of communities or cases during limited and bounded points of time and then attempt to draw general conclusions. But as Wilson notes 'several different situations may simultaneously co-exist at any given moment in time'; there are changing effects through time, and there is differentiation even within one community (Wilson, 1993: 40; Wilkinson and Pratiwi, 1995). We are dealing with different 'perceptual time zones'; tourism does not operate uniformly, nor consistently and nor does it generate the same effects everywhere (Wilson, 1993: 36–40; Greenwood, 1989: 197). A way out of this dilemma is precisely Cohen's approach in undertaking wide-ranging comparative studies. What happens to local communities will also depend on the stage of development of tourism, its scale, pace and organization, and whether or not it is under local or external control. Cohen formulates, for example, a generalized scheme of the development of tourism in Thailand, which he argues has moved from 'personalized' to 'impersonal', 'centralized' to 'dispersed', and 'homogeneous' to 'diversified' tourism, and from 'isolation' to 'regional integration' (2001a: 4–14). He summarizes this complex process as a 'touristic transition' which Thailand, given the importance of tourism to the national economy, and the rapid increase in tourism activities and numbers of visitors, demonstrates in an 'extreme' way (2001b: 172).

In this connection, Singapore studies by Teo, Yeoh and Lim of Haw Par Villa ('Tiger Balm Gardens') reveal a shifting, contested set of perceptions of this tourist space, complicated by the different views of domestic and international tourists, and the competing views among Singaporeans themselves. The Villa was established through local philanthropy, it was internationalized and commercialized for overseas visitors, then it became a site for the rediscovery of local cultural origins, and more recently it has surrendered to the personal influences of a small group of local operators (Teo and Yeoh, 1997; Teo and Lim, 2003).

Overall then there are different kinds of tourism and tourists with different priorities, and shifting perceptions of tourist sites; the character of destinations and host cultures also vary as do the power relationships between the different actors contesting a tourist space (see, for example, Teo and Leong, 2006). As we have seen from Cohen's perceptive work, our understanding of the concept of authenticity is enriched if we take account of the variations in tourist motivations. We now recognize that not all tourists are pilgrims undergoing rites of passage and journeys of discovery (1983); they might well be pilgrims in one context and pure pleasure-seekers in another. But the problematical nature of the distinctions made by the dispassionate Western observer about tourist motivations applies equally to those external distinctions made about the supposed perceptions and categorizations of the host communities. Bruner captures the issue precisely: 'If a Balinese troupe performs a dance drama in a temple, we call it religion; if in a concert hall we call it art; if in a beach hotel, we call it tourism. But the distinctions between religion, art and tourism are western categories, not Balinese realities' (1995: 238).

Tourists also differ on a continuum of dependency or degree of institutionalization, expressed most prominently in Cohen's early quadripartite classification of the institutionalized 'organized mass tourists', the less dependent 'individual mass tourists', the relatively independent 'explorers' and the free-wheeling, discomfort- and novelty-seeking 'drifters' (1974: 527–555). But even Cohen's classification did not capture the complexity of the category 'tourist'; it was followed by categorizations based on finer discriminations of tourist types and on different domains of tourism, including the ethnic, cultural, historical, environmental and recreational (Smith, 1977; 1989b: 4–6; and see Wood, 1980; 1984). Nevertheless, these attempts at classification, while necessary, have tended to lead to stereotyping and over-simplification, and by their nature have underplayed the dynamics and complexity of tourism as a process (see, for example, the recent literature on Southeast Asian backpacking: Cohen [2004]; Muzaini [2006]; Spreithofer [1998]).

Finally, tourism as well as being a differentiated subject is also embedded in other more general processes of modernization. This poses one of the greatest challenges to tourism research in that it is often problematical to disentangle the effects of tourism development from other processes of change, particularly with the rapid expansion and outreach of the international media and electronic communication. In the case of island communities and small scale tribal populations or minorities directly exposed to tourism activities (see Cohen, 2001a), the exercise to identify sources of change might be more straightforward, but even then these transformations are unlikely to be only tourism-generated. As Cohen said, in his study of hill tribe tourism, it is a 'difficult task . . . isolating the impact of tourism from other kinds of impacts on the tribal communities emanating from the wider society' (1979a/2001a: 117). Similarly, in her study of the performing arts and tourism in central Java, Hughes-Freeland proposed that 'it is of limited value to isolate tourism as an object of analysis. Its significance resides in the connections and disconnections it constitutes in the general processes of social change' (1993: 138).

State Action and Local Agencies

I have touched on the importance of the relationships between the state and its citizens in relation to the promotion of tourism and in the construction and transformation of ethnic identities. As Wood has said, 'The relationship between tourism and ethnicity is mediated by various institutions, but none more important than the state', and further that the relationships between tourism, ethnicity and the state are 'dynamic and ongoing, with highly variable outcomes' (1997: 2; Philip and Mercer, 1999).

However, there are other important actors in the development and transformation of cultures and identities, and often these are not given the attention they deserve.

As guides, interpreters and promoters, they mediate and present communities and cultures to tourists in such processes as 'communicative staging' or, as entrepreneurs, bureaucrats and policy-makers, they determine the kinds, scale, quality and pace of development of tourism provision (Dahles, 2001). There is a tendency not to consider these actors nor to identify particular individuals, unless they happen to be especially high profile: the case of Walter Spies (and Beryl de Zoete) and Bali immediately comes to mind (Hitchcock and Norris, 1995), and to a lesser extent Miguel Covarrubias, W. O. J. Nieuwenkamp, Gregor Krause, Vicki Baum, Margaret Mead and Gregory Bateson (Yamashita, 2003a: 26–41; Picard, 1996: 26–38). Hitchcock also refers to the Armenian hoteliers, the Sarkies, and their 'exclusive hotels', including the Raffles, in Singapore, Java, Burma and Malaya, and the Scottish entrepreneur, Muriel Pearson (aka K'tut Tantri) and her venture in Bali (1999: 207). The issue of agency is a complex matter because of the interrelationships between international, national and local actors, and the variety of roles and functions performed. In some cases, one individual may have a crucial influence on the development of a tourist site, in other cases a whole host of actors may be involved, but they are important in stamping their character and interpretations upon the site.

Cohen's study of 'jungle guides' in northern Thailand is an interesting case of agency and mediation because there, at least in the initial stages of tourism development, the state did not assume a leading role (1989/2001a; and see 1982/2001a; and see Cohen and Cooper, 1986; Holloway, 1981; Salazar, 2005). Rather it was the interaction between 'alternative' tourists (generally young travellers in search of 'authentic' experiences) and 'local entrepreneurs' which generated hill tribe tourism and jungle trekking (1989/2001a: 31). Cohen also noted, in the case of 'jungle guides' that the provincial authorities had not encouraged jungle tourism, but they 'half-heartedly acquiesced to its spontaneous development' (1982/2001a: 106). However, once it had developed the authorities began to intervene to regulate it and to professionalize the 'marginal' occupation of jungle guiding (ibid.: 108–109). Cohen has said, 'Enterprising travellers who penetrate new and as yet "unspoilt" areas frequently become the unsuspected pioneers of the touristic penetration of these areas by less adventurous individuals, who follow in their footsteps' (Cohen, 1989/2001a: 33). From the 1970s onwards these young travellers in Thailand then interacted with 'freelance local guides' and 'small jungle-tour companies' (ibid.: 38–39). Cohen stressed the importance of the personal qualities of the guides, their charisma, experience, reputation and linguistic abilities as well as the activities of a small group of tour companies which were key agents in developing and presenting 'images' of the hill tribes (ibid.: 59–61; 1983/2001a: 67–68).

In certain locales tourism appears to develop almost by accident. This early stage in the development of tourism is sometimes given insufficient attention, nor do we have much information on the origins, organization, ethnic identity and personal characteristics of individuals, particularly the local entrepreneurs, who are crucial in establishing and building tourism activities, and deciding on the kinds of tourism activities and the services to be offered, or who perhaps expand tourism interest at a later time. However, Hitchcock has undertaken some research on Chinese, Javanese and Balinese entrepreneurs in Indonesia (2000), as has Dahles on brokers, guides and 'romantic' entrepreneurs in her study of sex tourism in Yogyakarta ([1999; 2001: 101–119; 131–154; 188–213; see also Dahles and Bras on informal sector entrepreneurs in Yogyakarta and Lombok [1999]); Shaw and Shaw on local entrepreneurship in Bali (1999); and Adams on some key local players in the Toraja tourism industry (1997a, 2003, 2006). I shall, however, draw attention in a moment to some examples of agency in relation to Bali, Torajaland and Yogyakarta and their position in competing discourses about the interpretation of tourist sites.

Anthropology and Tourism in Context: Case Studies

The Main Sites and Concepts

Different parts of Southeast Asia have produced different kinds of work in the anthropology of tourism, partly in response to the different tourist resources which are promoted and displayed, but also, I suspect, because of the different interests and theoretical inclinations of the observers. Sofield notes that 'for the most part, each country [in the ASEAN Tourism Council] focuses on imaging its *differences*' (2001: 117). Within wider processes of globalization and within the sphere of the politics of identity, we are witnessing processes of social and cultural differentiation. Kahn has said of globalization that it 'is as likely to generate difference, uniqueness, and cultural specificity as it is to produce a genuinely universal or homogeneous world culture' (1998: 9). In addition, although all Southeast Asian states have an interest in the construction of identities and therefore in the 'image-making' dimension of tourism development, they do so to different degrees and in different ways (Wood, 1997: 11–24). In some cases state regulation and intervention are robust, in others much less marked so that local communities have more room for manoeuvre.

In terms of the concepts used to analyze tourism processes and their effects, the anthropological literature on Southeast Asian tourism, certainly from the early 1990s, seems not to have moved in radically new directions. The debates have been dominated by post-modern concerns with the construction and transformation of national and local identities and of 'images' of 'cultures' and 'traditions' (Hitchcock, 1999). Wood's eloquent statement on the conceptualization of these matters of cultural change and tourism still holds. He says that we should see 'people as active and strategic users of culture, participating in contexts where no single set of cultural interpretations has an inherent claim to truth and authenticity' (1993: 66). He continues, 'Not tradition

54

but its on-going symbolic reconstitution; not authenticity but its attribution; not inherited identities but relational, improvised and contested ones; not internalized values as much as available templates and strategies of action; not culture but cultural invention and local discourses – the central questions to be asked are about process, and about the complex ways tourism enters and becomes part of an already on-going process of symbolic meaning and appropriation' (ibid.: 66).

What has happened increasingly since Wood made this statement is an elaboration of this dynamic, contested, symbolically constructed concept of culture and identity by examining it in relation to the policies and image-making of the state in interaction with the responses of tourists and local communities (Picard and Wood, 1997a; Yamashita, Eades and Kadir Din, 1997), and in relation to such concepts as heritage, commoditization and globalization (Hitchcock and King, 2003a). Yamashita attempts to capture these demands in terms of 'dynamic ethnography', and following Clifford (1988), 'narratives of emergence and invention' rather than 'narratives of loss and homogenization' (2003: 8–10). Furthermore, 'tourist spaces' have been increasingly conceptualized as sites or zones of cultural strategy, contestation and image-making and -remaking in the context of the encounters, interaction and differentials of power between the different participating actors, and they present opportunities for engaging in debates about the conceptualization and interrelationships of the past, present and future (Teo and Leong, 2006; Erb, 2000). Local actors too develop their own views and create their own images of tourists in response to the 'tourist gaze' in what Maoz (2006) refers to as the 'local gaze' and the 'mutual gaze'.

It is no surprise that anthropologists have gone where the tourists go. Indeed, Crick suggests that in important respects anthropologists and tourists share similarities (1995; and Bruner, 1995: 224–241, and Harkin, 1995: 650–670), as do traders, travellers and tourists (Forshee, 1999; Forshee et al., 1999). Adams remarks pertinently that 'Both tourism and anthropology thrive on exotic imagery' (2006: 20). It is true that anthropologists have also studied populations of relatively minor interest in tourism terms or those communities which are only just entering the tourism market (see, for Indonesian examples from Flores, Allerton [2003] and Erb, on Manggarai, [1998; 2000; 2001; 2003] and Cole on Ngadha [2003], Bras [2000] and Hampton [1998] on Lombok, and Forshee on Sumba and Timor [2001; 2002]), but generally they have examined the major sites of tourist interest. In this regard anthropological studies of tourism among the Balinese and Toraja still occupy centre stage in Indonesia. Java, although a major centre of international and domestic tourism, has not received as much attention in comparison (but see Dahles, 2001; Hitchcock, 1997; 1998; Hughes-Freeland, 1993; Wiendu Nuryanti, 1998), and neither has northern Sumatra (but see, for example, Causey, 2003, and Hutajulu, 1995). In Thailand, the anthropological/sociological literature is dominated by Cohen's work (see, for example, 2001a). In Malaysia there is a scattering of research on urban-based and heritage tourism in such places as Penang and Melaka (see, for example, Worden [2003], Cartier [1996; 1997: 1998; 2001], Kahn [1997], Jenkins and King [2003], King [1993]), on the effects of beach tourism on local communities (see, for example, Bird [1989]) and increasing attention to such areas as longhouse or ethnic tourism in Sarawak (King, 1995; Carslake, 1995; Zeppel, 1995; 1997), but very little else. Singapore's post-modern 'touristscapes', constructed cultural and historical sites, and national and ethnic imaging have also commanded some attention (see, for example, Ooi [2001; 2002a; 2002b; 2003]; Leong [1997a, 1997b]; Chang [1997]; Teo and Yeoh [1997]; Teo and Lim [2003]; Teo and Huang [2005]).

Indonesia

The studies which have made a special contribution to our understanding of Southeast Asian tourism are those undertaken on Bali. These, and studies among the Toraja and the Javanese of Yogyakarta, must be located in the context of the Indonesian state's policies on national identity and culture, and its construction of 'regional' or 'provincial' cultures (King and Wilder, 2003: 216; 214–230; Dahles, 2001; Pemberton, 1994). Wood has said that, for the Indonesian government, 'religion' and 'region' are much more important than ethnicity (1997: 13–15). The strategy of the New Order government was to 'domesticate' ethnic diversity within a grand project of national image management and the construction of national tourist attractions. The state created a 'hyper-reality' which confirmed 'endless diversity' within 'harmonious unity' (Dahles, 2001: 38). But in the case of Bali local communities still have room for manoeuvre and resistance in creating and manipulating their own sub-regional ethnic identities. Although Indonesia is a large and culturally diverse country, much of what we know about its tourism is filtered through the lens of Bali. This has brought a particular character to studies of Indonesian tourism. Bali's unique quality as a focus of tourism activity and the ways in which it has been represented began to be established some 90 years ago. 'The image of Bali as a paradise, and of the Balinese as practising a colourful version of Hinduism in a sea of austere Islam, was generated in colonial times' (Howe, 2005: 5).

The important work of Picard, given his long involvement in research there and the availability of historical material on the Dutch 'Balinization' policy and the post-war Indonesian government policies of development and national integration, avoids the problems occasioned by Wilson's 'ethnographic time-traps' (1993). Picard has observed the changing trajectories and character of tourism in Bali and the debates about it since the 1980s, and placed it in a detailed historical perspective (1987; 1990a; 1990b; 1993; 1995; 1996; 1997; 2003). He has also been able to draw on a considerable amount of other research on Bali, including local materials in Indonesian, to flesh out and reinforce his conclusions and findings, and to re-evaluate the complex relationships between tourism and culture (see also, Hanna,

1972; Francillon [1979; 1989]; McKean [1973; 1976; 1977a]; Noronha, [1973]; Vickers [1989]; Yamashita [2003a]).

Picard's work on Bali has been preoccupied with the process of the 'touristification' of culture and the ways in which culture, in response to the demands of tourism and to national cultural policies, is manipulated, constructed and transformed. Perhaps nowhere else in Indonesia, with the partial exception of the Toraja, and nowhere else in Southeast Asia, has tourism become such an integral part of a culture that we can speak of a 'touristic culture' (1996; and see Howe, 2005: 142–145). The government's promotion of cultural tourism there, the scale and intensity of tourist attention over a relatively long period of time, and the contribution of a large number of influential individuals to the creation and display of elements of Balinese culture, have resulted in the Balinese discovering that they have something called 'culture' which they need to treasure and preserve as an integral part of their identity. Above all, they need to protect it from 'contamination' (Picard, 2003: 108–109; Howe, 2005: 131). Indeed, they have come to conceptualize their 'culture', 'tradition', 'art' and 'religion' in terms of concepts which were introduced to Bali from outside (from Sanskrit, Arabic, Dutch and Malay). This process and preoccupation have also led to a deep and on-going interaction and integration of 'that which belongs to culture and that which pertains to tourism' (Picard, 2003: 108–109), and an increasing emphasis on culture as 'spectacle' and on 'artistic and material productions' (Howe, 2005: 1–2; Shepherd, 2002b).

A note of caution here: we are not addressing the whole of Balinese culture. Tourists concentrate in particular parts of Bali, especially in the southern regions, as has the research on tourism. There are communities in Bali where there is very little if any tourism, and where the characterizations of Picard and others would not apply or not to such a degree. Indeed, given the recent devolution of powers to the district level in Indonesia, there is a real fear that such provinces as Bali will fragment and disintegrate, and Picard draws attention to the recent contestations about Balinese religion and the breaking up of the religious field, which have generated debates on the very conception of Balinese identity (2003). It seems to me that Bali, like the hill tribes of northern Thailand, needs a Cohen-like systematic comparison of different communities in different sub-regions of Bali with different experiences of tourism (but see Wall, 1996b).

With regard to the theme of agency in Balinese tourism, much has already been written about the intellectuals, artists and aesthetes who descended on Bali in the 1920s and 1930s. I shall not repeat the story here, other than to note that Balinese culture 'rather than simply being preserved, was recreated under the gaze of the artists and anthropologists such as Spies, Mead and Bateson, as well as by the tourists visiting the island' (Yamashita, 2003a: 37). This process of cultural creation and re-creation has continued through Bali's recent history, with the crucial contribution of opinion formers and leaders, among them the anthropologists Clifford Geertz, Raymond Noronha, Philip McKean, James Boon and Michel Picard himself. Picard says of McKean, for example, that his argument had 'considerable repercussions, both in Bali and beyond'; it contributed 'to making Bali an exemplary model of successful cultural tourism (. . .) Perhaps of even greater consequence is the fact that (. . .) McKean's conclusions appeared just in time to support the tourism doctrine elaborated by the Balinese authorities' (1996: 112).

Picard has also recently drawn attention to the Head of the Provincial Government's Tourism Office, I Gde Pitana, who was appointed in June 2001; a columnist on tourism issues for the *Bali Post*, and a 'respected academic' who was attempting to set a new course for tourism development, promoting 'a shift from a capital-intensive tourism to a people's "community-based tourism"' (2003: 113). The concept of local ownership and management of tourism facilities seems to have struck a cord with some prominent, senior Balinese in the provincial government, and it coincides with a more general emphasis in development practitioner circles on local participation, small-scale activities and sustainability. However, Picard questions whether the recent trend to develop mega-projects can be reversed, and that with the Law on Regional Autonomy implemented in 2001, 'district heads are more than ever eager to attract big-scale investments to their region' (ibid.: 114). What is particularly fascinating is who will win out in the struggles to determine tourism policies in Bali and the nature of Balinese identity among, for example, progressive intellectuals and Hindu fundamentalists. One of the foremost students of Balinese culture and tourism, I Nyoman Darma Putra, is a respected Balinese intellectual and one of the opinion leaders in the province; another is Satria Naradha, the chief editor and owner of the *Bali Post*.

In emphasizing the importance of contestation in the politics of identity and tourism development, it is important to have more detailed information on those involved in the debates and struggles, their backgrounds, their influence and who determines final outcomes. These are complex matters, but Picard notes that the launching of 'reformation' after President Suharto's downfall 'has unleashed a struggle amongst Balinese opinion leaders, concerning not only the desirable course of tourism development and a fair distribution of its revenue, but even more so the definition of their identity and the place of their island within Indonesia' (2003: 116). One notes in some of the more recent literature on Indonesia a growing interest in identifying and examining the 'opinion leaders', the intermediaries, the composition of factions and patron-client networks, and the contribution of outsiders, including anthropologists (Adams, 1995, 2006), in the struggles and rivalries generated by efforts to promote tourism and construct and maintain cultural identities. In addition, Wall, in considering future trends in tourism research refers to an emerging focus, and that is the 'role of intermediaries' in evaluating the 'meaning and significance of tourism' in Southeast Asia (2001: 320; Timothy and Wall, 1997; Dahles, 2002).

Another site of investigation has been the Toraja. They are a very different population from the Balinese – so-called 'tribal' or upland, and 'animist', though now mainly converts to Christianity, whilst the Balinese are in popular parlance 'peasants' and members of a world religion. It is as if those who promote tourism in Indonesia have seized on a dominant motif, consciously or unconsciously, in Southeast Asian anthropology – the contrast between 'peasant' and 'tribal', and between the 'great' and the 'little' traditions. In a predominantly Muslim Indonesia it is also certain of the non-Muslim minorities which are selected for tourist attention (see Kadir Din, 1989, on Islam and tourism in Malaysia). However, with the Indonesian government's policy on religion pressing all citizens to be members of one of the major monotheistic religions, the Torajan 'animist' beliefs and practices (*aluk*), expressed in such events as funerals, have been recognized by the Indonesian authorities since 1969 as 'an official "sect" of Hindu-Dharma, a category that interestingly includes Balinese religion as well' (Volkman, 1985: 167).

From the early 1970s Toraja 'began to be billed as an alternative to Bali for tried and true tourists, just as beautiful and more exotic, remote, and primitive' (ibid.: 166). The emergence of tourism in Toraja paralleled the early attention of anthropologists. They were first put on to the tourist stage by Eric Crystal (1989/1977), and then by Toby Alice Volkman (1984; 1985; 1987; 1990), Kathleen Adams (1984; 1993a; 1993b; 1995; 1997a; 1997b; 1998a; 1998b; 2003) and Shinji Yamashita (1994; 1997). Although touristification has not been a major theme here, and other influences including Christian conversion and labour migration have been at work, there has been an enduring interest in Torajan identity formation and the importance of ethnic identity markers (in this case house architecture, funeral rituals and ancestral effigies). An interesting dimension of the emergence and transformation of Torajan identity is that 'the tourist trade thrives on images of paganism that many Toraja rejected long ago and increasingly reject with the rising Christianity fostered by migration' (Volkman, 1985: 167). Christian Toraja, who have accumulated wealth whilst working away from their homeland, invest some of their resources in status- and tourism-generating funeral rituals, and Christian entrepreneurs, including hotel owners, make money from the presentation and support of a religion to which they no longer adhere. 'It would not, after all, be easy to entice European travellers with promises of Calvinist or Catholic mortuary rites' (ibid.: 167; 168).

In 1969 the Toraja were 'shielded from the outside world' and in 1971 only 58 tourists visited the region (Crystal, 1989: 155). Crystal notes that this figure increased rapidly and by 1975 over 2,500 visitors were recorded (ibid.: 141–142; 156). In the early 1970s Indonesian government planners began to consider developing cultural tourism there (Volkman, 1984: 165–166; Crystal, 1989: 141–142). Small numbers of intrepid visitors, the majority from continental Europe, particularly France, Switzerland and Germany, and also Australia, had already begun to arrive there by 1971 and in 1972 'several hundred foreign visitors witnessed a major performance of *ma'nen*', honouring *aluk* ancestors, in Pangala . . . [and] [s]till more attended the much publicized funeral of the man reputed to have been the last great southern puang [lord/owner] of "pure" noble blood: Puang Laso' Rinding of Sangalla' (Volkman, 1984: 165). In my view, Toraja tourism provides the most appropriate illustration of the importance of particular events and personalities in encouraging tourism interest: the filming of Puang Laso' Rinding's funeral by a British film crew sponsored by Ringo Starr and broadcast on French, Swiss and Belgian television; the publication in English and Indonesian of an article on the history and culture of the Toraja in 1972; and a piece in the *National Geographic* in the same year (ibid.; Adams, 1997a: 159). Another key event was the visit of the Indonesian Director-General of Tourism, Joop Avé, to South Sulawesi, and his declaration that Torajaland was 'the touristic prima donna' of the province (Adams, 1997a: 159). The celebrity status of the Toraja was then confirmed in tourist guidebooks, presenting an authentic, exotic 'other'; the representation of the Toraja also demonstrated the persuasive power of texts and the ways in which culture is commoditized (McGregor, 2000).

In a relatively rare example of the role of particular individuals in the development of tourism, Adams provides a fascinating account of the initiative of a prominent member of the local elite in putting his community of Ke'te' Kesu' on the tourist map. She discusses the enterprise of Ne' Raba Sarungallo, leader of the ancestral house of Kesu', in securing local government approval for his hamlet to become a 'tourist object', producing a written history of his house, and offering lectures on his home at 'tourism, architectural, and university seminars' (2003: 96–103). Indeed, '[a]s the reigning Kesu' noble and as an exceptionally knowledgeable elder, Ne' Raba was increasingly sought out by foreign and domestic researchers' (ibid.: 97). His achievement was 'successfully enshrining the name Kesu' on the touristic and anthropological map of Tana Toraja' (ibid.: 97). After his death in 1986 there was difficulty in finding a suitable successor and other elite families were competing for the tourism spoils. Ne' Raba's kin group engaged in a collective effort to maintain their position: this included staging a 'reconstruction ritual' for their ancestral house, with an explanatory 50-page booklet, which succeeded in attracting a large number of guests, tourists and representatives of the media, and also the founding of a museum to celebrate the history and culture of Ke'te' Kesu' and the place of the Sarungallo family within this (ibid.: 97–100). It appears that Ne' Raba's son, though 'a quietly reflective man in his early fifties', had begun to take on a more prominent role, training young people in the community in carving, and lobbying prominent Indonesians to secure the nomination of Ke'te' Kesu' as a UNESCO World Heritage site (ibid.; and see 2006).

Similarly Volkman makes reference to Pak Kila', a ritual specialist and follower of the traditional religion, educated and articulate, who had held 'several important political positions' in the local administration, including as Head of the Tourism Office (1985: 167–168). It was he who played a crucial role in ensuring that Torajan traditional religion was recognized by the Indonesian government as an official 'sect' of Hindu Dharma (ibid.). He did so as an adherent and passionate supporter of Torajan beliefs and practices, but his advocacy also had a spin-off for the development of tourism since this traditional religion, focused on elaborate mortuary rituals, attracts tourists and provides the essential elements in Torajan images presented to the outside world and to the Toraja themselves. As Yamashita says 'what was once religious ritual is becoming a spectacle to be viewed by tourists' (2003a: 121).

The role of individuals in the development of tourism and in the imaging of a tourist site are illustrated in Yamashita's narrative of the death of Puang Mengkendek, an aristocratic, Christian regent with whom he enjoyed a close association during his fieldwork, and whose funeral he attended in late October–early November 1992. Puang Mengkendek's eldest son and chief mourner Sampe (a pseudonym), who played a major part in organizing the funeral, was a Muslim. Yamashita says, capturing the power of tourism to hybridize culture, 'The Christian Puang Mengkendek's funeral was to be carried out by the Muslim son according to the Toraja traditional custom – a fantastic combination' (1997: 85). What this event also illustrates is the crucial role which individuals play in creating and sustaining cultural tourism. Sampe negotiates with a Japanese television company to film his father's funeral for a very large fee (ibid.: 86–87). He does so as a prominent Torajan businessmen, at that time a close associate of one of President Suharto's sons, and a director of 'a newly opened hotel in Tana Toraja' (ibid.: 87). Yamashita says, 'Anyway, for Sampe, performing his father's funeral and promoting his new hotel must have been closely interconnected' (ibid.: 87). The lesson which we take from this case is expressed in Yamashita's concluding comments, and one which we might focus on for future research; he says, 'In Puang Mengkendek's funeral, not only Toraja locals, but also the president of the hotel group from Jakarta, the local troops of the national army, international tourists, and the Japanese TV, played important roles in shaping the "meaning" of the ritual performance' (ibid.: 101). As Yamashita explains, Sampe has manipulated Torajan 'ethnic tradition' (ibid.: 102). He does need to be brought centre stage, and the role of prominent individuals in tourism promotion deserves more detailed analysis.

A study that addresses the issue of agency directly is Heidi Dahles's work, conducted between 1992 and 1996, on tour guides in Yogyakarta, a region which, under New Order rule, was not on the periphery, but at the very centre of tourism policy because it was 'in the heart of Javanese culture' (2001: 19). This was both an advantage and a disadvantage. The 'cultural heritage of the Yogyakarta area has shaped the (international) image of Indonesia, as government propaganda has used architectural structures like the temples and the sultan's palace and expressions of art like the Ramayana dance to promote Indonesian tourism world-wide' (ibid.: 20). Being centre-stage also entailed being subject to closer control in order to conform with government propaganda about the shape and content of national culture whose central ingredient was Javanese-based. Therefore, there was a 'limited diversity of tourist attractions' because '[i]nnovations have not been welcomed as they threaten the carefully planned tourist area and jeopardize the government-controlled objectives of tourism to Yogyakarta' (ibid.: 20). According to Dahles, the room for manoeuvre, at least in the officially controlled tourism or 'streetside' sector, including officially licensed tour guides, was limited. It was in the unofficial, *kampung* or low-class neighbourhoods where tourism began to flourish. What Dahles discovered was that, in the informal sector, there was a 'multivocality of images and meanings associated with the city and its attractions' (ibid.: 21). She adopts, with advantage, the Geertzian paradigm of the distinction between the 'firm' and 'bazaar' (1963a), demonstrated most clearly in her dualistic tourism model of the 'modern', 'quality', 'developed', 'dominant' and the 'traditional', 'marginal', 'underdeveloped', 'dependent' sectors (2001: 124–127).

According to Dahles it was in unofficial, 'backstage' tour guiding where the images and meanings presented by government-supported and -approved agencies were principally contested, though not exclusively. Dahles provides us with some detailed information on entrepreneurs in *kampung* and homestay tourism such as Pak Djono, who was the first to organize budget tours in the Sosrowijayan area, and Ibu Siska, who developed tours to local home industries and subsequently 'adventure tourism' and ecotourism (ibid.: 101–106). It is with this sector that the unofficial, unlicensed guides (occasional touts, odd-jobbers, professional friends, romantic entrepreneurs) developed their closest relationships, though the government attempted to institute control, procedures and training for the purposes of 'professionalization'. Tour guides, as we have already seen, have a crucial role in image-making; they are 'entrusted with the purest of public relations missions: to encapsulate the essence of a place and to be a window onto a site, region, or country' (ibid.: 131). Official guides to the main sites of officially sanctioned tourism such as the splendid temple complex of Borobodur were constrained in their narratives, though even here, they could 'sprinkle their narratives with subversive elements' (ibid.: 173). However, it was in the unlicensed arena that 'storytelling' flourished. What is intriguing in Dahles's analysis is her comment that these guides 'know how to read a social situation and have general conceptions about tourist motivations, national stereotypes, and tourist types which they turn to their advantage' (ibid.: 178). This comment in itself constitutes a very large research agenda and presents us with the 'folk' version of the tourism researcher. Unofficial guides then are part of a small-scale entrepreneurial culture and they present a counter-narrative to the officially sanctioned government ideology which comprises notions of national unity in diversity, law-abiding, enjoying modernity and prosperity, and of Yogyakarta as the centre of a homogeneous Javanese culture. Instead the *kampung* versions of Indonesia and Java convey 'the image of Yogyakarta as a city of migrants from all over Indonesia, struggling to make a living under harsh conditions and enjoying themselves while engaging in partly illicit trade and leisure activities' (ibid.: 211). Dahles concludes: 'the state control exerted on the discourses [of nationhood] has been more conspicuous in its effort than in its effect' (ibid.: 229).

Thailand

A rather different, more disparate set of studies on tourism in Thailand has been provided by Erik Cohen. Here we are not dealing with work on one ethnic group, or one location like Bali with a long-standing tourism interest and one which was set in motion as long ago as the inter-war years by the Dutch colonial administration, or with a focus on exotic pagan rituals as in the case of the upland Toraja, or with tour guides in Yogyakarta. Instead we have wide-ranging, indeed nation-wide studies of Thailand since the 1970s, comprising hill tribe village tours and jungle trekking in the north (2001a: 31–148), island and beach tourism on the southern islands (ibid.: 151–246), and sex tourism, principally in Bangkok (ibid.: 249–345). These constitute the three major elements of tourism in Thailand, though their degree of importance relative to one another has changed through time, and there are other tourist attractions, both in Bangkok and beyond, which have been developed since the 1970s. Tourism is mainly located on a north-south axis with three prominent nodes – Chiang Mai, Bangkok (including an extension to Pattaya) and Phuket (ibid.: 158). Rather than a particular ethnic group or a site providing a showcase or emblem of Thailand, it is the country itself which is marketed. 'Thailand has enjoyed, in the West, the image of an enchanted Oriental kingdom throughout much of modern history' (Cohen, 2001b: 156). Cohen also detects a shift in its imaging from an 'exotic' and 'erotic' tourist site to an 'amazing' one, with the accompanying deliberate construction and staging of 'major contrived attractions' (archaeological sites, historical parks, festivals, theme and amusement parks) as Thailand's tourism industry matures, and as it attempts to move away from its image as an 'erotic' destination (and see Leheny, 1995).

Cohen indicates a complicating factor in the study of tourism there, and one which has already been alluded to. 'The growth of tourism in Thailand did not occur in isolation – as it did in some small, isolated island states on which tourism is the principal or sole industry; rather, tourism grew hand in hand with the rapid economic development of the country, comprising the industrial, financial, communicative, and service sectors' (2001a: 24; Elliott, 1983). Cohen suggests, therefore, that it is a difficult task to evaluate the impact and consequences of what is 'a highly diversified, complex, and changing phenomenon . . . within the wider processes of economic development and social change in Thai society' (ibid.: 28). His overall assessment in the mid-1990s, using the notion of 'impact' rather than 'touristification', was that the effect of tourism on 'mainstream Thai culture has had some creative as well as debasing consequences'. However, the impact 'on the way of life of some small and vulnerable ethnic groups . . . can be seriously detrimental' (ibid.: 26–27). Indeed, 'the more accessible tribal villages often suffered extreme de-culturation' (2001b: 163; and see Dearden [1996], Dearden and Harron [1994] and Toyota [1996]). It would seem that the concept of touristification is not so appropriate for Thailand, nor has there been much attention to the role of individuals or entrepreneurs in the development of tourism there; tourism in Bangkok, for example, given that it has taken place in a highly cosmopolitan, urban environment, has not touristified Thai culture. It is one of many forces of change in the capital city. The effects of tourism are much more dispersed and disparate in an increasingly segmented tourism industry; the sustained influence of tourism in Bali, and to some extent in Torajaland, does not seem to have been replicated in Thailand where there has not been so much concentration on specific ethnic groups nor, given the degree of ethnic homogeneity in Thailand, has the Thai state been overly preoccupied with the imaging of cultural diversity within an overall national culture (Wood, 1997: 22). Comparing Picard's work on Bali and Cohen's on Thailand, there is a noticeable difference.

Overall Cohen, though recognizing processes of staging and cultural invention, keeps to a perspective which harkens back to the debates about 'impacts' and which sees tourism as having both negative and positive effects. He identifies processes of 'commodification of art, culture, and sex' but also the contribution of tourism 'to the preservation of crafts and customs which would otherwise have disappeared, as well as the emergence of new artistic styles (. . .) and cultural performances' (2001b: 170).

Malaysia and Singapore

In Malaysia and Singapore there has been an overriding preoccupation with pluralism and with state policies on tourism development and the role of tourism in identity formation, the 'objectification' of culture and ethnicity, and cultural change (see, for example, Kadir Din [1982; 1986; 1997]; Kahn [1997]; King [1993]; Leong [1989; 1997]). In plural situations like Malaysia and Singapore the state has a very strong interest in developing and promoting a national culture, even though it has to address the tension between this exercise and one which depends on permitting and promoting some cultural diversity as tourism assets. Much has been written on the colonial legacy in Malaysia and Singapore and the ways in which ethnic groups were constructed through processes of rationalization and categorization; these processes continued during the post-independence period when governments were engaged in nation-building (see King and Wilder, 2003: 193–230). From an earlier and much more complex, variegated ethnic mosaic the Malaysian government now recognizes three major ethnic categories: Malays (and other indigenes), Chinese and Indians; and, in Singapore, these three are augmented by a miscellaneous category labelled 'Other' in a quadripartite classification, CMIO ([C]hinese, [M]alay, [I]ndian, [O]ther).

Perhaps more than other countries in Southeast Asia the study of tourism in Malaysia and Singapore is also more closely associated with the creation of 'imagined communities' (Anderson, 1991), and research on tourism has been located more firmly in 'a larger cultural landscape' of ethnic diversity within an embracing national cultural unity (Wood, 1997: 22). Kahn, for example, emphasizes, in his examination of a preservation and restoration project of Muslim heritage in George Town, Penang, that it must be understood in terms of more general processes of 'culturalization' in Malaysia rather than specifically in relation to tourism (1997: 100–101; and see Jenkins and King, 2003). Although identities are contested and debated in Malaysia and Singapore, the role of the state seems to be dominant, and there is little evidence or interest in the anthropological literature on tourism of individual innovation and agency.

The major tourism activities are highly focused regionally and emphasize Malaysian culture, beach tourism (Penang, Langkawi, east coast peninsular Malaysia), heritage (Melaka, Kuala Lumpur and Penang) and environmental tourism (mainly in the national parks including Taman Negara and Kinabalu): these have been the main forms of recreation promoted by the government and tourist companies and agents (and see Oppermann, 1992). There has also been more limited attention to ethnic tourism, principally among the minority populations of Sarawak and Sabah; the dominant theme in this research has been the 'imaging' and 'staging' of exotic, primitive cultures – longhouses in the deep tropical rainforests in picturesque and unspoilt riverine settings; head-hunters and trophy skulls; tattooed, loin-clothed and costumed warriors; hunters with blowpipes; cock-fighting; bare-breasted women; pagan rituals; and dancing to the accompaniment of gongs and drums (see, for example, King, 1995; Zeppel, 1997).

Much of the literature on Malaysia has been focused at the national level rather than on specific ethnic groupings. There is also the issue of the promotion of tourism in a country whose main defining characteristics are rooted in Islam, a religion which rejects the notion that Muslim culture is a resource for 'staging' and for commoditization (Kadir Din, 1989; 1997). The image promoted by the Malaysian official agencies is therefore one of unity in diversity, a combination of the three major ethnic categories in a colourful, vibrant, interconnected and harmonious cultural tourism package (King, 1993: 103; 108–112). Islam is, however, distanced in the promotion of tourism, apart from references to mosques, festivals, and royal towns and palaces, and, according to Kadir Din, it has little direct affect on tourism policy and the direction of tourism development (1989). As I have said elsewhere, 'The fact that Islam is the national religion, and that Malaysia has to be conscious of ethnic divisions and sensibilities, lead to a more cautious and circumspect treatment of culture' (King, 1993: 108–109). Official tourism images focus on diversity and colour, but culture is presented in 'distinctly neutral' terms (ibid.: 110). Nevertheless, the importance which the Malaysian government attaches to indigenous history and the Malay cultural legacy, within the national culture, is expressed in a range of specifically Malay cultural products, including museum displays, especially in the former sultanate of Melaka (Cartier, 2001). As Worden says, the 'heritage representations shown in Melaka are (. . .) a product of the cultural policies and historical constructions of the 1970s and 1980s' in which the historic city is presented as a Muslim Malay project (2003: 39).

In Singapore, in contrast to Malaysia, cultural heritage, architecture, and ethnic enclaves have been swept away in a process of technocratic 'cleansing' and 'sanitizing' so that 'most physical manifestations of history' have been 'erased' (Wood, 1997: 21; Leong, 1997a: 520–522). 'The cleaning and cleansing of the city-state have been so successful that foreign travel guidebooks and foreign observers have commented on the tidiness and cleanliness of the city, observations that suggest the city is antiseptic and the culture sterile' (Leong, 1997b:78). Unlike any other part of Southeast Asia including Malaysia, Singapore's strongly interventionist government has not preserved or restored its heritage, but dramatically reconstructed and re-created it. What it does present to the tourist, as with Malaysia, is cultural diversity and deliberately constructed tourist sites. But Singapore does not herald cultural heritage, instead it presents an artificially constructed and managed cultural mosaic both for tourism and political purposes (ibid.: 84). As Leong says: 'When tourism in Singapore mines, manufactures, and markets ethnicity as commodities, it operationalizes the pre-existing CMIO model' (ibid.: 93).

Interestingly Singapore's elimination of heritage has caused it to display it in museums; but it does so in a very political way. In his analysis of the three major national museums in Singapore, Ooi indicates that the Singapore History Museum 'emphasizes Singapore's past' (and 'asserts the state boundaries and sovereignty of an island-state' separate from but a part of the Malay world); the Asian Civilizations Museum 'showcases Asian ancient civilizations' (and Singapore as 'a melting pot of peoples from different Asian cultures' expressed in the state ethnic ideology of CMIO); and finally the Singapore Art Museum 'exhibits contemporary Southeast Asian visual art' (and can 'offer the standards against which the art world must measure itself in appreciating Southeast Asian art as a genre'; it confirms Singapore's Southeast Asian identity) (2001: 176, 190). The Singapore government, therefore, through its cultural industry, both locates the city-state and regionalizes it. An essential element in Singapore's identity is a domestic cultural diversity which is then connected regionally to the rest of Asia, but the assumption is that the 'arts and cultures among the member countries in the region have some form of coherence and homogeneity' (ibid.: 184). The government's policy to develop museums 'is just one of many strategies to make Singapore unique. It is an attempt to display Singapore's multi-cultural Asian character, which has been dwarfed by skyscrapers, the widespread use of the English language and the country's growing significance as a global trading centre' (Ooi, 2003: 80). But the museums which tourists are encouraged to visit display a Singapore which is 'essentially Asian', distinct from its neighbours, and 'multi-cultural, independent and culturally vibrant' (ibid.: 88).

Conclusion

Despite, in my view, the relatively modest contribution of anthropology (and sociology) to the study of tourism in Southeast Asia in terms of empirical coverage and scope, the discipline has drawn attention to conceptually crucial issues in our understanding of tourism as a social and cultural phenomenon. These issues, or at least most of them, were identified very early on in Cohen's work, though he has tended to remain rather Thai-centric and has not brought his insights very firmly to other parts of the region. The key issues comprise the importance of systematic comparison (within and beyond a particular culture and country); tourism as a differentiated subject and as a process rather than an event; staging and authenticity; the importance of local strategies, agencies, perspectives and meanings; tourism's embeddedness within broader processes of change; and, given that tourism focuses on contestations over identities (national, provincial, local, ethnic), the significance of the roles of the state, factions, opinion leaders and entrepreneurs in giving form and content to the resources which tourism uses and deploys. The preoccupation with identities – their formation, transformation and contestation – will undoubtedly continue to provide a major interest in the anthropology of tourism in Southeast Asia.

Although tourism studies have now been accepted as a legitimate subject of investigation in anthropology, we still have much to do to locate the study of tourism within mainstream anthropology and within a comparative, cross-cultural enterprise. Yamashita's call to arms needs substantial support when he says 'Tourism, rather than being an eccentric object of study for anthropologists, is, on the contrary, essential if anthropologists are to restructure the objects of their research' (2003: 151). This goes to the heart of what a comparative, cross-cultural, locally sensitive anthropology should address in a globalizing world. Sofield, citing Graburn (1997), has the sense of it when he says, 'Tourism has played a major role in the "imaging" and "recreation" of "national cultures" and ethnicity in many Asian countries' (2001: 108). He continues, '"culture" is increasingly the province of the state rather than the community, its definition rendered not by its peoples but by its governments for political ends, with the energetic involvement of a number of agencies of the state including national tourism organisations' (ibid.: 109). Yet governments are working within and responding to both local and global pressures and demands, and a major future challenge for a comparative anthropology is precisely to embrace, within its vision and endeavours, the study of culture at the local, national, and the global levels.

3

Indonesian Souvenirs as Micro-Monuments to Globalization and Modernity: Hybridization, Deterritorialization and Commodification

Kathleen Adams

I set out to explore Ubud. The reason I chose this town was because in Bali, Ubud is known for it's [sic] arts & crafts. And boy howdy, were there a lot of art galleries all over the place. My friend Mike warned me that the art in Bali was amazing, but I had no idea what was ahead of me. Masks, statues of wood & stone, carvings, paintings, what the hell – do any of these people do anything besides create?? I felt like a kid inna candy store, and spent the next few days finding all sorts of amazing pieces of art. I managed to max out ALL of my credit cards. I bought so much crap that I had to have it all packed into a giant crate & shipped home by sea freight. When my 'shop till you drop' frenzy finally let up (aka: no more money), I packed my bag and headed for the north coast to a group of seaside villages . . .

(Travel blog posted by a male Californian in his twenties[1])

As the above post suggests, souvenirs and handicrafts are an intrinsic dimension of Southeast Asian tourism. Few visitors to this region return home without at least one or two local handicrafts or tourist trinkets tucked into the corners of their suitcases. And some visitors, as in the case above, find themselves transformed into frenzied consumers of tourist arts. Likewise, as hinted above, both domestic and foreign tourists' pursuit of mementos of their Southeast Asian travels has transformed the physical and economic landscapes of the places they visit. Many destinations along the Southeast Asian tourist trail – from Bali to Yogyakarta to Chiang Mai – have emerged as tourist magnets for the acquisition of local arts and handicrafts. In such locales, streets and lanes once lined with homes

69

and businesses oriented towards local household consumption needs now host rows of art galleries and tourist shops. Some of these tourist-oriented businesses present museum-like displays of spotlighted 'tribal' sculptures and glittering bejeweled items, while others are more akin to bazaar stalls, crammed with hand-made baskets, reproductions of antiquities, brilliantly-colored *ikat* textiles, wooden masks, and other trinkets. In this chapter I suggest that these artistic handicrafts, whether produced by local artisans or by more distant factories, can be productively examined as micro-monuments to modernity, embodying some of the salient characteristics associated with globalization and modernity.

Whereas early academic discussions of souvenirs and tourist-oriented arts tended to dismiss such products as bereft of meaning and value, pioneering work by Nelson Graburn (1976) and Paula Ben-Amos (1977) prompted anthropologists to reassess these assumptions. Ben-Amos's article, 'Pidgin Languages and Tourist Arts', made the compelling argument that souvenirs were more communicative than had previously been assumed and that they should be considered akin to pidgin languages, embodying elementary, often-stereotyped versions of producers' and purchasers' symbolic repertoires. In essence, she pushed for scholars to recognize that touristic trinkets can carry simplified messages between peoples of different cultural and linguistic backgrounds. Likewise, Graburn's edited volume, *Ethnic and Tourist Arts*, illustrated not only how different historical circumstances resulted in the emergence of these new artistic forms, but also how a range of meanings were embodied in these 'arts of acculturation'. As he and others later helped to illustrate, tourist arts can play a powerful role in sculpting outsiders' images of the places and peoples they are visiting (Graburn, 1976; 1987; Hitchcock and Teague, 2000). In addition, artisans have drawn upon their tourist-oriented arts to renegotiate, or in some cases reaffirm, outsiders' stereotypes of their identity and situation in the world (Graburn, 1976; Adams, 1998a; 2006; Causey, 1999; 2003; Hitchcock and Teague, 2000; Forshee, 2001). Since this pioneering work by Ben-Amos and Graburn, numerous anthropological and sociological studies have explored how souvenirs and commodified arts/ handicrafts are directly and indirectly tied to notions of ethnicity, gender, authenticity, and cultural heritage (cf. Cohen, 1983a; 1993; 2000; Stewart, 1993; Shevan-Keller, 1995; Hitchcock and Teague, 2000; Hitchcock, 2003). In this chapter, I draw on some of this prior work as well as my own field research to suggest that handicrafts and material culture found in tourist stalls and markets across Southeast Asia can be seen as material testaments to some of the dynamics of accelerated globalization.

Much has been written about the socio-economic transformations wrought by globalization. Scholars concerned with the arts have tended to concentrate on documenting how global socio-economic interdependence has prompted new trade movements of indigenous arts, reconfigured the value of so-called 'tribal arts', or transformed the physical forms and symbolic meanings of local crafts (Steiner, 1994; 1995; Marcus and Myers, 1995; Errington, 1994; 1998; Phillips and Steiner, 1999; Chibnik, 2003). Building on this work, I draw on examples from Indonesia to show how commoditization, hybridization, and deterritorialization – all features associated with globalization and modernity – are part and parcel of much of the material culture produced for sale to tourists.

Before turning to discuss specific Indonesian tourist-oriented arts, a brief survey of the terrain of globalization theory is necessary. Whereas early discussions of globalization tended to posit cultural homogenization as a leitmotif of globalization, more recent analysts have rejected this claim (cf. Robertson, 1994; Tomlinson, 1999). As numerous scholars, like the Dutch sociologist Jan Nederveen Pieterse (2003), have recently argued, a more common dynamic of globalization is what has been referred to as cultural 'hybridization'. For Nederveen Pieterse, hybridization can be thought of as 'global mélange' or 'global cultural interplay' (1993: 9), involving a mixing and merging of cultural forms from diverse locales. Homi Bhabha's writings also discuss hybridity, although his emphasis is on hybrid identities rather than art forms. His work underscores how hybridity is an area of tension produced by splits between two cultures in colonial contexts, as well as 'the sign of the productivity of colonial power, its shifting forces and fixities' (1994: 112). The notion of cultural hybridization shares some terrain with the concept of 'glocalization', pioneered by Roland Robertson (1995), among others. As an amalgamation of the terms 'globalization' and 'localization', the expression is said to be derived from the Japanese business term for adjusting global products for specific local markets. According to Shinji Yamashita (2003b: 6), the term derives from the Japanese word *dochakuka*, which translates as 'living on one's own land', and initially was used to describe adjusting one's agricultural techniques to local conditions. In recent years, a number of anthropologists have embraced this concept in their analyses of tourism dynamics (cf. Raz, 1999; Yamashita, 2003b; Ness, 2003). In many cases, today's tourist arts of Southeast Asia are hybridized and glocalized, as I will illustrate shortly.

As with hybridization, deterritorialization has also been spotlighted as an important cultural dimension of globalization (cf. Tomlinson, 1999). According to Mexican theorist Nestor Garcia Canclini, deterritorialization is 'the loss of the "natural" relation of culture to geographical and social territories' (2001). Ulrike Schuerkens defines this process as a kind of restructuring of space that entails 'the disappearance of fixed links of human beings to towns, villages and national frontiers' (2003: 212). As Schuerkens declares, 'spatial distances [now] include the world as a space' (Schuerkens, 2003: 212). In Southeast Asia today, as the examples that follow will show, cultural products sold to tourists embody this dimension of globalization as well.

Before proceeding to the ethnographic illustrations, a caveat is necessary. In arguing that we can productively approach Southeast Asian tourist trinkets as mini-monuments to a contemporary post-modern world in which travel, displacement and commoditization are salient themes, it is important to underscore earlier observations made by Anthony Reid (1988; 1993; 1994), Forshee, Fink and Cate (1999) and others regarding long-term dynamics in Southeast Asia. As these authors have compellingly illustrated, travel and the inter-regional marketing of local products are deeply-rooted and ancient traditions in Southeast Asia, although, as Reid has observed, 'Southeast Asia was not "discovered" by world trade systems' until more recently (1994: 268, cited in Forshee, 1999: 2). In short, the selling of material culture and handicrafts to travellers is not as recent a phenomenon as has been imagined. However, with the ease and affordability of travel brought by jumbo jets and charter flights, as well as with the projection of material images of destination handicrafts on the internet, the marketing and elaboration of Southeast Asian handicrafts have expanded dramatically. In the course of this recent expansion, then, Southeast Asian touristic trinkets have come to embody many of the key themes of the post-modern global world.

I now turn to embark on a whirlwind tour of some of the souvenirs emerging from parts of Indonesia. Like all tours, this one tends to favour certain destinations. This chapter concentrates primarily on examples from Tana Toraja, in upland South Sulawesi. However, I also make occasional, brief comparisons to work done by other scholars elsewhere in the region (including the Toba Batak region of Sumatra, the Eastern Indonesian island of Sumba, and East Timor). Since the 1980s, my research has concentrated on art, tourism and identity in the Toraja highlands, hence my focus on examples from this area. However, it is clear from the work of other scholars in other parts of Southeast Asia (cf. Cohen, 2000; Forshee, 2001; Causey, 2003) that the dynamics chronicled here are also relevant to the touristically commoditized arts of other regions of Southeast Asia.

Tourism and Commoditized Arts in Upland Sulawesi, Indonesia

Hailed as the 'second tourist stop after Bali', the Sa'dan Toraja homeland of upland Sulawesi attracted growing numbers of international and domestic tourists in the 1980s and 1990s. Whereas in 1972 only 650 foreigners visited the Toraja highlands, by the mid-1990s over 230,000 tourists were traveling to Tana Toraja annually.[2] However, in 1998, when Indonesia plunged into a period of political and economic unrest, only 24,626 foreign tourists and 38,187 domestic tourists visited the region. In the post-September 11th world, on-going Muslim–Christian violence in certain areas of Indonesia and the infamous October 2002 Bali discotheque bombing took a further toll on Toraja tourism.[3] However, Toraja entrepreneurs have not let the plummet in foreign tourist visits inhibit their promotion of their homeland and its artistic products: the internet sports multiple Toraja web–sites offering carved Toraja handicrafts and imitation Toraja antiquities for sale to those who are inclined to remain in their armchairs at home (Adams, 2006). Thirty-five years ago, carved Toraja

Figure 3.1: Toraja effigies of the dead (*tau-tau*)

kindred houses (*tongkonan*) and sculpted Toraja effigies of the dead (*tau-tau*) were known only to Indonesians, anthropologists and missionaries. Today no Southeast Asia travel log is without at least a paragraph devoted to the Toraja and their ritual and material culture. As a Sunset article declared, 'Here [in Tana Toraja] you can get an anthropologist's glimpse of an ancient culture, fantastic building styles, unusual burial customs and possibly witness a festive funeral' (Holdiman, 1985). Through tourism, travel shows and internet promotion, then, these images have rapidly become international icons of a seductively exotic culture. For many tourists, the purchase of a miniature carved ancestral house, a wall plaque sporting incised Toraja motifs, or an imitation Toraja effigy of the dead represents not only a physical memento of travel experiences, but also a physical embodiment of assorted ideas about the 'Other'.

The explosion of tourism in the 1980s and 1990s and the attendant commoditization of Toraja material culture have coloured the relationship between the Toraja and their material products, most notably their effigies of the dead (*tau-taus*) (see Figure 3.1). Brochures and posters issued by the Indonesian Office of Tourism, as well as popular guidebooks, all feature images of Toraja burial cliffs and effigies of the dead. For those Torajas who continue to practice Toraja traditional religion (*aluk to dolo*), the *tau-tau* is thought to be inhabited by the spirit of the particular ancestor it represents: in exchange for periodic offerings, the spirit offers protection from ills. For Torajas, these effigies are also closely associated with noble identity, since only elite Torajas were traditionally permitted to have sculpted wooden effigies at their funerals. However, for foreign visitors, *tau-taus* soon became haunting symbols of pan-Toraja identity and animism. By the 1980s local carvers had begun accommodating the tourist interest in these effigies. Some started sculpting miniature, stylized *tau-taus* clothed in bits of well-worn sarong fabric. Others experimented with suitcase-sized carvings of burial cliffs, complete with small balconies holding troll-like effigies. Still others began to make what has become known as *patung model Bali* (Balinese-styled sculptures), small doll-sized sculptures of Toraja villager 'types' (see Figure 3.2).

Figure 3.2: Doll-sized tourist carvings of Toraja 'village types'

Lolo was one of the first Kesu' area carvers I knew to recognize the potential income to be had from carving fake effigies. After years of working on Java, Lolo returned to the Kesu' area in the early 1980s and decided to try his hand at carving. He was inspired by a tourist who had arrived at Ke'te' Kesu' wanting to buy a statue (effigy). Over the next decade, he and the two assistants he had trained sculpted dozens of statues and fake *tau-tau*s, many of which were purchased by tourists. Such were his skills that he has even been hired to sculpt two *tau-tau*s for American museums. As Lolo did not have a family to support, he worked sporadically, largely to support his passion for cock-fighting. Despite his erratic involvement in carving, Lolo devoted much energy to creating authentic-looking weathered patinas for the effigies he and his assistants carved. In the late afternoons I would occasionally come upon Lolo and his assistants splattering their carvings with a mixture of palm-wine and rice grains, then turning their roosters loose to peck at them. On other days I would find them pouring urine on their sculptures. To further accelerate the aging process, they would bury them for several weeks. Their carvings emerged looking suitably haunting and were often sold in the family's tourist stall or in the art shops in town.

Lolo is not the only carver crafting such tourist treasures. Today, miniature hunchbacked men with canes, sturdy youths toting pigs, roughly hewn elders cradling cockerels, and old women bearing funeral offerings all crowd the shelves of local tourist shops. While domestic Indonesian tourists rarely purchase these sorts of souvenirs (possibly due to Islam's disinclination to represent human forms), these sculptures tend to spark the interest of foreign tourists. Even more intriguing to these tourists are the carved reproductions of grave-related antiquities, which they could fancy to be authentic.[4] Ironically, tourism's showcasing of the Toraja not only promoted the *tau-tau* as an emblem of generalized Toraja identity (rather than personal elite identity), but also played a role in transforming the *tau-tau* from a ritually significant entity into a commodified art object of economic significance.

By the 1980s, a wave of *tau-tau* thefts plagued the Toraja highlands.[5] Since that time, hundreds of *tau-tau* have been stolen and sold to European, American and Asian art collectors. Burial cliffs once crowded with effigies were pillaged, leaving local villagers anguished and perplexed. At some burial sites frequented by tourists, the Indonesian government has funded the carving of replacement effigies of the dead, prompting local controversy. At other sites, villagers have enclosed their remaining *tau-tau*s in cliff-side cages, to insure against further thefts. Despite international repatriation laws,[6] stopping the drain of *tau-tau*s to Europe, the United States and Canada seems a hopeless matter, particularly in the wake of the Asian economic crisis of the late 1990s and the political turbulence that has followed. As prices for basic goods spiralled and tourism dwindled to a trickle, economic desperation inspired new thefts. In addition, the nation's political instability and inter-ethnic violence rendered pursuit of *tau-tau* smugglers a low priority. As Torajas confided, there are obstacles to stemming the flow of effigies to the West at every level – international, national and local. International art dealers assert that the *tau-tau*s they sell were 'legally acquired', and those *tau-tau*s that are recovered frequently become entwined in lengthy legal processes. Stolen effigies that are acquired before leaving Indonesia often end up languishing in police warehouses, where they become 'evidence' awaiting the capture and trial of the thieves. And at the local level Torajas are themselves sometimes reluctant to reclaim their stolen *tau-tau*s, as returning them to the graves requires traditional religious rituals that many Christian Torajas are reluctant to undertake, as well as the installation of new security systems. Both of these courses of action cost money at a time when cash is in short supply. Thus a number of the *tau-tau*s that have been recovered continue to reside in crowded police warehouses.

Today, the Torajas' relationship to the *tau-tau* has come full circle: once 'protected' by these effigies, Torajas now find themselves in the reluctant role of *tau-tau* guardians. The Toraja experience is emblematic of the changing relationship between ethnic groups and their sacred art in other parts of Southeast Asia. Paul Michael Taylor's edited volume *Fragile Traditions: Indonesian Art in Jeopardy* (1994) chronicles parallel trends elsewhere in Indonesia. Likewise, a recent thought-provoking article by Jill Forshee discusses tourists' and international connoisseurs' collecting of stolen objects of value from Eastern Indonesia and East Timor in the 1998–2002 period (2002). In discussing stolen sculpted figures from East Timor and Sumba that made their way to tourist shops in Kupang, Bali and Jakarta, she observes that 'images of "violent" societies perpetuate a peculiar type of international value attached to arts, from image-charged places like Oceania or Africa, or from historical head-hunting societies in Sumba and Timor' (Forshee, 2002: 69). Elaborating on this increasing flow of often sacred collectible cultural objects to Indonesian tourist market centers, Forshee further reflects,

> I imagined that this commerce was laced with tragedy, finding an outlet in an international demand for what were in truth spoils of war. Underscoring this market was an ongoing state of mass violence that continuously produced charred or partially destroyed objects that enlivened the sales pitches of traders of arts. Burn marks or machete hackings characterizing carvings said to originate from East Timor attested to their authenticity in the arts boutiques catering to tourists in Bali, hundreds of miles to the west of Timor Island.
>
> (Forshee, 2002: 73)

As examples from Tana Toraja, Sumba, East Timor and elsewhere suggest, as Southeast Asian ethnic arts become increasingly commoditized and coveted by tourists and international collectors, their sacred value competing with their new economic value, more and more groups will find themselves becoming guardians of the spiritually potent creations that once promised protection. In essence, the process of commoditization of spiritual arts has dramatically transformed both insiders' and outsiders' perceptions of these material objects.

Souvenir Hybridization and Deterritorialization in South Sulawesi

Just as the touristic commoditization of indigenous arts has ultimately transformed peoples' relationships to their material culture as well as bringing about the birth of new 'trinketized' art forms, accelerated globalization (of which tourism is an intrinsic part), has also produced new hybridized art forms for the tourist art market. Significantly, many of these often hybridized forms are not produced locally, but in other regions of Indonesia. Thus, we find factories in the city of Surabaya (on Java) mass producing imitations of the hand-made *ikat* textiles of Sumba (in Eastern Indonesia), which are sold to tourists visiting Bali and other tourist destinations in Indonesia. And a stroll past the windows of tourist shops in Kuta Beach, Bali, reveals an array of carvings that have little to do with indigenous Indonesian artistic traditions, from carved mini surfboards and paintings of Western pop stars, to sculpted Tolkien-esque ork creatures bearing clubs and hair fashioned from jute.[7] While some of these new art forms are embraced by locals, others prompt trepidation and frustration, as the examples below will illustrate.

When I first visited Tana Toraja Regency in the early 1980s, I followed the path of many tourists and scholars before me. I flew from Bali to the South Sulawesi capital of Makassar (formerly known as Ujung Pandang). This capital is in, and adjacent to, the homeland of other Sulawesi peoples known as Makassarese and Bugis (historically Muslim populations with a long history of rivalry with the largely Christian Sa'dan Toraja of the highlands). After over-nighting in Makassar, like other tourists, I boarded a bus and headed for the Toraja highlands, some eight to ten hours away. Had I wanted to purchase souvenirs prior to or following my trip to the Toraja homeland, an array of tourist stalls could be found in the heart of old Makassar. In the early 1980s, these tourist shops were largely owned by Chinese, Bugis and Makassarese families. Crammed with dusty replicas of Toraja architectural structures, T-shirts, Bugis-made silver filigree necklaces depicting Bugis sailing vessels, an assortment of presumably-antique Bugis *krises* (daggers), *ikat* textiles, and other touristic treasures, these shops offered an overwhelming array of indigenous art items and served as collection depots for crafts and antiquities produced by peoples in and beyond the region.

By the mid-1980s, however, as tourist visits to the island were sky-rocketing, new lines of touristic trinkets appeared in these Makassar art shops. Among these new items were innovative Bugis-made wall plaques decorated with Toraja traditional houses (*tongkonan*s) and other Toraja motifs. The decorations on these circular lacquered wooden plaques were composed of rice husks, an artistic technique never seen in Toraja but with a longer tradition in the lowlands of Sulawesi (see Figure 3.3). In addition, in the 1980s Bugis silversmiths began crafting fine silver filigree miniature *tongkonan*s and *tongkonan* necklaces. Not only are these Bugis-produced necklaces sold in Makassar shops, but they were soon being marketed in tourist shops in Tana Toraja. These in-

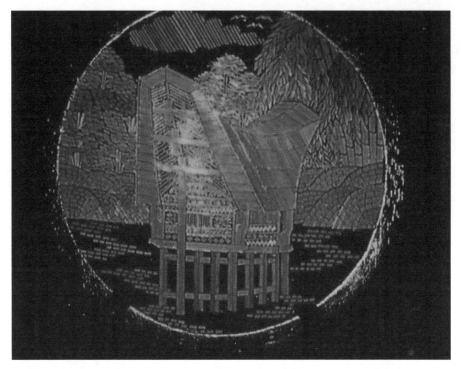

Figure 3.3: Bugis-made lacquered plate with rice husk picture of Toraja *tongkonan* (ancestral house).

novative hybrid art forms were born of Bugis and Makassarese attempts to cash in on the new Toraja-oriented tourist market. Toraja response to these new hybrid touristic creations was varied. Some Torajas purchased the silver filigree *tongkonan* necklaces as gifts for one another while others shunned them. Foreign and domestic tourists, however, were quick to buy them as souvenirs of their Toraja experiences, much to the dismay of Toraja handicraft makers in the highland. These new trends not only exemplify the hybridization borne out of growing tourist markets in Southeast Asia, but also illustrate some of the dynamics of deterritorialization, as arts presumed by outsiders to be Toraja-made are now produced far from the Toraja homeland by non-Toraja artisans.

With regard to this trend towards deterritorialization of Toraja tourist arts, for many of the highland Toraja artisans with whom I work, the most distressing incident occurred in 1995, when a Chinese resident of Makassar reportedly obtained a preliminary patent on Toraja carving patterns. As one Toraja carver told me with indignation, 'He wanted us to pay him royalties each time we carved our own carvings!' Outraged Torajas reportedly rallied, circulated a petition and delivered it to the Makassar judge who had granted the preliminary patent. (According to my Toraja carving mentors, the court eventually ordered the entrepreneur to withdraw his patent request and apologize.)

By 1996 tourist shops in Rantepao not only sold Bugis-made Toraja trinkets, but souvenirs with Toraja motifs produced by foreigners or manufactured in Javanese factories. T-shirt lines had vastly expanded and now included sophisticated composites of *tongkonan* motifs and Paleolithic-looking stick-figure warriors inspired by designs from heirloom Toraja *sarita* cloth. Often bearing phrases such as 'Toraja Primitive', many of these T-shirts are produced in the silk-screening ateliers of foreign graphic artists residing elsewhere in the province. As with the Bugis-made silver *tongkonan* necklaces, these 'foreign-made', icon-embedded clothes prompt various Toraja responses. While some young Torajas wear them proudly, unconcerned by their origins, others are more reluctant to embrace them.

As a case in point, a lively middle-aged Toraja midwife I knew delighted in wearing eye-catching cargo pants fashioned from green cotton cloth covered with small, traditionally coloured Toraja designs. When I admired the pants, she explained that a Javanese doctor who had been working in Tana Toraja for a number of years had 'invented' the new line of Toraja pants. Now manufactured at a factory on the island of Java, the pants are transported back to Sulawesi and sold in her parents' souvenir stall at a Toraja grave site frequented by tourists as well as in Rantepao tourist shops. My friend stood in front of me playfully modeling the pants, while I read the words displayed on the large exterior pocket tag out loud, '*Bayu* [clothing] Collection TORAJA'. Joining us, my Toraja research assistant smirked and dismissively declared, 'Those are made by a person from Java, *not* Toraja!' Turning to the midwife, he teased her for being so 'dumb' as to buy a Javanese-manufactured product masquerading as something Toraja. A month later, when it came time for me to return to the United States, my Toraja midwife friend tucked a similar pair of the pants into my arms as a farewell present. With a sly smile, she noted that in the United States no one would give me a hard time for wearing these pants. My research assistant, who was present, remained silent. A few days later, however, he presented me with a striking batik dress shirt. The shirt featured carefully executed traditional Toraja *pa` tedong* (water buffalo) designs drawn from house carvings. 'The Javanese will be mad when they see that shirt', he quipped. 'Now we Toraja are making batik shirts like the Javanese, but replacing their patterns with our own! Soon we'll be selling them in Jakarta!'

When I left Tana Toraja a few days later, my encounters with deterritorialized cultural pastiches and appropriations of cultural iconography and designs had not ended. While waiting in Makassar airport, I wandered over to a souvenir shopping island topped with a Bugis-styled roof. As I scanned the small portable gifts intended for the last-minute shopper, my eyes settled on a glass case filled with what looked, on first glance, like the tiny Peruvian worry dolls sold to tourists in Latin America (see Figure 3.4). Arranged in neat clusters were barrettes and pins of various sizes, each adorned with rows of squinty-faced dolls. Their miniscule heads were crafted of balsa wood, each wearing a small, triangular black cotton headdress. The dolls were clad in brightly coloured Bugis silk. I called the young Bugis attendant over for assistance and asked her about these new creations. As she explained, 'They are from Toraja and have to do with dead people . . . You see, in Toraja they put the dead in cliffs. These are those things they make that look like the dead people . . .' Realizing she meant that these Peruvian-inspired items were intended to depict *tau-tau*s, I asked why they were dressed in Bugis silk and not Toraja *ikat*. Whereupon I learned that they were made by lowland Bugis and not Toraja artisans.

The pins were a triumph in hybridity, using a Peruvian souvenir form and classic Bugis silks to showcase *tau-tau*, a Toraja form. As discussed earlier, in recent years a number of scholars have explored the concept of hybridity. Edward Said, among others, has developed the concept in his book *Culture and Imperialism* (1993), which underscores the role of colonialism, and more recently migration, in fostering hybrid identities. For Said, the contemporary conduits of hybridity are often migrants. I suggest that a slightly different form of temporary migrants – international tourists – are often the conduits of artistic/trinket hybridity, along with print and electronic media. Indonesian international travellers, both actual tourists and those who surf the Web, draw inspiration for

Figure 3.4: Bugis-made pins depicting Toraja effigies of the dead (in the style of Peruvian 'worry dolls')

new tourist art forms from visits to foreign tourist destinations and exotic Web pages. The entrepreneurs among them reinterpret and 'localize' these foreign products, crafting indigenized versions of the trinkets they have seen. In this sense, the Peruvian-inspired, Bugis-made pins also offer testimony to the dynamics of deterritorialization.

This chain of invention, manufacture, and sale – spanning islands, cultures and nations – is not unique to Sulawesi. Cohen has chronicled similar dynamics in Thailand, where he documents how Dan Kwien tourist pottery in Thailand was not only initiated by outsiders, but also how outsiders were the 'principal initiators of innovation and diversification' (1993: 138).[8] Likewise, Causey (1999) has also described how a Sumatran Batak carver invented a new-genre tourist sculpture drawn directly from a classic Balinese tourist art form. As he observes, not only was the carver inspired by Balinese tourist arts, but also by discussions with foreign tourists visiting the Toba Batak region. These tourists' presumptions about what 'primitive art' should look like were an ingredient in shaping this Batak sculptor's tourist-oriented products. While the phenomenon of artistic borrowings is not new,[9] the contemporary acceleration of touristic demand for mementoes of their travels has greatly amplified these long-distance chains of invention, manufacture and sale of handicrafts. Thus, as Tim Oakes (1999: 325) has chronicled, we find factories in the People's Republic of China employing rural women to embroider cloth for export to Southeast Asia and, as Hitchcock (2003) describes, we find Indonesian-manufactured batik sarongs decorated with beach motifs for sale to foreign tourists in Cuba.

Final Thoughts

In sum, a closer examination of the array of objects found in the tourist stalls and art shops along the Southeast Asian tourist trail reveals an assortment of dynamics associated with accelerated globalization, with hybridization and deterritorialization being especially prominent.

Far from being unimportant by-products of tourism, Southeast Asian touristic trinkets such as hybrid *tau-tau* pins, Javanese-manufactured pants with Toraja motifs, and Bugis-made filigree *tongkonan* necklaces are worthy of our attention, as are other commoditized ethnic art objects purchased by tourists and international collectors. The growth of the tourist art market in Southeast Asia has not only transformed the physical landscape of tourist sites in palpable ways, with the mushrooming of souvenir shops and tribal art galleries, but also entails more abstract transformations. In some cases the meaning, significance and treatment of indigenous material culture has undergone dramatic transformations, as we have seen with Toraja effigies of the dead. In other cases, the tourist market has produced new hybridized forms – forms which may be passed off as being rooted in local traditions but are actually the product of intercultural dialogues, sometimes inspired by foreign tourists' expectations of what 'tribal art' should look like.

In still other cases, a closer examination of Southeast Asian tourist-oriented arts offers testimony to the process of deterritorialization, with certain objects embodying distant chains of production and distribution. As we have seen via the examples presented here, Southeast Asian tourist objects offer testimony to the broader dynamics of globalization. In essence, they are micro-monuments to modernity.

Notes

1 Downloaded on February 1, 2005 from people.tribe.net/asshole/blog&topicId= 014b7492-5c41-4f18-9eb8-134d00395602.

2 Over 75 per cent of these tourists were domestic. These tourism statistics derive from the Badan Pusat Statistik in Tana Toraja Regency. Government tourism officials calculate these figures by comparing the number of tourist ticket sales at the most popular tourist sites with occupancy rates and guest logs at local hotels, inns and home stays (Rombelayuk, personal communication, August 15, 1995). It is probable that the number of domestic tourists is slightly inflated, as many Toraja residing outside the homeland regularly return for family visits and funeral rituals. While in Tana Toraja Regency, they often visit the more celebrated tourist villages to purchase trinkets for friends back home. Some of these returning family members also prefer to stay at local hotels. For an exploration of the factors and dynamics underlying domestic tourists visits to Tana Toraja, see Adams (1998b).

3 See Simamora and Nurbianto (2003).

4 For a rich analysis of tourists' pursuit of 'real' souvenirs of their travels and the ambivalences conjured up by fakes, see Causey (2003).

5 For more information, see Adams (1993) and Crystal (1994).

6 Indonesian government laws decree that objects more than fifty years old be banned from export, unless they have been evaluated for their cultural and historical criticality (see Directorat Perlindungan dan Pembinaan Peninggalan Sejarah dan Purbakala, 1993).

7 I thank Jill Forshee for alerting me to the latest trends in Kuta. As she observes, these cave-man like creatures bear no resemblances to any Indonesian people whatsoever (personal communication, January 30, 2006).

8 For a fascinating chronicling of a similar process in Mexico, see Chibnik (2003). Chibnik's book details the origins of the colorful Oaxacan carved wood figures, chronicling how this distinctive folk art is not actually a Zapotec Indian product (despite claims that it is), but rather was invented by non-Indian Mexican artisans for the tourist market.

9 See Sekimoto (2003) for a discussion of the long-term history of borrowings involved in comprising contemporary Javanese batik.

4

Terrorism and Tourism in Bali and Southeast Asia

I Nyoman Darma Putra and Michael Hitchcock

Introduction

Michel Houellebecq's controversial novel *Platform* (2002) manages to combine a lurid account of sex tourism with a horrific terrorist attack in Thailand. The book's protagonist Michel, who coincidentally bears the same first name as the author, falls in love with Valérie, an employee of a struggling tour company. On their return to Paris they embark on a love affair in which Michel persuades Valérie and her boss to devote their company's hotels in Thailand and the Caribbean to sex tourism. The new package holidays prove to be popular, especially with Germans, portrayed in the book as stupid and uncultured. One of Michel's characteristics is his rabid and senseless hatred of various 'others' (e.g. Germans, pork butchers and Protestants), but Muslims are the villains of the story, murderers of Michel's father and his mistress. While Michel's thoughts turn to domesticity and babies, young men with turbans – Muslim terrorists – blow Valérie and the hotel's prostitutes and their customers to bits. Whatever the merits of the book, which was originally published in French in 1999, the author is eerily prescient about how tourist resorts could become terrorism targets in Southeast Asia.

Houellebecq may be concerned with Thailand, which, although it has suffered attacks on nightclubs and centres of entertainment, has not experienced the same level of terrorist violence as other Southeast Asian countries, notably the Philippines. There the militant Islamic group Abu Sayyaf took 21 hostages, including 10 foreign tourists, from a diving resort in the Malaysia state of Sabah. The kidnap earned Abu Sayyaf US$ 20 million, reportedly paid by Libya (Rabasa, 2003: 54).

Thailand, however, is arguably one of the most iconic of Southeast Asian tourism destinations and the fact that the real terrorist outrages have happened elsewhere does not detract from one of the main messages of the book: tourists are easily attacked and some of what they engage in may be used as a justification for attacking them. This chapter is mainly concerned with events in Bali, but because Bali itself is as iconic as Thailand and the attacks in Bali have involved cross-border movements of terrorists within ASEAN, the authors argue that the recent attacks on tourists are as much a Southeast Asian event as they are an Indonesian one. The bombings in Bali represent not only the largest act of terrorism in Indonesian history, but also one of the largest attacks on a tourist resort in the region.

Many analysts moreover link the attacks in Bali to attempts by terrorists to re-organize the modern borders of Southeast Asia to create a substantial Muslim Caliphate (Rabasa, 2003), a position steadfastly opposed by the governments of the region, including the country with the world's largest Muslim population, Indonesia. Terrorism networks with local agendas that converge with those of al-Qaeda have surfaced with the arrests in Malaysia, Singapore and Indonesia of militants associated with Jemaah Islamiyah (JI) and thus Southeast Asia has emerged as a major battleground in the war on terrorism, which has major implications for the region's important tourism industry.

Tourism and Terrorism

There is a widespread view among tourism analysts that international visitors are very concerned about their personal safety (Edgel, 1990:119) and that '(. . .) tourism can only thrive under peaceful conditions' (Pizam and Mansfield, 1996: 2). Political stability and prosperous tourism thus go hand in hand and, though tourism is perceived as being particularly vulnerable to international threats such as terrorism (Richter and Waugh, 1986: 238), analysts accept that it may be impossible to isolate tourists completely from the effects of international turbulence (Hall and O'Sullivan, 1996: 120). Security and peace may be crucial for tourism and international travel, but national and supranational organizations concerned with tourism have little influence on peace and security agendas (Hall, Timothy and Duval, 2003).

One of the most widely cited cases of the effect of international strife on leisure travel is that of the Gulf War in 1991. The downturn that accompanied the outbreak of hostilities had an impact not only on the area immediately surrounding the strife, but on international tourism generally. Indonesia, for example, was among those affected by the war, though it was located a great distance from the scene of conflict. Tourist arrivals in Indonesia tumbled in the first half of 1991 despite its designation as 'Visit Indonesia Year', part of an ASEAN-wide tourism promotion strategy (Hitchcock, King and Parnwell, 1993: 4). Once the country had recovered from this turbulence, tourism continued to rise throughout the 1990s up until the fall of Suharto in 1998, helped in part by the security and stability provided by the military.

In view of tourism's sensitivity to crises, it is also widely held, particularly by tourism promotion boards, that the press has a particular role to play in helping alleviate the fears of travellers. In this respect the media is seen as being a major force in the creation of images of safety and political stability in destination regions (Hall and O'Sullivan, 1996: 107). Not only are obvious threats to tourism such as the press coverage of terrorism seen as a cause for alarm, but so is negative reporting in general. For example, following the onset of the Asian monetary crisis in 1997, Thailand became so alarmed about the future of its tourism industry in the wake of the poor publicity that it sought to counter the flood of bad news by the positive promotion of the country as a cost-effective destination (Higham, 2000: 133). Thailand's use of tourism simultaneously to boost its image and offset its budgetary deficit at a time of crisis is widely hailed as a success story, and the country has remained very sensitive about its image as a tourism destination.

Not all the strife that has a negative impact on tourism is concerned with tourism *per se*, though tourists have become targets to advance certain religious and political causes since the early 1990s at least, the most publicized case being that of Luxor in 1997 which left 58 foreign visitors dead. But even before Luxor terrorists were targeting tourists and, according to the Ministry of the Interior, had killed 13 of them, as well as 125 members of the Egyptian security forces, since 1991 (Aziz, 1995: 91). Five years were to elapse, however, until the first major loss of life of tourists from terrorism occurred in Southeast Asia, but when it did happen it was on a scale that overshadowed all previous attacks on tourists. As a result of the explosions of 2002 on the Indonesian island of Bali at least 201 people lost their lives, though the full extent of the casualties may never be known for sure because of the difficulties in identifying all the victims.

Ness has likened the attacks in Bali to a terrorist incident at Pearl Farm Beach on Samal Island in the Philippines, which she sets apart from more economically related incidents of tourism–related violence that have occurred in the Philippines and elsewhere. She also notes the 'family resemblance' of the Pearl Farm assault to the Marcos-era outbreak of arson attacks on luxury hotels in the 1980s by the politically-motivated Light-a-Fire Movement, as the activists came to be known (Ness, 2005: 119). This movement at times combined economic motives with political ones, as could well have been the case with the Pearl Farm attack, but the motives of the Light-a-Fire Movement were not only concerned with generating revenue for dissident groups. Ness makes the point that the Pearl Farm attack was more closely related to non-economically related forms of violence on tourism than with other forms, such as banditry (Ness, 2005). Ness characterizes the Pearl Farm attack as a form of locational violence directed against a particular kind of place and not a particular person or collection of individuals, but as this chapter argues the bombings in Bali were concerned as much with place as with certain kinds of people.

Because the trials of the Bali bombers were held in public and because professional journalists were able to interview the bombers it is possible to examine many of their motives with some clarity. The bombers initially claimed that they were attacking Americans, though the largest number of victims turned out to be Australians and the second largest, Indonesian. Despite this error what should also not be overlooked is that the American Consulate in Bali was also targeted that night. Placed around 100 metres from the American Consulate office, the bomb caused no casualties, but served as a warning to the United States that it was the target. As the casualty figures emerged a range of other political justifications were offered, such as an alleged statement by Osama bin Laden that it was indeed Australians who were being targeted because of their alliance with the United States. The motives may have been political but the outcome was also economic and Erawan (2003: 265) has argued that the bombings of 2002 had by far the biggest impact on Bali's economy of any recent crisis: in 2000 the tourism sector contributed 59.95 per cent of provincial GDP, but in 2002 it had fallen to 47.42 per cent.

The 2002 Bali Bombings

On 12 October 2002 three targets were bombed in the Indonesian island of Bali: the Sari nightclub and Paddy's Bar in Kuta and the American Consulate in Denpasar, not far from the former Australian Consulate office. The consulate bomb was largely ineffective, but the ones in Kuta were devastating. The bomb at Paddy's Bar did not at first appear to have had a great impact, but it had a deadly side effect. It drew people on to the streets so that when the next bomb at the nearby Sari Club went off more people were exposed. The explosives had been packed into a van that had been parked outside the packed nightclub, which was almost entirely destroyed by the blast and raging fire that ensued.

The victims represented twenty-two nations, but the brunt of the tragedy was borne by Australia with eighty-eight dead. The second largest loss of life with thirty-five dead was experienced by Indonesia, the majority of those who perished being Balinese islanders. What should also not be overlooked is that many of the Balinese dead were Muslims, drawn from a minority on the largely Hindu island of Bali. The third largest toll was suffered by the UK, which lost twenty-three of its citizens in the explosion. Not only are Americans (7) and many European countries (Germany, Sweden, France, Denmark, Switzerland, Greece, Portugal, Italy and Poland) recorded in the list of victims, but also are Canada, South Africa and New Zealand. There were also other Asian victims (Taiwanese, Japanese and South Korean), as well as South Americans (Brazilians and an Ecuadorean) (see Table 4.1).

Initially, the Australian Federal Police said the attacks had been well planned and expertly conducted, and were intended to cause the maximum number of casualties. The police spokesman, Graham Ashton, maintained that the bombs were placed skilfully to make the best use of the surrounding buildings and that technical experts had evaluated the quality of bomb making as 'above average' (CNN, 1 November 2002). The investigators thought that the larger blast, which decimated the Sari Club, was caused by the explosive chlorate that had been ignited by a 'booster charge' such as TNT. Ashton also reported that 400 kilograms (880 pounds) of chlorate was stolen in September from a location on Java, but he declined to give more background information. Later in court it was revealed that one of the bombers, Amrozi, had purchased one ton of calcium chlorate ($KClO_3$) in a shop in East Java, which he shipped along with other chemicals to Bali by bus.

In response to the high death toll among Australians, the Australian Federal Police joined forces with the Indonesian investigators under the leadership of Inspector General

Table 4.1: Countries of Origin of the Victims of the 2002 Bali Bombings

Country	Number of Victims
Australia	88
Indonesia	35
UK	23
USA	7
Germany	6
Sweden	5
Switzerland	3
The Netherlands	4
France	4
Denmark	3
New Zealand	2
Brazil	2
Canada	2
South Africa	2
Japan	2
Korea	2
Italy	1
Portugal	1
Poland	1
Greece	1
Ecuador	1
Taiwan	1
Total	**196**
Plus 3 unidentified victims and 2 bombers	**201**

Source: Planning Bureau of Badung Regency, 2003.

I Made Mangku Pastika. In spite of the bombers' apparent ingeniousness a central part of their plan failed and this drew Pastika quite swiftly to the first of the suspects, Amrozi bin H. Nurhasyim. As a mechanic, Amrozi had intended to foil detection by altering the registration number on the van that he purchased to transport the larger bomb. What Amrozi was unaware of was that the van had previously been used as a minibus and carried another number, which Pastika's team were able to connect to Amrozi. After his arrest and interview with the Indonesian police chief, Da'i Bachtiar, Amrozi quickly gave the police a detailed confession, which laid the basis for the subsequent investigation.

The Australian and American governments initially suspected that the bombings were the work of an al-Qaeda-linked terror group based in Indonesia, Jemaah Islamiyah (JI), but no organization at that stage had claimed responsibility for the attacks in Bali. One of the chief suspects was JI's alleged leader, Abu Bakar Ba'asyir, who was detained on October 18 after Indonesian investigators returned from questioning an al-Qaeda operative, Omar Al-Faruq, who had been handed over to the United States in June earlier that year. Al-Faruq maintained that he knew Ba'asyir well and alleged that the cleric had been involved in attacks on Christian churches in Indonesia in late 2000. The security forces of the United States, Australia, Singapore and the Philippines also claimed to have evidence of JI's links to al-Qaeda and that the group had established several cells throughout Southeast Asia and Australia. It remains uncertain whether Ba'asyir was linked to the Bali bombings and according to a International Crisis Group report of December 2005 he is said to have opposed the bombings and was thus unlikely to have been the mastermind behind them (Rabasa, 2003: 35). The Indonesian police, however, believe that he was involved, but whatever the reality the fact is that Indonesia's Supreme Court overturned a guilty verdict against Ba'asyir for conspiracy with regard to the 2002 Bali bombings. He was released in June 2005 after completing a 30-month jail sentence (Murdoch, 2006).

Approximately a year later, the world's press was stunned when one of the alleged bombers, Mukhlas, reacted with delight when his death sentence was read out in the court in the island's capital of Denpasar. His response mimicked the ecstatic reactions of his brother Amrozi, nicknamed the 'smiling bomber' by the press, who had been sentenced earlier and who had claimed that there were many people in Indonesia willing to take his place should he die. Mukhlas was the third bomber, along with his younger brother and the operation's mastermind, Imam Samudra, to be sentenced to death for inspiring his followers to attack Westerners supposedly to avenge the oppression of Muslims.

A noteworthy feature about Mukhlas and his followers is that once charged they did not seek to deny that they had been the perpetrators, even to the extent of correcting the judges to make sure that the record was accurate. With the exception of Ali Imrom, who confessed that the bombings had been against his Muslim teachings, the bombers claimed to be proud of their achievements. Presumably to draw attention to their religious motives, the alleged bombers donned Muslim-style clothes to attend court and were photographed carrying out their devotions. In contrast, Ali Imron wore a suit and tie in court, behaving politely and expressing remorse and even weeping a couple of times in public. Ali Imron also gave a press conference to describe how the bombs were made, demonstrating a filing cabinet similar to the one that was used in the bombings and other related equipment. He also rebutted claims that this was the work of foreign nationals and said that the bombers undoubtedly had the ability to make these explosive devices.

The Bombers' Motives

Seemingly satisfied with the number of foreigners killed, the bombers appeared to be unconcerned about the deaths of their own fellow citizens, many of whom were Muslims. Amrozi simply offered to pray for the dead Balinese, but the belief that he had done something worthwhile remained unshaken, expressing disappointment that he had not killed more Americans. As the trials took place many reporters claimed to be horrified by what they saw as the banal and callous behaviour of the bombers, and the *Asia Times* even likened them to Albert Eichmann and his complete lack of remorse about his crimes against Jewish people.

> While exact parallels may not be drawn, broad similarities are appearing in the current Bali bombing trial. The cavalier, almost frivolous, attitude toward human lives is rooted in the banal worldview of the alleged Bali perpetrators.
>
> (*Asia Times*, 3 June 2003)

In particular, Amrozi was quite open about what motivated him to conduct the attacks, claiming that he had learned about the decadent behaviour of white people in Kuta from Australians, notably from his boss while he was working in Malaysia. The Malaysian connection was important in another respect since he had worked alongside French and Australian expatriates in a quarry and had thus learned about explosives. Amrozi also maintained that it was these people who revealed to him what an easy target Bali was and he claimed to have become incensed about their stories of drug-taking and womanizing.

By 1996 Amrozi had convinced himself that it was the Jews who sponsored Westerners and that they were intent on controlling Indonesia. He began to hate Westerners and became convinced that violence was the only way to get these people out of Indonesia since diplomatic means had proved ineffectual. He revealed that the bombers comprised a core group of nine who were united in their hatred and were experienced in carrying out bombings. He claimed to have been involved in attacks in Jakarta, the Indonesian capital, and in the strife-torn regions of Ambon. He also maintained that he had participated in the Christmas Eve attack in 2000 in Mojokerto, Central Java, that claimed 19 victims, and admitted that he had had a hand in the attack on the Philippines Embassy in Jakarta and had actually mixed the explosives.

Kuta was selected as a location because there were a lot of foreigners there and when Amrozi heard that many of them had been killed he claimed to have felt very proud, though he prayed for the Muslim victims. Amrozi's hatred of Westerners may have been nurtured by his experiences in Malaysia, but he seems to have been open to other influences. For example, he attended the Lukman Nul Hakim *pesantren*, a traditional Islamic college, in the 1990s in Malaysia where Abu Bakar Ba'asyir was one of the teachers, but it remains unclear what he studied. Amrozi's hatred of Westerners could have been underpinned by radical Islamic teaching, but not all the bombers shared precisely the same outlook. Imam Samudra seems to have been more motivated by religious hatred and learned to manufacture bombs in Afghanistan. Also known by other aliases, Imam Samudra was trained as an engineer and had a university education.

The prosecutors in Denpasar alleged that Imam Samudra had selected the targets and organized the planning meetings and had remained in Bali for four days after the bombings supposedly to monitor the start of the police investigation. Imam Samudra was also suspected of being involved in a series of church bombings across Indonesia. On giving evidence at the separate trial of Abubakar Ba'asyir, Imam Samudra said that the bombings were part of a *jihad*, though he denied any connection with the militant group Jemaah Islamiyah. He responded to a question about the Christians who died in those attacks, by saying that 'Christians are not my brothers.' Imam Samudra is also the author of a 280-page book (2004), which he wrote in prison under the title *Aku Melawan Teroris* (I Oppose Terrorism). He cited the Koran in legitimizing his attacks and a *jihad* in Bali and reaffirmed that his target was the United States and its allies. According to his interpretation of his Holy Scripture, these enemies could be killed wherever they could be located. In his book, he refers to the Americans and their allies as 'nations of Dracula'. Searching at random, Imam Samudra discovered the the Sari Club and Paddy's Pub in Bali contained the largest homogeneous target of Americans and their allies (2004: 120). Referring to the large number of dead Indonesians, Imam Samudra wrote that it was 'human error' (English is in the original) and that he much regretted it (2004: 121).

The bombers may have responded differently to questions about their motives, but one who has offered a clear political explanation is Mukhlas. He was not only the eldest and most experienced of the three brothers, but was a veteran of Afghanistan where he claimed to have met Osama bin Laden.

> Osama bin Laden. Yes, I was in the same cave as him for several months. At the time, he wasn't thinking about attacking America. It was Russia at that time.
>
> (NineMSM, 23 May 2003)

In an interview recorded by Sarah Ferguson in prison nineteen months later, Mukhlas's reasoning was given in an English translation:

I want the Australians to understand why I attacked them. It wasn't because of their faults, it was because of their leaders' faults. Don't blame me, blame your leader, who is on Bush's side. Why? Because in Islam, there is a law of revenge.

(NineMSN, 23 May 2003).

This could well be a post-event rationalization given the bombers' earlier claims that they were attacking Americans, but may represent their motives accurately

The bombers also justified themselves by arguing that they were taking part in a *jihad*, a struggle to establish the law of God on earth, which is usually interpreted as meaning holy war (www.parstimes.com/history/glossary.html). *Jihad* is sometimes called the 'sixth pillar of Islam', a reference to the famous 'five pillars' that underpin the identity of a Muslim. *Jihad* has two meanings, the first being the 'greater *jihad*', a struggle of any kind, particularly a moral one, such as striving to be a better person, a better Muslim, the struggle against drugs, against immorality, and against infidelity. The second interpretation is the holy war itself, which is embarked on when the faith is threatened in accordance with Islamic law, Shari'ah and only with the approval of the appropriate religious authority (faculty.juniata.edu/tuten/islamic/glossary.html). The bombers do not appear to have had the necessary authority to carry out their attacks and after careful consideration Ali Imron confessed in court (15 September 2003) that the bombers had broken the terms of *jihad* and contradicted Imam Samudra's position. His apprehension may be summarized as follows:

1. In accordance with the terms of *jihad* the target must be clear and there must be authentic proof that those targeted are truly the enemies of Islam, but in the case of the Bali bombings the targets were unclear.

2. Under the terms of *jihad* a warning or *dakwah* is required before any attack but in Bali the bombers attacked without warning.

3. The killing of women is excluded under the terms of *jihad* unless the women concerned have taken up arms against Islam, as was not the case in Bali.

4. In accordance with *jihad* any killing has to be done in the best possible (most humane) way, whereas bombings involved a very nasty form of killing.

Ali Imron went on to say that 'whatever the motive behind the Bali bombings, the act was wrong because it breached the rules'.

Discussion on the meaning of *jihad* was at the time of the first Bali bombings fairly limited in Indonesia, but this changed after the second round of bombings on 1 October 2005 when videos of the suicide bombers' confessions recorded before the attacks were circulated, compelling religious leaders to comment. The majority of religious leaders in Indonesia spoke against the practice of suicide bombings and argued that the instigation of *jihad* was only acceptable when the nation was under attack. In contrast to what was happening in Iraq, they argued that *jihad* was not acceptable in Indonesia because there was no national threat.

Tourists as Targets

Since the bloody upheavals of the mid-1960s, Bali had been one of the safest islands in Indonesia, and remained untroubled by the violence that occurred during the Asian Crisis. Given the economic hardship that is widely experienced in the sprawling cities of neighbouring Java, it is perhaps not surprising that Bali's comparative security and prosperity may have encouraged a certain amount of envy. On top of this, many Balinese appear to have been unaware of potential threats from close at hand with many believing that theirs was a 'sacred island' that was protected by God from evil. This outlook seems to have been reinforced by an earlier experience of a failed bombing dating from the 1980s when a bomb from Java that was destined for Bali exploded on a bus before it reached the island. The rioting and bombing that took place elsewhere in Indonesia did not appear to be a problem in Bali and this may have led to complacency among the security services.

What also enhanced Bali's desirability as a target was its status as a renowned tourism destination with a truly global profile and thus any attack on it was likely to generate a high level of media interest, not least because of the presence of Western interests and Western tourists. The combination of its profile and prosperity may have made Bali a tempting target, but what seems to have made it compelling was that it was an easy target. This was compounded by the fact that other potential targets were becoming much harder to attack, especially in Jakarta. In response to the widespread strife that followed the fall of Suharto security measures were tightened to protect embassies and government institutions, making it more difficult to attack them. Tourist resorts and other visitor facilities in Bali were by comparison much easier to target and the tourists themselves, who were often present in large numbers, were difficult to protect without curtailing their freedom. They also had the advantage of following predictable behaviour patterns and a tendency to cluster.

Tourists are valuable in another way since there is often less of a local backlash when they are attacked because there are fewer innocent local victims – something that backfired in the case of the Bali bombings because of the high death rate among Indonesians. The presence of large numbers of Westerners moreover meant that any major disruption would attract foreign interest and thus publicize the terrorists' cause. The deaths of foreign nationals would not only attract attention, but would also generate external publicity that the government could not suppress. Interestingly, what has emerged from the trials in Denpasar is that tourists *per se* were not supposedly the intended victims, but Westerners and possibly Christians. These people were targeted because they were perceived as being associated with attacks on Muslims, and Amrozi made clear that he felt no remorse about killing them.

> How can I feel sorry? I am very happy, because they attack Muslims and are inhumane.
>
> (*Asia Times*, 3 June 2003)

The bombers anticipated that there would be more Americans in the club and bar, but when informed that the majority of their victims were Australians, one of them quipped:

> Australians, Americans whatever – they are all white people.

This indifference to the victims may reflect the anger and rage about the alleged abuses of the West, but it also seems to be couched in terms that appear racist. The Indonesian words used to describe a person by their physical attributes can be ambiguous and can range from the culturally neutral '*orang putih*', literally 'white person', to the more controversial '*bule*', which means 'albino'. In Indonesian usage 'albino' can be used relatively neutrally and often crops up in humour, but when applied dismissively as in the quotation above it can convey notions of inferiority. When interviewing Amrozi on 23 May 2003, Sarah Ferguson recorded him making apparently dismissive comments about whites, but in the translation the word 'whities' was used and it remains unclear what was actually said in Indonesian. Significantly, the widely used term for tourist, *turis*, which is often used to refer to white people only, does not appear to have been used in these interviews, which suggests that it was the victims' Western or white attributes that caught the attention of the bombers.

The 2005 Bombings

The island was attacked for a second time on 1 October 2005 when cafés along Jimbaran Bay and Kuta were attacked, leaving 20 dead including three suicide bombers, most of whom were Indonesian citizens (see Tables 4.2 and 4.3). The first explosion was at Raja's Restaurant in Kuta Square at 7.45 pm local time and was followed a few minutes later by two bomb blasts at cafés along Jimbaran Bay, south of Bali's international airport. This time the bombers killed fewer people, but the bombs were more advanced and contained ball bearings, some of which were found in the bodies of injured victims.

It took the police less than two days to announce that the bombings were the work of not only terrorists, but also suicide bombers. The police reached this conclusion after receiving a video recording from an Australian tourist who, with his friend and family, happened to be outside Raja's Restaurant photographing the nightlife of Kuta. The Australian accidentally recorded a man with a backpack, who was walking faster than ordinary people, entering the restaurant seconds before the attack. At a press conference held in Kuta General I Made Pangku Pastika, the Bali police chief, showed journalists how a suicide bomber carrying a backpack could be seen walking through guests having dinner in the restaurant, which was followed seconds later by an explosion. The victims

Table 4.2: Countries of Origin of the Killed Victims of the 2005 Bali Bombings

Country	Number of Dead Victims
Japan	1
Australia	4
Indonesia (including 3 suicide bombers)	15
Total	**20**

Source: Indictment against Mohamad Cholily (a suspect of Bali Bombings II), prepared by Bali Prosecutor Officer, 2006, 8.

were identified relatively quickly and the police took away the remains of the three chief suspects whose body parts and heads had been found on the sites. By circulating a poster with pictures of the three suicide bombers in colour the police hoped that they would be able to identify the bombers, but it did not work out like that. Several weeks passed and because little progress was made with regard to identifying the bombers their pictures were revised and clarified by removing the blood and debris from their faces. The police distributed more posters, but once again the public response was minimal. Since no family members or friends came forward to admit that they knew the bombers, the Indonesian public in general and the tourism industry in particular started to become very worried. It began to occur to the police that perhaps Indonesian citizens were simply unable, as opposed to unwilling, to identify the bombers, and this time there appeared to be signs of foreign involvement. The police and media opined that the bombs were the work of two Malaysian fugitives from the Bali bombings of 2002, Azahari and Noordin M. Top and that a new generation of bombers was involved.

Perhaps because of fears of a more global dimension to the attacks the 2005 Bali bombings enquiry was more secretive than the investigation of the bombings of 2002, which was rather open to the media. The police held daily and frequent press conferences, but the public received no significant information on those responsible for the latest round of bombings. The police only stated that there were no significant developments, and that they were continuing to question witnesses, whose number rose above 700. Alongside these enquiries, the police launched silent operations shaking out alleged Jemaah Islamiyah suspects throughout Java, although no arrests were announced until after the storming of Azahari's safe house in Batu in Malang, East Java. Azahari and one of his followers were killed during the raid and the police found dozens of vest-bombs, VCDs, books and a plan for a 'bomb party' for Christmas and New Year. Noordin remained on the run and as of mid-2006 had still not been apprehended.

According to the International Crisis Group South East Asia Project Director, Sidney Jones, Noordin Top now called his splinter group 'al-Qa'ida for the Malay

Table 4.3: Countries of Origin of the Injured Victims of the 2005 Bali Bombings

Country	Number of Injured
Indonesia	102
Korea	7
Japan	4
America	4
Germany	3
Belgium	1
France	1
Australia	29
Total	**151**

Source: Indictment against Mohamad Cholily (a suspect of Bali Bombings II), prepared by Bali Prosecutor Officer, 2006, 8.

archipelago', although he still regarded himself as the leader of JI's military wing. According to Jones, Noordin and the people around him adhered to the al-Qaeda tactic of attacking the United States and its allies and, being close to Indonesia, Australia was a prime target (Radio Australia, *AM*, 6 May 2006). The funding to mount attacks could have come from various sources, including al-Qaeda, as well as from the group's own activities. For example, prior to the Bali bombings of 2002, some of Imam Samudra's men robbed a gold shop in West Java and the proceeds helped to defray the expense of the attack. These costs included an estimated Rp 3–4 million to make a vest bomb, the rental of premises and the costs of surveying the target.

The details of the 1 October 2005 attacks were found in notes found at the scenes of the bombings and in the hiding places of those taken into custody. The notes reveal how JI members travelled to Bali to survey potential targets before reporting back to JI's master bomb-maker Azahari. They surveyed nightclubs, temples, shopping areas, sports venues, fast food outlets, souvenir shops and the airport. They concluded that Jimbaran Bay, the eventual scene of two attacks, was a good target because, 'Insya Allah' (God Willing), they estimated that there would be at least 300 people there (Wockner, 2006a). One of the four suspects of the 2005 attack, Mohamad Cholily, said he was with Dr Azahari when they heard news of the bombings on BBC Radio. He claimed that Azahari had shouted 'Allahu Akbar' (God is Greatest) and 'Our project was a success'. Cholily, who was learning bomb-making skills from 'the demolition man' Azahari, was arrested one month later. It was Cholily who led police to the safe house in East Java where the famous fugitive was hiding (Wockner, 2006b).

Azahari was killed in the raid but this did not alleviate the public's fears a great deal, largely because of the existence of the plan for the 'bomb party'. Even though the police confiscated numerous vest bombs, it was widely believed that Azahari must already have recruited dozens of people who were prepared to conduct suicide missions. Anxieties were also heightened by the video footage recovered in the operation because they contained the pre-recorded confessions of the three suicide bombers who attacked Bali: Salik Firdaus, Aip Hidayatulah, and Misno.

Widely circulated in the media, both in Indonesia and abroad, the confessions sent out the horrifying message that further attacks were possible. The Australian government responded by issuing additional travel warnings, leading to a decline in visitor arrivals, but there were important differences as compared with the 2002 attacks. For example, the massive exodus of tourists that had followed the 2002 bombings did not recur and it looked at first as if the tourism industry would not be so adversely affected. Eventually the numbers began to drop drastically due to the combination of the travel warnings and the televised confessions of the suicide bombers. Terrorism in its global context also appears to have exerted an influence as Indonesians were shocked by coverage of a female Iraqi suicide bomber who succeeded in bombing a wedding party in Amman. An Indonesian musician was included among her victims.

There was ongoing coverage in the Asian and Australian media of terrorist attacks and the hunt for terrorists and this undoubtedly helped frighten visitors away. Australia also continued to issue travel warnings about the possibility of further terrorist attacks in Indonesia, which was understandable given the fact that Noordin was still at large. On 29 April 2006, in a dawn raid at Wonosobo, Central Java, the police killed two suspected terrorists and arrested another two, but Noordin evaded capture. There was now speculation that this terrorist mastermind had either run out of followers or had a reduced capacity to launch further attacks.

The Christmas and New Year period is usually the busiest time of the year in Bali but the combination of the 2005 bombings and perceptions of a global terror threat began to have a severe impact on arrivals in Indonesia, and hotel occupancy in Bali fell below 40 per cent. Occupancy declined to 30 per cent in 2006 and what had been expected to represent a full recovery from 2002 had turned into a huge downturn. By 24 November Air Paradise International (API), the Bali-based and -owned airline, had mothballed its service totally and was forced to lay off 350 of its employees, some of whom were Australian employees. Garuda Indonesia reduced its flight frequency from 32 to 25 services per week between Bali/Indonesia and various cities in Australia, and their services between Bali and Japan dropped from 22 to 16 a week. Deprived of customers, many local tour agencies experienced hardship. The drop in passenger demand came from Bali's two main sources of tourists: Australia and Japan. Overall arrival figures dropped by almost 50 per cent, from around 4,500 per day to 2,000 per day in the months after the 2005 bombings and as a consequence Qantas and Australian Airlines also reduced the frequency of their flights to Bali. The decline was possibly as bad if not greater than that of 2002 (*Kompas*, 11 January 2006: 35). The attacks may have been directed at America and its allies, but in the process great suffering was inflicted on Indonesian people and the Indonesian economy.

Conclusion

The 2002 bombers offered different variations of the main reasons for their attacks ranging from a simple desire to hit back at Westerners for their supposed attacks on Muslims to a more politically sophisticated attack on John Howard's support for President Bush and Australian intervention in East Timor in 1999. Some of their explanations have been couched in terms of what appears to be racial hatred, though these threats and statements are somewhat vague. What is clear is that they decided to bomb a tourist resort because it offered a relatively soft target, but not because the victims were tourists per se, but because their numbers were likely to include large numbers of foreigners whose deaths would attract publicity to the terrorists' cause. Some disapproval over the alleged behaviour of tourists in Indonesia has been expressed, but it was the intended victims' nationality and perhaps racial type, their invaluable foreign-ness, that appears to have been upper-most in the bombers' minds. Tourists are also useful because they create more publicity than when only locals are involved. Such publicity is moreover difficult to suppress, thereby enabling terrorists to make their various causes known more widely. The tsunami disaster of 26 December 2004 seems to reinforce the notion that foreign tourists make for more media attention than say the terrible disaster in Darfur or previous disasters in China involving only nationals.

Despite the caveats, tourists were the main targets, perhaps not because they were tourists, but because their behaviour is predictable and they have a tendency to cluster. Their value is enhanced since ordinarily there is less backlash to attacking tourists than to indiscriminate bombing, which produces more 'innocent victims'. Bali seems to have been doubly attractive because any local victims would be likely to be Hindu and not Muslim. As it happened, the bombers miscalculated and ended up killing significant numbers of their co-religionists.

After the 2005 Bali attack police found a document called the 'Bali Project', which contained the reasons for targeting. The document began with the question 'Why Bali?' to which the answer was: 'Because it is the attack that will have global impact. Bali is famous all over the world, even more famous than Indonesia. The attack in Bali will be covered by international media and the world will get the message that the attack is dedicated to America and its allies' (Wockner, 2006b). This turned out to be an accurate prediction since media worldwide covered the Bali attacks immediately.

The impact of the Bali bombings of 2005 on the island's tourism sector seems to be far worse than that of 2002. After the 2002 bombings, multinational investigations and support from the international community helped to speed up the investigation and restore Bali's image as a safe destination. Tourism arrivals recovered quite quickly once the island seemed secure again. But after the 2005 bombing less help from the international community was evident due to a combination of factors: compassion fatigue in the aftermath of the tsunami, especially with Australia, which had contributed generously, and a general stretching of resources in a generally less safe environment. Possibly because the 2005 attacks had a limited direct effect on Australians, less help with police work was offered to Indonesia; a wide range of considerations, including the identity of the victims, would appear to complicate the recovery of tourism from a terrorist attack.

The common feature of both the attack in Thailand imaged by Houellebecq and the real attacks in Bali is that they occurred in mass tourism resorts and that terrorists exploited the opportunities that this kind of tourism provides: relatively easy targets, large numbers of potential victims, relatively small numbers of co-religionists, the publicity value of foreigners and the alleged hedonism of tourists that could be exploited rhetorically as a justification for killing them. What would be worth investigating is whether other kinds of tourism such as cultural tourism or eco-tourism, which are often hard to disaggregate precisely from mainstream tourism, are less vulnerable to such attacks and thus politically and economically more sustainable.

Authors' Note

The authors are especially grateful to the following institutions and organisations: Udayana University, Bali–HESG, the British Academy, ASEAN–EU University Network Programme, and London Metropolitan University. We are indebted to the Sutasoma Trust for supporting I Nyoman Darma Putra as the first Bagus Suatasoma Fellow. Thanks are also due to the late Prof Dr I Gusti Ngurah Bagus and Prof Ida Bagus Adnyana Manuaba of Udayana University for their generous support. The first version of this paper was presented at the International Sociology Congress Hawaii in 2005 and the authors are grateful to Linda Richter and her fellow panellists for their comments. A later version was presented at the South-East Asia seminar series in 2005 at St Antony's Asian Studies Centre, University of Oxford, and the authors are also very grateful for their comments.

5

From 'Kebalian' to 'Ajeg Bali': Tourism and Balinese Identity in the Aftermath of the Kuta Bombing

Michel Picard

Shortly after 11:00 p.m. on Saturday, 12 October 2002, a series of bomb blasts shook Bali, putting an end to the peace and prosperity the island had so jealously guarded over the years. The first bomb exploded inside Paddy's Bar, followed a few seconds later by the explosion of a vehicle parked in front of the nearby Sari Club, two popular night spots in Kuta Beach, the most famous resort on the island. Almost simultaneously, a third blast, thought to target the United States Consulate in the Renon District of Denpasar, apparently missed its mark, destroying instead only a tree in a vacant lot on a roadside. The bombs in Kuta killed 212 people from 22 countries, including 88 Australians and 35 Indonesians. They also injured 324 people and damaged 418 buildings.[1]

Traumatized by the horror of the carnage, the Balinese reacted at first with an outburst of anger toward the alleged perpetrators who, in their eyes, could only be outsiders. Then came a time of 'introspection' (*mulat sarira*), of intense soul-searching. Even though the attack was the work of outsiders, it led the Balinese to wonder if they brought this curse upon themselves and to ask what they must do to set things right. The bombing was seen as a warning that something must be out of balance in Bali, that all was not well on the island of the gods. Indeed, many regarded the strike as a punishment from the gods, a divine retribution for the sins of Kuta, where drugs and prostitution were allowed to flourish shamelessly. Too busy chasing the tourist dollars, the Balinese had disregarded their moral values and neglected their religious duties.

Thus, in the words of one distinguished 'cultural observer' (*pengamat budaya*), Balinese psychiatrist and medium Luh Ketut Suryani: 'The destruction happened because the Balinese people have already forgotten their Balineseness' (*Kehancuran terjadi karena orang Bali telah melupakan kebalian mereka*) (Sarad, 2002a: 24).[2]

By and large, the Hindu Balinese responded to the bombing with an intensified religious fervour. Starting on the very next day, a series of rituals and prayers was convened in various locations, either by private organizations or by the provincial government. These culminated on November 15 with an elaborate and highly media-tized purification ceremony (*Pamarisuddha Karipubhaya*), intended to clean the site of the bloodbath from all trace of pollution (*leteh*) and to restore the cosmic order by liberating the souls of the dead victims from their earthly bonds. As a result, the Balinese succeeded in appropriating the traumatic event, by accommodating it within their own frame of reference. In their eyes, by dealing appropriately with the situation in its *niskala* aspects – the numinous and invisible world beyond the senses – it followed that it would become settled in the *sekala* dimension – the concrete reality perceptible to the senses.[3] For the Balinese, ritual is no mere reflection of the material world but the real work (*karya*) of which the material world is the result (MacRae, 1997: 145).

Yet, if celebrating these cleansing rituals had comforted the Balinese and placated their gods, it had hardly resolved the problems generated by the bombing, namely the collapse of an economy based on tourism and the severe social crisis which ensued. In the days following the attack on Kuta, thousands of tourists scrambled to get a flight out of Bali. Within a week, daily foreign arrivals dropped from over 5,000 to less than 1,000. Within two weeks, hotel occupancy rates on the island fell from around 70 per cent to below 20 per cent. For months to come, Bali was shunned by foreign visitors. The island's tourism industry, including hospitality businesses, airlines, tour operators and travel agencies, was almost driven to the wall. Travel warnings and ad-visories issued by foreign governments, including Australia, the United States, some European countries and Japan, nearly paralysed the industry, hitherto the island's economic mainstay.

Faced with such a disastrous plight, a number of Balinese opinion leaders viewed their island's predicament as a timely opportunity to appraise its development prior-ities. Specifically, they started calling for a more balanced economic development, giving its due share to agriculture instead of relying too exclusively on international tourism. But the attack had not only hit Bali's tourism revenues, it had also con-vinced the Balinese that they were under siege and had to defend themselves against outsiders. The precariousness of their situation combined with a heightened feeling of insecurity sharpened their sense of identity. In that way, the Kuta bombing marked a watershed in the Hindu Balinese perception of themselves as a vulnerable ethnic and religious minority within the Indonesian nation-state.

In this chapter, I investigate how the Balinese addressed the manifold crisis – economic, social and cultural – entailed by the Kuta bombing. Specifically, I focus my investigation on the way they construed and asserted their identity after what became known on the island as *'Bom Bali'*.

Tourism Development and Its Discontents at the Close of the New Order

While the island of Bali has been famed as a tourist destination since the 1920s, it was only in the early 1970s that tourists started landing on its shores in significant numbers. This was the result of a decision taken in 1969 by the Indonesian government to open up the country to international tourism, primarily in order to address a pressing national balance of payments deficit. Banking on Bali's prestigious image as a tourist paradise, the government decided to make this island the showcase of Indonesia. With the backing of the World Bank, a team of foreign experts was commissioned to draw up a Master Plan for the development of tourism in Bali. Their report, published in 1971 and revised in 1974 by the World Bank, proposed to confine the bulk of the tourists to the south of the island, while providing for a network of excursion routes linking major attractions inland (SCETO, 1971; IBRD/IDA, 1974).

Yet, if the island of Bali was becoming firmly established on the world tourism map during the 1970s, it was only in the late 1980s that the development of tourism shifted to high gear, with a sharp up-surge in visitors' arrivals, followed by an even more rapid rise in hotel investment and other tourism-related facilities. Thus, between 1970 and 1980, the number of foreign visitors to Bali multiplied from fewer than 30,000 to over 300,000 a year, reaching about 1 million in 1990 and up to around 2 million in 1997, when the regular growth of arrivals started to slow down owing to the Asian financial crisis and the ensuing Indonesian political breakdown.[4] During the same period, hotel capacity increased from fewer than 500 rooms in 1970 to about 4,000 in 1980, jumping to 20,000 in 1990 and up to over 30,000 in 1997. All of this, on an island which is only 5,600 km^2 large, with a population of 3 million people at the time.

If one can delineate various reasons for this boom, the main one appears to be that, after the slump in oil revenues in 1986, the Indonesian government undertook actively to develop international tourism. Liberalization measures to promote trade and foreign capital investment in 1988 also spurred on the tourism industry in Bali. Leading international hotel chains established themselves on the island, enticed by the deregulation of the banking system and solicited by Asian investors, most of them backed by Jakarta-based conglomerates. Whereas the previous governor of Bali, Ida Bagus Mantra, had presided over a moderate and controlled growth of tourism, in 1988, alleging the pressure of demand, his successor Ida Bagus Oka scheduled 15 areas for development as 'tourism resort areas' (*kawasan wisata*) – which became 21 in 1993, covering one quarter of the total surface of the island. This initiative provoked intense competition amongst the resort areas, eager to attract a bigger share of tourism investment. It also led to a demand for cheap labour for building projects, which brought to Bali large numbers of migrant workers from other parts of Indonesia.

There is no question that tourism has boosted the economic growth of Bali, to the point of displacing agriculture as the leading sector.[5] At the close of the New Order, with the activities it has generated, such as handicrafts, garment manufacture and other cottage industries, tourism was estimated to contribute two-thirds of the Regional Gross Domestic Product of the province and over half of the income of the Balinese, while absorbing up to 60 per cent of the work-force if one includes its indirect spin-off effects. Meanwhile, the average per capita income on the island had moved from below the national average to one of the highest-ranking provinces.

However, the growing encroachment of foreign interests, as well as the uneven distribution of economic benefits within the local population and throughout the island, was becoming a matter of serious concern. The southern area, where the main resorts and most of the facilities are located, receives the lion's share of the tourism revenues. Furthermore, tourism has tended to accentuate social inequalities, with a widening gap between those Balinese with direct access to tourist dollars and those without.

Its disparity notwithstanding, the new affluence brought about by the tourism industry has fuelled the rise of a Balinese middle class, while furthering the spread of urbanization. In spite of the tight control exerted by the New Order régime over any expression of dissent and its forced depoliticization of society, despite also a very mediocre education system, hardly conducive to the voicing of critical personal opinions, and with a press conditioned to tread a narrow path between self-censorship and official rebuke, one witnessed the emergence on the island of something akin to a public opinion (Bagus, 1999). Even though Balinese public intellectuals – academics, bureaucrats and businessmen, NGO and student activists, artists and journalists, religious and community leaders – were enjoying some of the fruits of affluence engendered by their participation in the nation-state, they were intent on creating institutional space for themselves. As members of an ethnic and religious minority, they had become critically aware of the plundering of their island's natural and cultural resources in the name of 'development' and 'national interest' (Suasta and Connor, 1999).

Throughout the 1990s, growing feelings of discontent were voiced against the capital-intensive tourism development initiated from Jakarta and operated by foreign investors. A number of controversial tourism 'mega-projects' (*megaproyek*) made the headlines of the *Bali Post* and triggered the protests of Balinese public opinion – the Garuda Wisnu Kencana on the Bukit peninsula, the Bali Nirwana Resort at Tanah Lot, the Bali Turtle Island Development on Serangan island, the Bali Pecatu Graha

Resort, and the beach reclamation at Padanggalak, to name but the most infamous ones (Supartha, 1998). Since political opposition to the government was out of question during the New Order, these projects were generally objected to on account of the damage they inflicted upon the island's environment (Warren, 1998). But at the same time, the Balinese were becoming highly sensitive to any move they construed as an 'offence' (*pelecehan*) against their religion, particularly as a result of the tourist exploitation of religious sites and the ceremonies which take place therein. Complaining that Bali had become Jakarta's colony (Aditjondro, 1995), influential opinion leaders accused foreign investors and their Indonesian counterparts of having made a clean sweep of prime real estate at the expense of the Balinese, who were finding themselves progressively marginalized on their own land. They denounced the directives from Jakarta, which too often overrode provincial regulations, as well as the collusion between corrupt officials and powerful interests (Picard, 2003).

The fact is that, as a result of inadequate planning and lack of control, the environment of Bali has been heavily stressed, to the point that the island is now rife with air and water pollution, beach erosion and reef destruction, water and electricity shortage, saturation of solid waste disposal, not to mention traffic congestion, urban sprawl, overpopulation, crime and social tensions. Worse in the eyes of the Balinese is the transformation of land into a marketable commodity and its massive conversion, which has caused family as well as communal feuds and up-rooted the local population, alienated from land ownership.[6] Thus, it is commonly claimed that over 1,000 hectares of irrigated rice fields disappear every year, from a total area of less than 90,000 hectares. This shift in the function of rice fields has important implications for the production of food and the livelihood of farmers, and it poses serious threats to the perpetuation of traditional Balinese culture, which grew out of a communal-agrarian society (MacRae, 2003).

Crisis, Reform and Regional Autonomy

The fall of Suharto in May 1998, by bringing about the breakdown of the Indonesian state apparatus, entailed a major political restructuring, while unleashing centrifugal forces in the regions. It opened up an era of 'reform' (*reformasi*), marked by a revival in cultural, ethnic and religious identities, as well as by severe social turmoil, as old resentments and conflicts that had been simmering under a lid of political repression and cultural censorship began to surface in the open (Ardika and Darma Putra, 2004). What had started as a monetary crisis (*krismon*) rapidly blew up to become a 'total crisis' (*kristal*) (Hitchcock, 2001). Thanks to tourism, Bali was less affected by the crisis than other regions of Indonesia, as direct contact with international business networks had rendered the island's economy less dependent on state subsidies (Vickers, 2003). In fact, the devaluation of the Indonesian rupiah boosted Bali's tourism and export-based dollar economy, and many Balinese (and foreign) entrepreneurs were able to make large profits since they had access to foreign currencies (Connor and Vickers, 2003).

Moreover, Bali appeared to remain remarkably free of the political, ethnic and religious strife that engulfed the archipelago. The main reason for this state of affairs was not the fact that the Balinese people are Hindu and peace-loving, as they are prone to claim, but rather the widespread concern for sheltering the island's all-important tourism industry, on behalf not only of Jakarta and foreign-based conglomerates but also of Balinese politicians and business stakeholders. By stressing that Bali was prosperous and safe, the Balinese authorities appeared eager to dissociate their island from the turbulences affecting the rest of Indonesia. Thus, during the campaign preceding the general election in June 1999, one could see roadside signs bearing slogans such as 'Bali is safe: the tourists come' (*Bali aman: Turis datang*). This, notwithstanding the fact that Bali has had its fair share of social disturbances in these years of turmoil – mostly communal clashes fuelled by conflicting claims on land or on status, commonly euphemized as *kasus adat* ('customary law disputes') in the Balinese media (Warren, 2000) – but the authorities have been careful not to spread the news abroad. And even when this carefully nurtured image of the Balinese as a peace-loving people was at risk of being jeopardized, such as by widespread reporting of the riots that followed the failure of Megawati's bid for the presidency in October 1999, the troubles were readily blamed on 'foreign' (non-Balinese) *agents provocateurs*.

As a matter of fact, the problem was that Bali was indeed seen as prosperous and safe, so much so that the Balinese authorities were at a loss to prevent other Indonesians entering their island, attracted as they were by the seemingly inexhaustible gold mine of tourism.[7] The relative good fortune of Bali, at a time when the rest of Indonesia was in dire straits, increased the influx of migrant workers – mostly Muslims from Java, Madura and Lombok – in search of employment. At the same time, large numbers of Indonesian Chinese refugees from the anti-Chinese riots that marked the fall of Suharto in Jakarta and other main cities of Java sought refuge in Bali and settled there, putting additional strain on the environment and infrastructure of the already densely populated and urbanized area of south Bali. Whereas the Balinese did not appear to resent the arrival of these Chinese settlers, whose ancestors have been well integrated on the island for centuries, on the other hand, the increasingly conspicuous presence of Muslim labourers and petty traders sowed the seeds of ethnic and religious discrimination on the island, whose population was becoming more and more heterogeneous.[8]

Indeed, disturbing signs of a growing rejection of newcomers – referred to as 'outsiders' (*pendatang*) – have been noticeable since the late 1990s. As expressed in a recent critical self-portrait by representatives of the new generation of Balinese public intellectuals, the growing heterogeneity of the population on the island, in terms of ethnic belonging and religious affiliation, is producing, amongst many Balinese, 'a feeling of insecurity which manifests itself in the growing readiness to use their own culture defensively against the ethnical and religiously others' (Ramseyer, 2001: 11). To name only a few examples of this defensive attitude, all across Bali, notice boards have been posted at the entrance to villages which read *'pemulung dilarang masuk'* ('scavengers forbidden to enter'), warnings which are meant to deter non-Balinese Indonesians from intruding. Then, in January 2000, the municipality of Denpasar decided to impose a system of residence permits on migrants. A few months later, a poll was conducted by the *Bali Post*, which found that over 90 per cent of the respondents agreed that such a system should apply to the whole island (*Bali Post*, 12 August 2000). In addition, it was reported in Balinese and foreign media that vigilante groups regularly conduct raids in Denpasar and elsewhere in which house-to-house checks result in Indonesians of non-Balinese origin being harrassed and sometimes expelled from the island – when they are not simply put to death on accusation of thievery (Santikarma, 2001; England, 2001; Couteau, 2002).

As in other regions of Indonesia, the ineffectiveness of the weakened state in maintaining public order has led to the establishment in Bali of militia (*pecalang*), ostensibly aimed at protecting village communities from 'external' threats.[9] This kind of neo-traditional village militia was first employed to provide protection to Megawati's party, the PDI-P, when it held its congress on Bali in October 1998. It was not long, however, before *pecalang* became identified less with party politics and more with the control of non-Balinese migrants. Their role as a communal security force even became officially sanctioned in March 2001, when the government of Bali issued a provincial regulation on the Customary Village (*Perda 3/2001 tentang Desa Pakraman*) (Warren, 2004). According to this regulation, the *pecalang* have the authority to ensure law and order in matters of 'tradition' (*adat*) and 'religion' (*agama*).

This provincial regulation had been enabled by the new laws on Regional Autonomy (*UU 22/1999 and 25/1999 tentang Otonomi Daerah*), promulgated in May 1999 but implemented only on January 2001. Law 22/1999 abolished law 5/1979 on Village Governance (*UU 5/1979 tentang Pemerintahan Desa*), which had enforced a uniformity of government administration at the village level across Indonesia (Warren, 1990). Until then, Balinese villages were characterized by a dichotomy between customary and administrative authority. This state of affairs went back to the colonial times when, in order to govern the island efficiently, the Dutch had introduced uniform administration throughout Balinese society. A new type of village was created, the 'administrative village' (*desa dinas*), which ran parallel to the 'customary village' (*desa adat*). The Indonesian government, and particularly the New Order régime, went much further than its colonial predecessor in the penetration of society by the state, by subordinating *adat* to the requirements of national development and thus undermining the authority of the customary village (Warren, 1993). But the regional autonomy laws opened the way for a revision of the relationship between *adat* and *dinas*, by giving the Balinese an opportunity to restore the traditional prerogatives of their *desa adat*, which had been unduly appropriated by the state.

This was precisely the purpose of the *Perda 3/2001*, which attributes to the customary village full authority to 'run its internal affairs' (*mengurus rumah tangganya sendiri*). Yet, contrary to what had been advocated in some radical Balinese quarters and discussed at length in the *Bali Post*, it did not go as far as abolishing the *desa dinas* altogether. In order to give the newly restored customary village a more specific Balinese flavour, its name was changed from *desa adat* to *desa pakraman*. Unlike the word *adat*, which has both a colonial and an Islamic connotation,[10] the term *pakraman* claims its authority from old Balinese inscriptions and is derived from the Sanskrit root *krama*, meaning 'rule sanctioned by tradition' (Surpha, 2002; Janamijaya et al., 2003).

To all intents and purposes, the *desa pakraman* is conceived as 'the last line of defence of Balinese culture' (*benteng terakhir pertahanan kebudayaan Bali*). Yet, one of the most contentious points of the *Perda 3/2001* concerns the role attributed to the *desa pakraman* in controlling and limiting migration in the villages. According to the regulation, migrants – dubbed *krama pendatang* (outside members) or *krama dura* (foreign members) – are members of the *desa pakraman* with respect to social and territorial, but not religious, matters. Only the natives of a *desa pakraman* are 'entitled to partake in the village participatory trilogy of *"palemahan"* (land), *"pawongan"* (people) and *"parhyangan"* (pantheon), the unity of which makes up the village (*desa*)' (Couteau, 2003: 48).[11] The result is thus a demarcation between the residents originating from the village, *ex officio* members of its institutions, and the newcomers, barred from worshipping the gods considered to be the legitimate owners of the village.

This provision has been criticized on various counts. To start with, its ambiguity is blatant, in that it does not distinguish explicitly between the rights and obligations of Hindu Balinese coming from another *desa pakraman*, and those of migrants from abroad. Specifically, Balinese who want to keep migrants away from the villages contend that they are only expected to fulfil social and territorial obligations, whereas Hindu Balinese have to comply with religious duties as well, which are much more demanding in terms of both time and money. On the other hand, those observers more sensitive to considerations of human rights and democracy denounce the discrimination against non-Hindu Balinese settlers, who are stigmatized as outsiders as they are denied full participation in the village community. In any case, such controversy about membership of the *desa pakraman* testifies to the difficulties the Balinese are facing with the increasing heterogeneity of their society.

Special Autonomy or Independence?

Regional autonomy was meant by the Balinese not only to restore their customary village and curb the coming of migrants but it was also expected to provide an opportunity to control tourism development (Picard, 2005). Indeed, as we have seen, even before the era of *reformasi*, influential public intellectuals had denounced the takeover of the tourism industry by Jakarta and foreign-based conglomerates, and warned that the unrestrained influx of investment was unsustainable in the long term. They claimed for the Balinese the prerogative to further their own views on a tourism policy appropriate for their island and beneficial to its population. The solutions revolved around the need for an adequate planning and managing of tourism development, which implied both political will and legal authority from the provincial government to develop tourism in the interest of the Balinese people, whose participation should be promoted and given priority over foreign investors. Moreover, most incomes and taxes earned from the tourism industry should accrue to Bali instead of being siphoned off to Jakarta.

Accordingly, the Balinese had pinned high hopes on the laws on regional autonomy. With the newly acquired autonomy, it was assumed that the provincial government would be in a position to control the development of tourism on the island and to appropriate a larger share of its revenue. Unfortunately, it turned out that the laws devolved most of the authority not to provincial but to district (*kabupaten*) and municipal (*kota*) levels. For fear that a genuine transfer of authority to the provinces might entice some of them to break away from Jakarta, they were granted only a vague mediating role between the districts.

In fact, seen from Bali, the degree of autonomy accorded to the districts is far from clear, as is the power of the governor to conduct and to coordinate policies implemented at regional levels. And the situation is all the more confused regarding tourism, as it is not even mentioned amongst the fields falling under the authority of either the regions or the centre. In any case, as soon as the dispositions of the laws became known, Balinese opinion leaders started calling for a 'special autonomy' (*otonomi khusus*) status, in order to confer the autonomy to the province instead of the districts. One of the most vocal critics of the way regional autonomy was being carried out was the head of the Bali Provincial Government's Tourism Office, I Gde Pitana, a respected academic, appointed in June 2001 (Pitana, 2004). According to him, Bali should be dealt with in a holistic manner, as it is a small island with limited natural resources. Yet, as a province, it is divided up into eight districts and one municipality. Only the southern districts of Badung and Gianyar, as well as the municipality of Denpasar, have an adequate regional income, while the rest are destitute.[12] With autonomy being devolved to the districts, the widely unequal distribution of profits raised from tourism is inciting each district to compete in issuing permits for resort development, in order to boost their regional revenue. Moreover, for the same purpose, each district may impose various taxes and fees on hotels, restaurants and tourists. This will only increase regional imbalances, heighten inter-regional conflicts, and result in ruining the environment as well as creating social and cultural problems.

That these concerns might not be too far off the mark is testified by a recent incident. In order to remedy the imbalance created by the concentration of seaside resorts in the district of Badung, the governor had already required in the 1970s that 30 per cent of hotel and restaurant tax revenues (PHR) collected by Badung be redistributed to the other districts. For most of these districts, the contribution made by these proceeds is far larger than their own regional revenues (PAD). Now, in March 2001, the Badung regional legislative council (DPRD) proposed to reduce the district's tax distribution from 30 per cent to only 15 per cent. In retaliation, legislators from the neighbouring districts of Gianyar and Bangli, where many famous tourist attractions are located, threatened to impose levies on every tourist passing through their territory.[13] The governor reminded the protagonists that tourists are attracted in the first place to the island of Bali, not to the district of Badung or, for that matter, to any other district. And he promoted the idea that all tourism-related profits be submitted to the provincial administration, which would then equally distribute them to all districts. But eventually, in August 2002, during a meeting between the governor and all the district heads (*bupati*) together with the leaders of the regional legislative councils, it was agreed that the provincial government would relinquish its share of hotel and restaurant tax revenues collected by Badung, while the latter contribution would be reduced to 22 per cent and restricted to only six districts, Gianyar and Denpasar being henceforth considered sufficiently well-off.

Since this affair, similar incidents have underlined the weakness of the provincial authorities,[14] raising fears of a disintegration of Bali. Opinion leaders in Denpasar are concerned that each *bupati* might turn into a 'little raja', thus going back to the situation when Bali was fragmented between quarrelsome kingdoms, before the Dutch colonial forces put an end to their internecine wars by subjecting the whole island. Their concern echoes a study by Geoffrey Robinson, which attributes the recurrent political conflicts amongst Balinese, and the absence of strong regionalist or ethnic-based movements on the island, to the historical weakness of regional powers encompassing the whole of Bali (Robinson, 1995).

Concerns about the weakening and disintegration of Bali are all the more pressing since the demise of the New Order resulted in the politicization of Islam. This challenge, which is taken very seriously by the Balinese, gave rise to a proliferation of new political-cum-religious organizations on the island, accompanied by a profusion of publications on the Balinese identity, which reveal the anxiety of a society threatened in its structures as well as in its self-image. Amongst these publications, one notices a flurry of magazines and newspapers with a distinct traditional culture flavour, which began to mushroom with the inception of *reformasi*. Some are written in Balinese (*Kulkul, Buratwangi, Canang Sari*), a relative novelty on the island, where the vernacular is seen as fast disappearing under the onslaught of Indonesian and English. Even those published in Indonesian, such as *Bali Aga* or *Sarad*, target a local readership with topics that are strictly Balinese.

The Islamic menace reached a climax in October 1998, following the provocative remark made in the Muslim newspaper *Republika* by A. M. Saefuddin, a minister in Habibie's cabinet and a presidential candidate from the Islamic United Development

Party (PPP). He declared that Megawati was not a suitable presidential candidate because she worshipped Hindu gods. This was an allusion to the fact that Megawati – whose grandmother was Balinese – was seen praying in Hindu temples whenever she visited Bali. This insult against their religious identity raised an immediate outcry amongst the Balinese and triggered mass protests on the island. A committee of Hindu Balinese activists was formed, which threatened to fight for an 'Independent Bali' (*Bali Merdeka*) as long as Saefuddin had not presented his resignation. Eventually, the atmosphere cooled down, even though Habibie did not sack his minister, but the idea of an independent Hindu Bali in a predominantly Muslim nation had taken hold of the Balinese people's imagination – all the more so as the economic prosperity warranted by tourism made it appear as a feasible option (Vickers, 2002; Couteau, 2002: 243–244 ; 2003: 55–56).

The Kuta Bombing and its Consequences

Given such a state of mind, it should not come as a surprise that one of the first Balinese reactions to the Kuta bombing has been to shut out Bali from the rest of Indonesia and specifically to close the island to outsiders.[15] Thus, an influential Hindu Balinese leader, Putu Setia, wrote in the Indonesian news magazine *Tempo* a few days after the bombing: 'The most important thing for the Balinese people now is to isolate the island of Bali . . . from the tumult and abuse of Indonesian politics' (*Yang paling penting dilakukan orang Bali sekarang ini adalah mengisolasi Pulau Bali . . . dari hingar-bingar dan carut-marut politik Indonesia*) (in: Setia, 2002: VII).

In these circumstances, one could have expected a backlash by Balinese against Muslim communities when it transpired that the bombing had been committed in the name of Islam. The fact that this did not happen is due to a series of factors. First of all, even though there were 16 Balinese amongst the 35 Indonesian victims, none of them were natives of Kuta, and only two locals were injured. This was no doubt due to the fact that the shops and businesses around the bomb site did not belong to the local population, and that most of their employees were outsiders. Indeed, the bombing took place away from the settlement areas and furthermore, the nearby altars (*pelinggih*) remained relatively unscathed. Therefore, the village community did not perceive the attack as directed against them. Besides, not only were there several Muslims amongst the Balinese victims, but one of the first rescue volunteers to arrive on the site was an aid group headed by Kuta's Muslim community leader, Haji Agus Bambang Priyanto. And what is more, leaders of the regional and national Muslim organizations were unanimous in readily condemning the bombing.

But the most significant factor was certainly the calls for restraint from the local and provincial authorities and the cautious attitude of the Balinese media, intent on avoiding inter-religious and inter-ethnic conflicts. Early morning the very next day, a group of prominent public intellectuals, religious leaders from various denominations, security officers and government officials, who had gathered in the governor's office, made a solemn appeal to the population, urging them to remain calm and to preserve unity and solidarity on the island. In the weeks following the bombing, the provincial government and various local organizations managed to provide the people with inter-religious vigils and ritual outlets, through which they could channel their emotions and strengthen the cohesion between different communities. Moreover, the police's seriousness and effectiveness in investigating the bombing and arresting its perpetrators played a crucial role in defusing the tension-filled situation. Last but not least, the Balinese were very much aware that any ensuing inter-communal strife would further aggravate their economic problems and might virtually destroy the island's prospect of getting tourists back. This was especially so at a time when Bali was being scrutinized by the international media.

Yet, behind an appearance of composure, discriminative measures were taken against non-Balinese migrants through the authority of the *desa pakraman* and the empowerment of their *pecalang*. After some deliberations, the provincial and district governments decided that any residents who were not duly registered in the administrative unit in which they lived would have to obtain a residence permit (KIPEM), costing Rp. 50,000 (about US$5) for three months for non-Balinese and Rp. 5,000 for Balinese (*Sarad*, 2003a). In addition, restrictions were enforced on migration from Java via Gilimanuk harbour, allowing only those with valid identity cards and guaranteed jobs to enter Bali. But it seems that after a few months this policy of population control was no longer rigorously enforced, as the prevention of internal migration to Bali appeared impossible to implement. And in their survey of inter-communal relations on Bali after the bombing, Hitchcock and Darma Putra did not find any evidence behind the rumours of mass deportations of *pendatang* (Hitchcock and Darma Putra, 2005). While there was indeed an exodus of non-Balinese labourers and petty traders in the wake of the bombing, it was due to the collapse of the tourism industry more than any crackdown on illegal settlers.

Beyond the sharp initial decline in tourist arrivals and the impact on the hotel and travel industry, there was an immediate shrinking in demand for industries that cater for tourism, such as handicrafts and the building trade. Responses and pledges of assistance to the direct and anticipated impacts of the bombing came from a wide range of actors, including the Indonesian government, international donors, private charitable donators and civil society organizations locally and overseas, reflecting the level of worldwide support and solidarity for Bali and Indonesia after the terrorist attack.

A few days after the bombing, Indonesia's Minister of Culture and Tourism, I Gede Ardika, a native Balinese, held a press conference in Bali outlining a four-stage tourism recovery plan. According to the minister, complete recovery would only occur in 2004 with the next three months dedicated to industry rescue efforts, the first six months of 2003 for rehabilitation, and the last half of the year for normalization. The final phase of recovery would be committed to the expansion of Bali's international tourism market, once the island's image as a safe and attractive tourist destination had been fully restored. In order to bridge the time necessary for Bali's recovery, the minister urged the Indonesian tourism industry to undertake an unprecedented marketing campaign aimed at the domestic market.

Meanwhile, a so-called Bali Tourism Recovery Committee was set up in Jakarta by key figures from government and business circles, who coined the slogan 'Bali For The World'. They came to Bali with lots of money and little understanding of the real issues facing the Balinese people. With the help of celebrities from the media and show business, they invited to the island top Indonesian and international entertainers to celebrate the New Year holidays in the presence of President Megawati and several members of her cabinet. This initiative, and a few other promotional events of the same kind, was given a mixed reception by Balinese public intellectuals – not the least, by the head of the Bali Tourism Office – who accused the committee of being more interested in making money in the name of Bali than in really helping the Balinese people. In addition, they objected to the slogan 'Bali For The World', which they construed as selling out Bali for the sake of tourism (Wedakarna, 2002; Sarad, 2003a; Darma Putra, 2004a: 217–220).

After a sharp slump in foreign arrivals, tourism began to recover in the first months of 2003, but the war in Iraq and the SARS epidemic outbreak that swept through Southeast Asia – not to mention the terrorist attack on the Marriott Hotel in Jakarta in August – compounded the effects of the bombing. One year later, while international tourist arrivals were on the rise, they still remained well below past levels. Moreover, the quality of these visitors had changed. In place of tourists from Australia, Europe and the United States, now the best part were from Asia. These Asians were coming for five days on discount packages, while Westerners used to stay longer and had a higher spending power. Thus, tourism revenues, and therefore incomes, were lagging behind the tourist numbers significantly.

In October 2003, a joint report was issued by the World Bank, the United Nations Development Programme and the United States Agency for International Development (UNDP/World Bank, 2003). This report aimed to provide an independent assessment of the current overall condition of Bali's tourism sector within the local economy; evaluate donors' and government's response in dealing with the effects of the bombing; and suggest medium- to long-term strategies for sustainable recovery in the island's economy. Upon releasing the report, the country director for the World Bank said that there had been no comprehensive policy response to Bali's economic crisis, because of poor co-ordination, planning and budgetary mechanisms amongst the various levels of government – central, provincial and local.

The report found that Bali was facing a harsher, longer economic crisis than initially expected. Average incomes across Bali were down 40 per cent while 30 per cent of workers were affected by job losses, and children were increasingly dropping out of school. Unemployment impact was more often expressed in terms of reduced income and underemployment, rather than formal termination. Amongst those losing their jobs, many had returned to their home villages. There, they had to rely on their relatives or try to make a living as farmers. But, toiling in the muddy rice fields was by no means easy, especially after one had become accustomed to the financial rewards and prestige attached to a job in tourism. Eventually, they were forced to work at menial jobs, sell household goods, allow their wives to go to work or just rely on their dwindling savings.

More worrying than the crisis itself was the fact that it had not led to a fundamental reassessment by the Balinese policy-makers about the island's development priorities. The aim of the recovery plan was to return as fast as possible to the pre-bomb number of tourists. Former questions about the sustainability of tourism growth were only given lip service. But on the contrary, the report's final recommendation was for Bali to seek a more sustainable model of tourism instead of pursuing the chase for ever more tourism dollars. While admitting that tourism presented the greatest short-term opportunity for supporting economic recovery, the report warned that a return to past conditions was not an option and recommended that Bali diversify its economy in order to make it more resilient. Accordingly, it stressed that a concerted effort must be made to wean Bali off its overdependence on tourism by developing opportunities in handicrafts and agriculture. And in conclusion, the report stated that: 'Bali needs to balance its future development strategy to (i) promote greater equity in the distribution of the benefits of tourism, (ii) develop an environment supportive of investment, (iii) support other sectors to mitigate against the inherent risks of the tourism sector and (iv) create effective rural development policies that benefit those not benefiting directly from tourism' (UNDP/World Bank, 2003: 66).

By the time international agencies were assessing the current economic situation in Bali, a group of concerned Balinese opinion leaders and policy-makers were formulating their own views on the direction they wanted their island to take.

Ajeg Bali

On 1 August 2003, a seminar entitled '*Strategi Menuju Ajeg Bali*' (Strategy towards a strong and everlasting Bali)[16] was organized at an international hotel by the *Bali Post*. The papers presented at this seminar were then published in a special edition of the *Bali Post* to celebrate its 55th anniversary on 16 August. They were reprinted in book format in January 2004 (Satria Naradha, 2004), along with a collection of essays by prominent public intellectuals (Darma Putra, 2004b). In his editorial, the chief editor (and owner) of the *Bali Post*, A. B. G. Satria Naradha,[17] explained that the purpose of the *Ajeg Bali* strategy is to defend and preserve the identity, the environment and the culture of the Balinese people. The problem is that the Balinese have forgotten their 'Balineseness' (*kebalian*), 'which is based on their religion, their tradition and their culture' (*berdasarkan agama, adat dan budaya*). They have to strengthen themselves if they want to avoid being overcome by the cultural hegemony of globalization, with its trail of consumerism, commercialism and commodification. The present critical situation of Bali is due not only to the bombing, but also to the fact that the Balinese people have lost control of their island, which is overloaded with constructions, invaded by migrant workers and exploited by foreign investors. Now, Bali is on the verge of destruction (*di ambang kehancuran*), and the Balinese are becoming foreigners on their own land (*orang Bali merasa terasing di tanahnya sendiri*). In short, Bali must be rescued (*Bali harus diselamatkan*).

While admitting that the *Ajeg Bali* concept was still being debated and was given divergent interpretations, Satria Naradha denied that it meant a return to a by-gone era. In his view, the *Ajeg Bali* strategy aims at achieving a harmonious holistic development of the island, by avoiding overdeveloping tourism to the detriment of other economic sectors, such as agriculture and cottage industries. In addition, the Balinese authorities should fight for a special autonomy (*otonomi khusus*) for the province, which should become autonomous by reducing its dependence on Jakarta and the outside world. If Aceh has been able to obtain a special autonomy on account of Islam, Bali should get it as well on account of the fact that it is an island of Hinduism surrounded by a sea of Islam.

It seems that the slogan *Ajeg Bali* was initially voiced in May 2002, when the *Bali Post* launched its own television station, *Bali TV*, the first private regional channel on the island, with a proclaimed mission 'to bring forth a strong and everlasting Bali' (*mewudjudkan Ajeg Bali*). And one of the regular programmes of *Bali TV* is a cultural talk show called *Ajeg Bali*. But it is only after the Kuta bombing that *Ajeg Bali* has become a pervasive catchword, which one encounters not only in *Bali Post* articles and *Bali TV* talk shows, but also in seminars and public events, as well as in electoral meetings.[18] Besides, Satria Naradha appears to have a political agenda in launching his *Ajeg Bali* campaign. He was concerned not only with the predicament of post-bomb Bali but also with the political fragmentation of the island, which had been exacerbated by *reformasi* and *otonomi*. In order to strengthen Bali and symbolize the unity of the Balinese people, he invited high-ranking officials and dignitaries (the governor, the district heads and the mayor of Denpasar, the Indonesian president and cabinet ministers, the sultan of Yogyakarta, etc.) to sign stone inscriptions (*prasasti*) endorsing the *Ajeg Bali* campaign ('*Dengan Semangat Persatuan Mari Kita Ajegkan Bali*') (Darma Putra, 2004a: 226). This is a practice inspired by former royal patronage, which was taken over by the New Order régime to commemorate official events. These inscriptions are now set in the front walls and columns of the head office of the Bali Post Group, a monumental building called the *Gedung Pers Bali K. Nadha*, located in the suburbs of Denpasar.

Thanks to Nyoman Darma Putra, and in the company of the anthropologist Graeme MacRae, I had the opportunity to interview Made Nariana, Marketing Director and Public Relations of the Bali Post Group, at their head office, on 22 June 2005. According to him, *Ajeg Bali* is basically about 'preserving Balinese culture, so that Bali does not lose its Balineseness' (*melestarikan kebudayaan Bali agar Bali tidak kehilangan identitas kebaliannya*). This is in fact an old story, the end product of an on-going movement of self-identification that goes back to the colonial period, when the inquisitive gaze of foreigners in their midst – Dutch administrators and orientalists, Christian missionaries, American anthropologists, Western artists and tourists, not to forget Javanese school teachers and civil servants – impelled the Balinese explicitly to account for the definition of what it meant to be Balinese. And it underwent a discursive shift in the 1970s, when the Balinese authorities faced the challenge of tourism.

Accordingly, the question that needs to be adressed is whether *Ajeg Bali* – as a response to the Kuta bombing – represents a stage markedly different from previous discourses on Balinese culture and identity, or whether it is but a case of new wine in old bottles (Allen and Palermo, 2004: 6). To answer this question, one has first to deconstruct the discourse of *kebalian*. Far from expressing a primordial essence as its present proponents would have it, this conception of 'Balineseness' – construed as the primeval and indivisible unity of 'religion' (*agama*), 'tradition' (*adat*) and 'culture' (*budaya*) – is in fact the outcome of a process of semantic borrowing and conceptual recasting which the Balinese had to make in response to the colonization and the Indonesianization as well as the touristification of their island. As I have delved extensively into this issue elsewhere (Picard, 2000), here I shall but outline the dialogic construction of Balineseness by briefly reviewing the circumstances in which Balinese have engaged in a course of self-identification following the inclusion of their island into a modern state.

The Emergence of *Kebalian*

What should be stressed from the outset is the fact that the forced incorporation of Bali into the Dutch colonial empire, completed in 1908, was instrumental in bringing about the emergence of a sense of religious, ethnic and cultural identity amongst the Balinese people. Whereas the Dutch knew little about Balinese society, they had certain ideas about what it should be like, and they undertook to make it conform to their preconceptions. For them, Bali was a world apart, unique and fragile, which should be protected against pernicious foreign influences and the traumatizing impact of modernity, through the enlightened paternalism of colonial tutelage.

Before colonial administrators started to deal with Balinese society, it had been imagined by orientalists, who regarded the island of Bali as a 'living museum' of Hindu–Javanese civilization, the only surviving heir to the Hindu heritage swept away from Java by the coming of Islam.[19] In their eyes, Hinduism constituted the core of Balinese society, the guardian of its cultural integrity and the inspiration of its artistic manifestations. Accordingly, it had to be shielded from the intrusion of Islam, which had strengthened its grip on most of the archipelago, as well as from Christian missionaries, eager to settle on the island.

In the guise of redeeming what they regarded as the Balinese traditional order, the Dutch determined to teach the Balinese people how to keep on being authentically Balinese. Such was the aim of the cultural policy known as 'Balinization' (*Baliseering*), which was expected to produce a renaissance of Balinese culture. Conceived by orientalists, this policy was intended for native youth, who had to be made conscious of the value of their cultural heritage by means of an education focusing on Balinese language, literature and the arts.

This conservative policy carried on in Bali by the colonial state was to have long-lasting consequences. For one thing, by looking for the singularity of Bali in its Hindu heritage, while conceiving of Balinese identity as formed through an opposition to Islam and Christianity, Dutch orientalists and administrators established the framework within which the Balinese were going to define themselves. Furthermore, by attempting to preserve Bali's singularity from the rest of the Indies, the Dutch ended up by emphasizing it far more than they had ever envisioned, all the while turning it into a challenge for the Balinese.

Despite the Dutch attempt to insulate Balinese society from disturbing foreign influences, Bali actually underwent rapid and profound changes as a result of increasing interference in native affairs by the colonial state (Boon, 1977; Vickers, 1989; Schulte Nordholt, 1994; Robinson, 1995). In particular, the requirements of a modern administration were instrumental in the emergence of a Balinese intelligentsia, since the colonial state needed educated natives to mediate between the local population and their European masters.

During the 1920s, some Balinese educated in colonial schools set up organizations and started publishing periodicals dealing with matters of religion and social order. The Balinese authors who have commented on these organizations have tended to stress the conflict which opposed the commoners (*jaba*) to the nobility (*triwangsa*), expressed through their respective publications – *Surya Kanta* (1925–1927) and *Bali Adnjana* (1924–1930) – while construing that conflict in terms of a contest between 'modernist' and 'traditionalist' factions. True, the polemic between *Surya Kanta* and

Bali Adnjana concerned mainly 'caste' privileges, which had been aggravated by the colonial policy and which the commoners wanted to abolish in the name of 'progress'. Yet, one should be wary of focusing too much on this so-called 'caste conflict', at the risk of overlooking the fact that all these organizations shared a common concern for Balinese identity and were eager to preserve its foundations (Picard, 1999).

In striving to make sense of the changes brought about by the colonial encounter, these educated Balinese viewed themselves as members of a singular entity – the 'Balinese people' (*bangsa Bali*). Until then, their identities were particularistic, in the sense that the Balinese identified themselves as members of a village, of a kinship group, or of a temple network, rather than as 'Balinese'. Their collective identity, based on the awareness of sharing common characteristics and adhering to unifying symbols, started to take shape during the colonial period, when they attempted to define themselves as different from both the foreign colonizers and the other 'peoples' from the Indies (Howe, 2001).

In their publications, *jaba* and *triwangsa* described themselves both as a religious minority, the stronghold of Hinduism threatened by the aggressive expansionism of Islam and Christianity; and as a particular ethnic group characterized by their own customs, which made them at once distinct from and comparable to other ethnic groups in the Indies. More precisely, they construed their identity – which they began calling *kebalian* – as being based simultaneously on *agama* and on *adat*. Now, the very fact of the Balinese resorting to these foreign terms to define their identity testifies to the conceptual shift occurring on the island after its take-over by an alien power.

Introduced to Bali by the Dutch, the word *adat* replaced a varied terminology for variable local customs, which governed the relationships between social groups and infused the sense of communal solidarity in the villages. The incorporation of a miscellaneous assortment of local customs into a generic term altered their meaning for the Balinese: what had been, until then, an inter-play of significant differences deliberately fostered between villages was becoming the locus of Balinese ethnic identity, in the sense of a customary body of inherited rules and institutions governing the lives of the Balinese. As for the word *agama*, which is of Sanskrit origin, it has acquired in Indonesia the generic meaning of 'religion' through its association with Islam and with Christianity later on. By adopting that word, the Balinese were attempting to elevate their own religion to an equal standing with these world religions, and thus to resist their proselytism.

Now that they had the words to refer to both 'tradition' and 'religion', the problem for the Balinese was to discriminate clearly between their respective fields. Their inability to do so stemmed from the fact that up until then they did not regard religion as a bounded domain that could be set apart from other aspects of their life and labelled with a specific name (Picard, 2004). Indeed, for the Balinese *adat* partakes of a religious world view, in the sense that it refers at once to a divine cosmic order and to the social order established accordingly by their ancestors. This is to say that Balinese religion is highly localized, as it consists of rites relating specific groups of people to one another, to their ancestors, and to their territory (Guermonprez, 2001). Furthermore, religion is a customary obligation for the Balinese, in the sense that participation in its rites is a consequence of membership in a local community as well as in a kinship group. In this respect, it is doubtful that religion was a boundary marker for the Balinese before they started viewing Islam and Christianity as a threat (Vickers, 1987; Couteau, 1999; 2000).

While they were busy sorting out what pertains to true 'religion' and what to 'tradition', the Balinese had yet to discover that they also had a 'culture'. The fact is that during the 1920s, culture (and art) as a specific topic had been conspicuously absent from the reflections of the first generation of Balinese intellectuals on their identity. It is only in the 1930s, with the promotion of the island as a tourist destination, and thanks to the interest and appreciation of Dutch Orientalists and American anthropologists, not to forget Western artists, that the Balinese added in the category of *budaya* as a component of *kebalian*. Yet, just as the Balinese language had no term for 'religion' or 'tradition', it also had none for 'culture' or 'art'. Thus, while the word for 'religion' (*agama*) had been borrowed from Sanskrit and that for 'tradition' (*adat*) from Arabic, the notions of 'culture' (*cultuur*) and 'art' (*kunst*) were initially acquired from Dutch, before being appropriated from Malay, as *budaya* and *seni* respectively.

Religious Affiliation and Ethnic Belonging

By giving rise to a sharper contrast between 'us' and 'them', the colonial encounter not only helped the Balinese to conceive of themselves as a 'people', a neatly bounded entity, but it also contributed to a drawing of boundaries between conceptually distinct semantic fields, undifferentiated until then. Yet, if the Dutch had de-politicized *adat* by dissociating political power from customary authority, religion remained merged with tradition in the colonial period. Once they had become Indonesian citizens, the Balinese would be compelled to distinguish explicitly between religion and tradition: in order for their rites to accede to the status of *agama*, they had to be detached from what was considered as belonging to the domain of *adat*.

After Indonesia's proclamation of independence, the question of the religious foundation of the new state came rapidly to a head, opposing the 'Muslims' to the 'nationalists'. The former wanted to establish an Islamic state, whereas their opponents argued in favour of a state in which religious and secular affairs would be kept separate. This confrontation resulted in a compromise: the Indonesian state placed belief in 'One Almighty God' (*Ke-Tuhanan Yang Maha Esa*) first amongst its founding principles (*Pancasila*), without making Islam an official or even a privileged religion.

As a concession to the Islamic parties, however, a Ministry of Religion was set up in 1946, with three sections – for the Muslims, the Protestants and the Catholics. The Ministry stipulated the following conditions for a religion to be recognized: it must be monotheistic, have a codified system of law for its followers, possess a holy book and a prophet, enjoy international recognition and, further, its congregation should not be limited to a single ethnic group.

According to these conditions, Balinese religion was considered to belong to the domain of *adat* and not to that of *agama*. Consequently, if the Balinese did not want to become the target of Muslim or Christian proselytizing, they had to reform their religion in order to make it eligible for the status of *agama*. Thus, during the following years, the Balinese kept pressing the Ministry to recognize their religion, while a number of reformist religious organizations were making their appearance. Stressing the theological significance as well as the moral implications of religion, they strove to restrain the ritualistic propension of their fellow Balinese, while interpreting their Hindu–Javanese heritage in reference to Islamic and Christian tenets. They enjoined the Balinese to come back to the fold of Hinduism, by renewing their contact with India. Finally, after intense lobbying – and thanks to President Sukarno, whose mother was Balinese – the 'Balinese Hindu religion' (*agama Hindu Bali*) was recognized by the Ministry of Religion in 1958, shortly after Bali had become a province of its own.

The following year, the main religious organizations on the island merged into a single council, the *Parisada Dharma Hindu Bali*, in charge of co-ordinating all the religious activities of the Balinese Hindus. The *Parisada* undertook to compile a holy book, standardize the rites, formalize the priesthood and provide religious instruction to the population – all this amounting to a 'scripturalization' of Balinese religion, a shift of focus from orthopraxy to orthodoxy (Bakker, 1993).

Through their struggle to have their religion recognized, the Balinese have come to define their ethnic identity in terms of a localized version of Hinduism. But it is precisely from the moment they identified themselves as a Hindu island in a sea of Islam that one can date a disjunction between the Balinese religious and ethnic identities. This is because their identification of ethnicity and religion would soon be hindered by a two-fold process: on the one hand, the affiliation of other Indonesian ethnic groups to Hinduism would tend to dissociate it from the Balinese, while on the other, the fragmentation of the religious landscape on their island was making the link between religious affiliation and ethnic belonging ever more problematic for the Balinese.

While the name *Hindu Bali* implied recognition of the ethnic component of Balinese Hinduism, it would not be long before the Ministry of Religion would put pressure on the Balinese to nationalize their religion. At the same time, the presence of Balinese communities outside of their island enabled the *Parisada* to extend its influence to other parts of the country. In 1964, the council changed its name to

Parisada Hindu Dharma, thus forsaking any reference to its Balinese origins. And when, the following year, Sukarno announced the names of the religions that were to qualify for official government sponsorship, it was *agama Hindu* and not *agama Hindu Bali* that was retained.

Throughout the New Order period, *agama Hindu* would remain the primary marker of Balinese public identity, while growing ever apart from its Balinese origins. On the one hand, by increasing the Balinese awareness of their position as a religious minority, the pressure of Islam drove them to close ranks under the banner of *agama Hindu*, which characterizes them as a non-Muslim and non-Christian minority within the Indonesian multi-religious nation. Yet on the other hand, once detached from any ethnic reference, *agama Hindu* was no longer the sole property of the Balinese. In fact, its recognition brought it new recruits in the wake of the anti-communist massacres of 1965–1966, which marked the advent of the New Order régime. Thousands of Javanese nominal Muslims 'converted' to *agama Hindu* for fear of being branded as 'atheists', an accusation synonymous with 'communists' in Indonesia. In the following years, the Balinese and Javanese Hindus were joined by several ethnic minorities, who took refuge in the Hindu fold hoping to be allowed to conserve their ancestral rites, *agama Hindu* being reputedly more accommodating than Christianity or Islam.

The diffusion of *agama Hindu* outside of Bali would continue to such an extent that the Balinese started fearing that they might lose the control of the religion they had themselves established. After having opened a branch in every province of the country, the *Parisada Hindu Dharma* became in 1986 the *Parisada Hindu Dharma Indonesia*. The Indonesianization of what had initially been the organ of Balinese religion prompted the rise of non-Balinese as well as of commoners within the hierarchy of the *Parisada*, which had been controlled until then by the Balinese nobility. This evolution was confirmed in 1996, when the *Parisada*'s headquarters was transferred to Jakarta in order to place *agama Hindu* on an equal footing with the other official religions. From then on, there would only remain in Bali a regional branch of the *Parisada*.

During the 1990s, the rise of Islam in Indonesia would trigger a 'Hindu revival' (*kebangkitan Hindu*) (Setia, 1993). This revival has resulted in religious divisions amongst the Balinese, with the spread of various devotional movements inspired by neo-Hinduism of Indian obedience (*sampradaya*). Their devotees are no longer satisfied with a nationally recognized religion but aspire to universalize their religious identity by breaking the ties which bind it to Bali (and to its *adat*), so as to bring it in line with the allegedly 'authentic' Hinduism of India. It appears that neither the traditional religion, attached to the correct execution of the rites, nor its official version, concerned with ethics and theology, are able to satisfy a growing faction of the Balinese middle class, in quest of religious devotion and personal conviction as well as of universalism (Howe, 2001). So much so that the *Parisada* has become challenged in its reformist project, with the defection of numerous intellectuals, who criticize both its political subservience to the Indonesian state and its passivity towards the offences inflicted upon *agama Hindu*.

The political and religious effervescence fuelled by the demise of the New Order resulted in an open conflict between supporters of divergent conceptions of the Balinese religion, which would eventually tear the *Parisada* apart at the time of its eighth national congress, in September 2001. The Balinese branch of the *Parisada* objected to the decisions adopted by the congress, namely the nomination of a layman at the head of the *Parisada*, until then a monopoly of the *Brahmana* high priests (*pedanda*), not to mention the massive presence in its leadership of commoners and non-Balinese. In November of the same year, the Balinese *Parisada* held its regional congress at Campuan, near Ubud. Accusing the leadership of unduly Indianizing *agama Hindu*, the Campuan congress demanded the nomination of a *pedanda* at the head of the *Parisada*. By the close of the congress, the nobility, and particularly the *pedanda*, had taken control of the Balinese *Parisada*. Soon afterwards, the central *Parisada* disowned the *Parisada Campuan* and convened its own regional congress in March 2002 at Besakih, the main sanctuary on the island. After the *Parisada Besakih* had ratified the decisions of the national congress, it was acknowledged as the one and only official Balinese branch of the *Parisada*. Since then, each of the two Balinese *Parisada* has been claiming to be the legitimate representative of the Balinese Hindu community, while attempting to win the support of the Balinese people for their respective positions. While the *Parisada Besakih* has the backing of the *sampradaya* as well as of the urbanized intelligentsia, the *Parisada Campuan* is unquestionably more in phase with the Balinese population at large.

Thus it is that what had started as a struggle of the Balinese for the recognition of their religion led to a conflictual division of the Balinese religious identities. Religion is no longer in Bali a unified field of practices and beliefs, but it has become an arena where the stakes are simultaneously political, ethnic and religious. Such a breaking up of the religious field has bred a debate on the very conception of the Balinese identity, which has ended in dissociating the religious affiliation of the Balinese from their ethnic belonging.

Cultural Tourism

During the New Order period, while 'religion' and 'tradition' were drifting further apart, the one striving for universalism, the other delving into exclusivism, 'Balinese culture' (*kebudayaan Bali*) was being actively promoted by both the state and the tourism industry. Inasmuch as Bali is a province of Indonesia as well as a tourist destination, Balinese culture was treated as a resource, and expected as such to contribute both to developing international tourism in Indonesia and to fostering the national Indonesian culture.[20]

Unlike Sukarno, who wanted to forge an Indonesian identity by eliminating the 'ethnocentricity' (*sukuisme*) inherited from the colonial period, Suharto undertook to create a national culture based on regional cultural traditions. Rather than denying the appeal of ethnicity as a focus of allegiance by suppressing its manifestations, the New Order endeavoured to domesticate ethnic identities by enlisting their contribution to the process of nation-building. Yet, while the expression of ethnic identity appeared to have found official sanction, it was tolerated only as long as it remained at the level of cultural display. Thus, the visual and decorative aspects of Indonesian ethnic cultures – such as dance and music, costumes, handicrafts and architecture – benefited from an unprecedented degree of official promotion. This is what is called in Indonesian *seni budaya*, which amounts to a vision of culture as art (Acciaioli, 1985), targeting two audiences: first and foremost, Indonesians themselves, expected to endorse a contrived version of what they are told is their national 'cultural heritage' (*warisan budaya*); and, second, foreign visitors enticed into the country to admire its famed 'tourist objects' (*obyek wisata*).

But even this is only one side of the story, as we are not really dealing here with Indonesia's 'ethnic cultures', but rather with what Indonesian officials call 'regional cultures' (*kebudayaan daerah*). Now, through the pervasive reference to *kebudayaan daerah*, what was actually enacted, in conjunction with the process of national integration, was a policy enforcing at once uniformization within each province and differentiation between the provinces. The New Order state was aiming to induce in each of its provinces a distinctive homogeneous provincial identity, based on a notion of culture stripped down to *seni budaya*, at the expense of the diverse ethnic cultures enclosed within their boundaries. Such provincial identities were promoted by the regional governments and proposed to the nation for consumption, as well as to the local populations they allegedly represent for authentication.

In this respect, Bali's situation is unique, in that its name stands for an entity that is at once geographic, ethnic and administrative – in addition to designating the touristic showcase of Indonesia. Therefore, depending on the context, *kebudayaan Bali* could refer either to the culture of the Balinese people as an ethnic group, or to the regional culture of Bali as a province of Indonesia, or else to the main attraction of the island of Bali as a tourist destination.

Bearing this in mind, one is in a better position to assess the Balinese response to what they called the 'challenge of tourism' (*tantangan pariwisata*). One has to know that the Balinese authorities had not been associated with the decision taken in Jakarta to convert their island into the tourist gateway to Indonesia. In order to take advantage of Jakarta's decision, they decided to make the island's culture the focus of tourism development. From the start, Balinese policy-makers and tourism stakeholders evinced an ambivalent attitude toward tourism, which they perceived as being both fraught with danger and rich in promising prosperity. On the one hand, the artistic and religious traditions that had made Bali famous world-wide provided its main attraction in the eyes of tourists, thus turning Balinese culture into the most valuable asset for the island's economic development. But on the other hand, the invasion of Bali by foreign visitors was seen as a threat of 'cultural pollution' (*polusi kebudayaan*). To prevent such a fatal outcome, the Balinese authorities devised a policy of 'cultural tourism' (*pariwisata budaya*), which was intended to develop tourism without debasing Balinese culture, by using culture to attract tourists while fostering culture through the revenue generated by tourism (Picard, 1996).

Besides expressing a genuine worry, the focus on cultural tourism was an attempt on the part of Balinese policy-makers and tourism stakeholders to protect their island's main symbolic capital – and of its financial stakes – from Indonesian officials and foreign investors. They were conveying the message that, in the unfortunate event that the touristic exploitation of Bali's cultural resources should lead to their depletion, this would bring about the ruin of the tourism industry itself. Hence, declared the Balinese, it is in everyone's interest to preserve, foster and promote Balinese culture (*melestarikan, membina dan mengembangkan kebudayaan Bali*).

The rhetorical power of persuasion of cultural tourism was intended not only for Jakarta but for the Balinese as well. By defining Balinese cultural identity in reference to the 'challenge' of tourism, the discourse of cultural tourism united the Balinese people under the banner of their culture, while its promoters could claim to speak in the name of the superior interests of Bali. As Adrian Vickers once remarked, no Balinese worthy of the name could refuse to adhere to the ideal of 'Balinese culture': 'Nobody on Bali would seriously think to challenge the idea of Balinese culture. Even those people who oppose tourism and see themselves as defenders of tradition are supporters of the idea' (Vickers, 1989: 195).

Ajeg Bali or *Ajeg Hindu*?

At first sight, *Ajeg Bali* would appear to be a mere follow-up of the discourses of *kebalian* and *pariwisata budaya*. In Bali, traditional values have periodically been drawn upon at critical moments, and the new slogan seems to carry the same message as before in a new guise.[21] Indeed, in Balinese *ajeg* means 'constant', 'permanent', just like the word *lestari* in Indonesian, which brings *Ajeg Bali* very close to the watchword *pelestarian budaya* ('cultural preservation'), in vogue during the New Order.

Yet, in the meantime the situation has changed rather markedly, and *Ajeg Bali* differs on at least two counts from previous articulations of Balinese culture and identity. On the one hand, since the Kuta bombing the Balinese are clearly on the defensive and their plea has a stronger sense of urgency – of desperation even – than ever before. Accordingly, the discourse of *Ajeg Bali* captures a much harder-edged notion of Balineseness, one that is under siege on a number of fronts and in need of guarding itself against the perils assailing the island from all sides – such as globalization, tourism, Jakarta, Islam and terrorism.[22] The bombing has hurt the Balinese not only in their economic mainstay but even more so in their honour, if not in their virility. It shook their nerves and raised their sense of *jengah*, which is a peculiar Balinese feeling of shame mixed with anger. Hence the call for the Balinese to rise again (*bangkit kembali*), to stand up (*berdiri*), in short, to be erect (*ajeg*). Whereas *kebalian* was just seen as a statement of the obvious, *Ajeg Bali* is performative.

On the other hand, *Ajeg Bali* is much more divisive than former slogans ever were. Even though the policy of cultural tourism did not really stand up to the expectations of its initiators, the ideological discourse which it supported is still being eagerly embraced by most Balinese. And when tourism development in Bali was contested in the 1990s, it was precisely in the name of cultural tourism. Now, contrary to Satria Naradha's purpose, the *Ajeg Bali* campaign, which appeals to the Balinese people to show a united front in the face of external threats, has given rise to both scepticism and criticism from various quarters on the island (Allen and Palermo, 2005).

Firstly, for a number of Balinese (and foreign) analysts, *Ajeg Bali* is really no more than an empty shell, a rhetorical device, to which public figures are just expected to pay lip service. They point to the fact that, apart from the vaguely phrased intentions to protect Balinese culture, very few practical solutions were suggested by the participants of the *Ajeg Bali* seminar in August 2003 (*Sarad*, 2003c; 2003d). In truth, besides having become indeed an unavoidable reference in Balinese public discourses, as well as the topic of further seminars (including one called precisely '*Ajeg Bali*, between slogan and implementation'), *Ajeg Bali* has resulted in few initiatives. In addition to *Ajeg Bali* competitions amongst schoolchildren and prizes awarded to *Ajeg Bali* teachers, the main practical measure has been the launching by Satria Naradha in May 2005 of a co-operative (*Koperasi Krama Bali*), to strengthen the economic standing of the Balinese people vis-à-vis their competitors by granting soft loans to needy local petty traders and entrepreneurs. Thanks to these grants, it is hoped that the Balinese would no longer be tempted to sell their land to foreign investors.[23]

Apart from these limited initiatives, *Ajeg Bali* has remained mostly a catchword, which appears moreover to mean different things to different people. For some, it is a statement of ethnic and cultural identity, a way to remind the Balinese to be faithful to their *kebalian*; for others, it is a filter through which to select from external influences those that fit Balinese cultural values; for yet others again, it is an aspiration for Bali to become peaceful and prosperous with the return of the tourists (Darma Putra, 2004a: 227).

As for the critics, they come from two main fronts: from cosmopolitan and progressive public intellectuals, such as Made Kembar Kerepun (*Sarad*, 2003d), Gusti Ngurah Bagus (*Sarad*, 2003d), Nyoman Wijaya (*Sarad*, 2003d; Wijaya, 2004), Ketut Sumarta (*Sarad*, 2003d), AA GN Ari Dwipayana (*Sarad*, 2003d; 2005), Degung

Santikarma (2003b; 2003c), Ngurah Suryawan (2004); and from Hindu religious leaders, like Putu Setia, Ketut Wiana, Made Titib or Ida Pandita Nabe Sri Bhagawan Dwija Warsa Nawa Sandhi (*Raditya*, 2004; Titib, 2005).

To start with – and Satria Naradha's claim to the contrary notwithstanding – progressive public intellectuals reproach *Ajeg Bali* for freezing Balinese society by preserving out-dated customs and values, in order to buttress the abusive privileges of traditional elites whose power has been jeopardized by *reformasi* and *otonomi*. Quite a few of them see in *Ajeg Bali* a return to the Dutch cultural policy of *Baliseering*, which they denounce as an attempt to turn Bali into a living museum for the sole enjoyment of tourists. They recall that the *Baliseering* policy, which had the backing of the conservative nobility assembled behind *Bali Adnjana*, was rejected by the modernist commoner movement *Surya Kanta*, whose leaders wanted to adapt the Balinese people to the changing times. Further, they charge that, in fostering social stability and normative consensus, the *Ajeg Bali* campaign results in putting down any dissent and criticism, by accusing its opponents of disturbing the romantic image of Bali promoted by the tourism industry.

According to these opponents, the problem facing the Balinese is not one of preservation – as if Bali was already *ajeg* and had to be kept that way – but of transformation, in order for them to become better equipped to confront the challenge of globalization. Instead of complaining about migrant workers and foreign investors taking over the tourism industry and appropriating its revenue, the Balinese people should acquire the professional proficiency which will allow them to compete for job and business opportunities with their challengers. Otherwise, they will be pushed aside by outsiders and will become foreigners on their own land, just like the Hawai'ians before them.

Furthermore, these same critics object to the reified and essentialized vision of *Ajeg Bali* as a homogeneous and harmonious society threatened from outside, which they say is not only illusory but dangerous. It is a xenophobic ideology, which fosters primordial ethnic and religious identification by erecting boundaries between Balinese and non-Balinese, and by sparking Hindu fundamentalism as a response to Islamic pressure. This protectionist stance is illusory, for Bali's plight does not come from beyond its shores but arises from within Balinese society itself. Witness the incidence of social strife on the island, which rose sharply after the collapse of the New Order. Thus, in December 2003, the Balinese magazine *Sarad* dedicated its main feature to debating intra-Balinese conflicts (*Sarad*, 2003e; see also *Sarad*, 2005a; 2005b). Its investigators registered no less than 88 violent mass conflicts since 1997, most of them having to do with customary law disputes, the so-called *kasus adat*.

Ironically, while progressive intellectuals associate *Ajeg Bali* with the rise of Hindu fundamentalism, the real Balinese Hindu fundamentalists accuse its promoters of fostering Balinese cultural and ethnic identity to the detriment of the Hindu religion.

Thus, the Hindu magazine *Raditya* made its December 2004 headlines on the question: '*Ajeg Bali* or *Ajeg Hindu?* (*Raditya*, 2004).[24] According to its editor, Putu Setia, if the purpose of *Ajeg Bali* is to preserve and strengthen Balinese culture, then it concerns Muslim and Christian Balinese as much as it does Hindu Balinese. If this is the case, Bali is doomed to become like Java after the fall of Majapahit under the pressure of Islam, when the Javanese held on to their culture while discarding their religion. On the other hand, if the aim is to curb the coming of Muslim migrants and to limit the construction of mosques on the island, *Ajeg Hindu* should be promoted instead. Indeed, as long as the Hindu religion is still *ajeg* in Bali, the Balinese culture will be *ajeg* as well (*sepanjang agama Hindu masih ajeg di Bali maka kebudayaan Bali akan tetap ajeg*), as Balinese culture is based on Hinduism (*kebudayaan Bali bersumber dari agama Hindu*).

The Predicament of Balinese Identity

The contradictory criticism *à propos* of *Ajeg Bali* attests to the disintegration of the discursive construction of *kebalian*. While progressive public intellectuals are attempting to adapt their island to the challenges of a globalized world, Hindu fundamentalists are busy inventing a universal religion true to their idealized vision of Vedic India, whereas most Balinese are inclined to find refuge in the parochial ideal of their traditional village community. Since what defines them as a non-Muslim and non-Christian minority in a multi-religious nation is no longer their exclusive property, while their religious identity has become controversial, it is understandable that, faced with an aggression from outside, the Balinese are withdrawing into what is most exclusively theirs, that is, not *agama Hindu* but *adat Bali*.

Such is the predicament of *kebalian* that, due to the dissociation of their ethnic and religious identities, the Balinese are left hanging between two alternative referents, *adat* and *agama*. Yet, neither of these referents is unequivocally defined, as testified by the difficulty in establishing who rightly belongs to the *desa pakraman* on the one hand, and on the other, by the divergent conceptions of the Balinese religion, which ended in a schism between two opposing factions within the *Parisada*. How did the Balinese become entangled in such a predicament?

In compelling the Balinese to account explicitly for what it meant to be Balinese, the colonial encounter was instrumental in bringing about the emergence of a sense of religious, ethnic and cultural identity amongst the Balinese people. Once they had become Indonesian citizens, Balinese power holders and opinion leaders endeavoured to homogenize the components of their 'Balineseness', in order to assert the distinctive character of Bali as a Hindu island in a Muslim-dominated nation-state. Up to the end of the New Order things were still reasonably clear-cut, in the sense that Balinese public opinion would usually blame outsiders for the problems increasingly facing their island.

In those days, the main bone of contention between Bali and Jakarta centred on the control of tourism development and the appropriation of its revenue on the one hand, and on the recognition of Balinese singularity on the other. Gathered under the banner of 'cultural tourism' (*pariwisata budaya*), Balinese policy makers and tourism stakeholders were unanimous in calling for the preservation and promotion of Balinese culture.

With the collapse of the Indonesian state apparatus, and the onset of *krisis, reformasi* and *otonomi* which ensued, cracks started exposing that façade of consensual unanimity. It is as if, once their identity had been thoroughly established and recognized – thanks to the success of their island as a tourism destination – the unity of the Balinese as a people was breaking up. Not that Bali had ever been the seamless and harmonious society depicted in the tourist brochures, but now the intra-Balinese conflicts were becoming too conspicuous to be ignored or even to be swept under the carpet by putting the blame on outsiders. This being the case, it is significant that, while status contests have hit the media with renewed vigour since the demise of the New Order, articulations of class conflicts within Balinese society have not surfaced in public discourses, which have remained clearly framed in terms of insiders versus outsiders.

The bombing of October 2002 would initially alleviate these internal dissensions, by inspiring an outburst of solidarity amongst the Balinese, standing together against its perpetrators. In these trying circumstances, the *Ajeg Bali* campaign appears as a cultural revival movement fostering a monolithic identity based on *agama Hindu* and *desa pakraman*, which attempts to protect the Balinese from external threats by presenting a united front to the outside. The Balinese are thus urged to take shelter in a closed-in definition of their identity, at a time when the boundary line between the inside and the outside of Bali is becoming increasingly difficult to draw and to enforce, due to the growing heterogeneity of the people who have made this island their home, not only fellow Indonesians of various ethnic background and religious persuasion, but also foreign expatriates.

Tourism has thus entailed paradoxical consequences in Bali. While opening up the island to the outside world and increasing its dependence on a global market, it has induced an inward-looking focus amongst the Balinese people. According to the felicitous expression of Henk Schulte Nordholt (2005), Bali is like an 'open fortress', whose multifarious problems cannot be solved by such slogans as *Ajeg Bali*.

Afterword: 1 October 2005

As I was finishing this chapter, Bali was hit for the second time. On Saturday night, 1 October 2005, two blasts went off almost simultaneously at Kafe Nyoman and nearby Kafe Menega in a crowded seafood night market on Jimbaran Beach, with a third one exploding in Raja's restaurant in downtown Kuta a few minutes later.

The damage was fortunately far less massive than the first time, with many fewer casualties, most of whom were Indonesians.

The Balinese reacted in the same fashion as they had done before, with prayers, offerings and purification ceremonies. As for the tourists, their reactions were more muted than previously, as if the world had become used to terrorism over the past three years. Unlike what happened in October 2002, there was no mass exodus. Nonetheless, two weeks after the bombing, arrivals were down 40 per cent and average occupancies had fallen from 90 per cent to 50 per cent. The decline persisted in the following months, with a 40 per cent drop in foreign visitors for the last quarter of 2005 as compared to the same period one year before. While damage to Bali's tourism industry was still being assessed, tourism stakeholders expected that the business downturn this time around would prove less severe and of shorter duration than that experienced following the first bombing.[25]

More than ever, security became the central issue, as it was considered the key to the recovery of tourism. Bali's police chief called on the provincial government to introduce regulations allowing a strict control of non-Balinese migrants. He further announced that a Bali Security Council would soon be in operation, charged with coordinating general security policies on the island.

Meanwhile, renewed references to *Ajeg Bali* featured prominently in Balinese public discourses. A seminar entitled 'Challenges and opportunities for *Ajeg Bali* in the global era' (*Tantangan dan Peluang Ajeg Bali dalam Era Global*) was held on October 8, which resulted in the foundation of an 'Institute for the Strategic Study of *Ajeg Bali*' (*Lembaga Kajian Strategis Ajeg Bali*).

Author's Note

The writing of this paper benefited from stimulating exchanges over the years with numerous Balinese and foreign intellectuals. In this respect, I would like to thank particularly I Gusti Ngurah Bagus, Ida Bagus Adnyana Manuaba, I Gde Pitana, I Nyoman Darma Putra, I Nyoman Wijaya, Degung Santikarma, I Wayan Juniartha, I Ketut Sumarta, I Made Nariana, Putu Setia and Ida Pedanda Gde Made Gunung, as well as Jean Couteau, Diana Darling, Jean-François Guermonprez, Michael Hitchcock, Leo Howe, Graeme MacRae, Henk Schulte Nordholt, Adrian Vickers and Carol Warren.

Notes

1 See Sulistyo (2002), Sudhyatmaka Sugriwa (2003), Sujaya (2004), as well as Moor (2003), Anggraeni (2003) and Allan (2005) for detailed accounts of the bombing and its aftermath.

2 After having been stated in the *Bali Post*, the main daily paper on the island, Suryani's opinion was widely circulated abroad when she was quoted in an interview to *The*

Australian, published on October 22: 'This is the punishment of God because we have not developed cultural tourism but we have brought in many things outside our Balinese culture . . . We now have prostitution, gambling, paedophilia, drugs, [plans for a] casino. These things are not Balinese. These things are brought in by foreigners. It disturbs our culture.' (Ellis, 2002). As a matter of fact, such a reaction is not that different from the contempt expressed by the perpetrators of the bombing toward the immoral behaviour of the foreign tourists in Bali.

3 Thus, it seems that many Balinese attributed to this ceremony the success of the chief of police, I Made Mangku Pastika, in finding and arresting the perpetrators of the bombing. See Moor (2003) for a detailed report on the arrest of the perpetrators.

4 Disconcertingly enough, we do not know how many tourists visit Bali each year, be they foreign or domestic. The only precise figures given by the Bali Provincial Government's Tourism Office (*Dinas Pariwisata*) concern foreign visitors entering Indonesia through Bali on direct international flights, registered by the provincial immigration services. These numbered 1,230,316 in 1997. These figures, therefore, do not take into account Indonesians or foreigners arriving on domestic flights, or arrivals at Gilimanuk by the ferry coming from Java, not to mention tourists from cruise ships mooring at Benoa or Padang. According to various surveys, it seems that the proportion of foreign indirect arrivals has been decreasing since the 1990s. On the other hand, the number of domestic tourists has been on the rise during the same period, to the point that they probably outnumber foreign visitors. In addition to the uncertainties as to the number of tourists visiting Bali each year, there are also unexplained discrepancies regarding the number of hotel rooms in the non-starred sector between the Central Bureau of Statistics (BPS) and the Bali Tourism Office.

5 According to the Regional Development Planning Board (*Bappeda*), while in 1970 the agricultural sector supplied about 60 per cent of the Regional Gross Domestic Product, its contribution had been reduced to less than 20 per cent in 1997. At the same time, barely one-third of the work-force on the island was still employed in agriculture (Bappeda, 2004).

6 Due to land speculation, numerous Balinese owners are no longer able to pay the Land and Building Tax and are consequently forced to sell to investors or middlemen (Suasta, 2001).

7 In the very words of the Governor: 'Being prosperous is a dilemma for us. We cannot prevent people from coming and working in Bali. Indonesia is a united country, and as such we cannot close our door on others. Everybody has the right to make a living here. But in all honesty, the influx of seasonal migrant workers has created serious population, environmental and security problems. It is difficult for us to precisely register the number of these migrants, who usually reside in the already densely populated areas of Denpasar or Badung regencies. We don't have adequate infrastructures, including for housing, water and sanitary facilities, to support them. As a result, we see so many new squatters in the city of Denpasar, creating slum areas. A lot of them are jobless and could possibly affect the crime rate on the island.' (*The Jakarta Post,* 14 August 2001).

8 There is no reliable evidence as to the scope of these migrations to Bali. The only figures made public, from the Regional Office of the Department of Religion (Kantor Wilayah Departemen Agama Propinsi Bali), provide some indication regarding the religious affiliation of the population in the province. According to this office, the proportion of Muslims amongst the population of Bali has remained constant over the years, at around 6 per cent. The same source indicates a proportion of 15 per cent Muslims in the municipality of Denpasar (*Bappeda*, 2004). These figures are, in all likelihood grossly underestimated, and other sources give 10 per cent Muslims for Bali and 25 per cent for Denpasar, while the proportion of Hindu Balinese on the island would be 87 per cent and only 67 per cent in Denpasar (*Sarad*, 2002b: 19). Whatever the case, there is a general consensus amongst Hindu Balinese that they are on the wane in their own island, and will even soon become a minority in Denpasar. And not a few of them accuse 'Jakarta' of intentionally undermining their position.

9 There is a growing literature on the *pecalang*, both Balinese and foreign: Darling, 2003; MacDougall, 2003; ICG, 2003; Widnyani and Widia, 2003; Santikarma, 2003a; Suryawan, 2005.

10 *Adat* is a word of Arabic origin, appropriated by Islamized populations in the Indonesian archipelago to refer to indigenous 'customary law' as opposed to imported 'religious law' (*hukum*, *syariah*), and which was introduced to Bali by Dutch administrators.

11 On this topic, see the January and March 2003 issues of *Sarad*, which deal with *desa pakraman* and *pendatang* (*Sarad*, 2003a; 2003b).

12 Taken together, these three areas appropriate roughly 50 per cent of the province's budget (APBD) and 90 per cent of the regional revenues (PAD).

13 As they like to put it: 'The tourists only urinate and defecate in our district, while they spend their money in Badung.' (*Kami hanya dapat kencing dan beraknya wisatawan, sedangkan pendapatan diterima Badung*.)

14 For example, the *bupati* of Klungkung is pushing to open a casino on the island of Nusa Penida, despite the opposition of the governor and the majority of Balinese opinion leaders.

15 Such a futile temptation is sneered at by some Balinese intellectuals, who are quick to point to what they dub the '*Nyepi syndrom*'. *Nyepi* is the Hindu Balinese New Year, a day of silence when *pecalang* patrol the island to make sure that everyone keeps their lights turned off and does not venture out into the open. Since the demise of the New Order, the Balinese authorities have succeeded in closing Bali's harbours and airport on *Nyepi*'s day, thus stopping any traffic from entering the island. On that day, the Balinese realize their dream of controlling their island by keeping foreigners at bay. As one *pecalang* told Degung Santikarma: 'It's too bad *Nyepi* is just one day' (Santikarma, 2003a: 16).

16 *Ajeg* is a Balinese word, which translates in Indonesian as *tegak* (upright, erect) or *kukuh* (strong, firm) (Warna, 1990: 9). The term has a further connotation of permanence and persistence (Bawa, 2004: 251).

17 Satria Naradha is the son of Ketut Nadha, who founded *Soeara Indonesia* in 1948, which after undergoing several name changes became in 1972 the *Bali Post* (Putra and Supartha, 2001). He took over the paper in 1993 and gave it a more assertive orientation, stressing the need to 'defend Balinese identity' (*menjaga identitas Bali*) and to 'preserve Balinese culture' (*melestarikan kebudayaan Bali*). Since then, and particularly since the onset of *reformasi*, the *Bali Post* has become the main channel for the Balinese ethnic revival. While the majority of its contributors are public intellectuals, and while it mostly attracts an educated and urban readership, its influence reaches the Balinese community at large and goes a long way in shaping public opinion on the island. Over the years, Satria Naradha has built a powerful provincial media group, which includes a TV station, several radio stations, and a number of newspapers and magazines.

18 One of my favourites is '*Wujudkan Ajeg Bali / Pilih Presiden Berdarah Bali / Megawati Soekarnoputri*' ('Create a strong and everlasting Bali / Choose a President with Balinese blood / Megawati Soekarnoputri'), which one could read on banners erected during the 2004 presidential election. To drive the point home, the word *berdarah* (to be of a certain blood, of a certain ethnic background) was written in red letters.

19 In their opinion, Hindu religion had been brought to Bali in the 14th century by Javanese conquerors from the kingdom of Majapahit, who had also imposed a division of society into four 'castes', in conformity with the Indian model of the *varna*. According to this model, the Balinese nobility is composed of the triwangsa (literally, the 'three peoples' – Brahmana, Satria and Wesia), as opposed to the commoners (*jaba*, literally the 'outsiders', that is, those who are outside the sphere of the courts), who make up the bulk of the population.

20 The meaning of the word *kebudayaan*, commonly translated as 'culture', is at once normative and evolutionist, in the sense that it refers to the process through which ethnic groups are expected to acquire the qualities deemed necessary to institute the order and civilization that is consonant with the ideal of the Indonesian nation. One should not, therefore, expect to find in this word the idea of a cultural specificity characteristic of each ethnic group, nor that of cultural relativism. In this respect, *budaya* and *agama* are both equally tokens of civilization, which Indonesian ethnic groups are expected to strive for in order to be conferred a stamp of good citizenship.

21 In Indonesia, social problems tend to be treated as moral problems. Hence an inclination for a normative approach, expressed through the recurrent use of injunctions, such as harus, *mesti* ('must'), *perlu* ('necessary'), harap, *moga-moga* ('let's hope'), *jangan* ('don't'). Hence also a taste for incantatory maxims and mottoes, which seem to be acquiring a life of their own, as if the situation would be under control once it has been labelled. Thus, from one slogan to the next, it is difficult to escape a certain sense of *déjà-vu*.

22 As a matter of fact, there is very little reflection on the part of the Balinese authorities on terrorism in general, or even specifically on Islamic terrorism. They appear to be mostly concerned with demonstrating to foreign tour operators that security is now warranted in Bali and with convincing potential visitors that they will be safe on their island.

23 As the saying goes, in *Ajeg Bali* parlance: 'The Balinese sell their land to buy sate, whereas the newcomers sell sate to buy land' (*Krama Bali jual tanah untuk beli sate, warga pendatang jual sate untuk beli tanah*).

24 *Raditya* was launched in 1993 (initially under the name *Aditya*) by a group of Balinese, commoners based in Jakarta for the most part, who had founded in 1991 the Forum of Indonesian Hindu Intellectuals (*Forum Cendekiawan Hindu Indonesia*). Advocating a perspective at once universalist, individualistic and egalitarian, the Forum's leaders were critical of the *Parisada*, whom they accused of being more a pressure group made up of conservative members of the Balinese nobility than a genuine religious body, as well as of promoting a traditionalist conception of Hinduism, still very much affected by its original Balinese parochialism. They can be characterized as 'fundamentalists', in the sense that – in the fashion of Dayananda Sarasvati, the founder of the *Arya Samaj* in India – they want to go 'Back to the Veda', which in truth had never been known in Bali before the Hinduization of the Balinese religion in the 1950s.

25 After having slumped down to 993,185 in 2003, foreign direct arrivals to Bali set an all-time record in 2004, at 1,458,309 visitors – 3.21 per cent better than the previous record set in 2000 (1,412,839). Meanwhile, international newspapers and magazines had been releasing articles bearing such titles as 'The Rebirth of Bali' (The *New York Times*, 27 March 2005) or 'Recovering Paradise Lost' (*International Herald Tribune*, 1 April 2005). And given the figures for the first nine months of 2005, analysts were confident that this year would break new records. Due to the bombing, Bali ended 2005 with 1,386,499 foreign direct arrivals, a decline of 4.92 per cent from the previous year. As for Indonesia, total foreign tourist arrivals dropped 8.23 per cent in 2005, totalling 4.88 million as compared to the 5.32 million tourists arrivals achieved in 2004.

6

Tourism Policy-Making in Southeast Asia: A Twenty-First Century Perspective

Linda Richter

Introduction

In the early 1990s I attempted to describe policy-making on tourism in Southeast Asia and, although a chapter eventually emerged (Richter, 1993: 179–199), I was mostly forced to write charts that summarized the basic facts for each country. In the last five years, however, several books have emerged that focus on tourism in Southeast Asia. Still, broad comparative studies of policy-making in the region are rare.

Part of this problem hinges on how one defines policy-making. Some consider it to be what governments agree to do, but plans are often little more than creative writing. Others say policy is what the government actually attempts, which is often quite different, reflecting altered circumstances, new administrations, changes in political costs and benefits, and budgetary realities. This comes closer, I think, but I consider public policy as being what the government both decides to do and *not* to do. I shall return to this later as I discuss specific policies. However we define it, whatever stakeholders we include, the topic is extremely complex. The central problem for discussing public policy in Southeast Asia is that it is incredibly varied – politically, economically, linguistically, geographically, religiously, historically and in terms of the factors and processes by which tourism is being developed (Hitchcock, King and Parnwell, 1993).

A few examples make my point. Politically, the nations of Southeast Asia range from communist Vietnam and Laos to the despotic military junta which renamed Burma 'Myanmar' in 1989. There has been alternating civil-military rule in Thailand with a king offering royal continuity. There are strongly controlled 'Asian-style' democracies in Malaysia and the tiny island state of Singapore. There are rowdy and often inept democracies in Indonesia and the Philippines complete with home-grown insurgencies, and arguably constitutional monarchies in Brunei and Cambodia. East Timor's (Timor Leste's) political system is still a work in progress (Richter, 1999; Williams, 2004: 120). Economic systems range from socialist-lite, to state-controlled governments like Myanmar, to varying degrees of capitalist societies in the rest of the region. Languages and scripts are numerous within nations and among them.

Geographically, the range is from land-locked Laos to archipelagoes like the Philippines and Indonesia with most of the nations having both mainland and islands. Active volcanoes offer both striking attractions and potentially lethal dangers in several countries. The 26 December 2004 tsunami made clear that even tectonic plates can alter policy-making dramatically for both nations and non-governmental organizations (NGOs). In the case of Indonesia it even led to the end of a decades-long insurgency on Sumatra. Old goals were rendered obsolete by the staggering new needs for both the government and the insurgents.

Islam is the dominant religion of the maritime or island region whilst the major religion in mainland Southeast Asia is Theravada Buddhism, with Mahayana Buddhism in Vietnam, and as part of the complex mix of elements in the religion of immigrant Chinese. Hinduism as a practised religion survives on the Indonesian island of Bali, and is also found among Indian immigrant communities. Roman Catholicism is the main religion in the Philippines, although Islam is dominant in some of the southern Philippine islands. There are several varieties of Christianity among minority groups, especially the upland populations of both mainland and island Southeast Asia. There are also followers of numerous sects and animist believers.

Historically, most of the nations except Thailand have also experienced long periods of colonialism (up to 400 years) from a variety of European powers. Britain colonized what is now Malaysia, Singapore, Brunei and Burma; the French conquered Vietnam, Cambodia and Laos; and the Dutch ruled Indonesia. East Timor was a Portuguese colony from 1556–1974, and under Indonesian misrule until 1999. The Philippines endured 350 years of Spanish conquest and another 50 by the Americans. Portugal created a seaborne empire from the sixteenth century and until the mid-1970s held on to its remaining territory of East Timor. It is no wonder that their public bureaucracies and political cultures vary so much. Nor are their boundaries undisputed (Richter, 1993; Musa, 2003).

Thus, finding patterns of tourism policy-making in the midst of this variety of governmental experiences is very challenging. Still, some characteristics are obvious: top-down policy-making, some national planning, belated attention to environmental and indigenous factors and much corruption. Singapore, while rather authoritarian by Western democratic standards, is unusual in its political stability, economic and social discipline and successful development of both the economy in general and tourism in particular (Chang, 2004).

In the next section I provide a broad analysis of tourism public policy-making across three stages of development. Included are several policy decisions these nations confronted in their decision-making. Then in the subsequent section of the chapter several sustainability challenges to policy-makers will be examined. These problems are complicated by tourism but threaten the nations as a whole. Finally, some of the aspects of the region's tourism will be noted that encourage cautious optimism.

Stages of Tourism Policy-Making

Colonial Tourism and Its Aftermath

Traditional rulers in these nations may have visited religious shrines or sought seasonal respite from the heat, but it was not until European conquests and colonization that discretionary travel as opposed to trading and pilgrimage flourished in Southeast Asia (Stockwell, 1993; Saunders, 1993; Douglas and Douglas, 2000). In her book, *The Great Hill Stations of Asia*, Barbara Crossette (1999) explains how highland retreats became tourist summer homes and in some cases the eventual locations of colonial administrations during the hottest seasons. Thus, it appears that one of the earliest public policy decisions was for the civil administration to head for the hills! Then, as now, a failure of the outsider to adapt to the climate led many to succumb to illness. For example, the British and Dutch were particularly notorious for signalling their superiority by refusing to 'go native' and dress for the tropics. This often cost them their lives. Rudyard Kipling, in his poem 'Padgett M.P.', gives a withering critique of those 'who tried to hurry the East'.

Crossette's book details life in the Cameron Highlands of Malaysia, Dalat in Vietnam, Maymyo in Burma, Baguio in the Philippines and Bogor in Indonesia. These colonial outposts continued after the independence of these nations and have evolved into resorts of differing success and character. Some like Maymo have been almost abandoned as hated relics of colonialism. Others have become improbable recreation centres at variance with the local cultural values. For example, the largest casino in the world is in the highlands of Malaysia. Linkages to that early era still persist in place names, museums, and in the histories. Today tourists continue to come to the hill stations, though some, like Bogor, have become virtual suburbs, given the sprawl of the major cities.

Modern tourism existed from the post-World War I era but it was not until the independence of these countries (the Vietnam War in Thailand's case) and the arrival of the wide-bodied jet in the 1960s that international tourism became significant. Still, most of these nations were unable to attract many tourists because of their political situation. Xenophobia kept Burma off limits until much later. Today, the illegitimate junta that rules the country desperately wants tourism but now it is the tourist that is considering the political meaning of such visits (Henderson, 2003; Hall, 2000).

134

Militancy and unrest led Indonesia to refrain from promoting tourism until after 1969. Crime, corruption, insurgencies and martial law from 1972–1986 discouraged Philippine tourism. This, despite the presence of major American bases in the country and a Philippine dictatorship obsessed with its image and eager to promote tourism. The government sought to lure former Filipinos back with its Balikbayan programme and former World War II soldiers and their families with their Reunion for Peace incentives, but success eluded President Marcos (Richter, 1982; 1989; 2001).

The Vietnam War and its spill-over impacts delayed the development of tourism throughout Indochina. This was before the recent penchant some have for danger-zone travel (Adams, 2001; Pelton, Aral and Dulles, 1998; Pelton, 1999). The Federation of Malaya got independence in 1957, delayed because of communist insurgencies, and found its link to Singapore intolerable after only two years, following the formation of the wider Federation of Malaysia in 1963, when Singapore and the two former British crown colonies of Sarawak and British North Borneo (Sabah) were brought together with the former Malayan Federation. Malaysia divorced from the largely Chinese Singapore in 1965, but still faced devastating ethnic riots in 1969 which poisoned its tourism prospects for some time. The Indian, Chinese and other minorities in the Malay-controlled country chaff at the pro-Malay government policies. Heritage sites also continue to emphasize Malay experiences (personal observation from 1969 and 1999).

Tiny, flat Singapore, devoid of much natural beauty and relentlessly modernist had destroyed much of its cultural and historic sights in favour of commercial and block housing. However, following its short-lived association with Malaysia (1963–1965), it developed into an amazing tourist success based on challenging Hong Kong as a shopping and commercial centre and providing a level of cleanliness and political stability that was the envy of the region (Hall and Oehlers, 2000). Today, nearly three times as many tourists visit annually as there are residents and Singapore continues to forge a tourism success as the 'Gateway to Southeast Asia' (Chang, 2004: Henderson, 2001; Timothy, 2000; Lew, 1999).

Thailand, never colonized, has seldom had democratic government for very long but its many coups have been largely bloodless and so tourism has not been deterred. Tourism has grown from less than 60,000 in 1961 to more than eleven million in 2000 (*Travel Industry Yearbook*, 2001: 162). The Vietnam War spurred much of the early, and often unsavoury, sex tourism to Thailand (Hall, 1992; Lim, 1998; Richter, 1989). As the rest and recreation base, hundreds of thousands of Americans and other allies poured through Thailand from 1963 to 1975. Tourism became the largest source of revenue for Thailand after 1980 as commercial travel supplanted the American military (Richter, 1993).

Planned Tourism/Unplanned Implementation

From 1970 on tourism in Southeast Asia stopped being something that just happened to being something consciously planned (Burma and Brunei would be exceptions for another 15 years). To some extent many of the countries developed similar top-down strategies: national plans, government developed infrastructure and/or incentives for development of tourism facilities (Bramwell, 1998; Wanhill, 1998).

Most nations built on some of their colonial-based seasonal resorts (Crossette, 1999). These countries had several policy decisions to make (Richter and Richter, 1985). First, did they want a centralized or decentralized tourism development plan? Most opted for a national level plan often with a Ministry of Tourism or something similar. This was consistent with the governmental structure of most of the nations in Southeast Asia.

A second decision was to determine the target of tourism promotion. In most cases it was the international tourist over the domestic tourist, reflecting the relatively small middle class in each nation with the financial security to travel. This would change slightly with growing affluence. Also, the Western tourist was initially preferred over the Asian tourist. At the beginning of major tourism development only Japan had a sizeable tourism-generating population in Asia and the scars of its wartime influence in Southeast Asia made Japanese travellers unwelcome in the early years. Also, such tourists were overwhelmingly male and often involved in sex tourism. Boycotts and demonstrations against Japan took place (Richter, 1989; Lim, 1998). As other nations became involved in trafficking and sex tourism and as Japan became more affluent, marketing to Japan was accelerated.

A third and related question of policy was the type of tourist clientele. The overall strategy of promotion and infrastructure development was designed to attract luxury-seeking tourists, not pilgrims, students, backpackers or individual travellers. This decision was reached not because of research but rather because of the personal tastes of the governing elites. Not all nations were as celebrity-seeking in their orientation as the Philippines, but of those active in tourism, there was no push for camp sites, but rather golf courses. This decision to cater to the up-scale tourist would result in massive foreign exchange leakage (Richter, 1989).

Tourism was always advanced as an economic bonanza, but job maximization was not a high priority in the national plans, nor were the training institutes that developed in some countries like the Philippines really geared to assuring national control of tourism. Even today, much of the infrastructure is controlled by transnational companies through their management contracts or franchises (Cukier, 2002).

There was an attempt, if only for patronage or counter-insurgency reasons, to develop tourism in many parts of the countries. A major policy question attached to tourism distribution was whether tourists themselves should be clustered in almost self-contained tourist belts and enclaves or integrated as much as possible into the population. A case could be made for both strategies. In conservative Muslim societies, enclaves were seen as separating the polluting impacts of the tourist from the rest of the population. For example, gambling could be put out of major Malaysian cities and Muslims banned from participating (Crossette, 1999). Tourists could be lured to

Hindu Bali in Indonesia and on that island further encouraged with World Bank aid to stay in the enclave of Nusa Dua. Outside of Yogyakarta, tourists were guided to the World Heritage Sites of Borobodur and Prambanan, not Islamic shrines. In fact, residents near many of the Hindu and Buddhist sites were explicitly not permitted to hold religious ceremonies there (Kagami, 1997).

Enclave tourism was also practised in Burma, the Philippines and Thailand. Restrictions on itineraries and access in Myanmar persist to this day. In martial law Philippines every effort was made to keep tourists in a few areas. There was even a wall built from the Manila airport covered with pictures by schoolchildren so the real poverty was hidden. Crimes against tourists were met with stiffer sentences. In Thailand and the Philippines special tourist police protected the visitors. By shielding visitors from the poverty and the consumption patterns of the tourist from the population, it was thought all would go more smoothly. Erik Cohen has in fact argued that such a strategy is probably wise since it protects the naive tourist from the more unsavoury and dangerous elements of the local population (Cohen, 1996). Unfortunately, no one is protecting the naive residents from the more destructive tourists.

Moreover, the problems of enclave tourism grew obvious. Very little money, services or benefits trickled out of the enclaves to the local population and often whole settlements of residents were removed for the resorts built for the tourists (Henderson, 2003; Richter, 1989). Enclave tourism tended not to defuse insurgencies but to radicalize ordinary people, as the Philippine 'Light a Fire Movement' illustrated in the early 1980s and the Bali bombings may do once more (Richter and Waugh, 1991; Richter, 1992; Hitchcock and Darma Putra, 2005). Though Michael Hitchcock claims that the bombers' statements demonstrate that tourists were not the primary target, his own sources note that tourists were seen by the assailants as depraved (see also Chapter 4 in this volume). Also, the tourist enclaves allowed the bombers to murder primarily Westerners, especially Australians, with less collateral damage to Muslims than another target might have meant (Hitchcock and Darma Putra, 2005).

Government-sponsored tourism led the private sector in the early days and there was little if any consideration of how tourism could be made accessible to the local people or how their input could be valued. Governments tended to have their own national airlines and assumed control of most of the national marketing. Pre-internet, the chief players were the government and a few multinational hotel, tour, and financial service companies.

To most, it must have seemed as if the only policy objective was 'more', the only implementation schedule was 'as soon as possible', and the only evaluation was in terms of arrivals and gross receipts. More information was in fact available, but political considerations too often trumped more considered analysis. Frequently, planned development was accelerated or changed at the behest of powerful stakeholders.

The Philippines under Ferdinand Marcos was a classic example (Richter, 1982; 1989; 1999). Tourism infrastructure that would not be viable under any scenario for another decade was built in Manila to impress the World Bank–IMF financiers to continue aid to the government following martial law. It worked. The presence of tourists was also designed to legitimize the Philippine government, something present-day Myanmar apparently seeks to do (Henderson, 2003). President Marcos was able to convert hotel financing into patronage of key supporters while foreclosing on opponents. After his overthrow in 1986, the People Power revolution that ousted him would itself be an attraction and the President's home with all its excesses was made into a temporary museum (Richter, 1999; 2001). Ironically, the President's Palace was closed as a museum after a few years when it was discovered that the lavish spending it represented actually instilled awe rather than revulsion in some of the visitors.

Indonesia at first confined tourism to largely non-Muslim areas but as those areas flourished the government developed Bali Plus – a plan to broaden the tourism attractions to other parts of the country. This was to defuse critics worried more about the few gains Muslims were getting from tourism than the potential for polluting effects.

Myanmar desperately needed foreign exchange – so much so that it has used slave labour and the relocation of millions to build new resorts and encourage foreign investment. It has not worked. Henderson (2003) describes the external efforts to lead a boycott of the country and the efforts of its most famous prisoner, Nobel Peace Prize winner and opposition leader Aung San Suu Kyi, to put pressure on the regime to liberalize. Neither side has much to show for its efforts to use tourism as a policy tool.

Vietnam, Cambodia and Laos are at a disadvantage in developing tourism given the war-torn character of some of their landscape. Also, a socialist outlook finds tourism a mixed blessing with its demonstration effect and aggravated inequality. Still, in recent years, travel to Vietnam has soared. It is based on the fascination of a beautiful land so long off-limits, but also the country has promoted heritage tourism around what some call 'thanatourism' – the Viet Cong tunnels, China Beach and other war sites so familiar to hundreds of thousands of French, American and Australian troops (Laske and Herold, 2004; Mok and Lam, 2000).

As in Vietnam, but thirty years earlier the Philippines utilized thanatourism – the Reunion for Peace promotion – in its efforts to lure both Japanese and Allied soldiers and their families back to World War II sites like Corregidor, the Bataan Death March route and the Leyte Landing that heralded General Douglas MacArthur's return. In both nations, there is an effort to contrast the memories of war-torn societies with the triumph of nationalism over the oppressor. The governments now in power cannot help but look better than when under siege. Also with time, foreign exchange earned from former enemies is scarcely less welcome than that of allies.

Malaysia has had to neutralize its multi-ethnic heritage against an overwhelming Malay political control and tourism has offered a way simply to move around or beyond it. Malaysia has concentrated primarily on recreational attractions, and more recently ecotourism, over its contested cultural mix. Yet it also promotes an image of cultural harmony, a balanced combination of cultural traits from the three major ethnic categories, and the more exotic character of Borneo longhouse dwellers. Non-Muslim gambling also fits this political agenda (Kadir Din, 1997; Dowling, 2000).

Despite all the overt decisions reflected in special plans, five year goals and so on, the political objectives are seldom acknowledged. They have to be teased from the use of tourism by the presses which are often controlled to convey legitimacy to the government. They are sometimes reflected in the budget but all financial decisions are not always clearly identified – making Harold Lasswell's injunction to look at who gets what, when and how rather difficult (Lasswell, 1936).

This leads to another point – what *does not* happen?. The decision *not* to let certain issues even get on the agenda, *not* to do something planned, *not* to budget for some articulated goal, or *not* to acknowledge unpleasant or embarrassing side effects of the policy process are just as important to understand but much harder to research than decisions publicly implemented. 'Non-decisions' have resulted in several nations being notorious for their sex tourism, paedophilia tours and trafficking in women and children despite the fact that prostitution is officially illegal in all the countries (Bachrach and Baratz, 1963; Richter, 1989; 2003; 2004; 2005; Lim, 1998; Hall, 1992; *WTO News,* 2004, 4th quarter: 6; and Richter and Richter, 2003).

In fact, the situation which accelerated but did not start during the Vietnam War is now so widespread and aggravated by the internet that some tourist-generating countries are choosing to prosecute sex tourists who go to Southeast Asia since the Southeast Asian nations too rarely can be depended upon to enforce their own laws (Richter, 2005). A Kuta Beach in Bali is not overtly planned; a Pattaya in Thailand does not happen overnight but flourishes because of official corruption, and the notorious motels in Manila became ubiquitous when the Minister of Tourism owned many and exempted them from the martial law curfew (Richter, 1982).

In a region where smoothly ordered relationships are highly valued, serious government or elite attentions to the seamier or criminal side of tourism is considered indiscreet. Cohen explains this process further: 'Even in contemporary Thailand, whenever a new emergency occurs, the government tends to respond by the establishment of a new agency to deal with it or by promulgation of a new law or regulation after which (. . .) little effective action is taken. Thus, while prostitution was outlawed by Marshal Sarit in the 1960s, the number of prostitutes increased, openly and virtually unhindered (. . .) even as Bangkok came to be known as the "Brothel of Asia", a commander of the Bangkok police in the 1980s announced with a straight face that there is no prostitution in Thailand since it is an outlawed activity' (Cohen, 1996: 79). Until very recently, there has been a similar pattern of inactivity in much of

Southeast Asia with respect to AIDS despite the fact that it was clear what a threat the disease posed. Implementation, be it with AIDS, prostitution or job-creation, is not a priority if it alters elite control or reflects badly on the nation.

Tourism in the Twenty-First Century

Several of the countries of Southeast Asia today have what tourism analysts might refer to as 'mature' tourism infrastructures, though Vietnam, Laos, Cambodia, Myanmar, East Timor and Brunei might still be characterized as emerging. Facilities are well-developed in most countries for the up-scale and middle class tourist. Until 2001, arrivals grew dramatically as a per cent of global tourism with Singapore and Thailand leading the way (*Tourism Industry Yearbook*, 2001). The growth of terrorism globally, the emergence of SARS, and the looming threat of an avian flu pandemic have cost the region greatly despite the greater sophistication of policy-makers and priorities focused on tourism.

There is a growing wealth in the region which has encouraged more domestic travel and a more deliberately regional tourism development approach. This has long been a goal of organizations like the Association of Southeast Asian Nations (ASEAN), but internal competition has inhibited much progress. Now collaboration and co-ordination seems to be occurring both as a consequence of planned and unplanned developments (Henderson, 2001; Teflen, 2002; Timothy, 2000; 2003; Teo, Chang and Ho, 2001c).

Attractions are being developed but are increasingly geared to the regional traveller, such as golf and gambling. Ecotourism is becoming a more important component of the tourist scene as its appeal to up-scale travellers is noted. Thus, it is not great planning and political will, but more a recognition of traveller tastes that is encouraging such development (Dowling, 2000; Kadir Din, 1993; 1997).

Public policy continues to guide tourism development, but the private sector is playing an ever more important role. Most of the government-owned accommodations have been privatized, as have the airlines. The latter are increasingly exposed to internal competition (Kua and Baum, 2004). Deregulation of the industry is uneven, but all to some degree are adopting freer trade, foreign ownership and other features of globalization once considered intolerable.

Niche tourism is also on the up-swing and fortunately is not confined to the still active sex tourism industry. Spa tourism in particular and luxury tourism in general are on the increase. Worries about the effects of such conspicuous consumption seem to have faded before the lure of hard currency. A special and growing niche in the Philippines, Singapore and Thailand is health-related tourism. Many of the finest doctors in those nations were trained in the United States and Europe yet the costs for even the most pampered care there are a fraction of American costs (PBS, February 21, 2005). In 2000, one Bangkok hospital had more than 165,000 foreign patients. Package tours for health care are being promoted by the Tourism Authority of Thailand and by Thai Air (The *Travel Industry Yearbook*: 162).

Another growing niche is cruise-ship tourism, although the receipts from cruise ships typically are far less to the host country since housing and most services are provided on board (Singh, 2000). Public policy seems to have been less a factor in the growth of cruising than the overcapacity of cruise ships following the 11 September 2001 attacks in the United States.

The attacks on the Pentagon and the World Trade Center also highlighted the vulnerability of many of the predominantly Muslim Southeast Asian countries, the Southern Philippines and more recently Southern Thailand to radical Islamic plots against tourists and the countries from which they come. The Bali bombings, the kidnappings in the Philippines and the capture of terrorist suspects in several of these nations served to depress tourism.

There is increasing research on the efforts policy-makers are making through international bodies like the Association of Southeast Asian Nations (ASEAN). Among other things, ASEAN has made promotional sketches of all member nations which are rather revealing in what they both include and exclude. While describing in detail the political structure of most of the member nations, ASEAN promotional materials conveniently eschew descriptions of the governments of Cambodia, Laos, Vietnam and Myanmar and are totally uncritical of any nation's tourism product. This is perhaps to be expected, but it is nevertheless illuminating. There are also more limited efforts to forge so-called 'growth triangles' that encourage regional promotion and co-ordination of tourism itineraries and transport (Henderson, 2001: Teo, Chang and Ho, 2001c: Dallen, 2000; 2002). However, these fledgling attempts suffered a major setback with the global recession of the late 1990s and the severe Japanese financial crisis during the 1990s (Lew, 1999).

Sustainability Issues for the Public Sector

Many public policy issues can be considered sustainability issues. The literature is replete with discussions of reef protection, the problems of deforestation, issues of water and energy supplies. Social issues also are increasingly noted as central to keeping tourist attractions from being terrorist targets or centres of ordinary crime. The issues I examine all concern aspects of health, yet they are often neglected in discussions of sustainability (*WTO News*, 2004: 7). They are also issues which cannot be dealt with on a country-by-country basis but must be taken up regionally and globally. They are expensive to deal with, require unprecedented co-ordination and political will and are absolutely vital to the protection of tourism but also national stability and prosperity.

I highlight only four of these health and sustainability issues. First, consider the 26 December 2004 tsunami. This and other natural disasters require a region-wide seismic and general weather monitoring system. While the presence of tourists and victims from so many nations explains the unprecedented outpouring of aid, the poorest citizens in its wake are the least apt to recover their livelihoods. Also, tourism – so much of it coastal in nature – may be a long time recovering. Thus, the once considered optional linkages with ASEAN and PATA are now seen as more critical if they help link Southeast Asia to Pacific monitoring systems in Japan and Hawai'i (PBS, March 29, 2005). The first anniversary of this disaster found tourism severely depressed in Indonesia and Thailand. However, significant progress has been made in infrastructure development and education for health and weather disasters. The co-ordination of NGOs, all levels of government and international assistance from the United Nations and member nations illustrate significant advances in crisis policy-making and implementation.

The second major regional health issue is 'smaze' [smog-haze], the unhealthy thick smoke that blanketed much of the region for months following uncontrolled burning in Indonesia in the late 1990s. It may also have been responsible for the crash of a Garuda Airlines flight that killed all aboard (Causey, 2005). Smaze caused many deaths, countless respiratory problems and was an undisputed tourism disaster for a region already struggling with polluted cities. Though some years are worse than others, smaze has become a chronic environmental and economic problem. Clearly, ASEAN members must act to prevent and if necessary sanction countries whose practices threaten the water and air of other nations. (I say this as a citizen fully aware of the failings of my own government to reduce acid rain both within the United States and in Canada, or to combat the global warming to which the United States is the largest contributor).

A third and present threat is the terrible trafficking in women and children. Paedophilia tours, the rise of sexual slavery and with it AIDS has allowed a belated but deadly scourge to infect the region (Richter, 2003; 2004; 2005). As noted earlier, the response of the Southeast Asian nations involved has been inadequate. This situation raises issues of enforcement, criminality, and disease that few governments are willing to acknowledge (Richter and Richter, 2003; Cockburn, 2003: 2–29).

After the Marcos dictatorship in the Philippines was overthrown, the government of President Cory Aquino greatly cleaned up the government advertising involving women. No more was a 'fresh peach on every beach' a government promise (Richter, 1982; 1989). Moreover, the town of Pagsanjan Falls which was a major paedophilia setting was removed from tourist maps put out by the government. Still, much more needs to be done. Critics of American bases in the Philippines predicted that their ousting would remove much of the nation's prostitution, but that has not happened. Tourism has always attracted much more prostitution than the bases (Richter, 1989).

Trafficking is a threat both to women and children and to clients especially with the soaring AIDS rates. Many clients assume younger victims will be disease-free, but that is not the case. They just may be more vulnerable. The World Tourism Organization, the United Nations, the Centers for Disease Control and the World Health Organization have all been involved in efforts to deal with these problems. Countries have in recent years sought to assure that trafficking across their borders does not limit the right of victims to get police help. More nations also are attempting to prosecute those of their own citizens who commit crimes against children in other nations. The non-governmental organizations of the region have done more than the affected governments to curb this problem. Still today, girls and women from Myanmar are trafficked to the brothels of Bangkok and then abroad as are women from the northern hill tribes of Thailand (Meyer, 2001; Richter, 2003; 2005; East–West Center Conference on Trafficking in Women and Children in Asia and the Pacific, October, 2003). So-called 'entertainers' and their families in the Philippines are coerced or lured to Japan and Europe. Lao and Cambodian women are also trafficked abroad.

The fourth health-linked public policy issue for Southeast Asian tourism is also the most open-ended and challenging. It reflects the powerful twin pressures for both deregulation and globalization: international public health. As such, it extends from terrorist threats to a myriad of health issues brought on by the travel of millions to countries whose citizens may lack the necessary immunity to the diseases the tourists bring. Deliberate bio-terrorism gets the most attention and clearly it has daunting implications for tourism, but inadvertent bio-terrorism is just as lethal and more likely (Smith, 1995; Richter and Waugh, 1991; Richter, 1992; 2003).

Tourists are going to places of considerable risk from accidents and disease. They are doing so without adequate warnings by their governments who want smooth relations with Southeast Asian nations. Those host nations are similarly not taking precautions to warn tourists or indeed their own citizens of the health risks they may face. As virgin jungles are cleared for resorts and golf courses, diseases once confined to animals far from inhabited areas are now riding home with tourists (Richter, 2003).

A staggering fifty per cent of international travellers are estimated to have some type of accident or illness, some resulting in death (Edgell, 1999), yet tourist-receiving countries and tourist-generating countries pay much more attention to the condition of pets and agricultural products than to the tourist (Richter, 2003). Dogs must have up-to-date shots and in many destinations face quarantine. Yet, studies I have done of endemic disease – specifically malaria – show no correlation between prevalence and morbidity statistics and the requirements for entry into a country. More amazing has been the decline in requirements for re-entry. In less than a day a disease anywhere in the world can be across the globe. Some are the result of ordinary exposure, and the drop in mosquito eradication regimens. Now many deadly parasites are hopping a ride anywhere: Lassa fever in Germany, malaria in Canada, West Nile fever in the United States and dengue fever throughout much of Southeast Asia (Richter, 2003). The threat in spring of 2005 was Marburg Disease from Angola for which there is no treatment or protection. As Harvey Fineberg of the Institute of Medicine (Washington, D.C.) put it: 'nature is the worst terrorist you can imagine' (Shute, 2005: 42).

The most recent tourist-related threats to public health have come from East and Southeast Asia. SARS (Severe Acute Respiratory Syndrome) in 2003–2004 inflicted a dramatic toll on tourism, although it fortunately killed relatively few people due to an unprecedented effort by governments throughout the world to keep the threat contained. The epidemic became a global menace when an elderly man staying at a Hong Kong hotel infected fellow guests at a wedding (Fidler, 2004: 187). Hundreds of millions of chickens were killed in China and Hong Kong as well as in other nations to keep the disease in check. However, China's reluctance to admit to the initial problem and take an immediate proactive role allowed the disease to spread as far as Toronto. The tourist industry globally is estimated to have had losses of $40 billion from SARS, much of that in airline, convention and hotel cancellations in Southeast Asia (Shute, April 4, 2005: 40–47; Puska, 2005: 85–134).

Now we are faced with an even deadlier disease – avian flu from Vietnam. The World Health Organization, the Centers for Disease Control and other bodies have warned repeatedly that a pandemic is entirely possible. They argue that the threat is probable because pandemics come in cycles and we are overdue for a major one. Moreover, although avian flu has appeared before, it is unusual in already jumping from chickens and other birds to a variety of mammals including humans. Morbidity is 72 per cent and we have no vaccine to confront it (Shute, 2005). With relatively little fanfare we could be facing a pandemic comparable in scope and morbidity to the Black Death, the bubonic plague that stalked and killed a quarter of all Europeans in the fourteenth century (*Kansas City Star*, 22 February 2005). Already the toll on tourism is dramatic, especially in Thailand, Hong Kong, Vietnam and Indonesia where bird flu has already killed some people. As other nations wait for what some see as an inevitable spread, travel is cancelled or postponed.

Sustainability has thus moved from being a buzzword illustrating an awareness of environmental and social problems associated with tourism to a much larger question of public global health, co-ordinated regional and global decision-making, and sophisticated monitoring of issues from terrorism and crime to heritage protection and facilitation of the travel of hundreds of millions.

A Wary, Weary, but Hopeful Forecast

Despite these challenges, several new characteristics of Southeast Asian policy-making with respect to tourism are encouraging. First, there is a growing, although still limited, regional effort to address not just promotional and marketing issues but also questions of disease, trafficking and pollution. There is a recognition that no one nation can deal with these problems alone and they will only be addressed if none of the nations is put at a comparative disadvantage in confronting them. In spite of the regional cultural mores, AIDS, trafficking, and environmental concerns are on the policy agendas about which governments are actually taking some basic steps. In general, the push for this action has come from NGOs both inside and outside each individual country and through international groups like ASEAN, the WTO and the United Nations.

Secondly, although tourism has soared in the region and has grown to be a much more important sector to virtually all these economies, the countries have retained relatively diversified economies and diversified sources of tourists. It is critical to maintain this diversity. The Japanese recession hurt but it did not destroy Southeast Asian tourism. Hopefully, SARS and avian flu will not either.

Thirdly, also encouraging is the fact that domestic tourism is increasing, heritage protection is growing and regional travel is strong – all factors that would seem to broaden the distribution of political and economic benefits from tourism. The justification for international tourism can never be to furnish a cheap playground for the elites of the world. Governments can and must do more to make opportunities for their own people to travel and have recreation. Some governments, as in Britain, have almost an automatic policy response to achieve needed balance. Parks and recreational facilities are opened as the population in certain communities reach a critical mass. Other countries have promoted work camp tourism and socially responsible travel both within and outside their borders. Models for responsible tourism do exist. The will to look at them and develop others depends on the political strength of the society at large and on how much groups insist on a role in the governments' plans. Even small ethnic groups and local populations have some clout and they also have important international NGOs that, as in ecotourism, can take up their cause (Causey, 2003; Kadir Din, 1993; 1997).

Still, no critique of tourism should be allowed to blame tourism policies alone for the social ills of society. Tourism is but one among many forces bringing profound social changes. There is much reason for optimism that future tourism policy-making will be better integrated with the environment and local public if only because governments have learned all too painfully what a fragile industry it can be – subject to disease, terrorism, sabotage, environmental decay and corruption. They have also come to appreciate tourism's contribution to job growth, preserving built and natural heritage and contributing to an important constituency for health and resource protection.

Author's Note

This chapter is developed from a speech given at the Conference on Tourism in South-East Asia: Local, Regional, and Cross-National Perspectives, 14–15 April 2005, Ohio University, Athens, Ohio. The author is deeply indebted to Professor Kadir Din, Distinguished Professor in Residence, and to Ohio University's South-East Asia Program for their invitation to participate and for their generous hospitality.

7

The Development of Private Tourism Business Activity in the Transitional Vietnamese Economy

Jonathan Bennett

Introduction

This chapter examines the development of private tourism business activity in Vietnam since 1986. I first briefly outline how the organization of the tourism industry in Vietnam has been restructured since 1986. I highlight how, in the regulation[1] of tourism activity in local spaces, regulatory power has shifted from the centre to municipal and provincial people's committees. In particular, I discuss how despite the creation by the central government of a formal framework of laws and directives to guide the establishment and running of private businesses, local state institutions and officials have been afforded significant capacity to interpret and mediate these laws and directives.[2] As a result, for entrepreneurs wanting to develop private tourism businesses, local state officials have emerged as key conduits with whom they must negotiate in order to establish and run their businesses. This I find has heightened the role of *quan he xa hoi* – social ties and relations – with entrepreneurs cultivating pre-existing ties and creating new ties with a range of local state officials as a way of facilitating the establishment and running of their tourism businesses.

Restructuring the Regulation of Tourism

Until 1986, the central government tourism institution – the Vietnam Tourism Company, renamed the General Department of Tourism after reunification – had possessed total regulatory power over the entry of all foreign visitors coming to Vietnam, allotting foreign visitors and groups to one of the state tourism companies under its control.[3]

However, with the introduction of Doi Moi after 1986, tourism was immediately recognized and highlighted as an economic sector offering considerable potential in the transitional economy.[4] Consequently, as with other potentially lucrative economic activities emerging out of the transition to a capitalist economy, powerful municipal and provincial constituencies within the Party-state, in particular in Ho Chi Minh City, supported by allies within the central government, exerted considerable political pressure for much greater regulatory control over the development of tourism activity in local spaces (pers. comm., university lecturer, 2000).

In attempting to maintain political cohesion and the hegemony of the Party-state, the central government has acceded to the demands of these political constituencies and significant institutional restructuring has taken place in regulating tourism in the transitional economy, with in particular the central government tourism institution, now renamed the Vietnam National Administration of Tourism – VNAT – (*Tong cuc Du lich*) – relinquishing its previous monopoly control over tourism activity within the national space and instead ceding a significant degree of regulatory control in local spaces down to municipal and provincial people's committees. This was evinced as early as April 1987 with the enactment of Central Government Resolution 63, with the recommendation to

> quickly reorganize the system of tourism management from the centre to the local and on the basis of moving towards the abolition of centralized management, transfer entirely to self-financing socialist businesses; clearly differentiating the state management functions of the General Department of Tourism with the independence of tourism businesses.
>
> (Anonymous: *Nhung ngay thang vas u kien dang ghi nho* (dates and events worth remembering), *Tap chi Du lich*, 1999: 6)

Thereafter, it was reflected in the enactment of central government decrees, such as Decree 05/CP in October 1992 and Resolution 45/CP in June 1993 under which the majority of state tourism companies were transferred from the control of the central government to municipal and provincial people's committees (EIU, Indochina: Vietnam, Laos, Cambodia, 1996–1997; *Tong cuc Du lich*, 1997: 47; *Tap chi Du lich*, 1999: 4; 6; Nguyen and Brennan, 2000: 8; 17; Cooper, 2000: 175).[5] Secondly, with the enactment of Decree 09/CP in February 1994, the VNAT assigned total regulatory control to municipal and provincial people's committees in implementing tourism directives enacted by the VNAT in approving the setting up and administering the running of all domestic tourism businesses: hotels and domestic tour operators in local spaces (EIU, Vietnam: Country Report, 1st quarter, 1995: 29; *Tong cuc Du lich*, 1997: 71).

Consequently, with the enactment of decrees such as Decree 09, the formal regulatory framework created for the tourism industry in the transitional economy has conferred municipal and provincial people's committees as the key institutions regulating tourism activity. This has occurred in a context where municipal and provincial people's committees act both as the key tourism actors in local space, through the hotels and tour operator businesses directly under their control and as the key institutions regulating the establishment and running of tourism businesses in local space.

Municipal and Provincial People's Committees as Regulators of Private Tourism Businesses

The enhanced regulatory control and autonomy possessed by local state institutions and officials have, in large part, come about as institutional and legislative forms are being restructured and reconfigured in the process of transition from a socialist to a capitalist oriented economy.

Vague Wording of Central State Resolutions

During the Doi Moi era, an increasing number of overlapping (*chong cheo*) and shifting political alliances and factions, linking central and provincial constituencies within the Party-state, have emerged (Kolko, 1997: 66; 68). These have arisen largely out of competition over business interests in the nascent capitalist economy and the maintenance and consolidation of control over resources and gate-keeping positions in lucrative areas of the transitional economy (Templer, 1998: 90; 91; Riedel and Turley, 1999: 35; Gainsborough, 2002: 360; Dixon and Kilgour, 2002: 608).

Within the central government, this has contributed to a crisis in national policy- and decision-making as it has been extremely difficult for the central government to broker policy consensus among the competing and polarized interest groups, alliances and factions and their constituencies within the Party-state (Leifer and Phipps, 1991: 10; Williams, 1992: 24; Kolko, 1997: 27; 43; Phong and Beresford, 1998: 58; Templer, 1998: 97; Riedel and Turley, 1999: 6; Dixon, 2000: 293; Dixon and Kilgour, 2002: 611). As a result, in attempting to maintain a relative degree of political cohesion among these disparate groups, the central government has been compromised in its construction of a coherent framework to regulate the establishment and running of private businesses such as tourism businesses in the transitional economy.[6] Instead, the policies and directives issued by the central government have been watered down and become intentionally vague, opaque and ambiguous, generally expressing only broad intentions and occasionally containing contradictory statements.

For example, Decree (*Nghi dinh*) 02/CP enacted in January 1995 formalizes the legal requirements which an entrepreneur has to satisfy in order to establish a private business, including a hotel or tour operator business. However, the list of requirements detailed under the Decree is vague and imprecise, simply comprising minimum standards relating to infrastructure, equipment, the quality of services, environmental health and safety conditions, a suitable location, as well as minimum standards of professional expertise and training for any potential business owner (*Tap chi Du lich*, October 1995: 2; *Tong cuc Du lich*, 1997: 76). Similarly, while the 'Tourism Law' (*Phap lenh Du lich*), enacted at the beginning of 1999 was hailed as 'creating a clear legal framework for tourism activities' ('*tao hanh lang phap ly choc hung ta tien hanh lap lai trat tu trong hoat dong du lich*') (Tran Van Dan, 1999: 7), most of the articles in the twenty-seven page document are vague, outlining general pronouncements and objectives with imprecise instructions regarding implementation or information on how objectives contained in the Law are to be realized.[7]

Consequently, interpreting central government directives has been largely left to individual state institutions and officials. This has heightened levels of inconsistency in interpretation, haphazard implementation and the discretionary and arbitrary powers of local state officials (Kolko, 1997: 125; *VIR*, 17–23 July 2000: 10; Dixon and Kilgour, 2002: 610). Through their control over bureaucratic levers, these processes have as a result acted to consolidate and expand the regulatory power of local state officials over private business activities.[8]

The lack of clarity by the central government in building a formal legislative framework to regulate private economic activities such as tourism was reflected in an article in 2000 in the *Vietnam Investment Review*, entitled 'Anyone Know Which Law To Follow?' in which the writer Diệp Anh outlined how:

> There is widespread confusion in the business community about the meaning of rules and regulations and what exactly is required under the law. At the same time, the legal system is neither transparent, consistent nor stable. Conflicting requirements are laid out under different decrees and regulations undergoing alteration. Even if a private business takes considerable care to follow the law and attempts to fulfil all requirements, it is not certain that it actually has.
>
> (*VIR*, 19–25 June 2000: 6)

Cumbersome and Bureaucratic Nature of Regulatory Processes

While the central government is attempting to create a formal regulatory framework with a clear and transparent delineation of responsibilities between state institutions, administrative processes continue to be both bureaucratic and cumbersome, evoking legacies of the former central planning system. Moreover, administrative processes are still complicated by the overlapping jurisdictions of various state institutions; both between central government institutions such as ministries and between municipal and provincial authorities, where officials at different institutions act contrary to one another (*VIR*, 8–14 January 2001:1). As a result, the bureaucratic and arbitrary nature of interpreting laws and directives is manifested in inaccurate and incomplete decision-making. A decision made by one official is subject to over-rule by another official in another institution or even from the same institution, as a result of different interpretations. At the same time, as the regulatory environment for private business is continually evolving as changes and amendments are made to laws, this has in turn exacerbated uncertainty and unreliability for entrepreneurs (Gates, 1996: 213; Levine, 1998: 1; Templer, 1998: 136).

All these factors have compounded the difficulties for entrepreneurs attempting to establish and run private businesses. Despite having been officially sanctioned by the central government since 1988, entrepreneurs have in reality encountered a hostile regulatory environment. In large part this has been due to the fact that local state officials retain significant control over administrative levers, acting as conduits that entrepreneurs must negotiate before establishing and running businesses. In the course of setting up or running a private business, the regulatory environment allows for a large number of gatekeepers: officials from local state institutions with significant arbitrary and discretionary powers over the bureaucratic process. Each individual official has considerable capacity to facilitate or hinder any stage of the process (Scholtes, 1998: 194; Templer, 1998: 135; Levine, 1998: 1). Entrepreneurs are consequently reliant on officials to negotiate smoothly through the process.

In the mid-1990s, it was found that: '. . .setting up a small guesthouse in Ho Chi Minh City required the submission of forty different documents that were stamped with eighty-three official chops and signed by 107 bureaucrats from twenty-six different offices. At almost every step, officials would demand a "fee". Officials have almost unlimited discretion to block licenses. . .' (Templer, 1998: 137). Thus, perhaps unsurprisingly, it has been found that as a result of the difficulties faced by entrepreneurs in dealing with the bureaucratic system, the vast majority of private businesses which have emerged since 1988 have grown out of connections with the Party-state (Kolko, 1997: 124; Dixon and Kilgour, 2002: 603; 612). Most private businesses have been set up by relatives of state and party officials or as a result of ties between entrepreneurs and state and party officials (Kolko, 1997: 122; Riedel and Turley, 1999: 49).[9]

I now move on to discuss this last point in more detail. I examine how for private tourism business owners, the building of social ties – *quan he xa hoi* – with local state officials has constituted an important institutional mechanism in the regulation of private tourism business activity in the transitional Vietnamese economy. Private tourism business owners are cultivating pre-existing ties and creating new ties with a range of officials as a way of facilitating the establishment and running of their businesses. The findings presented here are based on data collected from interviews with private hotel and tour operator business owners and managers in Hanoi, Hue and Ho Chi Minh City.

The Role of *Quan He*

Establishing a Private Tourism Business

For the vast majority of private tourism business owners interviewed in Hanoi, Hue and Ho Chi Minh City, possessing *pre-existing ties* with officials working in local state institutions involved in the approval and establishment of private businesses had constituted an important pre-requisite in their decision to establish a tourism business. 65 per cent of respondents in Hanoi, 60 per cent in Hue and 80 per cent in Ho Chi Minh City considered 'relations with local state officials' to have been very (*rat*) important (*quan trong*) and influential (*anh huong*) in their decision to establish a private tourism business. An additional 25 per cent of respondents in Hanoi, 15 per cent in Hue and 20 per cent in Ho Chi Minh City considered relations to have been relatively (*tuong doi*) important and influential.

Explaining why this was the case, the following quotation typifies the kinds of responses that were given by the majority of private tourism business owners:

> In theory, according to official regulations, the support given to any business of any type should be the same. However, in reality the level of support differs markedly depending on the extent and closeness of relations between the owners of a business with the relevant institutions and individuals working in them.
>
> (HBTTIC, Hanoi, a private tour operator)[10]

The quotes serve to illustrate how, despite the creation by the central government of a formal framework of regulations governing the establishment of private businesses, local state officials retain significant capacity to mediate these regulations and to exercise arbitrary and discretionary decisions. For entrepreneurs, local state officials consequently possess the capacity to facilitate or hinder any stage of the establishment process. As a result, for private tourism business owners, possessing pre-existing ties with local state officials working in institutions involved in the approval and establishment of private businesses was considered important as it provided a greater degree of certainty and reliability that all procedures required in the setting up of a business could be completed quickly and smoothly.

Sites in the Creation of Ties between Tourism Businesses and Local State Officials

Among private tourism business owners interviewed, the majority of pre-existing ties cultivated with local state officials had been created through the sites of *university* and *workplace*.

University

A significant number of private tourism business owners cited ties with friends made at university, now working in state institutions, as having facilitated the establishment process. These friendships formed ten, fifteen or even twenty years before had provided private tourism business owners with support in establishing their businesses.[11] Ties had again, in particular, ensured that all bureaucratic procedures had been completed quickly and smoothly. This is reflected in the comments below, which were typical of the views expressed by research respondents:

> I had a number of relations with former university classmates and relations, who work in the provincial taxation office, the city police and in relevant departments in the Provincial People's Committee. They helped with regard to completing all procedures and paperwork related to establishing the business. They introduced and promoted the hotel to their friends and business relations and thus provided the hotel with a supply of guests in the initial stages of operation.
>
> (BD Hotel, Hue, a private hotel)

Workplace

Almost all private tourism business owners mentioned how pre-existing ties with state officials formed through previous work had facilitated the establishment of their businesses. Ties had once again ensured that all bureaucratic procedures had been completed quickly and smoothly. Ties had been invoked with former colleagues in state institutions and also with officials encountered through previous work in other private businesses.

Work in State Tourism Institutions. The highest proportion of respondents – Hanoi (40 per cent), Hue (62 per cent), Ho Chi Minh City (60 per cent) – cited ties formed with state officials through previous work at state tourism institutions as having been cultivated when establishing their private tourism businesses. In Hanoi, one respondent had worked for five years in the Hanoi Bureau of Tourism. Another respondent had worked as a tour guide for Hanoitourist for two years.[12] In Hue, one respondent had worked in the Hue Bureau of Tourism and for five years at one of the large state tour operators in Hue. Another respondent had worked as an accountant at one of the large state hotels in Hue for four years. A third respondent had gained a considerable amount of experience as the chief accountant for the provincial state tour operator. In Ho Chi Minh City, one respondent had worked for four years as a tour guide for one of the large state tour operators. Another respondent had been a manager in a large state hotel for three years.

While working at state tourism institutions, respondents had formed ties with officials working in state tourism institutions with direct control over administrative procedures involved in establishing a private tourism business. For respondents, invoking these ties had significantly facilitated the establishment process by ensuring that all procedures had been completed quickly and smoothly. This is illustrated in the following quotation:

> As I had worked for the Hanoi Bureau of Tourism before establishing the business, I had good relations with a lot of officials working in tourism institutions, for example, at the VNAT with the assistant director and also with a number of other officials there. At the Hanoi Bureau of Tourism, I knew almost everybody. As a result of these connections, I had extremely favourable conditions in which to set up my tourism business. My relations in the VNAT and the Hanoi Bureau of Tourism helped in applying for and obtaining a licence to establish my business. They helped with all the procedures required to obtain a licence to set up the business. They ensured that my application was dealt with favourably and that the process was quick, straight-forward and problem-free.
>
> (HBTTIC, Hanoi, a private tour operator)

Private tourism business owners had also received support from family members working in state tourism institutions. Around 25 per cent of respondents in Hue and 20 per cent of respondents in Ho Chi Minh City were running businesses, while their spouses continued to work in local state tourism businesses or institutions. As the quote below illustrates, this had allowed respondents to 'tap into' (*khai thac*) the ties of their spouses with officials in local state tourism institutions once again ensuring that the process of establishing the private tourism business had been completed smoothly.

> In setting up the hotel, I had the support of my husband, who was working for the TTH Provincial Tourism Company. Through my husband, I had good relations with a number of officials working in the Hue Bureau of Tourism. These relations are former classmates and colleagues of my husband. These relations facilitated the establishment of the business a lot by completing the approval of applications for licences quickly and without causing difficulties.
>
> (TGH, Hue, a private hotel)

Negotiating the Unofficial Regulatory Environment without Personal Connections. In the absence of 'close relations with officials working in the state authority institutions connected with the tourism sector', entrepreneurs 'waste a lot of time, effort or expense' and need 'to resort to shelling out extra expenses in order to get officials at the relevant authorities on side' (SMH, Hue, a private hotel). This was reflected in comments made by a small number of respondents, who, during the establishment process had faced difficulties not in negotiating the whole process but particular stages of the process. For example, in the case of the TH Tourism Company, a private tour operator in Ho Chi Minh City, illustrated in the quote below, ties formed by one of the owners with officials at local state tourism institutions when working in a large state tour operator had been considered as an important factor in the initial decision of the owners to establish the business. Indeed, close ties with officials at the Bureau of Tourism in Ho Chi Minh City had enabled the business to mediate official

VNAT regulations and obtain an ITOL.[13] However, a lack of ties with officials with control over administrative procedures at other stages in the establishment process had seriously impeded the smooth completion of these procedures.

> Having worked as a tour guide for the HB Tour Company in Ho Chi Minh City for four years, I had a lot of friends also working in the industry; including at the Bureau of Tourism in Ho Chi Minh City, the HB Tour Company and Saigontourist. My connections at the Bureau of Tourism helped me obtain an international tour operator licence, despite the fact that the business was ineligible under official regulations.[14] However, as I did not have relations with officials working in other authority institutions, I did not receive any particular assistance from officials in these institutions and the process of setting up the business took a lot of time and money.
>
> (TH Tourism Company, Ho Chi Minh City, a
> private tour operator with an ITOL)

The above quote once again illustrates that local state officials retain considerable arbitrary and discretionary power over the completion of administrative procedures required by entrepreneurs in order to establish private businesses. It serves to demonstrate why for entrepreneurs without pre-existing ties, negotiating particular stages of the establishment process and completing administrative procedures can be extremely arduous, protracted and expensive. It again illustrates why for private tourism business owners, possessing pre-existing ties with officials working in those local state institutions involved in the process of establishing a private tourism business is considered so necessary.

Work Experience in Private Businesses. Thirty per cent of respondents in Hanoi, 38 per cent in Hue and 20 per cent in Ho Chi Minh City mentioned how they had cultivated pre-existing ties with local state officials formed through previous work in private businesses when establishing tourism businesses. As the following two quotes from interviews conducted in Hanoi and Hue illustrate, while previously working in private businesses, respondents had formed ties with those local state officials possessing control over administrative procedures involved in establishing a private business. Consequently, after deciding to establish their tourism businesses, these ties had ensured that the establishment process was completed smoothly and quickly. As mentioned by the owner of the CV Hotel in Hue, ties had helped to minimize the amount of expense and cumbersome bureaucracy encountered throughout the establishment process. The importance for private tourism business owners in possessing pre-existing ties with those local state officials involved in the establishment process was illustrated in the comments made by the owner of the TX Hotel in Hue that ties with officials from the Hue Provincial People's Committee, the City Police and the Taxation Department were 'quite an important factor' in his decision to establish the hotel.

> Relations formed with officials at a number of institutions such as the Hue Provincial People's Committee, the City Police and the Taxation Department, through my previous business and trading activities, helped a lot in the establishment process. They completed all procedures quickly allowing the hotel to start operating on time. Having relations was quite an important factor in my decision to establish the business.
>
> (TX Hotel, Hue, a private hotel)

Similar views were expressed by the owner of another private hotel in Hue:

> Through my previous business experience, I had formed a lot of relations with individuals working in the Hue People's Committee, the provincial economic arbiter (nowadays the Bureau of Planning and Investment), the Provincial Police . . .[15] This help enabled me to open and start running the hotel in a short time. In particular, it helped to reduce the time in completing all procedures necessary to set up the business (. . .) and also helped to reduce the expenses, which had to be shelled out by the business to the relevant authorities and also reduced the amount of cumbersome bureaucracy encountered during the establishment process.
>
> (CV Hotel, Hue, a private hotel)

Running a Private Tourism Business

In facilitating the running of a private tourism business, for private tourism business owners, the building of *quan he xa hoi* with local state officials has similarly played an important role. However, evidence from interviews with private tourism business owners suggests that social ties are being *created* rather than cultivated out of pre-existing ties as in the establishment process. Ties are chiefly being cultivated with officials from the local district taxation department, in the case of private tour operators and the local district taxation department together with the local police in the case of hotels.

The Cultivation of Social Ties with Officials by Private Tourism Business Owners

Particular officials from the local taxation office and the police are assigned to specific tourism businesses to carry out the bureaucratic procedures.[16] This consequently affords these officials significant arbitrary and discretionary powers over the completion of bureaucratic procedures at individual tourism businesses and, as in the establishment process, considerable capacity to facilitate or hinder the completion of bureaucratic procedures. Private tourism business owners are therefore reliant on officials from the local taxation office and the police in completing bureaucratic procedures quickly and smoothly, allowing owners to concentrate on attracting and serving customers.

Most private tourism business owners interviewed described a situation where, after establishing their businesses, in the initial stages of operation officials from the local taxation office and the police visiting these businesses for the first time or the first few times carried out procedures in a way which caused considerable inconvenience and disruption for business owners. A number of respondents described how officials would attempt to waste as much of their time as possible in scrutinizing documentation and in making repeated and excessive requests for additional paperwork and information. In doing so, for business owners and their staff, more and more time was diverted to dealing with the exacting bureaucratic demands of officials and less time to actually running the business.

A number of private hotel owners also talked about how police officers had attempted to cause inconvenience and disruption by carrying out frequent, surprise inspections on their businesses. One private hotel owner, interviewed in Hoi An, described how in the initial stages of operating the hotel, on a number of occasions the police officers responsible for collecting details of the guests staying at the hotel arrived at the hotel late in the evening and insisted on visiting all the bedrooms in the hotel to verify that the guest figures submitted by the hotel owner corresponded with the actual number of guests staying at that time. This was done to cause considerable inconvenience and embarrassment both to guests in their rooms at the time of the inspections and to hotel staff, and ultimately had the potential to damage the reputation of the hotel.[17]

Confronted by the arbitrary bureaucratic interference of officials from the local taxation office and the police described above, most private tourism business owners interviewed described how they had attempted to resolve difficulties and minimize the interference and disruption caused by these officials in the running of their businesses by cultivating social ties with those officials responsible for carrying out administrative procedures on their businesses. As is illustrated in the following quotation, ties are cultivated through regular 'social' interaction with the offering by private tourism business owners of meals, entertainment and envelopes containing small sums of money to local state officials. For private tourism business owners, this helps to ensure that all bureaucratic procedures carried out by officials can be completed smoothly without wasting the time of and minimizing the difficulties, interference or disruption caused to business owners, allowing them to focus on running their businesses.

> Officials in the City Police and the taxation department used to cause difficulties when carrying out their inspections. However, I have solved these problems and every time officials come to my hotel, I invite them to a meal or give them an envelope containing a little money . . . with both the Police and the taxation department, the ultimate objective is for both sides to benefit and in helping to develop good relations between our business with these institutions. In this way, these institutions no longer cause any difficulties at all.
>
> (TG Hotel, Hue, a private hotel)

Circumvention of and Non-Compliance with Official Regulations

Ties cultivated with local state officials are also allowing private tourism business owners, with the complicity (*thong dong*) of local state officials, to avoid full compliance with, and in a number of cases, to circumvent (*lach luat*) completely central government laws and directives. This is illustrated in the following quotation.

The level of compliance with central government regulations does not depend on how rigorously an institution carries out inspections. It depends on the extent of ties between business owners and officials. Potentially, violations of regulations from any institution no matter how rigorously they carry out inspections could result in fines or the business licence of a business being revoked. How much these matters can be 'smoothed over' is the decisive factor in the level of compliance by any business.

(MA Hotel, Ho Chi Minh City, a private hotel)

One important factor cited by a number of respondents as 'encouraging' non-compliance by private tourism business owners implied in the quote below, as well as illustrated in the quote above from the director of the MA Hotel in Ho Chi Minh City, is that, with local state officials responsible for monitoring compliance of central government laws and directives, the informal regulatory environment in most cases allows for transgressions of laws and directives to be 'smoothed over' (MA Hotel) through ties cultivated with local state officials by private tourism business owners.

The treatment of violations of the regulations carried out by the relevant state institutions is not as yet very thorough and does not deter or set an example for other businesses to comply with the regulations.

(TL Hotel, Hue, a state hotel)

This once again serves to highlight why, with local state officials retaining considerable capacity to mediate the official laws and directives being enacted by the central government, informal practices, exemplified by the cultivation of social ties by private tourism business owners with local state officials, constitute such an important mechanism in the regulation of private tourism activity. Moreover, it serves to illustrate how local state officials continue to seek to profit through their control over bureaucratic processes.

Complicity between local state officials and private tourism business owners is particularly prevalent in the completion of taxation procedures. As illustrated in the quote below, an informant, talking about how relations between private business owners and taxation officials typically unfold, described a situation very similar to the one outlined earlier in this section.

With private businesses, officials from the local tax department will initially make as much trouble as possible scrutinizing accounts and generally wasting a lot of time for the business owner. Eventually, the owner and the official from the tax department will come to a mutually beneficial arrangement whereby the procedures for paying tax can be dealt with quickly and the amount of tax owed by the private business in any month can be reduced as long as the official from the taxation department gets a little extra remuneration.

(Personal communication, investment consultant, 2002)

This was supported in comments made by private tourism business owners, as illustrated in the quote below.

I did have problems in the past with officials from the taxation department in calculating the amount of tax the business was liable for. Now both sides have resolved these problems for mutual interest. We have managed to have the actual amount of tax the business pays reduced and the official has also benefited by pocketing an amount of money. Now we have come to this agreement, the procedures in calculating the business's tax liabilities are carried out very smoothly and amicably.

(LA Hotel, Ho Chi Minh City, a private hotel)

As discussed earlier in this section, as a way of overcoming the arbitrary bureaucratic interference of officials from the local taxation office, for private tourism business owners the cultivation of ties with these officials ensures that bureaucratic procedures can be completed smoothly. In addition, it allows owners to transgress official state regulations and benefit financially by avoiding full compliance with tax regulations.

As illustrated in the preceding quotes and in the quotes below, ties cultivated by private business owners with taxation officials are principally constituted through financial benefits. However, they remain 'social' in the respect that, firstly, there is the idea of reciprocity with ties securing a regular (monthly) stream of benefits for both parties. Private tourism business owners benefit as taxation procedures are completed smoothly and the amount of tax they pay is reduced. Taxation officials gain a fee, consisting of a proportion of the tax saved by the tourism owner. Secondly, there is the notion that regular interaction between a private tourism business owner and a local taxation official, in this case constituted by monthly visits by the official to the tourism business owner's premises, helps to regularize the behaviour and expectations of both parties. A private tourism business owner will be comfortable in the knowledge that taxation procedures will be completed quickly and smoothly. As is illustrated in the second of the quotes below, he will also have an expectation regarding the amount of tax he will be able to save, whilst a taxation official will have a reasonable idea regarding the remuneration he is likely to receive.

With regard to the taxation department and the local police, my business and officials from these institutions have come to an agreement whereby both sides get financial benefit in return for avoiding fully complying with the regulations, i.e. reducing the amount of tax the hotel has to pay, through the inaccurate registration of guests, i.e. under-reporting the number of guests who have stayed at the hotel, as a way of under-reporting revenue earned by the hotel in turn in order to reduce the hotel's tax liabilities. These measures have helped to raise the amount of income retained by the hotel's owners.

(VD Hotel, Hue, a private hotel)

Another instance is say the official tax bill for our company is VND1,000,000 but one of the owners of our company could negotiate with the official responsible for our company at the local district taxation office to reduce the bill by say VND400,000 and give that official VND200,000. Therefore, our company's tax bill is reduced to VND600,000 and we pay only VND800,000 including the payment to the official.

(HMTTC, Hanoi, a private tour operator)

Heightened Competition

According to a number of respondents, one additional factor, which in the contemporary era has heightened the importance for private tourism business owners of cultivating ties with local taxation officials as a way of reducing the amount of tax paid, has resulted from the increasingly competitive nature of the Vietnamese tourism industry.

In the early 1990s, the streamlining of the official regulatory environment for private businesses coincided with a significant growth in foreign visitor numbers together with optimistic projections regarding future growth. This encouraged the establishment of significant numbers of, in particular, private tourism businesses. However, in the mid-1990s, while the growth in the number of tourism businesses continued unabated, the growth in foreign visitor numbers slowed down, leading to downward pressures on prices and erosion and squeezing of profits to very low levels. Since that time, tourism businesses have operated in a difficult and intensely competitive business environment. As illustrated in the quote below, this has encouraged private tourism business owners to cultivate ties with local taxation officials in order to reduce the amount of tax paid not only in order to compete with other tourism businesses, but in a lot of cases simply to survive.

> The entry of a lot of new tourism businesses, particularly private businesses has created intense and unhealthy competition (canh tranh khoc liet khong lanh manh), which has affected the performance of all tourism businesses. As a result of the deteriorating business situation, tourism businesses are turning to more illicit ways of maintaining their financial situations by for example colluding with taxation officials and avoiding complying with their legal obligations and responsibilities, in not fully declaring their true revenues in order to withhold paying tax.
>
> (TQ Hotel, Hue, a state hotel)

Once again as discussed throughout this section, the non-compliance of central government laws and directives in this way has been facilitated by a regulatory environment in which informal structures and practices, such as the cultivation of social ties by private tourism business owners with local taxation officials are, in the transitional Vietnamese economy, mediating more formal structures, such as central government laws and directives, in the regulation of economic processes in local spaces.

The Completion of Administrative Procedures

The control retained by officials from a number of local state institutions, including departments within the local people's committee, the local bureau of tourism and the local immigration office, in completing a range of bureaucratic procedures required by private tourism business owners in the course of running their businesses was similarly in evidence in the responses given by respondents. As the following quote illustrates, once again, as a way of negotiating the informal regulatory environment, cultivating ties with those officials involved in completing particular bureaucratic procedures has constituted an important mechanism for private tourism business owners.

> As an example, one of the owners or a member of staff at our business cultivates ties with an official at a particular state institution and deals with this official. Thereafter, he only has to give this official a small sum of money to resolve quickly any issues arising from our work, getting a visa issued quickly at the office of immigration or completing some other procedure quickly, for example.
>
> (HMTTC, Hanoi, a private tour operator)

As with the ties cultivated by private tourism business owners with officials from the local taxation office and the police, among the majority of respondents interviewed ties with officials from, for example, the local bureau of tourism and the local immigration office are being created by private tourism business owners rather than cultivated out of pre-existing ties based on shared affiliation.

As in the ties cultivated by private business owners with taxation officials, discussed in the previous section, in the preceding quotes and in the case study below, ties are principally constituted through financial benefits. Nevertheless, they are 'social' in the respect that, firstly, there is the idea that they are being created and cultivated to produce lasting, useful relationships rather than simply to carry out one-off business transactions that, secondly, can as a result be invoked in the short and long term to secure a regular stream of material benefits to both parties: for private tourism business owners, ensuring that all bureaucratic procedures are completed quickly and smoothly; and for officials, small sums of money.

The following quotation reports conversations with an informant working at a local immigration office in Hanoi. It provides a further illustration of the significant arbitrary and discretionary powers possessed by local state officials, in this case at the local immigration office in completing bureaucratic procedures in processing applications for visa extensions requested by local tour operators. As a result, ties cultivated by private tour operator business owners or members of their staff with individual officials at the immigration office constitute an important mechanism enabling private tour operator business owners to negotiate the informal regulatory environment. Cultivating ties ensures that visa applications can be processed quickly and smoothly.

> With a one month visa extension for foreign visitors in Vietnam, the official cost shown on the visa stamped on a passport is US$10. A tour operator company dealing in visa extensions has the discretion to charge foreign customers any amount to complete this service. For example, a tour operator company may decide to charge a customer say US$18. A member of staff at the company will then go to the immigration department. An official at the immigration department will agree to process the application on condition that he is paid a level of remuneration for completing the task. The level of remuneration is generally determined by the extent of the relationship

between the official and the member of staff at the tourism company, i.e. the closer the relationship, the lower the amount of remuneration sought. In the majority of cases, particularly where a tour operator company regularly carries out visa extensions for foreign customers, ties between a private tour operator and a particular official at the local immigration office will most probably have already been created. There will be a a pre-agreed arrangement or understanding between the official and the tourism company regarding the level of remuneration – say US$2 as well as payment for the time required by the official to complete the task.

(Personal communication, immigration official, 2001)

The statement above reinforces the notion that ties between private tourism businesses and local state officials are being created to produce lasting relationships, through which both parties are able to secure a regular stream of material benefits. In the above quotation, for the private tour operator, as well as ensuring that visa applications are completed quickly and smoothly, a profit of US$6 is earned by the tour operator on each visa; while an official at the immigration office profits by US$2 per visa processed. In addition, the statement illustrates how regular interaction between private tour operators and officials from the immigration office helps to regularize the behaviour and expectations of each party. As illustrated in the quotation, where ties between a private tour operator and an official at the local immigration office are well-established with the tour operator regularly submitting applications for visa extensions, the expectations of both parties will have become regularized: the private tour operator will be aware of how much time and what level of remuneration is required by the official and the official in turn will have a good idea of the 'fee' he will receive for processing the visa application.

Conversely, as is implied in the immigration official's statement above, in the absence of ties between private tour operators and officials from the local immigration office, through their arbitrary and discretionary powers over the process of completing visa applications, officials have considerable capacity to hinder the process for private tour operators. First, officials retain discretion over how quickly or slowly they complete applications, which for tour operators may cause uncertainty and unreliability in the visa services they offer to foreign customers. Second, in the absence of ties, for private tour operators the level of remuneration required by an official from the immigration office is likely to be both uncertain and higher than in the case where ties have been created, thus reducing the profit earned by a tour operator on its visa services, in comparison with a tour operator who has created ties with officials. Once again this serves to illustrate the importance for private tourism business owners in the transitional Vietnamese economy of cultivating ties with local state officials as a way of negotiating the informal regulatory environment in smoothly completing bureaucratic processes in the course of running a private tourism business.

Conclusion

In the transitional Vietnamese economy, private tourism business activity is developing in the context where local state institutions and officials in local spaces such as Hanoi, Hue and Ho Chi Minh City have been afforded significant capacity to mediate, interpret and implement the framework of laws, policies and directives created by the central government to regulate private tourism business activity. As a result, private tourism business owners are reliant on the 'support' of local state officials to negotiate smoothly through the processes of establishing and running their businesses. In attempting to gain this support, the building and cultivation of social ties – *quan he xa hoi* – with local state officials has constituted an important mechanism.

Data collected from interviews with private hotel and tour operator business owners and managers in Hanoi, Hue and Ho Chi Minh City demonstrate that, in establishing their businesses, for the vast majority of private tourism business owners, pre-existing ties, formed at school, university or from previous work, with officials working in local state institutions involved in the approval and establishment of private businesses enabled them to negotiate bureaucratic processes smoothly. While, in running their businesses, ties created with a range of local state officials, in particular, local taxation officials and the police, have allowed private tourism business owners to complete administrative procedures smoothly.

Notes

1 This term 'regulation' comes from French language in the sense that the concept of 'regulation theory' was first discussed in the late 1970s and early 1980s by academics within the Parisian 'regulation school'. Consequently, when talking about 'regulation' the meaning intended is not the English meaning of 'control' or 'restrict'. Instead, here the French word 'regulation' translates as 'regularisation' or 'normalisation' (Jessop, 1995: 309). This is the meaning I wish to convey throughout this chapter.

2 By local state, I am referring in particular to municipal and provincial people's committees. I do however acknowledge the regulatory power and autonomy possessed by the local state at lower administrative levels.

3 In June 1978, the General Department of Tourism came into being as the central government tourism institution managing the tourism industry throughout the whole of newly reunified Vietnam (Anonymous (DLVN), *Tap chi Du lich*, July 1998, 'Vietnamese tourism on the road to restructuring and development' (*Du lich Viet Nam tren duong doi moi va phat trien*): 5; 15).

4 At the seminal 6th Communist Party Congress in December 1986, which launched the Doi Moi reform programme, one announcement made was to 'Quickly make

good use of the favourable conditions of the country to expand tourism by mobilising domestic investment capital and by co-operating with foreign countries' (*Nhanh chong khai thac cac dieu kien thuan loi cua dat nuoc de mo rong du lich bang von dau tu trong nuoc va hop tac voi nuoc ngoai*) (Anonymous: *Bhung ngay thang vas u kien dang ghi nho* (Dates and events worth remembering), *Tap chi Du lich*, 1999: 4).

5 'CP' as in Decree 05/CP stands for *chinh phu* which signifies the central government.

6 Policy-making relating to general business aspects of a private tourism business is carried out by central government institutions other than the VNAT, for example, the Ministry of Trade and the Ministry of Planning and Investment as private tourism businesses are subject to general business laws, such as the Company Law and the Law on Private Enterprise (*Tong cuc Du lich*, 1997: 70).

7 The Ordinance on Tourism – the Tourism Law (11/1999/PL-UBTVQH 10) was approved and promulgated under (02L/CTN) on 20 February 1999.

8 This continues regulatory norms and practices in which municipal and provincial people's committees have traditionally been afforded considerable space to interpret central government policies and resolutions. While policy-making has traditionally been centralized, decision-making, however, has been extremely decentralized. Central government resolutions have traditionally been disseminated down bureaucratic and hierarchical lines with the highest levels receiving comprehensive details of the new resolutions, lower levels only a general outline and non-Party-state members receiving little or no information. Resolutions are disseminated in a range of meetings comprising central and lower level institutions: ministries, provincial leaders or branches or local levels etc. Therefore within each administrative level there is considerable scope for interpretation in accordance with local conditions and the priorities of particular administrative levels or institutions. After the discussions, a circular is issued by each institution, which guides implementation of a new directive by an institution's officials. The circular also reflects an institution's particular interpretation of the new central directive. This may be significantly different from the interpretation intended by the central government (Phong and Beresford, 1998: 73–78; VIR, 17–23 July 2000: 10).

9 Until March 2002, it was officially illegal for Party members to engage in private business activity (Abrami, 2003: 96).

10 With tourism businesses and owners from which quotes and case study material are presented, pseudonyms are used in order to protect the anonymity of these companies and individuals.

11 Estimated using the mean age of entrepreneurs interviewed of 42, 43 and 38 in Hanoi, Hue and HCMC respectively.

12 Hanoitourist is one of the largest state tour operators in Hanoi.

13 An 'International Tour Operator Licence' (ITOL) permits a tour operator to carry out tour business organised from overseas.

14 In this case due to the insufficient turnover of the business. Officially the VNAT will only issue an ITOL to a business achieving an annual turnover of at least VND1 billion. The turnover for the Tu Hai Tourism Company disclosed to me during the interview was only VND250 million in 1998 and VND400 million in 2000.

15 The respondent had previously been engaged in a number of different professions, including construction and trading.

16 Officially, once a month, officials from the local taxation department inspect the accounts and business results of the tourism businesses under their control to assess the level of business tax the tourism business is liable for. With regard to the police, at the end of every day a hotel is required to submit the details of all guests staying at the hotel for registration purposes. There is overlap between these functions as the tax department refers to the register of guests submitted by the hotel to the police in order to ascertain how many guests have stayed at the hotel in the previous month as an indication of the revenue earned by the hotel.

17 The interview was carried out at the MH Hotel in Hoi An.

8 Tourism in the Lao People's Democratic Republic

David Harrison and Steven Schipani

Introduction

The overall aim of this chapter is to assess the current role of international tourism in relation to development – specifically economic growth and poverty eradication – in the Lao People's Democratic Republic. More specifically, the focus is on how tourism is organized within the country, with particular reference to the Asian Development Bank, SNV (the Netherlands Development Organization), the Lao National Tourism Administration and the private sector, and the extent to which donor-assisted, community-based tourism contributes to the alleviation of poverty.

The Lao People's Democratic Republic (Lao PDR, or more commonly 'Laos'), a landlocked country of 236,800 sq. km., shares borders with Myanmar (Burma) and China in the north, Thailand to the west, Vietnam to the east and south, and Cambodia to the south. It has a tropical monsoon climate, with a rainy season from May to November and a dry season from December to April. Its terrain is characterized by mostly low calciferous mountains that rise to a maximum height of just over 2,900 metres, with some fertile plains, river valleys and plateaux scattered throughout the landscape. Nearly half the country remains forested, with a system of 20 National Protected Areas in place that encompasses 13 per cent of the nation's total land area. Of all its physical features, the most dominant is the Mekong River, which flows north to south for nearly 1,900 kilometres and, for 919 kilometres, forms a common border with Thailand. The capital city is Vientiane, located on a curve of the Mekong River that borders Thailand's northeastern city of Nong Khai.

The population of some 6.2 million is ethnically mixed, and there is much debate about how they should be described, especially with regard to the linguistic/cultural relationships to one another (Evans, 1999: 1–31). Following early Lao government practice, and using geomorphological criteria, the *CIA World Fact Book* simply categorizes the population as 'Lao Loum (lowland Lao) 68 per cent, Lao Theung (upland Lao) 22 per cent, Lao Soung (highland Lao) and ethnic Vietnamese/Chinese 1 per cent' (www.cia.gov/cia/publications/factbook/print/la.html). By contrast, the official guide book to Lao PDR refers to 49 ethnic groups in four linguistic families, notably the Lao–Tai, the Mon–Khmer, the Tibeto–Burmese and the Hmong–Ioumien (National Tourism Authority of Lao PDR, undated: 9). More technically, using ethno-linguistic criteria, Chazée (2002: 1) refers to the Lao as a sub-group of Tai speakers

Figure 8.1: Map of Lao PDR.

and 'a minimum of 131 ethnic minorities and sub-groups which can be divided into numerous clans and lineages', adding that in 1995 'the national census guidelines distinguished 47 main ethnic groups and a total of 149 sub-groups'. He concludes: 'If the ethnic minorities are taken to be all those who are not Lao–Tai, then they are the majority at 65 per cent' (Chazée, 2002: 14).

The Geo-Political Context

Seen alternatively as peripheral to or a lynchpin of mainland Southeast Asia (Jerndal and Rigg, 1999: 35), Laos emerged in the 1970s from a long period of war and civil unrest, prompted largely by the involvement of outside powers in its affairs. Disputed over by the Siamese and the French in the late nineteenth century, in 1893, after a series of Franco–Siamese treaties, it became a French Protectorate. It was briefly occupied by Japan during World War II, and subsequently obtained limited autonomy from the French in 1949. In 1953 it became fully independent, only to enter a protracted civil war, which largely reflected great power interests in the region. In the north-east, the communist Pathet Lao were aligned with Ho Chi Minh's movement in Vietnam and the Soviet Bloc, while to the south the anti-communist, Royal Lao Government forces were supported primarily by the United States.

By the mid-1960s, Laos was massively drawn into the Second Indochina War, fought primarily between the United States and Vietnam. During this 'secret war' that raged in Laos, Thai and Hmong mercenaries were supported by non-uniformed military personnel and 'advisers' based in western Laos and the capital, with American pilots carrying out large-scale bombing missions from bases in Thailand and Vietnam. The Ho Chi Minh Trail network in Laos and North Vietnam was subjected to sustained aerial bombardment, which included the use of defoliants and anti-personnel munitions. Pathet Lao recruits were trained by and fought alongside the North Vietnamese army, which had tens of thousands of troops stationed in Laos, and which proved more than a match for the American-backed forces, despite the latter's superior weaponry (Warner, 1997; Hamilton-Merritt, 1999).

The Push for Development and the Role of Tourism

A ceasefire was agreed in 1973 and led to two years of coalition government. However, in 1975 the Pathet Lao, under the political banner of the Lao People's Revolutionary Party, gained control, dissolved the monarchy, and formed the Lao People's Democratic Republic on 2 December 1975. From then until the mid 1980s the government followed a strict Marxist–Leninist political and economic ideology, but since 1986, and especially after the collapse of the Soviet Union, there has been a sustained attempt to move from a command economy to a more market-orientated system. One-party government continues, with a slow emergence of a more open democratic system. Nevertheless, despite occasional small-scale domestic unrest up to 2000, Lao PDR is currently experiencing political and social stability and, with considerable international assistance, widespread poverty is being addressed by Government and NGOs throughout the country.

Since 1996, the government has set itself a series of targets: to eradicate poverty, to reduce dependence on overseas development assistance, and to move out of the category of 'least developed country' by 2020 (Government of Lao PDR, 2003: iv–v and 1–4). Substantial poverty reduction has undoubtedly occurred, partly because of increased social stability, but also because government policy, with substantial overseas aid, has had some success. From 1991 to 2000, for instance, real Gross Domestic Product grew at an annual average of 6.3 per cent, and those living in poverty declined overall from 46 per cent of the population in 1992 to 33 per cent in 2002–2003. Most social indicators confirm the trend (Asian Development Bank, 1999a: 3; World Bank, 2005: 4–6).

Much remains to be done. There are stark differences across and within provinces (especially between north and south), between urban and rural areas, and across ethnic minorities (World Bank, 2005: 4–6). And although in 2003 the United Nations Development Programme up-graded Lao PDR to the status of country characterized by 'medium human development', poverty is still prevalent, and Lao PDR scores much lower on the Human Development Index (133) than neighbouring Thailand (73), China (85), Vietnam (108), Cambodia (130), and even Myanmar (129) (UNDP, 2005: 220–221).

International Tourism as a Tool for Development in Lao PDR

Lao PDR has officially welcomed international tourists only since 1989 (Hall, 2000: 183), and the country's first national tourism plan was published in 1990, placing emphasis on the development of a modest tourism industry based on high-end, tightly controlled group tours. However, by 1995 tourism had become a priority for economic development (Schipani, 2002: 18) and the second *National Tourism Development Plan*, published in 1998, focused more widely on four major types of tourism (conventional sightseeing; special interest tourism, for example, eco- and adventure tourism; cross-border tourism; and domestic tourism) to generate foreign exchange and stimulate economic activity. It was considered that together they would bring socio-economic benefits that could be spread across the population and would also enhance conservation of the natural and built environment (Lao PDR/ UNDP/WTO, 1998: 37). Indeed, by 1999 tourism was reportedly the country's most important earner of foreign exchange, ahead of garments and wood products,

Table 8.1: International Tourism in Lao PDR

Year	Day Visitors*	Overnight Visitors*	Total Visitors
1990	n/a	14,000	n/a
1991	n/a	38,000	n/a
1992	n/a	88,000	92,000
1993	67,000	36,000	103,000
1994	110,000	36,000	146,000
1995	286,000	60,000	346,000
1996	310,000	93,000	403,000
1997	270,000	193,000	463,000
1998	300,000	200,000	500,000
1999	355,000	259,000	614,000
2000	546,000	191,000	737,000
2001	501,000	173,000	674,000
2002	521,000	215,000	736,000
2003	440,000	196,000	636,000
2004	658,332	236,484	894,806
2005	807,550	287,765	1,095,315

* Those categorized by the World Tourism Organization as 'day visitors' are regional tourists who enter the country by road, and in fact they may stay one or two nights. By contrast, those classified as 'overnight visitors' are mainly from outside the region.

Source: World Tourism Organization 1996: 96; 1999: 104; 2001: 103 and 2005: 103; Lao National Tourism Administration 2006.

and had moved from the position of fourth to first in this league table over only three years (Lao PDR, UNDP and WTO, 1999: 6).

By the opening years of the twenty-first century, there was further recognition of tourism's potential to reduce poverty in Lao PDR. In 2004, the Government's *National Growth and Poverty Eradication Strategy (NGPES)* noted:

> Tourism is now a major contributor to national income (7–9 per cent of GDP) and employment. Tourism is a labour intensive industry and contributes directly to poverty reduction. The Lao PDR's tourism strategy favours pro-poor, community-based tourism development, the enhancement of specific tourism-related infrastructure improvements, and sub-regional tourism co-operation.
>
> (Lao PDR, 2003: 104).

A year later, the *National Tourism Strategy for Lao PDR* was to reiterate the role of properly planned tourism in reducing poverty and promoting national development. The strategy recognized the appeal of ethnic minority groups, traditional culture, and the wide range of archaeological and religious sites, and stressed promotion of the country's arts, crafts and numerous natural attractions to attract visitors (Allcock, 2004: 12–13; 18; 43).

The early statistics of tourist arrivals to Lao PDR were unreliable and varied considerably according to their source, but recent national data are more consistent. Clearly, tourist arrivals have increased dramatically over the last few years, even though the overall trend has been distorted by the world-wide impact of the terrorist attacks in the United States (2001) and the War in Iraq and, more regionally, by terrorist attacks in Indonesia (2002, 2005) and the SARS epidemic in Asia (2003). In 2005, there were more than a million international arrivals in Lao PDR, an increase of more than 50 per cent on the 2000 figure. The total amount of revenue that the tourism industry generated in 2005 is estimated at over US$146 million, making it the country's primary source of foreign exchange (Lao National Tourism Administration, 2006: 18). Most visitors (82 per cent) come from within the region, primarily from other ASEAN countries, but there are significant numbers of relatively high-spending tourists from Europe (12 per cent) and the Americas (5.5 per cent) (Lao National Tourism Administration, 2006: 6). Recognizing the value of these relatively small but growing markets, the government has prioritized Japan and Australia (with Thailand) in Asia, France, the UK and Germany in Europe, and the USA and Canada in the Americas (Lao National Tourism Administration, 2006: 14).

Much of Lao PDR is poorly developed with only basic transport infrastructure. Tourism development is most concentrated in the Municipality and Province of Vientiane, at the UNESCO World Heritage Sites of Luang Prabang Town and Vat Phou in Champassak, and in Savannakhet City (Lao PDR's second largest), with Savannakhet Province serving as a major entry point for visitors from Vietnam and Thailand. As indicated in Table 8.2, in 2005 Vientiane Municipality (21 per cent), Vientiane Province (11 per cent), Luang Prabang (15 per cent), Champassak (12 per cent) and Savannakhet (6 per cent) together accounted for 65 per cent of all accommodation establishments in Lao PDR, while the Vientiane–Luang Prabang corridor alone, which includes Vang Vieng, accounted for about half all establishments. (Lao National Tourism Administration, 2006: 18–19).

While the government's commitment to community-based tourism (CBT) has a high profile, tourism development in these destinations has been left largely to the private sector, normally locally-owned small and medium sized enterprises, while the introduction of tourism into outlying areas tends to have been taken up by such organizations as the Asian Development Bank, UNESCO, and non-governmental organizations.

The Organization of Tourism in Lao PDR

Numerous stakeholders have an interest in tourism in Lao PDR, and many are in the public sector. At the central level, they include government departments and ministries,

Table 8.2: Concentration of Tourism in Lao PDR, 2005: Selected Indices

Province	Visitors	No. of Hotels & Guest-houses	% of Total	No. of Rooms	Occu-pancy Rate %	Average No. of Rooms
Attapeu	13,740	12	1.1	190	50	16
Bokeo	89,027	24	2.2	309	67	13
Bolikhamxay	63,579	26	2.4	435	65	17
Champassak	99,044	126	11.6	1,616	29	13
Houaphanh	3,175	39	3.6	338	29	9
Khammouane	13,633	18	1.6	394	43	22
Luang Namtha	49,258	50	4.6	536	57	11
Luang Prabang	133,569	163	15.0	1,722	70	11
Oudomxay	54,721	63	5.8	703	52	11
Phongsaly	9,452	36	3.3	273	29	8
Saravanh	8,000	22	2.0	230	42	10
Savannakhet	133,569	67	6.2	1,257	60	19
Sayabouli	15,914	47	4.3	431	37	9
Sekong	6,526	17	1.6	172	37	10
Vientiane Muncipality	653,212	224	20.6	4,891	64	22
Vientiane Province	92,657	115	10.6	1,807	52	16
Xieng Khouang	24,174	32	2.9	441	40	14
Saysomboun	n/a	7	0.6	83	n/a	12
TOTAL		1,088	100.0	15,828		15

Source: Lao National Tourism Administration, 2006: 18–19.

most notably the Lao National Tourism Administration (formerly the National Tourism Authority of Lao PDR), which comes under the Prime Minister's Office and is led by a Minister. Ministries and departments dealing with agriculture, forestry, science, technology, the environment, finance, foreign affairs, transport, communication, health and handicrafts are also involved, while at the local level there is a similar range of provincial and district authorities and government departments (Allcock, 2004: 67–68). In addition, there are branch offices of the Lao National Tourism Administration in the country's sixteen provinces and in the Municipality of Vientiane.

Aid agencies, too, are active in supporting the development and promotion of tourism in Lao PDR. By far the best known project has been the UNESCO–LNTA Lao Nam Ha Ecotourism Project (NHEP), in Luang Namtha Province (see also

Parnwell, Chapter 12 in this volume). Started in 1999 with funds provided by the New Zealand Official Development Assistance Programme (NZODA), now the New Zealand Agency for International Development (NZAID), the Japanese government through the International Finance Corporation's Trust Funds Programme, and with additional technical assistance from UNESCO, the project demonstrates how treks to ethnic minority villages with trained local guides can bring much-needed cash income to the villagers, and facilitate conservation efforts within a National Protected Area (NPA). As external reviewers noted in 2002, 'the Nam Ha Ecotourism Project has established a first-class working model for ecotourism activities in areas of great cultural and natural richness' (Lyttleton and Allcock, 2002: 6). Indeed, its status as a role model is recognized in the recent *National Ecotourism Strategy and Action Plan*, prepared by the Lao National Tourism Administration with assistance from SNV (National Tourism Authority of Lao PDR, 2005: 4).

Tours developed by the NHEP are now operated by a locally-managed guide service under the supervision of the Luang Namtha Provincial Tourism Office. Now into its second phase (2005–2008) the NHEP is focusing on improving public-private sector co-operation, strengthening natural resource and protected area management in the Nam Ha NPA, and developing a tourism master plan for Luang Namtha Province. The Nam Ha model continues to receive strong support from the Lao Government and has been adopted by Green Discovery, the tour operator in Lao PDR most involved with community-based ecotourism products. With financial assistance from NZAID, a community-based ecotourism programme similar to Nam Ha is set to begin in Xieng Khouang province in mid-2006. Both Nam Ha Phase II and the Xieng Khouang Heritage Tourism Programme utilize technical assistance and monitoring sourced through the Office of the UNESCO Regional Advisor for Culture in Asia and the Pacific. These two programmes are part of the wider NZAID Lao country strategy that focuses on pro-poor tourism and natural resource management in Luang Namtha and Xieng Khouang provinces. With a commitment of up to US$ 1 million a year until 2010, New Zealand has emerged as one Lao PDR's main pro-poor tourism donors.

Several other ecotourism projects, based on similar principles and with similar aims, are promoted by aid agencies. These include a CUSO initiative (a Canadian volunteer organization), working in Attapeu Province, DED (the German Development Service) in Phou Khao Khouay National Park, near Vientiane and also in Oudomxay Province, GTZ (German Development Agency) and Vientiane Travel and Tour, its private sector partner, developing an ecotourism programme for eight Akha villages in the Muang Sing area of Luang Namtha, and small European Union projects in Vieng Phoukha District, Luang Namtha and in Phongsaly Province (www.ecotourismlaos. com accessed 3rd March 2006). However, the organizations most heavily involved in Lao tourism, both centrally and in the provinces, are the Asian Development Bank

(ADB) and SNV. The ADB is putting most of its resources earmarked for tourism into Luang Namtha, Luang Prabang, Khammouane and Champassak, but is also planning to extend its work through supporting 'pro-poor demonstration projects' in the provinces of Phongsaly, Houaphanh and Xieng Khouang (Asian Development Bank, 2005: 45). SNV, an independent NGO that traditionally has received most of its income from the Dutch government, focuses on small-scale, community-based tourism in parts of Lao PDR not currently on the main tourist trail – notably Savannakhet, Khammouane, Houaphanh and several villages outside the city of Luang Prabang.

The Asian Development Bank

In 2002, the ADB funded a feasibility study of priority tourism infrastructure projects in Lao PDR, Cambodia and Vietnam (Asian Development Bank, 1999b) and has since committed up to US$30 million in low interest loans and technical assistance to the Mekong Tourism Development Project. It is now a major presence in the Greater Mekong region, and is committed to developing tourism as a means of poverty reduction (Asian Development Bank, 2002a: 24). About a third of this amount is ear-marked for Lao PDR (Asian Development Bank, 2002b: 12).

As in Cambodia and Vietnam, ADB's focus in Lao PDR is on four distinct spheres of activity, as indicated in Figure 8.2, and is designed to be implemented over a five-year period. The first emphasis is on providing loans to improve tourism-related infrastructure, and primarily involves building or improving roads and airports. Currently, three projects are under way, in the Provinces of Luang Namtha, Khammouane, and Luang Prabang.

The second focus is on the development of pro-poor, community-based tourism, and for this purpose ADB has a team of four international and four national consultants working closely with local project implementation units (PIUs), which are comprised of staff from provincial tourism offices in Luang Namtha, Luang Prabang, Champassak and Khammouane. These PIUs co-operate with private and public sector agencies, oversee guide training and awareness programmes, and ensure, where appropriate, that women and ethnic minorities are empowered to participate in tourism activities.

The third emphasis is on strengthening regional co-operation, improving cross-border tourism facilities and harmonizing standards, and developing human resources in the Lower Mekong region, while the final sphere of activity is providing institutional support to implement the three major project components.

SNV (Netherlands Development Organization)

SNV has operated in Lao PDR since 2000, initially as SUNV (through a co-operative programme with United Nations Volunteers). The organization is especially committed to providing technical advisers for the development of community-based ecotourism in rural areas. It supported the Nam Ha Ecotourism Project by providing a Handicraft

Part A Tourism-related infrastructure improvement	Part B Community-based tourism	Part C Sub-regional co-operation for sustainable tourism	Part D Financial and administrative support
1. Luang Namtha: airport extension/ improvement 2. Road access to Konglor Cave, Khammouane 3. Improved road access to Kuangsi Falls, Luang Prabang	1. Institutional strengthening and community participation programme 2. Awareness programme: benefits/ conservation 3. Pro-poor tourism products: identification and development 4. Small-scale tourism-related infrastructure 5. Capacity building: micro enterprise and communities 6. Gender: development and participation 7. Ethnic minority participation and programme 8. Marketing and promotion plan 9. Promotion of community-based tourism networks and ecotourism stakeholder associations 10. Project performance monitoring system	1. GMS faculty for tourism cooperation 2. Improved tourist facilities at border posts 3. Establish GMS marketing and promotion network 4. Establish GMS hotel classification system 5. GMS tourism plan 6. Statistics improvement and harmonization 7. Diversification of Agency for Coordinating Mekong Tourism Activity (AMTA) 8. GMS tourism human resource development	1. Implementation assistance and institutional strengthening. 2. Consulting services for project management support 3. Incremental administrative costs and project administrative equipment

Figure 8.2: Lao National Tourism Administration – ADB Mekong Tourism Development Project (MTDP)

Production and Marketing Adviser, and has since moved into several Provincial Tourism Offices (PTOs) and national level government organizations (www.snv.org.la). In Luang Prabang, for instance, its advisers co-operate with the provincial authority in trying to extend the benefits of tourism, currently focused on the World Heritage city of Luang Prabang, to out-lying villages in the Province. In Houaphanh they have helped the PTO formulate a tourism development plan and are assisting in improving information and services at the network of caves once used by the Pathet Lao as command centres during the Indo-China wars, while in Savannakhet, SNV advisers are developing treks to three protected areas in conjunction with villagers and local guides. Similar activities are occurring in Khammouane, as part of the Mekong Tourism Development Project.

All such activities are designed to increase earning opportunities for the rural poor, diversify their sources of income, build local management capacity and expert-ise in tourism (for example, in guiding and heritage conservation), and empower local communities. They are complemented by technical assistance provided by SNV to the Lao National Tourism Administration in Vientiane, which promotes the National Ecotourism Strategy (National Tourism Authority of Lao PDR, 2004), and the work of the newly-formed inter-ministerial Ecotourism Technical Co-operation Group, which also receives technical assistance and further support from SNV and Mekong Tourism Development Project advisers. SNV also helped to establish the Lao Sustainable Tourism Network, and in May 2006 launched a three-year programme, funded by the European Union, to improve the marketing and promotion capabil-ities of the Lao Association of Travel Agents (LATA), strengthen the organization's management, and institute mechanisms for information-exchange between tour operators and the LNTA. Such examples, along with its co-operation with UNWTO through the STEP Programme, in disseminating the new Lao Tourism Law (ap-proved by the Lao Parliament in January 2006), show how SNV assists the LNTA in co-operating more closely with the private sector.

Importantly, it should be noted that, except for the work in Savannakhet and Houaphanh, many of the activities carried out by SNV's international and national advisers are funded by ADB through the Lao government, an arrangement that emerged during the first phase of the ADB-financed Mekong Tourism Development Project. In effect, the ADB and SNV have leading (even dominant) roles in the development and trajectory of tourism in Lao PDR – in so far as it is oriented towards rural, pro-poor community-based tourism.

The Lao National Tourism Administration

Over the past decade, the National Tourism Authority has been situated either in the Ministry of Commerce or the Prime Minister's Office. In 2005, the National Tourism Authority of Lao PDR was re-named the Lao National Tourism Administration and up-graded to Ministerial level within the Prime Minister's Office. Its organizational structure is shown in Figure 8.3. The LNTA is the main government agency responsible for regulating tourism in Lao PDR, in co-operation with several other government departments and ministries. These include the Ministries of: Agriculture and Forestry; Information and Culture; Security; Commerce; Communications, Transport, Post and Construction; and the Science, Technology and Environment Agency (STEA), which is also administered from the Prime Minister's Office. In every province there are tourism offices that work with the LNTA and other related government authorities to regulate tourism in the provinces. At the time of writing, there were about 65 full time, dedicated staff employed by LNTA.

Tourism Planning and Co-operation

The task of the Department of Tourism Planning and Co-operation is to develop the National Tourism Strategy and create tourism master plans for the provinces and specific sites throughout the country, often with the assistance of international organizations, through the Division of International Co-operation. For example, SNV provided technical assistance in drafting the National Ecotourism Strategy and Action Plan, and the current National Tourism Strategy and Action Plan was formulated with national and international technical assistance from ADB's Mekong Tourism Development Project.

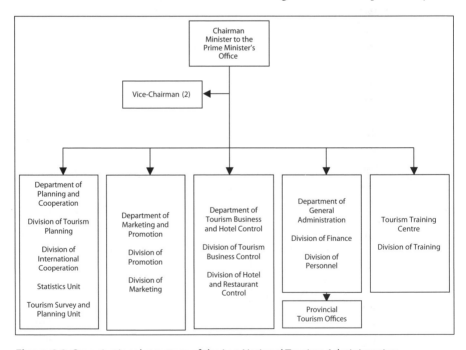

Figure 8.3: Organizational structure of the Lao National Tourism Administration

Licensing and Legal Affairs

The LNTA licenses tour companies, tour guides, tourist accommodation and restaurants, and sets appropriate standards, guidelines and codes of conduct for them. For example, it publishes a compulsory code of conduct for tour guides and is in the process of setting up a hotel rating system based on good practice elsewhere in the ASEAN region.

Marketing and Promotion

Most marketing and general promotion of the Lao tourism industry is carried out by LNTA, which produces informational materials and participates in conferences and exhibitions. It also maintains tourist information centres across the country and two websites (www.tourismlaos.gov.la and www.ecotourismlaos.com). However, more specific tourism products and services are marketed and promoted directly by the private sector, i.e. tour companies, hotels and restaurants, which produce their own advertisements and brochures and develop and maintain their own websites.

Training

Although hoteliers and such in-bound tour operators as Green Discovery provide some training in tourism-related activities, most is through the government and its NGO partners. National tour guides, for example, are trained and registered by the LNTA, which runs an annual tour guide course in Vientiane. Apart from a modest registration fee, costs are met from the LNTA's own budget. It also periodically conducts hotel and restaurant management training sessions for the private sector, as well as short tourism management courses for government employees and the private sector.

Guides trained at national level can operate throughout Lao PDR. Others may be trained at provincial and village levels, through projects supported by such organizations as the ADB and SNV. These may include private sector guides, but candidates going through this process are licensed to operate only at provincial or village level, according to where they were trained. Human resources may also be strengthened in other ways, for example, in language training and study tours.

At the village level, the LNTA supports local communities with targeted capacity building, thus enabling them to participate more in the tourism industry. Appropriate activities include education and training for disadvantaged and poor groups (particularly women), who can then obtain secure employment in the hospitality, guiding and handicraft sub-sectors.

The Private Sector

Three features concerning private sector involvement in Lao tourism are prominent. First, although SNV, ADB and the government are committed to working with the private sector, LNTA's linkages with tourism businesses remain tenuous, and it might be argued that, at least initially, aid agencies and the government have looked at the private sector with a degree of suspicion. For their part, private sector tour operators and tourism-related businesses used to complain at a lack of visible outputs and tangible support from LNTA, especially in marketing and promotion, and regulatory or training activities. However, while the ADB's Mekong Tourism Development Project is primarily focused on infrastructure projects, product and human resource development, it is also committed (as elsewhere in the region) to developing tourism through the establishment of a Lao Tourism Promotion and Marketing Board, which is intended to increase participation by the private sector and give it a stronger voice on issues related to tourism policy. At the time of writing such Boards had yet to materialize.

Secondly, it is clear that Lao PDR's tourism sector has not attracted substantial foreign direct investment (FDI). This might be explained by the relatively late conversion of the government to a market orientation, but the ILO study quoted above also indicates that, in 1996, 'the existing legal and policy framework favours large enterprises' (Enterprise Development Consultants Co. Ltd. et al., 2002). Through legislation enacted by the Government in 2004, international investors were offered even more favourable terms including the possibility of 100 per cent foreign ownership and tax holidays up to 7 years, followed by very low profit taxes thereafter (Lao PDR, 2004). However, at the time of writing, despite the country's immense potential for tourism, there has been little FDI in its historical, cultural and natural attractions, and such incentives seem not to have succeeded (GMS Business Forum and Directory, 2006).

Thirdly, and in contradistinction to the absence of FDI, since 1986, when a market-oriented economy was introduced in Lao PDR, small, locally-owned businesses have expanded at a phenomenal rate. By 1996

> there were 146,000 micro/small enterprises employing the equivalent of 259,000 full-time workers and accounting for 6 per cent to 9 per cent of GDP. This is over ten times the 22,000 that were employed by larger enterprises. Indeed, the micro/small enterprise sector accounted for 86 per cent of rural and 13 per cent of urban employment . . . 90 per cent of these are family businesses which tend to be multiple enterprises. However, they provide supplementary rather than principal household income. 63 per cent are female-owned and account for 56 per cent of total employment in this sector.
>
> (Enterprise Development Consultants Co. Ltd. et al., 2002)

By 2005, the importance of small/micro business was even more pronounced. This is especially evident in the tourism sector, at least in the provision of accommodation, food and beverages. In 1998, for example, there were only 307 accommodation establishments in the country, whereas by 2005 there were 1088 (Table 8.2). Interestingly, the average number of rooms was a mere 15, and exceeded 20 only in Khammouane and Vientiane Municipality. Even in Luang Prabang, with the second biggest concentration of establishments in the country, the average was only 11 rooms (Lao National Tourism

Administration, 2006: 18–19). The message these figures convey is evident in all of Lao PDR's main tourism centres: in the accommodation sector (and in restaurants), small/ micro businesses are the norm. Foreign investors may be conspicuous by their absence but, despite the lack of formal mechanisms for obtaining credit, the poor infrastructure, and relatively untrained human resources, local investment in tourism is booming.

Tourism and Poverty in Lao PDR

As tourism is considered a tool for reducing poverty, it is legitimate to ask if it does actually benefit the poor and alleviate their situation. From the evidence available, it seems clear that throughout Lao PDR tourism is perceived to benefit the poor. In the Akha villages visited by the team evaluating the first phase of the NHEP, for example, 'villagers interviewed felt that the tourists dramatically improved their income' and in one village the income from tourism relative to non-tourism sources was as high as 40 per cent (Lyttleton and Allcock, 2002: 42). An equally positive response emerged from interviews with government officials in Vientiane municipality and the provinces of Vientiane and Champassak, as well as numerous village groups in these provinces. Officials in the Lao National Tourism Authority and the Mekong Tourism Development Programme noted tourism was part of the country's Poverty Eradication Strategy, and all cited the Nam Ha Ecotourism Project as the primary example of how hill tribes had been able to increase their income through treks, becoming guides, and providing food and accommodation to tourists. Provincial officials echoed such sentiments, and also cited numerous examples of villagers providing handicrafts for sale to tourists, and agricultural products to guest houses. And from discussions with villagers in the Vang Vieng District of Vientiane Province, and in Champassak, the widespread view emerged that tourism (driven here by the private sector, rather than government and aid agencies) increased the incomes of many stakeholders, *including* but not specifically *targeting* the poor, provided taxes for central and provincial government, and employment for a wide range of people providing goods and services to the tourism sector.

Such perceptions are supported by objective evidence. In Luang Namtha, for instance, the site of the longest established ecotourism venture in the country, monitoring by the NHEP shows that the incomes of many in the participating villages have been considerably increased as a result of its activities (Lyttleton and Allcock, 2002: 17–19; Schipani, 2005: 6–11), and this model has been adopted widely throughout Lao PDR. Indeed, a crucial criterion in selecting villages for inclusion in the Mekong Tourism Development Project was the potential income the poor could derive from the development of community-based tourism programmes in their villages. Families able to provide food, meals, accommodation, guide services, handicrafts and transport were initially identified through a participatory process led by project staff, and were later selected by villagers to provide such services to tourists. The amount of gross and village revenue generated by the tours was then closely monitored, as was revenue at destinations that received infrastructure, promotional and tourism planning support. After an 18-month product development process, local tour operators began selling the new tours and destinations. Tables 8.3 and 8.4 summarize the direct financial benefits those communities, tour operators and the public sector received from tourism activities supported by the project.

It is important to recognize that some destinations were already receiving tourists before the project began working in these areas. However, for communities located on tour routes shown in Table 8.3, the situation was entirely different, and almost all of the village revenue shown in this table is attributed to the tours and operational mechanisms introduced by the project.

In villages involved in donor-assisted CBT in Lao PDR, poverty is alleviated through tourism, and account must also be taken of those 'soft' ecotourists who go to villages when visiting other attractions, for example waterfalls or caves. However, and crucially, most tourists to Lao PDR are *not* involved in donor-assisted, community-based tourism. Depending on which figures are taken as the total of tourist arrivals (Table 8.1), those who do visit such villages at some time are between 7 per cent and 22 per cent of all visitors. Evidence from the Nam Ha project (where monitoring is most advanced) indicates that about 12 per cent of all tourists to the province actually spend *part* of their time in the project villages. And expenditure by visitors at destinations supported by the MTDP is only about 0.3 per cent of the total revenue generated by tourism, a tiny proportion of total expenditure.

In effect, this means that whereas many community-based tourism projects have been specifically designed to bring benefits to poor communities (but not *necessarily* the poorest, which may lack tourist 'attractions'), enterprises developed by the private sector have a major role in alleviating poverty. In the ASEAN–EU project indicated earlier, for example, it was found that tourism was especially important in Vang Vieng municipality and in the nearby (and undoubtedly poor) Hmong village of Ban Pha Thao, as well as in several villages in the Siphandon region of Champassak. Residents of these areas had no doubt about its importance. Villagers of Ban Pha Thao, for instance, estimated that 40 per cent of the village cash income came from the sale of embroidery produced by the women for sale to tourists or, through intermediaries, to the USA, and the importance of embroidery to the household economy was evident in households in the sample survey. And in the village of Don Det Tok, in the Siphandon region of Champassak, discussed in more detail elsewhere (Harrison and Schipani, 2007), tourism was the main source of income in 22 per cent of sampled village households, the second source of income in another 11 per cent, and in 38 per cent of all households surveyed at least one individual was working in the tourism sector.

Table 8.3: A Summary of the Financial Benefits from Select New Tours Developed by the Mekong Tourism Development Project (March 2005–February 2006)

Name of Tour	No. of Tours	No. of Tourists	Gross Revenue (US$)	Village Revenue (US$)
Luang Namtha				
Pu Sam Yord 3-4-day trek	82	508	19,271	8,010
Nam Ha Camp Forest Camp	10	48	2,635	814
Akha Trail – Nam Mye Caves	6	20	1,016	301
Luang Prabang				
Chomphet 2-day Trek	15	58	2,438	282
Muang Ngoi 2-dayTrek	19	86	2,626	1,632
Kwang Si Nature Walk	24	93	1,886	234
Phou Hin Poun 2-day Trek	8	65	2,972	920
Khammouane				
Buddha Cave 1-day Trek	10	48	643	163
Kong Lor-Natan Homestay	8	172	2,313	1,506
Konglor Boat Trip	-	343	3,430	3,430
Champassak				
Don Daeng Island Camp	8	90	657	564
Xe Pian 2-day Forest Excursion	10	59	1,885	826
Kiet Ngong Elephant Rides	766	1,515	7,504	7,284
Pu Khong Mountain 1-day Trek	8	38	838	558
Total, 14 Products	974	3,143	50,113	26,523

However, whereas in donor-assisted CBT poor people are specifically targeted as beneficiaries from tourism, this is not so in the private sector. Indeed, while it was generally believed that tourism *would* bring benefits, provincial and district officials often assumed that the economic benefits from tourism would automatically spread to all members of the community, including the poor. In fact, while quantitative data exist for many of the CBT projects supported by the ADB and SNV, there is little information on how income from other tourism enterprises is distributed throughout Lao PDR. Clearly, in centres of tourism, where accommodation and restaurant sectors are dominated by small enterprises, run largely with family labour, tourism benefits are considerable but they have not really been quantified (but cf. Harrison and Schipani, forthcoming). More in-depth research is needed to ascertain how far others also benefit, for example through purchases of local agricultural crops, handicrafts and such services as village visits, treks and river trips and tubing.

Table 8.4: A Summary of Financial Benefits at Tourist Destinations Supported by the Mekong Tourism Development Project (March 2005–February 2006)

Location	No. of Tourists	Total Revenue (US$)	Village Revenue Estimates (US$)	Permits / Entrance Fees (US$)
Luang Namtha				
Green Discovery Co.	756	18,108	10,184	366
Nam Ha Ecoguide Service	1366	25,662	18,796	1,148
Muang Sing Ecoguide Service	567	12,941	8,195	0
Vieng Phoukha Ecoguides	79	6,885	2,272	125
Luang Prabang				
Muang Ngoi Kao Village	7,800	195,000	97,500	0
Khammouane				
Buddha Cave/Na Kang Xang	40,000	48,000	40,000	8,000
Champassak				
Ban Mai Singsampanh Market	14,000	168,000	84,000	0
Total	64,727	474,596	260,947	9,639

Lao Tourism: Potential and Issues

The natural and cultural attractions of Lao PDR are considerable. There are vast areas of tropical monsoon forest, numerous ethnic minorities, unspoiled countryside (apart, that is, from the areas bombed by the USA during the Secret War), and a virtually undeveloped hinterland away from the main tourist honeypots. Not surprisingly, perhaps, the country's tourism industry is expanding. It is characterized by a burgeoning, small-scale, locally-owned accommodation sector, essentially concentrated in a few tourism centres (notably Vientiane and Vientiane Province, Luang Prabang, Champassak and Savannakhet), which cater to an increasing number of somewhat young, relatively well-educated, independent, budget travellers, who are interested in the natural, archaeological and cultural attractions of the country (National Tourism Authority of Lao PDR, 2003: 21).

In the tourism centres, the private sector predominates. By contrast, in outlying areas it is government policy, with assistance from the ADB and SNV, to develop CBT, and while the numbers of tourists visiting such projects is relatively small, the projects themselves are considered, by government officials and NGOs, as important as role models for further development in the private sector. It seems that unless external constraints have an impact on tourist demand, visitating will continue to increase for the foreseeable future. Indeed, as indicated in Table 8.5, with tourism accelerating in Cambodia and Vietnam and a mature industry already existing in

Thailand, it is likely that the trend towards multi-country tours will continue to emerge, with Bangkok as the gateway to the region.

It is perhaps the likelihood of further increases in tourist arrivals that simultaneously and paradoxically carries a threat to future tourism development. As far as pro-poor, donor-assisted CBT is concerned, promising projects are now operating, but the future is not entirely rosy. As indicated above, the government has left most tourism development to the private sector, and the emerging tourist 'product' has much to recommend it. However, there are some signs in parts of Lao PDR, for example in the Siphandon area of Champassak, that uncontrolled tourism development may have negative impacts, despite the financial benefits it generates for the poor. Guest houses built too close to the river can pollute the water, and riverbanks are subject to erosion. And while local entrepreneurs are currently driving the sector, if large injections of foreign capital are made in the region (and they are undoubtedly being sought), a new impetus will be given to tourism development. In short, while it might be seen as imperative to encourage investment in tourism in Lao PDR, efforts must *also* be made to put efficient regulatory processes in place to ensure that expansion of the tourism industry, whether emanating from international donors and aid agencies or the private sector, is a sustainable form of development.

More specifically, several issues arise from the preceding discussion. The first concerns the kind of tourism development apparently preferred by Lao tourism authorities, while the second, which is related, focuses on the role of the state in future tourism development. Thirdly, important issues emerge from the current relationship of the donor-sponsored, community-based tourism sector to the much larger but less coherent (and to some extent lower-profile) private sector, *especially* over the extent to which the former can really be distinguished from the latter as a form of *pro-poor tourism*. Finally, and more generally, attention needs to be paid to possible problems emerging from the expansion of roads and other forms of communication, funded largely by the ADB, which will inevitably further incorporate Lao PDR in the regional and global economy and thus, at the same time, expose it to some of the problems found elsewhere in the region.

First, there is some ambivalence about the kinds of tourists Lao PDR wishes to attract. A wide range was targeted in the second *National Tourism Development Plan* (Lao PDR/UNDP/WTO, 1998: 37) but elsewhere it is suggested that Lao tourism policy should focus on 'pro-poor, community-based tourism development' (Lao PDR, 2003: 104). Others stress that higher spending regional and long-haul tourists, with an interest in nature and culture-based activities, will bring considerable economic benefits and yet have minimal negative impacts. At the same time, however, it is realized that the tourism facilities available in Lao PDR are more appropriate for low-spending, independent travellers, or 'backpackers', and this kind of visitor is also welcome,

Table 8.5: Tourist Arrivals in the Lower Mekong Region: Selected Years

	1995	1999	2000	2001	2002	2003	2004
Cambodia	222,000	368,000	466,000	605,000	787,000	701,000	1,055,200
Lao PDR	356,000	614,000	737,000	674,000	736,000	636,000	894,806
Vietnam	---	1,211,000	1,383,000	1,599,000	2,627,988	2,428,735	2,927,873
Thailand	6,952,000	8,651,000	9,579,000	10,133,000	10,873,000	10,082,109	11,737,413

Source: WTO: 1999a; 2002; 2005; ASEAN Tourism Statistics www.aseansec.org/tour_stat/ Total (accessed 26th February 2006).

provided they respect local customs. Whether or not these local perceptions about backpackers holds true merits further research, especially as evidence from elsewhere suggests that while they prefer budget accommodation, they are also likely to stay longer, and spend more on local crafts and souvenirs, than other tourists (Hampton, 1998: 653; Scheyvens, 2002a: 151–155; Westerhausen, 2002: 53–57).

Secondly, as indicated earlier, the efforts of the state, along with the ADB, SNV and other aid agencies, are primarily directed at developing small-scale, donor-supported, community-based tourism enterprises. There is a case for arguing that there should be a more integrated policy, in which the state continues its support for such projects, but *also* creates an enabling environment for the operation of that sector of tourism – the major part – which is dominated by the private sector. So far, perhaps because of financial constraints, state support for the private sector seems to have been limited to producing tourism brochures and, more recently, to attendance at tourism fairs.

Thirdly, it may be that elements of the distinction often made between donor-supported CBT projects and private sector enterprises, at least in Lao PDR, should be reassessed. It is commonly felt, for example, that the former are 'pro-poor', contributing to poverty alleviation, while the latter are frequently considered a less than wholesome tool for 'development'. Such a reassessment is needed for several reasons. Conventionally, it can be argued that NGOs are useful stakeholders in CBT development, and such community-based tourism clearly requires a large amount of technical and financial resources to support surveys, develop products, run training courses, and construct small-scale eco-lodges and other tourist facilities. Without such assistance (even prompting) from NGOs and other international partners, many CBT projects might be delayed or remain on the drawing board. The private sector often lacks the necessary financial and technical resources, and may not even consider such projects potentially worthwhile. By contrast, the argument continues, NGOs and the public sector are well suited to establish best practice models, research CBT regulatory frameworks, and act as mediators to ensure that equitable benefit-sharing mechanisms are put in place. At that point, the business side of CBT can be handed over to the communities themselves, and to private sector tour operators, who obtain a new product to sell at little initial cost to themselves.

This may be so. However, evidence from elsewhere indicates that NGOs are not always best placed to carry the twin burdens of supporting and marketing CBTs. In 1998 in the South Pacific, for instance, a five-day workshop involving government representatives, national tourism organizations, aid agencies, donors and community representatives examined several donor-assisted prestigious CBT projects then operating in South Pacific islands, and concluded that most, in fact, were examples of top-down development, that few – if any – were financially viable or sustainable, that the agendas and time-scales operated by aid agencies bore little resemblance to local requirements, and that most NGO representatives lacked the entrepreneurial and other skills required to run successful businesses.

> A key finding of the workshop was that there are very few examples in the Pacific of successful developments of community-based ecotourism operations in areas of high conservation value. Furthermore, there were few participants prepared to say "yes" to the question of whether these few ecotourism operations would be sustainable once donor assistance ended.
>
> (Tourism Resource Consultants, 1999: 5)

Problems may arise even at the start of a donor-supported CBT enterprise. The assessment by an NGO representative that a site will be commercially viable can be confirmed *only* when it is sufficiently established and seeking tourists. Only then, after a considerable investment of money and human resources, might the private sector be involved, and only then, too, might marketing problems become apparent.

Just as doubt can be cast on the medium- to long-term sustainability of at least some donor-supported 'pro-poor' CBT projects, private sector involvement in tourism may have more 'pro-poor' credentials than is generally recognized. In many parts of Lao PDR, for example, small, locally-owned guest-houses, funded by the sale of livestock and not at all dependent on donor support, play a crucial role in expanding the cash economy and benefiting the poor. Responding to market demand, they emerge from within local communities, cater for the majority of the country's tourists, usually by purchasing local goods and services, and also supply visitors to donor-supported CBT projects. As discussed in more detail elsewhere (Harrison and Schipani, forthcoming), there is a strong possibility that the role of such enterprises in alleviating poverty has been underestimated. Instead of being considered unwelcome competitors of 'alternative' tourism, they might more accurately be regarded as partners in tourism development, and thus accorded some of the technical advice and support provided on a regular basis to donor-supported community tourism projects.

Finally, as the Lao infrastructure is developed, roads built, and airports and river facilities expanded, the impacts of such changes need to be carefully monitored. Communications are usually two-way, and while they facilitate the movement of tourists and goods, they also enable others to move around more easily. Roads, for example, mean increased trade and more intra-regional travel. More commercial traffic on the roads is likely to lead to pollution, disrupt village life, and increase demand for commercial sexual services. Anecdotal evidence and personal observation suggests this demand is already being met.

This is not to suggest that tourism causes prostitution. As Brown makes clear, while local characteristics vary, prostitution has long been established throughout Asia (2000: 1–28) and the background and extent of sex tourism in Southeast Asia, especially Thailand, is sufficiently well known to require little supporting evidence (Meyer, 1988; Truong, 1990). In fact, as both Meyer (1988: 370) and Brown (2000: 11) clearly indicate, most prostitution in the region is provided for local clients rather than tourists. That said, prostitution is clearly exacerbated by tourism, and sex workers catering for Western tourists are able to earn more than those catering only for local clients. At present, though, it would seem the commercial sex trade in Lao PDR is mainly limited to Lao nationals and foreign labourers, and involves few international tourists.

More generally, as the country becomes more 'connected' to the region through transport networks and labour exchange, increased movement within Lao PDR, and across its borders, for commercial and tourist purposes, will undoubtedly expose Lao communities to trends already apparent, for example, in Thailand and Cambodia. Such trends will undoubtedly increase the attraction of the world outside, especially for the young, and increase the threat of an HIV/AIDS epidemic. At the same time, without effective control or planning, more tourists coming through Thailand, where uncontrolled mass tourism has 'led to the degradation and transformation of the principal natural attractions' (Cohen, 2001c: 170), could simply replicate the process in Lao PDR.

Conclusions

It has been argued in this chapter that, since the mid-1980s, tourism has become increasingly important in the economy of Lao PDR, to the extent it is now the country's main earner of foreign exchange, and that the significance of the tourism sector, and its role in poverty alleviation, is likely to continue. It has also been suggested that there is some ambivalence in government and non-government circles about the kind of tourism most appropriate to Lao PDR. On the one hand, considerable efforts (and funds) have been directed by government, by the Asian Development Bank, and by aid agencies (most notably SNV) in developing community-based tourism (CBT). On the other hand, ADB is also heavily involved in developing infrastructures that will facilitate the movement of tourists within Lao PDR and across the region, and in encouraging closer links with the private sector. Indeed, whereas most CBT projects are developed in outlying parts of the country, tourism development in areas of high levels of tourist concentration, most notably Vientiane Municipality and Province, Luang Prabang, Champassak and Savannakket, is largely in the hands of small, largely-unregulated, family-owned and family-operated enterprises, the importance of which to poverty alleviation and more general 'development' still remain to be researched but is likely to be considerable and under-estimated.

Numerous questions, then, need to be asked about the relationship of community-based tourism (CBT) to 'conventional' tourism (CT) – which in Lao PDR is predominantly independent travel and backpacking tourism. First, how far does CBT depend on CT? It could certainly be argued that the former develops only by 'piggy-backing' on the latter. Secondly, is it the case that while CBT is essentially rural, CT is urban-based? Tourism statistics and the interests of the cultural tourists who make up much of the CT sector would seem to suggest this is so. Thirdly, will successful CBT lead to CT? At present, it seems too early to say, but it is a distinct possibility. Fourthly, to what extent can it be argued that *both* sectors of Lao tourism – CBT and CT – are only partially capitalist? The former, with its support from the ADB and the aid agencies, can be considered (at best) only partially orientated to markets or profits, while CT, dominated by small guest houses employing (frequently unpaid) family labour, could equally be regarded as proto-capitalist. Indeed, is there merit in the suggestion that both sectors of Lao tourism might be regarded as contributing to poverty alleviation, and are different forms of 'pro-poor' tourism? If so, one way of bringing these apparently disparate sectors together would be to develop a network of donor-supported CBT projects with firm and expanding links to the private sector, leading to different forms of private-public (or NGO) partnerships. At present, although there is recognition of the need for an overlap between the two, *very* little occurs in practice.

Finally, is Lao tourism – whether CBT or CT – 'sustainable'? It is certainly growing but (as yet) has not reached the level of 'development' (and the associated problems) that have characterized so much of Thai tourism (Cohen, 2001c), or that can be perceived in the urban expansion and over-development of Cambodia's Siem Reap. It is not too late to avoid these dangers, and the goodwill to do so is present throughout Lao tourism. However, a successful strategy for sustainable tourism development has to be predicated on an integrated approach which not only takes due cognisance of the role of CBT, but also understands the role of and co-operates with the thousands of owners of small guest houses and hotels which dominate Lao tourism and who cater for most of the country's tourists.

Authors' Note

David Harrison, a co-author of this paper, first worked in Lao PDR in June 2002 as a consultant with the Asian Development Bank, and later, from 2003 to 2005, as part of an ASEAN–EU Universities Network Programme, 'Building Research Capacity for Pro-poor Tourism'. Funded by the European Commission, this project involved five partner organisations from Europe and South East Asia: the International Institute for Culture, Tourism and Development, at London Metropolitan University; the University of Liège (Belgium); the University of Social Science (Vietnam); Udayana University (Bali, Indonesia) and the National University of Laos. Data on tourism and poverty alleviation were obtained in Lao PDR in July and August 2004, and special thanks are due to Dr Sengdeuane Wayakone, of the National University of Laos, and Dr I Nyoman Adiputra, of Udayana Univiersity, who also participated in the Lao part of the research project. Further information on the project can be obtained from www.iictd.org

9 Southeast Asian Tourism from a Japanese Perspective

Shinji Yamashita

Introduction

Today international tourism has become a gigantic socio-economic phenomenon. According to UNWTO (World Tourism Organization), 842 million tourists travelled across national boundaries in 2006. This figure is expected to reach one billion in 2010 and 1.6 billion in 2020.[1] It is the age of global tourism. Nevertheless, people do not necessarily travel freely all over the world. By analyzing Japanese tourist practices in Korea, Okpyo Moon (1997: 178) has pointed out that the nature of the host-guest relationship and the cultural implications of tourism vary depending on who travels, and where. Therefore, one needs to pay attention to the local situations in a particular context. This chapter examines the socio-cultural implications of Japanese tourist practices in Southeast Asia.

Japanese Overseas Tourism and Southeast Asia

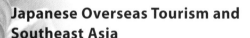

The history of Japanese overseas tourism goes back to the early twentieth century. In 1906, just after Japan's victory in the war with Russia (1904–1905), the *Asahi Shinbun* Newspaper Company organized the first overseas tour to Korea and Manchuria, in which 347 people participated. This was the birth of Japan's overseas tourism, motivated by a desire to visit the sites of the military exploits of the then Japanese empire and to compare developing Japan with its less developed Asian neighbours (Ariyama, 2002: 43–45). With the expansion of the Japanese empire in the first half of the twentieth century, this kind of colonial tourism developed, though the number of overseas tourists at that time was quite limited.

189

After Japan's defeat in the Pacific War in 1945, overseas tourism was restricted for most Japanese, but in 1964, the year of the Tokyo Olympics, the restrictions were removed. In that year, 128,000 Japanese went abroad. Over forty years since then, the number of Japanese overseas tourists has been growing continually. In 2006 there were about 17.5 million Japanese tourists going overseas.[2] The main reason for this rapid development of Japanese overseas tourism was no doubt Japan's economic growth, the increased power of the Japanese yen, and the change of leisure patterns in Japanese society during this period. However, international tourism today is quite sensitive to the political, economic, and even epidemiological conditions in the world. For example, the terrorist attacks of September 11 in 2001, the Bali bombing in October 2002, the SARS (Severe Acute Respiratory Syndrome) epidemic in Asia in 2003, and the second Bali bombing in October 2005, all had a serious impact on international tourist mobility.[3]

As for the countries which Japanese overseas tourists visit, the United States is the number one destination. In 2005,[4] 3.9 million Japanese visited the United States, including 1.5 million going to Hawai'i.[5] After the United States, China (3.4 million in number), Korea (2.4 million), Hong Kong (1.2 million), Thailand (1.2 million), and Taiwan (1.1 million) are the high-ranking popular destinations for Japanese tourists. The Asian region constitutes about 70 per cent of the total overseas tourist market for Japanese, while Europe is assumed to be the most expensive and prestigious destination.[6]

With regard to the Southeast Asian region, 3.6 million Japanese (about 20 per cent of the total Japanese overseas tourists) visited the region in 2005.[7] Among Southeast Asian countries, Thailand is the most popular country. 1.2 million Japanese travelled to Thailand. Other major destinations are Indonesia (622,000 in number), Singapore (589,000), the Philippines (415,000), Malaysia (340,000), and Vietnam (320,000).[8] Vietnam has become increasingly popular in recent years since the start of its open door policy.

The English term 'Southeast Asia' was used for the first time during the Pacific War by military strategists when the Allied Forces established the 'Southeast Asia Command' in Ceylon in 1943. The current Japanese term '*Tônan Ajia*' was introduced after the War as a translation of the English term 'Southeast Asia' , while Hajime Shimizu (2005: 83) pointed out that the Japanese term 'Southeast Asia' – '*Tônan Ajiya*' – was actually used in the teaching of elementary school geography from around the end of World War I until the beginning of Pacific War.[9] Generally, however, before and during the Pacific War, the region was known as *Nan'pô* (the 'Southern regions') or *Nan'yô*, (the 'South Seas'), a region which belonged neither to the East nor the West, the two civilized worlds known to Japan at that time.

Historically, Japanese involvement in the South began in the 1860s, although there had been accidental contacts between Pacific islanders and Japanese fishermen before that. Japanese labour emigration to Hawai'i started in 1868, the first year of the Meiji period. Because of increasing population and limited resources at home, the Japanese government at that time adopted a policy of international emigration. In the 1880s and 1890s, a group of ideologues advocated *nanshin* or 'southward advance'. They emphasized the economic and political backwardness of the Southern regions, and suggested that their development should be the task of Japan. In this view, Japan's advance into the Southern regions can be seen as a method of establishing itself as a 'civilized' country compared to the underdeveloped and backward South. In 1910, Yosaburô Takekoshi popularized the image of what is now Southeast Asia by publishing his *Nangokuki* ('On Southern Countries') based on his journey to Shanghai, Hong Kong, Singapore, Java, Sumatra, and French Indochina (Takekoshi, 1942).

Japanese colonial expansion to the South started with Taiwan in 1895, and continued with Micronesia in 1919.[10] It reached Southeast Asia in 1941, the year the Pacific War broke out. The South was considered as a part of the *Daitôa Kyôeiken* or the Greater East Asian Co-prosperity Sphere. As Minato Kawamura (1993) has argued, in this history of southern expansionism Japan needed a 'primitive and backward South' in order to feel more civilized and advanced. Therefore, dual processes proceeded simultaneously, one of 'orientalizing' other Asian and Pacific regions and the other of 'de-orientalizing' Japan, by conceptually disassociating it from them.

As I have examined elsewhere (Yamashita, 2004), the popular image of the South in Japan was formed through these historical processes. In this image, Southeast Asia is actually ambiguous in terms of cultural distance: it is sometimes assumed to be 'far' ('different'), a remote backward place, but sometimes 'near' ('similar'), the presumed original land of the Japanese people and culture. The Japanese image of Southeast Asia was in this way constructed on the basis of this ambiguous consciousness which I would call 'Japanese Orientalism'.

In the contemporary tourist map in Japan, Southeast Asia is usually classified as 'Asia', though sometimes as 'the Southern Islands'. In particular, there is a category of 'Asian resorts' which actually includes Southeast Asian resorts such as Bali in Indonesia, Phuket in Thailand, Penang and Langkawi in Malaysia, and Cebu in the Philippines. These Asian resorts are often described within a clichéd discourse of 'paradise'. As a tourist brochure expresses it: 'Getting up with chirping of birds, napping on the beach. Nature, people and hospitality, everything is warm. Asian resorts always welcome you gently. For your satisfaction, let's go.' (Jalpkak I'll, *Asian Resorts*, 2005 April–September edition). Here the various hard realities faced by the Southeast Asian countries are erased, leaving a tourist paradise. As a result, many tourists do not even know, for instance, the country to which Bali belongs. For most tourists, Bali is just a resort paradise without a nationality. There is usually no mention of the historical past in which Japan once colonized the region.

In what follows, I discuss the socio-cultural implications of Japanese tourist practices in Southeast Asia by taking the examples of first, Bali in Indonesia, second, Sabah in

Malaysia and third, Bangkok in Thailand. In the examination of these cases, I pay attention particularly to the changing contexts of tourist practices which are caused by changes in Japanese society as well as in the receiving host societies in Southeast Asia.

From Package Tour to Healing Tourism: Bali, Indonesia

Bali is a well known international tourist site in Indonesia. Historically, tourism in Bali goes back to the 1920s or the 1930s when it was discovered as 'the last paradise' by Western artists and scholars such as the German artist Walter Spies, the Mexican illustrator Miguel Covarrubias, the Canadian musicologist Colin McPhee, and anthropologists such as the Americans Jane Belo and Margaret Mead and Briton Gregory Bateson. Under their 'gaze' (cf. Urry, 1990), Balinese culture was re-created for artistic as well as tourist audiences (Yamashita, 2003: Chapter 3).[11]

After the independence of Indonesia, the first five-year development plan under the Suharto regime began in 1969. In this plan, tourism was seen as an important source of foreign exchange earnings for Indonesia, and Bali was designated as the most important of Indonesia's international destinations. The Balinese Provincial Government adopted a policy of development through tourism with a special emphasis on cultural tourism. Since then, Bali has grown successfully as the most important international tourist destination in Indonesia.

However, Balinese tourism has recently experienced serious challenges: the Indonesian economic crisis in 1997, the effects on tourism of September 11 in 2001 and the bombing in the Balinese resort of Kuta in October 2002. As a result of these incidents, tourism in Bali has entered a period of instability. After the bombing incident, the hotel occupancy rate fell drastically. In 2003, the year in which the SARS epidemic occurred in Asia, the number of visitors to Bali went down to 993,000, though in 2004 it recovered to 1.46 million, almost the same level as in 2000.[12] However, the second bombing in October 2005 threatens again to be a further negative influence on tourism in Bali.[13]

In this situation, the number of visitors from Europe and Australia is in drastic decline, while the number of visitors from Asia, especially from Japan and Taiwan, is increasing. In particular, the visitors from Japan have dominated the Balinese international tourism landscape in recent years. Of the 1.46 million 'direct foreign visitors' to Bali in 2004, 326,000 (22 per cent) were from Japan, while 268,000 (18 per cent) were from Australia and 184,000 (13 per cent) were from Taiwan.[14] Therefore, present day tourism in Bali cannot be discussed without taking Japanese tourists into account. The 'last paradise' created by the Western gaze is now being 'Japanized'.

I have examined elsewhere the distinctive features of Japanese tourists in comparison with Westerners on the basis of my research in 1994–1995 (Yamashita, 2003: 89–94). Here I summarize the points which are relevant to the current discussion. First of all, there are differences in the length of stay and the notion of vacation. For

Westerners, stays of one or two weeks are normal, compared with between four to six days for Japanese. In short stay package tours, Japanese tourists are busy seeing sights. When they make their hotel reservations, they generally specify that they must have a room facing the sea, but, as the Balinese guides comment cynically, they may not have any time to look at it, because they are out of the hotel from the early morning to late in the evening! Tourism – *kankô* in Japanese, which literally means 'seeing lights' – may be another kind of 'work' for workaholic Japanese (Sontag, 1973: 10), though this feature is changing as I will suggest later.

The stance toward Balinese culture and the focus of Balinese tourism differs between Japanese and Westerners as well. Misa Matsuda (1989: 43–45) has suggested that tourism in Bali for Japanese should be analyzed not only in relation to exoticism but also to nostalgia. To Westerners, Balinese culture with its *barong* dance (lion dance), Hindu temples, and rice terraces may look exotic, but to the Japanese the *barong* dance is reminiscent of the Japanese lion dance (*shishimai*), the Hindu temples may remind them of those in Kyoto and Nara, and rice terraces are quite normal in the Japanese rural areas. Nostalgia rather than exoticism is thus a more important factor for Japanese tourists. In terms of shopping, the Japanese buy souvenirs not only to remember their travels but also for obligatory social reasons. Therefore, the amount they buy may be considerable. The Japanese make up 20 to 30 per cent of the foreign tourists in Bali, but they are said to account for 50 per cent of the money spent on souvenirs.

In the international tourist landscape of Bali, there is a sort of national or ethnic territorialization of tourist space. For example, when Japanese tourists start to arrive, Western tourists tend to leave for the 'unspoiled' areas where there are no Japanese. If the mass of Japanese start to go to Ubud, Western tourists go to Candidasa in eastern Bali, or sometimes to the island of Lombok. On the other hand, Japanese tourists do not like tourists from Taiwan, and when they are with a Taiwanese group in a restaurant, they may claim that they are noisy or untidy. Furthermore, foreign tourists (whether Japanese or Western) and domestic (i.e. Indonesian) tourists tend to use different classes of hotels and restaurants. International tourism is a space in which people of different nationalities meet together, but in reality they are segregated as well. It emphasizes the socio-cultural differences not only between the hosts and guests but also among the tourists themselves.

These kinds of observations are based on stereotypes and there may be a significant level of individual variation. Further, the group-oriented package tours targeted at Japanese mass tourists underwent a change in the 1990s, with more stress on individual free choice. In 1991, *Jalpak*, the Japan Air Lines group tour operator, coined a new brand name '*I'll*' with a connotation 'I will choose' for their tourist commodity. In this change, a recent tourist brochure describes Bali as 'the island which touches your heart' with a stress on the word 'heart' or *kokoro*: 'The popularity of Bali has increasingly spread. People who have experienced the island find their hearts moved, and they come back to visit the island one more time, and then another. We can regain the things we have lost one by one, surrounded by the gods, by nature, and by the wise people who have chosen to live among them. As if in a second homeland, the days pass with our hearts completely at peace' (Jalpak I'll, *JAL Bali*, 1996 April–September edition). Here Bali is presented as a 'spiritual homeland' for Japanese tourists who visit it repeatedly.

Another remarkable characteristic of Japanese international tourism is the active involvement of young women in their twenties and thirties. They occupy approximately half of the total women overseas tourists (Kokudokôtsûshô, 2005: 36). Bali is especially popular among young Japanese women. A women's magazine once published a special issue on going to Bali in search of 'healing' or *iyashi*: 'Both love and work are a struggle. Self-healing is difficult while at the same time you are fighting. Mobile phones, the departure bells in crowded trains, the electrical noises at pedestrian crossings – if you are tired of everything like this, give up and leave Japan. Bali is only about ten hours' flight from Narita. There, with the dazzling blue sky and the scents, people welcome you with warm and nostalgic smiling faces. While the balmy breezes blow, yogurt and the essence of tropical flowers, and the natural beauty treatment provided by the sea will be the best cure for your body. This is your natural reward for your tired body. So if you want to heal yourself, cross the sea' (*Rinku*, 1996 July–August edition). Bali is here seen as a place of healing where young Japanese women can recover from the battlefield of the work place in Japan.

In the relaxed atmosphere of a place of healing they are also in search of *adventure*. This results in many romances in Bali. It is against this background that the phenom-enon of Japanese brides in Bali has developed. In 1995 when I carried out research, there were more than four hundred such cases, as I have examined in detail elsewhere (Yamashita, 2003: 94–100).[15] After their marriages to Balinese men, many of the Japanese brides work in the tourist sector in places such as souvenir shops, boutiques, restaurants and 'homestay' accommodation. It is interesting to note, however, that many of them have no intention of giving up their Japanese nationality and becoming Indonesians: they are not conscious of abandoning the country they have migrated from. They should perhaps be seen not as migrants but rather as 'long-stay' tourists searching for their own 'real' selves. So a recent tourist brochure therefore states: 'This is a paradise. You will discover another version of yourself that you do not know' (Jalpak I'll, *Asian Resorts*, 2005 April–September edition).

From Timber Industry to Ecotourism: Sabah, Malaysia

The State of Sabah, located in the northeastern part of Malaysian Borneo, is becom-ing a new site of international tourism in Southeast Asia. Since the early 1990s, Sabah has introduced a policy to develop tourism in place of the timber industry, which formerly provided the basis of the economy. By pursuing this policy, the State Government of Sabah intends not only to profit from tourism but also to conserve the tropical rain forest in Borneo, the second largest in the world after the Amazon, which has been critically reduced because of decades of over-logging. In this context, ecotourism deserves special attention.[16]

The 'Visit Sabah 2000' project put emphasis on promoting ecotourism with the theme, 'Malaysian Borneo: The New Millennium Nature Adventure Destination', which focused on tropical forests and seas with unique wild animals and plants such as orangutans, the rafflesia flowers, and pitcher plants (*Nepenthes villosa*). According to STPC (Sabah Tourism Promotion Corporation; currently Sabah Tourism Board), the primary aim of this event was to create tourist awareness of Sabah. Ecotourism is thus 'a highly specialized segment of tourism . . . based on people's interest in nature and conservation and their willingness to travel to pursue this interest' (Chong, 1993: 3). Looking at Sabah's tourism statistics, the number of visitors to Sabah increased from 520,000 in 1995 to 1.77 million in 2004. The number of international arrivals increased more than four times from 182,000 in 1995 to 792,000 in 2004.[17] Sabah tourism grew steadily during these years in spite of negative factors such as the Asian economic crisis in 1997, the terrorism of September 11 in 2001, and the SARS epidemic in 2003.

In the Sabah tourism market, Asian tourists play an important role. In 2004, 82 per cent of international visitor arrivals in Sabah were from Asian countries.[18] Visitors from neighbouring ASEAN countries made up 54 per cent of the total. In particular, 37 per cent (290,000 in number) came from Indonesia. However, they were not necessarily tourists but guest workers. The same is the case with Filipinos (51,000).[19] The Taiwanese were a major tourist group, and they accounted for 10 per cent (79,000) of the total.[20] Tourists from Mainland China (35,000) and South Korea (30,000) have also increased in recent years. Tourists from Japan numbered 44,000.[21] Most Japanese who visit Sabah come to dive at the Islands of Mabul and Sipadan, famous diving spots. Westerners, including Europeans, Northern Americans, Australians and New Zealanders, accounted for approximately 28 per cent of the total. Among Europeans, the British (28,000, including the Irish) were the largest group, reflecting their previous colonial connections. Western tourists have increased in recent years, particularly the Australians (34,000) who have shifted their destination from Bali to Sabah, after the Bali bombing incident in 2002.

During my research from 1999 to 2004, I was a participant observer of several ecotours. Here, I will take up the cases of Sukau in the Kinabatangan Basin and the Islands of Mabul and Sipadan. First, throughout the Kinabatangan River Basin near Sukau, which is located 135 kilometres from Sandakan, there remain tropical rainforests which function as wildlife sanctuaries. The tourists are mostly Europeans, and sometimes Japanese. They go on a cruise along the Kinabatangan River in motor canoes and enjoy watching the wildlife. In the guest book of the eco-lodge, many of these tourists recorded their experiences. A guest wrote, for example: 'Wonderful to stay two nights here far into the jungle of Borneo. This is an unforgettable experience, really something out of the ordinary. So far away from traffic and pollution this truly is a place for relaxation.' Another noted: 'I hope that this centre in the forest is the model for the next Millennium.' The Kinabatangan River Basin thus provides tourists with rich tropical fauna and flora to be watched, a place of relaxation far away from metropolitan centres, and a sustainable model for the future.

However, one should note that animals were in fact driven into the remaining forests because the original forests were cut down for logging and then for the planting of oil palms particularly from the 1960s to the 1980s. Actually seas of oil palm plantations now surround the Kinabatangan River Basin forests. Looking at the forests in this way, one cannot help feeling that ecotourism is ironically a final form of exploitation of Sabah's tropical rainforests. Or one may point out that what tourists do under the name of ecotourism is rooted in what the anthropologist Renato Rosaldo (1989: 68–87) has called 'imperialist nostalgia' in which imperialists are searching for something that they have in fact destroyed. Japanese also are responsible for the destruction of forests, for they have imported and consumed a huge amount of Sabah timber.

Second, on the Island of Mabul, which is located thirty minutes by boat from Sempurna on the east coast of Sabah, there is a resort called Sipadan Water Village.[22] Built in the local Bajau people's style of *kampung ayer* ('water village' or houses built over the sea on piles), the Water Village was opened as a Japanese–Malaysian joint venture. At the time of my research in 2000, the tourists there were mostly from Japan.[23] In Japan, diving has created a new category of tourism over the last fifteen years or so and Sipadan and Mabul have become famous among Japanese divers. One of the tourists who came from Chiba, the Metropolitan Tokyo area, made the following comments: 'It is wonderful to stay at the Water Village. In the sea I could meet various kinds of fish. I saw their eyes through a camera in the water. That was a fabulous healing experience.' Another stated: 'Commuting in Tokyo is quite stressful. At home we always put on the television without watching. Here are neither commuting trains nor televisions. I like such a life. That is why I come here repeatedly.'[24]

Interestingly, the majority of the workers in this resort were Filipinos. There are many Filipinos who migrate to look for jobs in Sabah. The fact that they speak English well is particularly suitable for the international tourism business. Therefore it is Filipinos who welcome the visitors at this Malaysian resort.[25] Actually, on the Island of Mabul there are Filipino settlements with approximately 2,000 people. The 'ethnoscape', to borrow Arjun Appadurai's term (1977: Chapter 3), of the Water Village is therefore transnational: it was established as a Japanese–Malaysian joint venture mainly for international tourists serviced by Filipino guest workers within a Malaysia–Indonesia–Philippines border zone.

In this ecotourism paradise, a shocking incident took place in April 2000. An armed Filipino Muslim group led by Abu Sayyaf, which was said to be related to the terrorist group Al Qaeda, captured twenty-one people, including ten Western tourists, on the Island of Sipadan and took them hostage, bringing them to the Island of Jolo, in the southern Philippines. In September 2000, a similar attack had occurred on another island. These terrorist attacks broke the dream of ecotourism and reminded us of another reality of the current world system.

In fact, ecotourism is regarded as a special niche market for wealthy tourists who come from the rich North. As the Japanese anthropologist Mitsuho Ikeda (1996) argues from his research in Costa Rica, ecotourism is a cultural product of Western middle-class values and ideology toward the natural environment. Therefore, it is a good example of Pierre Bourdieu's concept of the 'class distinction of taste', because travel, like knowledge of food, wine, arts and music, may assist in differentiating one's sophisticated self from others who lack such knowledge or appreciation (Bourdieu, 1984; see also Mowforth and Munt, 1998: 130). In Sabah, the Taiwanese are generally not interested in ecotourism. They are typical mass tourists who come to spend holidays in a group. It is the European and Japanese tourists who show their interests in ecotourism. However, there may be a further distinction between Europeans and Japanese: Europeans are much more concerned with forests, while Japanese are concerned with the sea.[26]

Although ecotourism is getting known in Japan, the Japanese tourist industry is reluctant to adopt the word 'ecotourism', because of its image in the Japanese tourism market as a sort of specialist tourism to unexploited areas without sufficient marketable demand. So in their tourist brochures they usually use the term 'nature tourism' rather than ecotourism. Further, one should also recognize that ecotourism has been developed on the basis of the modern Western conception of nature as opposed to the world of human existence. However, the concept of nature varies from culture to culture. In Japan, nature is traditionally not regarded as opposed to human existence, which is itself part of nature.

In this regard, it is interesting to note that some ecotour programmes in Japan are concerned with *sato-yama*, the 'village-mountain', which was traditionally utilized by the villagers as a sort of village commons for gathering necessities such as firewood. Humanized nature was thus preserved by utilizing nature. *Sato-yama* is in this way seen as a model of natural and human coexistence which can be revitalized in the context of tourism (Shimomura, 2002). Further, in Japan there is the animistic belief that natural places such as forests, rivers or the sea are places in which spirits or deities reside. Nature is therefore also conceived of as a domain for the supernatural.

One may find a similar kind of conceptualization of nature in Southeast Asia as well. In this respect, it is interesting to refer to the homestay programme, newly introduced in Sabah in 2002. In this programme, some villages offer community-based ecotourism in their areas. *Miso Walai Homestay* at Batu Puteh Village in the Kinabatangan River Basin, for instance, may be the most successful case. In this homestay programme, tourists can participate in local village life and encounter nature and the culture of the local community with local ecotour guides. Activity programmes include a river cruise, cultural performances, jungle trekking, handicraft making, paddy planting, farming and wedding ceremonies.[27] Although the homestay programme still lacks skill in basic marketing planning, it is an interesting attempt to develop community-based ecotourism on the basis of local conceptions of nature for their local benefit.

From Sex Tourism to Lifestyle Migration: Bangkok, Thailand

Thailand is undoubtedly the most successful country in Southeast Asia in terms of tourist development. International tourist arrivals in Thailand increased from 81,000 in 1960 to 11.7 million in 2004.[28] The growth accelerated especially after 1987 when the 'Visit Thailand Year' project was carried out. The tourism sector has been the number one foreign currency earner since 1982 (except for 1991). The 2004 revenue from international tourism is estimated at 384 billion baht. In terms of the number of international arrivals to Thailand by country of residence for the year 2004, Japan (1.2 million in number) was ranked number two, following Malaysia (1.4 million), and then Korea (911,000), China (780,000), Singapore (738,000) and Hong Kong (665,000). Visitors from Asian countries of the total international arrivals to Thailand amounted to 60 per cent, while the Western share was 29 per cent. From the Western countries, the largest group was from the UK (635,000), followed by the USA (567,000), Germany (450,000), Australia (397,000) and France (252,000).[29]

As many analysts have pointed out, sex tourism has been an important element in Thai tourism. It developed in the 1960s, especially after the Thai Government and the American Army agreed on 'rest and recreation vacations' for American soldiers in 1965. During the Vietnam War, prostitution was popularized, even though legally prostitution in Thailand was prohibited in 1961. After the Vietnam War ended in 1975, the entertainment business for international tourists instead of American soldiers was promoted by the Thai Government in order to gain foreign currency and also to meet the needs of the jobless sex workers. It was one of the remarkable features of Thailand's international tourism that the proportion of male tourists has been much larger than that of females: in the heyday of sex tourism in the first half of the 1980s, the male proportion was over 70 per cent (Tourism Authority of Thailand statistics cited in Kusaka, 2000: 60).

In his book on prostitution and tourism in Southeast Asia, Thanh-Dam Truong (1990: 178) quoted examples of advertisements for sex tours published by European tourist agents in the 1970s and 1980s. For example: 'Thailand is a world full of extremes and the possibilities are unlimited . . . especially when it comes to girls. Still it appears to be a problem for visitors in Thailand to find the right places where they can indulge in unknown pleasures. It is frustrating to have to ask in broken English where you can pick up pretty girls. Roise has done something about this. For the first time in history, you can book a trip to Thailand with erotic pleasures included in the price (Roise Reisen, West Germany).'

Japanese tourists were also involved in sex tourism in Asian countries, particularly in the 1970s and 1980s: this occurred first in Taiwan, then in Korea, and later in the Philippines and Thailand, to such an extent that an anti-sex tourism movement developed among feminists in Japan (Matsui, 1993: 61–122). Concerning Japanese sex tourism in Bangkok, Yôko Kusaka has reported, based on her informant who was once a tour operator in Bangkok: 'The staff of the local tour operators in contract with Japanese tour agents welcomed Japanese tour groups at the airport to accompany them to the hotels by a big bus. At the hotel, Thai girls with the job of "special services" waited for them and they accompanied each tourist from the group to their rooms. Also, a big bus was prepared to visit massage parlors in the city and the group returned to the hotel in the bus after they received the special services' (Kusaka, 2000: 58).

The Japanese sexual invasion into other Asian countries occurred in parallel with Japanese economic expansion in the region. Japan also exported the Japanese type of sex industry to satisfy the needs of these Japanese 'business soldiers'. In Taniya Ward in the city of Bangkok, for example, the Japanese style of entertainment business was developed (Kusaka, 2000). Bangkok thus became a world famous 'sex paradise' with the image of gentle Thai girls in the 'land of smiles'. It is said that 200,000 women work in this tourist-oriented sex industry.[30]

However, sex tourism has been criticized by feminists as well as human rights activists. Furthermore, in the 1990s the threat of AIDS and the efforts of the Thai Government to change the touristic image of Thailand led to a decline of sex tourism. Sex tourism is therefore giving way to other kinds of entertainment business.[31] In this change current Japanese tourist guidebooks on Thailand have come to put the emphasis on high quality resort tourism at luxurious hotels, gourmet tourism in Thai cuisine, health tourism together with women's beauty-treatment clinics and Thai-style massage, and shopping tourism of 'Asian tastes' goods which have become popular in Japan.

Along with these changes, there is an increasing number of Japanese tourists to Bangkok who are attracted by the Thai style of living. Mayumi Ono (2005) has examined young Japanese who pursue such an alternative lifestyle in Thailand. According to her, this is a new form of non-labour migration from countries with highly developed economies to those with less developed and still growing economies. They go to Bangkok because they just want to live there for a while to study the language and work (sometimes illegally), or because they are attracted by Thai culture, lifestyle, environment and people. One of her informants, a thirty-eight-year-old man, explained his motivation for living in Thailand as follows: 'I feel more comfortable and relaxed living in Thailand than living in the West. Bangkok is such a lively city that I've never felt inconvenience living here. Bangkok is modern enough that I can enjoy my life. Five years ago, I visited Thailand for the first time in my life. Since then I [have] lived in Thailand several times. I always missed Thailand while in Japan. I migrated to Thailand intending to live here permanently. I do not want to go back to Japan because Japan has a gloomy atmosphere with a long lasting recession' (Ono, 2005: 7).

Moving from gloomy Japan to lively Bangkok, this man and others sought an alternative life. In this sense they are what Machiko Sato (2001) has called 'lifestyle migrants'. Another of Ono's informants, a thirty-two-year-old woman, stated: 'I thought Japanese lose out on their lives. Since Thai people are so relaxed and human, I felt ridiculous that I was so enthusiastic and self-sacrificing for my job. I realized that I do not like work. Thailand taught me to be more relaxed, how to enjoy my life, and that you do not need to work. Living here is my second life, so I want to do something enjoyable' (Ono, 2005: 8).

Since the bubble economy burst in the early 1990s, Japan has been in a long period of economic recession and stagnation. In this atmosphere of social depression, some young people have lost their aim in life and have doubts about the values which have supported Japan's modernity and economic growth. They head for Thailand and discover a people who live according to other principles of life such as *mai pen rai* ('do not care') and *sabai* ('comfort' or 'pleasant'). They are attracted by this kind of Thai style of living.

A book on 'Bangkok-goers', edited by the Japanese travel writer Yûji Shimokawa, includes the story of a young man who stays at a guest house in Kaosan Street in the city, while enjoying doing nothing. In Japan he works in a car factory in Kanagawa prefecture as a part-time worker. He earns one million yen (approximately 8,300 US dollars) per year by working for a few months. Then, he goes to Bangkok with a tourist visa which allows him to stay for two months. After two months he extends his visa one more month. If it expires, he goes to a neighbouring country such as Cambodia, Laos, Myanmar or Malaysia to get a new tourist visa. This makes it possible to stay for six months in all. If he runs out of money, he comes back to Japan to earn (Shimokawa, 2001: 152). This kind of young man is called *furita* (a part-time worker without fixed occupation) in Japan. They, together with the NEET ('Not in Education, Employment, or Training'), have become a socio-economic problem in Japan. The young Japanese who head for Thailand should be examined as a part of this phenomenon.

Southeast Asian Tourism from a Japanese Perspective

As has been mentioned, historically Southeast Asia for Japanese was an ambiguous place in terms of cultural distance. It was regarded as a backward region as compared with advanced Japan. At the same time it was considered as the 'homeland' of Japanese culture (cf. Iwata, 1975). In the contemporary tourist market, Southeast

Asia is packaged as a 'paradise' – natural as well as cultural – in which Japanese tourists can relax and enjoy holidays in the magical time-space machinery of tourism. What are then the distinctive features of the Japanese way of encountering Southeast Asia in the context of tourism? I will make three major points.

Firstly, unlike Western tourists who tend to see Southeast Asia as an exotic place in their tradition of Orientalism (Said, 1978), Japanese tourists are likely to experience Southeast Asian culture as something familiar rather than exotic. Of course, there are differences in language and other cultural traits between Japan and Southeast Asia. However, underlying these surface differences, they feel that there is a fundamental similarity. Within this framework Japanese tourists often regard Southeast Asia as a *natsukashii* or nostalgic place where they can find what they have lost in Japan's modernization. In contrast, Europe or the United States is regarded as a more 'advanced' world, therefore a place of *akogare* (longing, aspiration, or goal) in the sense that the West has been providing Japan with a model of development since the Meiji Restoration (1868). Further, there is the contemporary cultural proximity created newly by the Japanese cultural industry, from Hello Kitty children's goods to *karaoke*, and from *Doraemon* comics to the television drama, 'Tokyo Love Story'. Japanese tourists feel at ease when they find this Asian popular culture in common.

Secondly, the keyword for contemporary Japanese tourists who visit Southeast Asia is *iyashi*, or 'healing'. In all the cases examined in this chapter, we have come across the theme of healing repeatedly. Recent Japanese tourist brochures make use of the word 'healing' to attract tourists. For example: 'Flowers, greens and smiles of people heal you in Balinese time' (Jalpak I'll, *JAL Bali*, 2005 October–2006 March edition); 'Asian Resorts: Cheerful heart comes back with healing tours provided by Look JTB' (Japan Tourist Bureau, *Look JTB, Asian resorts*, 2005 April–2006 March edition); and 'Asian Paradise: Full of nature: Warmness of People. Here is a healing resort which cures your broken heart' (Kinki Japan Tourist, *Holiday, Asian Paradise*, 2005 October–2006 April edition). The link between healing and tourism is not necessarily new in Japan. From the Edo period (1600–1868) on, there was a tradition of hot water cures and people visited hot springs (*onsen)* to 'rest their bones'. Even today, going to hot springs is still the most popular purpose for Japanese domestic tourism. What is new is that contemporary Japanese find resting places to recover themselves abroad, particularly in Southeast Asia, where time flows differently – more slowly and easily – than it does in Japan, and economically it costs them less.

Thirdly, in recent Japanese international tourism, the distinction between travelling and dwelling, or tourism and migration, has become blurred. This may be the case with the young Japanese women in Bali and with the young 'long-stay' travellers/ dwellers in Bangkok as examined in the previous sections. This is also the case of the 'long-stay' tourism in which retired elderly people have been moving to foreign places such as Thailand, Malaysia or Indonesia, in search of meaningful lives after retirement (Yamashita and Ono, 2006). They are coming to the fore as part of the recent changing demographic and socio-economic patterns in contemporary Japan. Host countries in Southeast Asia have provided a special kind of retirement visa such as 'non-immigrant "o-a" (long stay)' and 'non-immigrant "o" (pension)' in Thailand, 'Malaysia my second home programme' in Malaysia, and *lansia* or *lanjut usia* (retirement) in Indonesia. These tourists belong to the category of persons on the move in the sense that James Clifford (1977: 2) has termed 'dwelling-in-travel' and become lifestyle migrants to whom a classic definition of the tourist as one who returns home after the experience of a change can no longer be easily applied.[32]

To sum up, Japanese tourists see Southeast Asia not as a place of exoticism, but rather a place to which they feel a cultural proximity. They are likely to find the 'good old Japan' that contemporary Japan has lost in Southeast Asia. One can see here both Japan's superiority over Southeast Asia in terms of economic development on the one hand, and nostalgia for the old Asian socio-cultural traditions which Japan has lost due to development on the other. This may be a contemporary version of the Japanese ambiguous consciousness toward Southeast Asia which has its roots in Japan's colonial occupation of the region. Within this perspective, the current Southeast Asia has thus become a sort of receptacle for socio-cultural 'refugees' (Sugimoto, 1993: 175) from the rich but stressful Japan under the name of a tourist 'paradise'.

Conclusion

It is noteworthy that in the Southeast Asian tourism market tourists from Asian countries play a major role. Asians travel in Asia. This fact may be important for the study of Southeast Asian tourism, but has not yet been investigated in any detail. This chapter has examined tourism in Southeast Asia through the lens of Japanese tourists who are a major group within Southeast Asian tourism. For contemporary Japanese tourists Southeast Asia is staged as a 'paradise' usually without the historical relations between Japan and Southeast Asia. It is not difficult to see here what Johannes Fabian (1983) has termed the 'denial of coevalness'. Southeast Asia in this context is a sort of fantasy world in which 'Japanese Orientalism', once prevailing in the history of Japan's colonization of Asia, is still at work within a new form of international tourism.

However, the real Southeast Asia is of course not a paradise and does not represent Japan's nostalgic past either. Japan and Southeast Asia exist in the same contemporary world system. This fact may become much more important if we turn our eyes from tourism to migration as is the case with 'long-stay' tourism or lifestyle migration. Although research on tourism and migration has been carried out separately, linking the study of tourism with migration may give us a new perspective on the contemporary lifestyles of 'living transnationally' in the age of global mobility in Asia.

Notes

1 World Tourism Organization website: www.world-tourism.org.

2 Japan National Tourist Organization website: www.jnto.go.jp.

3 Since 1998 the number of Japanese overseas tourists has been going up and down due to unstable factors such as economic crisis, war, terrorism and the SARS epidemic mentioned. Particularly in 2003 the figure dropped to 13.3 million (19.5 per cent down from the previous year) due to the Iraq war and the SARS epidemic in Asia. According to 2006 statistical data, the latest available, the number of Japanese overseas tourists recovered to 17.5 million, the second highest figure following 17.8 million in 2000 (Japan National Tourist Organization website: www.jnto.go.jp).

4 I use 2005 statistical data here, because 2006 statistical data are not complete in terms of destinations to visit. See Japan National Tourist Organization website: www.jnto.go.jp.

5 During the period from 2000 to 2006, there were obvious changes taking place in Japanese overseas tourist destinations, which reflected sensitively conditions throughout the world after September 11. The number of Japanese tourists to the USA went down from 5.1 million in 2000 to 3.8 million in 2005. The number of tourists to Hawaii (1.5 million) also went down. On the other hand, the number of visitors to China increased to 3.4 million (Kokudokôtsûshô ed., 2005: 34; Japan National Tourist Organization website: www.jnto.go.jp). A tourist shift from the USA to China may also reflect Japan's recent economic shift in the same direction. In 2006 China (3.75 million) surpassed the USA (3.67 million) in terms of the number of Japanese visitors.

6 Japan National Tourist Organization website: www.jnto.go.jp. The Asian region is important for Japan's inbound tourism as well. The 2005 statistical data show that 69 per cent of the international visitors to Japan were from Asian countries.

7 ASEAN–Japan Center website: www.asean.or.jp.

8 As for minor destinations, 138,000 Japanese travelled to Cambodia, 23,000 to Laos, and 20,000 to Myanmar (Burma) in 2005 (Japan National Tourist Organization website: www.jnto.go.jp).

9 The use of the term, however, is quite complex, as Shimizu writes: 'The [Japanese] term 'Southeast Asia' – 'Tônan Ajiya' – had first to be erased from elementary and middle school textbooks during the occupation leaving no trace of the regional concept created by the pre-war Japanese. Then 'Tônan Ajia' was introduced to post-war Japan as a translation of the English term 'South East Asia' and a concept compatible with the United States' global strategy' (Shimizu, 2005: 105). Therefore, we have to distinguish the current Japanese term 'Southeast Asia' from the former one.

10 Actually, Palau had been under Japanese occupation since 1914.

11 I have already published a book on tourism in Bali (Yamashita, 2003). This section is based mainly on the discussion in Chapter 7 of the book which deals with Japanese

tourists. Fieldwork in Bali was carried out in five separate research trips between 1988 and 1996, funded by the grant-in-aid for scientific research from the Japanese Ministry of Education, Culture, Sports, Science and Technology, in cooperation with LIPI (the Indonesian Institute of Sciences), Jakarta, Indonesia. I revisited Bali in 2005 and 2006.

12 Bali Tourism Board Website: www.bali-tourism-board.com.

13 In 2005 the number of direct foreign tourist arrivals to Bali decreased to 1.39 million slightly down from the previous year (Bali Tourism Board Website: www.bali-tourism-board.com). However, I do not have data enough to discuss the influence of the second bombing incident at the time of writing this chapter. My description and analysis of Balinese tourism in this chapter, is therefore, concerned with the period before the second bombing. See the chapter by Darma Putra and Michael Hitchcock in this book.

14 Bali Tourism Board Website: www.bali-tourism-board.com.

15 The number of marriages between Japanese women and Balinese men seems to have increased after my research in 1995. Tôko Shirakawa (2002: 153) reported that there were about forty cases in 1998, and about fifty cases in 1999.

16 This section is based on an abridged version of the paper presented at the 9th biennial conference of the International Academy for the Study of Tourism, held in Beijing, China, June 30 to July 6, 2005. A fuller version will be published as part of the conference publication (Yamashita, forthcoming). The fieldwork in Sabah on which this section is based was done during six separate trips from 1999 to 2004, funded by the grant-in-aid for scientific research from the Japanese Ministry of Education, Culture, Sports, Science and Technology (later by the Japan Society of the Promotion of Science) in cooperation with Institute of Development Studies (IDS), Kota Kinabalu, Sabah, Malaysia.

17 I have used the statistical data from my research in Sabah. According to the latest statistical data available now, the number of visitors to Sabah increased up to 2.09 million in 2006. However, international visitors slightly decreased to 751,000. See Sabah Tourism Board website: www.sabahtourism.com.

18 Calculation from the statistical data by Sabah Tourism Board for 2004.

19 In 1997 it was estimated that of Sabah's total population of 2,663,800, approximately 30 per cent (784,100 in number) were non-Malaysian immigrants, including 410,000 illegal immigrants – 290,000 Indonesians and 120,000 Filipinos (Kurus, 1998: 161–162).

20 The share of Taiwanese tourists was 27 per cent in 2000 but the figure dropped in 2003, presumably due to the SARS epidemic that year, though Taiwanese people remained a major tourist group in Sabah in 2004. However, in 2006 Taiwanese tourists decreased to 47,000. Except for Indonesia and Philippines, the top three countries of international visitors to Sabah in 2006 are: Brunei (67,000 in number), South Korea (57,000), and Taiwan (as mentioned). See Sabah Tourism Board website: www.sabahtourism.com.

21 This is quite a small number if one remembers the fact that about 300,000 Japanese visited Malaysia that year.

22 Although the resort is not located on Sipadan but on Mabul Island, the name of Sipadan is used, because Sipadan is much more famous as a diving spot. The Island of Sipadan is located about thirty minutes by boat from Mabul.

23 However, in a later visit to Mabul in August 2004, I found the situations changed. The number of Japanese tourists had decreased and instead there were remarkable numbers of Italian tourists. There were also Singaporeans and West Malaysians.

24 Interview, September 2000, Mabul.

25 In my August 2004 visit, however, I found that Filipino workers had decreased, while Malaysian workers increased. This was due to the recent change in Sabah Government immigration policy in which it has become difficult for employers to hire foreign workers because an expensive employment fee for guest workers has been imposed.

26 Therefore, in Sabah, tour operators specialize in different kinds of tourist markets, which correspond to tourism commodities divided along ethnic lines such as European, Japanese and Taiwanese. Japanese diving tourists may be included in the category of eco-tourism, even though they usually regard themselves as 'divers' rather than 'ecotourists'.

27 It is run by Koperasi Pelancongan Miso Walai Homestay or Miso Walai Homestay Tourism Cooperation. According to the chairman of the Cooperation, they accepted 425 visitors in 2002, and 530 visitors in 2003. The Cooperation earned about 110,000 RM or 29,000 US dollars in 2003.

28 In 2006, the latest statistics available, international arrivals to Thailand numbered 13.8 million. Tourism Authority of Thailand website: www2.tat.or.th

29 Tourism Authority of Thailand website: www2.tat.or.th

30 There is no exact figure for the number of prostitutes. Kusaka (2000: 68) has given figures from various sources. The Thai Ministry of Welfare mentioned the figure of 63,941, based on the research in 1998. In the same year a research team from Mahidon University provided an estimate of 90,000. The maximum figure reported so far is 2.8 million. Professor Pasuk at Chulalongkorn University estimates 200,000, based on the number of brothels recognized by the police.

31 Erik Cohen (1993) analyzes the subtle changes in the relationship between tourist-oriented prostitutes and their clients.

32 The Japanese publisher Diamond Inc, known for a popular travel guidebook *Chikyû no arukikata* (Globe trotters travel guide) series, has started to publish a new series of guidebooks featuring 'long-stay' tourism called *Chikyû no kurashikata* (Globe dwelling guide).

10

Cultural and Gender Politics in China–Vietnam Border Tourism

Yuk Wah Chan

Introduction: The Political Space of Border and Gender

After a decade of border shutdown, the Vietnamese–Chinese borderline was reopened in 1991 following a series of diplomatic negotiations between China and Vietnam. Border tourism began to grow after that and gradually developed into one of the development strategies of the border regions in the north of Vietnam. Lao Cai, the capital town of Lao Cai province, is situated opposite the county of Hekou in the Chinese province of Yunnan across the Red River. A town devastated by the border war of 1979, Lao Cai now sees a regular flow of Chinese tourists walking over its border-crossing bridge. The Chinese tourists, with their colourful caps and tour guides holding colourful flags, brighten up the main streets and market of the small border town. They hover over the souvenir shops and snack stalls in the market and bargain fiercely with their Vietnamese hosts.

To the Vietnamese, the Chinese have been familiar neighbours for many centuries. However, the Chinese coming to Vietnam as mass tourists is a novel experience. Not only has border tourism brought about a new boom to the economy of the border regions, it has also created a social space for the interactions of the Chinese and the Vietnamese within a new trans-border political economy, and has become a locus for exercising new forms of power. This chapter analyses the political space of border and gender within the interactive space of trans-border tourism. It examines how the growth of tourism has effectively sexualized and sensualized the border with the increasing availability of wealth and the

206

rising economic expectations in the borderlands. Both Chinese men and Vietnamese women have been utilising different forms of capital to engage in trans-border sex games and trade.

Borders, which have become increasingly important in academic studies (see, for example, Wilson and Donnan, 1999; 1998; 1994; Ganster and Lorey, 2005; Heyman and Cunningham, 2004; Staudt and Spencer, 1998; Walker, 1999; Evans, Hutton and Eng, 2000), are often intriguingly ambiguous. The re-opened Sino–Vietnamese border is supposed to facilitate economic integration and reduce differences through cultural and technological exchanges, but it is also immediately producing new cultural and gender divides. This chapter firstly examines the prominence of Vietnamese brothels and the sexualization of the borderlands within tourism discourses and activities, which have rendered these spaces as peripheral sex 'playgrounds', catering to the sexual desires and economic dominance of Chinese men. Secondly, it looks into how some Vietnamese female tourism workers engage in sensual flirting and love games with Chinese men in pursuit of material gain. The abundant in-flows of travellers and tourists have provided Vietnamese women with a pool of richer males. Some women have been successfully using physical appeal to solicit the favour of Chinese men and manipulating their relations with their Chinese lovers and potential lovers through the strategic use of flirting, sex jokes, love games, and physical intimacy. Although these women have been facing moral and cultural tensions and scepticism in the local tourism community, their initiatives in transgressing the triple 'borders' of territory, morals and sex to look for riches have liberated them from the submissiveness of the ideal-type Vietnamese woman and the 'bitterness' of Vietnamese women's fate. Rather than accepting life as it is, they take the initiative to work on their own 'modernization' schemes.

This chapter argues that border tourism has created a new niche accommodating the (economic and sexual) desires of both Chinese men and Vietnamese women through trans-border sexual and sensual contacts and connections. On the face of it, such connections might have suggested a new form of dominance of rich Chinese men over Vietnamese women reflecting the historical Chinese dominance over Vietnam. However, as illustrated below, the current translation of Vietnamese–Chinese contacts into trans-border gender relationships envisages more complex cultural and gender politics and accommodates the desires of borderland women who yearn for a quick step to a more modernized life.

In the last decade, with the expansion of a mobile population and intra-regional travel in Asia, there has been a great boom in Asian tourism. In 2004, Asia and the Pacific headed world tourism expansion with a growth rate of 28 per cent (WTO, 2005a), and it is estimated that China alone is going to produce 115 million out-bound tourists by 2020 (quoted in Greenlees, 2005). As a new category of travellers in the global tourism space, the interactions between the Chinese tourists and the local people of the destinations add considerably to the complexity of the global

Table 10.1: Numbers of Chinese and Vietnamese Tourists in Lao Cai Province (1994–2002)

Year	Vietnamese Tourists	Increase (%)	Chinese Tourists	Increase (%)
1994	4,200			
1995	6,400	52.4	4,200	
1996	9,300	45.3	9,700	131
1997	15,700	68.8	16,800	73.2
1998	26,300	67.5	33,700	100.6
1999	41,800	58.9	63,200	87.5
2000	69,300	65.8	98,400	55.7
2001	91,200	31.6	163,712	66.4
2002	112,700	23.6	176,316	7.7

Source: Statistics from Lao Cai Commerce and Tourism Department and one of the state-owned tourist companies in Lao Cai, 2003.

human interactions and cultural transformations. The trans-border gender politics depicted here is one of the first attempts to illustrate such complexity.

Border Tourism in the New Political Economy of the Vietnam–China Borderlands

Border tourism is a special form of tourism arranged for the nationals of Vietnam and China for visiting each other's country. It is arranged with special types of border travel documents; no passports or visas are required. In the early years after the border re-opening, many Chinese visitors came to Lao Cai town for a one-day visit. Since 1998, due to a relaxation of Vietnamese travel policies, Chinese tourists have been allowed to visit some interior cities in the north of Vietnam, including Hai Phong, Ha Long and Hanoi. In the past few years, Chinese tour groups visiting the south have also been increasing.

Since the advent of border tourism, the number of Chinese tourists going to Vietnam through the land border of Lao Cai has continued to rise. In 2002, the number reached 176,316 – over 40 times the number of Chinese tourists in 1995 (see Table 10.1). Chinese tourist groups are most abundant during the three Golden Holiday Weeks of China, i.e. the National Day holiday, Lunar New Year holiday, and the Labour Day holiday. In the week of National Day holiday in 2002, more than 10,000 Chinese tourists visited Vietnam through Lao Cai. Typical package tours provided by the travel agencies of Lao Cai include the following:

One-day tour in Lao Cai town

Two-day tour in Sa Pa town (a mountainous region of ethnic minorities in Lao Cai Province)

Five-day tour in the north of Vietnam (Lao Cai–Hanoi–Ha Long–Hai Phong)

According to the *Regulations on Tourism Management in Lao Cai Border Crossing Economic Zone* (PCLCP, 1999: 142–144), only travel companies with the international travel license issued by the General Department of Tourism of Vietnam are authorized to organize border travel programmes for Vietnamese and foreign tourists. All Chinese tourists who cross the Lao Cai international border have to travel in scheduled tours arranged by authorized tourist companies and should travel in groups of not less than five. Tour groups are also required to follow the instructions of Vietnamese tour guides, and are not supposed to travel without the arrangement of Vietnamese tourist agencies. Despite such written regulations, it is not uncommon to see individuals or a few business travellers who cross the border in small groups (less than five) and arrange their trips with local travel agencies with specific business purposes in mind.

In 2001, the number of travel companies in Lao Cai had expanded to over a dozen. Local people had great expectations about the development and expansion of the Chinese tourist market. However, due to a number of malpractices among some of the agencies (such as operating without formal registration and insurance), the number of registered travel companies decreased to seven after a crackdown campaign by the Lao Cai government. All the travel companies of Lao Cai had to operate in conjunction with the Hekou China International Travel Agency, which had split into seven off-shoot companies. Chinese tourists who registered with the Hekou travel agencies were packed into groups (large groups during the festive days can be as large as one to two hundred people), and handed over to the tourism companies in Lao Cai, which provided tour programmes and tour guides. Among the scheduled programmes, the one-day tour in Lao Cai and the five-day tour to the northern cities are the most popular. Although Sa Pa is an internationally well-known touristic destination, and is visited by quite a large number of Westerners every year, not many Chinese like to visit it. The Vietnamese tour operators explain that Chinese people have enough minorities to see in their own country and those in Vietnam do not differ much from those in China.

Sexualizing the Border

Borderlands as Peripheral Sex 'Playgrounds'

Although Vietnamese travel agencies do not provide packaged sex tours, sex in the borderlands is readily available due to the presence of both Chinese and Vietnamese prostitutes in the border towns. Many tourists, both men and women, who go on a trip to Vietnam have heard that prostitution is very common in Vietnam, and is especially cheap at the border areas. One young Chinese woman who came to Lao Cai with some friends for a half-day visit said, 'Yes, it is common sense for us. Ask them (pointing at her male friends), all of them know about the prices. Before we cross the border, the tour guide in Hekou already talked about how cheap Vietnamese prostitutes are.' A Chinese male tourist said, 'There is a common saying in China: "Vietnam sacrifices one generation of young women for the well-being of the next three generations."'

Chinese men who visit Vietnam generally hold expectations of some sort of sexual adventure. The tour guides of both of Hekou and Lao Cai will not fail to tell how Chinese male tourists are obsessed with *zhao xiaojie* ('looking for misses'). 'Among five Chinese tourist groups, four will ask us to bring them to find Vietnamese women', Wei, a young Chinese tour guide in Hekou said to me. 'I will say to them that I don't know where to find Vietnamese prostitutes when I don't want to help them. I will let the Vietnamese guide deal with them.' A Vietnamese female tour guide said, 'It is easy to make Chinese (male) tourists happy; they just need to eat well, sleep well, have fun and women.' When she said this, there was a trace of contempt in her voice and on her face. A Vietnamese male tour guide said, 'When they ask us to bring them to the red light zone (*hongdengqu*), we will tell them that it is not included in our scheduled programme. If they want to find women, they can go on their own, but we will not guarantee their safety.' Despite the contempt in which some Vietnamese tour guides hold the *zhao xiaojie* culture of Chinese men, they will help their guests when they want to get better tips. There are also a number of tour guides as well as tour bus drivers who actually encourage the tourists to *zhao xiaojie*.

One of the very first experiences I had in Lao Cai was *zhao xiaojie* for a group of Chinese male tourists. They were part of a larger tour group which came to Vietnam to explore investment opportunities. They spent a night in Lao Cai in the hotel that was opened by an informant's family. I was asked by the family to do some translation since the Chinese did not speak Vietnamese and the receptionists did not speak Chinese. That night, seven men from this group asked me if there were *xiaojie* around. A staff member of the hotel, also a close informant of mine, helped me bring the seven Chinese men to *zhao xiaojie*. Most of the men were enjoying some iced beer in the heat of that hot summer's night by the roadside cafes while I and my informant went in and out of the hair and massage salons nearby. My informant asked the girls the prices of different types of sexual services. After being informed of the prices, some men in the group suggested going to a karaoke bar instead. My informant suspected that the prices might be too high for these men.

Indeed, *zhao xiaojie* has often been a hidden agenda of Chinese tour groups, especially of groups containing only males. Even within groups that include women, Chinese men often ask the tour guides to provide such a programme for them at night, leaving their female members at the hotel rooms to chat. One Chinese man said, 'If it were not for women, why did we come to Vietnam? What else is there to see here?' Many Chinese tourist groups to Vietnam were arranged and financed by work units. Due to the cheap Vietnam tour costs, such tours are part of the welfare provision for workers as a form of yearly bonus. It is not unusual to see groups comprised solely of men. One such group that I observed was not interested at all in the travel programmes arranged by the travel agency. The few animated moments were the time when they flirted with some pretty restaurant waitresses. One night in Ha Long, a few members of the group asked the tour guide to bring them to *zhao xiaojie*.

The Vietnamese Sex Market

Although Chinese discourses have highly sexualized Vietnam and border tourism, the most openly run sex business in the borderlands is actually in Hekou, rather than in Lao Cai. It is situated in a three-storey building compound commonly known as the 'Vietnamese market' (*cho Viet Nam* in Vietnamese; *Yuenan jie* in Mandarin). The ground floor is lined with shops and stalls selling Vietnamese goods, while the second and third floors are full of small rooms owned by or rented to the bosses of Vietnamese prostitutes. There are usually two to three prostitutes in each of these rooms; some lying casually on the sofas, while others sit in front of the mirror painting their faces with make-up. Along the staircases leading to the upper floors of this building, one can see young Vietnamese women with heavy make-up and sexy outfits grabbing the arms of men passing by or hugging their one-night 'honeys' in their arms.

Both Vietnamese and Chinese men come here for sex, but the majority are Chinese. I came to this market of brothels to meet Thu, a friend of an informant. Thu was a twenty-one-21-year-old woman and a newcomer. She told me that she planned to work here for a period of time until she had saved enough money to return to her village in northern Vietnam to start a small business. As a newcomer, Thu looked quite different from the other women. She did not wear heavy make-up and dressed very ordinarily. I was told that many young Vietnamese women who came to work in the market had purposes similar to those of Thu. These women were from poor Vietnamese villages and believed that working as a prostitute would be a quicker way to improve their economic status and the livelihood of their families. I also met Nga and Hien who were working as hair-washing women. Nga said that the salon was opened by her aunt and she came to help her just for the summer. Nga and Hien were both in their early twenties and they said that they were not doing any sex services. But if they did meet some Chinese men who really loved them, they would not mind marrying them even if they were a bit old, like forty. They said that in Vietnam men beat their wives quite often[1] and that Chinese men were better than Vietnamese men in this regard.

Many of the brothels in the market were run by Vietnamese women who themselves had been prostitutes. They had become the bosses of the brothels usually after getting a Chinese husband or a stable lover. They ran the business by hiring other Vietnamese women to work for them. Some brothels were run by Chinese men who rented rooms to Vietnamese prostitutes. There were two ways for the prostitutes to work for these bosses. New girls usually took monthly salaries (around one million *VND*[2]) from the bosses, regardless of how many guests they served. They did not need to pay for rent or for meals. Those who were more experienced and had their own connections with the guests did not take salaries, but shared the money they made with their bosses.

The prices for quick sexual services varied from 30,000 to 80,000 *VND* (around US$2 to US$5.5). Some Vietnamese women who served their guests for the whole night might charge 200,000 to 300,000 *VND*. In Hekou, apart from Vietnamese prostitutes, there were also Chinese prostitutes who usually charged higher prices than their Vietnamese counterparts, from 200 to 300 *RMB*. They did not work in the market but at hotels and their own places. One male boss of a brothel told me that Chinese men tended to think that Chinese prostitutes were cleaner, and did not have AIDS. 'They're stupid to believe this', he said. One Vietnamese informant said that Vietnamese prostitutes in Hekou knew very little about AIDS. 'They just pray for luck since customers don't like to use condoms.'

In both Lao Cai and Hekou, propaganda billboards on AIDS alert were displayed on the streets close to the border crossing. In the Vietnamese market in Hekou, condoms were distributed by the local health department, but not all who worked in the market were eager to get them. One brothel boss said, 'Yes, they have free condoms for us, but we never go and get them. We don't need them. I have a special herbal formula. It can cure any sexual disease. Only drink one packet, you can get well right away. I sell it for fifty *yuan* to friends. For people I don't know, I sell it at seventy *yuan*.'

In one brothel room, I talked to a Chinese man from Hunan. He was sprawling on the sofa and was obviously drugged and talked in a hazy mood. There was a newly hired young Vietnamese woman in the room who was obviously in a bad mood during my visit. The Chinese man complained that the young prostitute was too stupid and did not speak any Chinese. The Hunan man said, 'Here, everything is freer, in the interior of China, going to the prostitutes is not as free as this. Here we are free. We spend money in ways we want.'

Discursive Estrangement of the Ideal Vietnamese Woman

The traditional images of Vietnamese women have been embedded in emotional words such as *phai chiu* (have to bear it), *an kho* (eat bitterness), *chiu kho* (bear bitterness), *kho qua* (very bitter), *qua kho* (really bitter). Very often when I heard these words said by a Vietnamese woman, they were charged with intense feelings and immediate sympathy was expected. The images of Vietnamese women being faithful wives, dutiful daughters and devoted mothers in a male-dominated society have been consistently recorded by scholars (Barry, 1996; Gammeltoft, 2001; Pettus, 2003; Luong, 2003b). The themes of self-sacrifice, industriousness, physical and mental endurance dominate the everyday discourse of Vietnamese women; they are said to be particularly apt at adapting to harsh environments and will sacrifice their happiness for the well-being of the family. Historical heroine figures, such as the Trung sisters who resisted the Chinese invaders, have often been glorified for their courageous and selfless patriotism. During the socialist period in the 1960s and 1970s, state promotion of the ideal of femininity extended women's responsibility from the sphere of the family to the wider context of national production and defence (Gammeltoft, 2001: 272). Not only were women obliged to follow the traditional Confucian moral model, they were also supposed to take up the 'all-capable, all-responsible' role under the socialist teaching of 'Five Goods' and 'Three Great Responsibilities' (Pettus, 2003: 37–50). Such a woman, the ideal Vietnamese woman, is destined not to live for herself, but to display a heroic femininity under the shadow of the father, the husband, the son, as well as the Nation.

Like China, Vietnam for centuries has absorbed Confucian values, thus, in theory, the submissiveness and subordination of Vietnamese women should be as institutionalized as those of Chinese women within the Confucian gender ideology. Some Vietnamese women have even taken it for granted that they have become the sole upholders of Confucian values. A twenty-one-year-old female university student said to me, 'Do you know we Vietnamese women have the principles called *tam tong tu duc* (three submissions and four morals)? We are not free to do what we like.' In this young woman's mind, Hong Kong Chinese women like me or Chinese women in mainland China are not as engaged in keeping traditional values as the Vietnamese.

Because of the intense physical and emotional burden that Vietnamese women have to bear, physical weakness and pains (like headaches, stomach aches, and dizziness) are common health problems among them (Gammeltoft, 2001). Besides physical pains, they also suffer from a psychological inadequacy that has to be addressed through alternative channels. Although the life goal of many Vietnamese women is to have a caring husband and happy family, the reality does not always allow such a dream to come true. Vietnamese women are often put in the predicament of living in an unfulfilling reality. As O'Harrow (1995: 170–174) has explained this oppression has made them seek private space where they secretly yearn for a dream lover. However, there is a persistent gap between the ideal lover and the real husband. For married women, such a dream and gap have occasionally been connected with their taking lovers. And since their society operates more on shame than on guilt, extra-marital affairs will be accepted as long as they are kept secret.

Social and economic changes often bring changes to women's traditional roles and they impact on gender relationships. In an age of globalization and an open economy,

Vietnam has found itself engaged in rapid socio-cultural and gender transformations. Urban Vietnamese women, especially those working in the commercial sector, are pioneers in bringing changes to the society and family since the market in the age of globalization has been lifting women from their traditional roles and morals (Pettus, 2003: 175–205). Thriving trade and commerce in the Vietnam–China borderlands have also freed many women from domestic constraints and made them more independent and self-reliant (Xie, 2000: 326). Urban women are said to be particularly troubled with the existential struggle between self and family, and husband and lover. Yearnings for true love and demands for sex no longer flow silently within a woman's mind, but are discussed more openly among women and in publications (Phan and Pham, 2003). More women are now trapped between 'traditional concepts of love and marriage and modern standards of sexual behaviour' (Phan and Pham, 2003: 216).

Gender relationships and women's social and cultural roles are products of socio-economic relations. In the border town of Lao Cai, the traditional image of Vietnamese women keeping to the principles of self-sacrifice and submissiveness can no longer be directly applied to many young women who take the border as a new space for extending personal space and power. The growing economy has led many to believe that chances for obtaining riches and modern life are freely available at the borderlands. One young woman who came from the village of Nam Dinh to work in a commerce and tourism company opened by a relative said, 'I have never seen so much money in my life. There are a lot of people, a lot of money and chances.' In the post-reform era, while Vietnamese social and government sectors have been looking to China for technology, capital and knowledge, women in the borderlands also look to China for lovers and husbands, as they believe that China has a bigger pool of richer men. Border tourism brings in Chinese men, more importantly rich businessmen, and sustains some women's fantasies for the improvement of their economic life.

Sensualizing the Border

Pretty Women's Strategies in the Borderlands

Being young and pretty are personal assets in the borderland tourism industry. It is also believed that female tour guides with pretty faces and lovely voices can get good tips from the tourists. In Lao Cai, the state-owned travel agencies do not allow female tour guides to go on long trips. Long tours to Hanoi and Ha Long are deemed to be too hard and dangerous for young women. However, for private companies, pretty young women on the contrary are seen as a company asset, and are assigned to work on long tours. It is believed that Chinese men like to have the company of young female tour guides.

During the long bus trips (around ten hours) from Lao Cai to Hanoi, tour guides entertain the tourists with singing and joke-telling, including telling sexual jokes.

One of those I heard went like this: A young girl was advised by her mother to take care of herself. When a man wanted to touch her breast, she had to say aloud 'Don't'. When a man touched her bottom, she should cry out loud 'Stop'. The problem was that the mother had not told the girl what to say when she was touched in both places, so she kept on crying out 'Don't stop'. Sex jokes like this were repeatedly used to entertain guests on the long and tiring bus trips, irrespective of whether there were only men on the journeys or men in the company of female tourists. I never heard people complaining about these jokes. Some very young female guides who were too shy to tell sex jokes would just keep singing to entertain their guests. There were also tour guides who did not seem to be enthusiastic to please their guests.

Some female tour guides used flirting games to elicit bigger tips from the men. These included certain levels of physical intimacy, like playful hugs and touches. A gentle voice and sweet smiles would also be used to impress targeted men on the trips. Innocence, gentleness and subservient attitudes would be strategically displayed in order to arouse the sympathy of the guests, and to fulfil the stereotyped images of Vietnamese females constructed by travel brochures and agencies. Some male Chinese tourists were particularly excited to talk to Vietnamese women who had soft voices and who spoke not particularly fluent Mandarin. Mispronounced words and wrongly placed accents were often sources of fun and jokes, and the Chinese men enjoyed them.

Some female tourist guides enjoyed the opportunities provided to them by their job to make acquaintances with relatively rich Chinese men. Linh, a beautiful twenty-one-year-old tour guide, had been working as a guide since she was eighteen. With three years of experience, she had already been considered as a senior tour guide in the locality. Linh's work provided her with many opportunities to get to know Chinese men from different provinces of China and of different backgrounds. Linh was skilful at making a good impression on her male guests. She had a good sense of humour and many Chinese men liked her since she could express herself humbly and often in a soft voice in the presence of the Chinese men. She would keep contact with some of her male guests for a while to see how the relationships could be developed. She called these Chinese men 'big brothers' (*dage* in Mandarin; *anh* in Vietnamese), who would sometimes send her gifts. With good tips and commissions from a trip, Linh bought herself new bags, shoes and hats from Hanoi, and adorned herself with fashionable earrings and necklaces.

Besides large tour groups, there are also small groups of business travellers or individual businessmen who go to Vietnam to explore investment and trade opportunities. These are called business tourists, who need special arrangements with the tour company for securing experienced tour guides. Sometimes female tour guides accompany such individual tourists, or small groups. Ha was a twenty-six-year-old female staff member of a travel and trading company. She often accompanied individual or a few business travellers to Hanoi and other parts of Vietnam. Being able to speak different Chinese dialects and always dressing up in a sexy fashion, she insinuated herself into many a Chinese man's favour. One man said to me that he liked Ha because, like him, she could speak a little bit of Cantonese. Ha was particularly good at playing flirting games with the Chinese men and she enjoyed keeping a handful of Chinese boyfriends in different cities and towns in China. One of her favourite pastimes was writing love letters to these lovers, who would in turn call her up once in a while. She asked me a few times to write love letters for her since her Chinese was not good enough to express her feelings. These letters were often filled with kitsch expressions of love, exaggeration and lies.

Ha and her colleagues also enjoyed sending and receiving flirting messages through their mobile phones. In Lao Cai, Chinese mobile phone numbers could still work in places near the border-crossing. Many Vietnamese tourism workers and traders possess Vietnamese as well as Chinese mobile phone numbers. The use of mobile phones has provided much convenience for trans-border business and trade, and has also promoted trans-border sensual exchanges. Short messages sent by Ha and her colleagues to men in China often included addresses like 'Do you miss me', 'Do you love me', 'I miss you', 'I really want to see you'. To Ha, Chinese lovers and wooers were personal assets. She received gifts and money from them. Among her lovers, one paid for her mobile phone bills, another bought her clothes and cosmetics. She believed that these two men really cared for her; otherwise they would not pay for her.

Sending and receiving short mobile phone messages across the border have become popular pastimes of local young people in the borderlands and are part of the courtship rituals played out between Chinese men and Vietnamese women. Translating love messages from Chinese to Vietnamese for my Vietnamese female informants was part of my leisure activities in the field. The convenience provided by mobile phones and the increased accessibility of trans-border contacts through phone messages have in fact facilitated more frequent communication between the people of the two sides. It is something that both the Chinese and the Vietnamese have never enjoyed before. Apart from enhancing business contacts, the new technology has also promoted cross-border contacts between men and women who are willing to be involved in the newly created trans-border romance and sensual lies.

Power and Sex within the Tourism Business

Although there were seven different travel agencies in Hekou in 2003, all of them were under the influence of a small number of key figures in the Hekou international travel agencies and tourism officialdom. In order to ensure good business, all Lao Cai travel companies were obliged to maintain close and co-operative relations with these powerful Chinese men. Within the Lao Cai tourism community, there was speculation about some travel agencies using the sexuality of young female staff to obtain and maintain such good relations. Rumours also ran that the female managers of two travel companies in Lao Cai were in fact *ban gai* (girlfriends) of these Chinese tourism bosses. The term *ban gai* in Vietnamese conveys rather vague meanings. It means a wide range of relationships, from female close friends to lovers, and it may or may not imply a sexual relationship. Although the term implies some kind of intimacy, such intimacy does not necessarily lead to serious relationships as the term *nguoi yeu* (lover) does. *Nguoi yeu* implies more stable and committed relationships. Whether being *nguoi yeu* or *ban gai* of the Chinese tourism bosses (most of them are already married), such relationships are seen as pragmatic and economically oriented.

The two young female managers mentioned above were considered the most successful tourism managers during my field research in 2003. They received most tour groups every month. During the Chinese New Year in 2003, they received as many as 800 tourists in a day. On the surface, their success was due to the low prices they offered. But within local tourism circles, most workers believed that they had kept 'special' relationships with the 'big guys' of the Hekou tourism companies. One middle-aged female travel agency manager commented, 'I am different from those young women. They worked for me before and learned how to run a tourism business from me. I am old already. They are still young. They know how to keep good relations with those Chinese men. All Chinese men are promiscuous. They like to travel on to women's bodies!'

Because of their special power and positions in the borderland tourism business, it was obvious that these Chinese tourism bosses were in dominant position with regards to the control of both the tourism business and trans-border sex games. It is not hard for them to get a handful of *ban gai* and *nguoi yeu* across the border. A number of Vietnamese women, on the other hand, were willing to play a part in such games in order to have access to the resources (business and power) offered by such intimate relationships.

Indeed, it was not only Vietnamese female tourism workers who had to take a subordinate position to these Chinese men, but all travel agencies in Lao Cai had to please them from time to time with gifts and bribes. Popular gifts included mobile phones, alcohol, cigarettes, dried meat, dogmeat, seafood, and envelopes of money. Every time these men crossed the border to visit Lao Cai's tourism agencies, it was understood that a free lunch and free drinks should be offered to them, and bags of gifts would be presented after lunch. One informant said to me that he hated entertaining these big guys. Because of their greediness, the profits of his company were gradually being eaten away. 'Out of one million [*VND*] we make, 500,000 will be used for buying gifts for them!' One tourist guide grumbled that he was often ordered by the manager to take these Chinese men for drinks. One strategy to avoid them was to 'disappear' before they reached the office.

Confronting the Gender Space in the Borderlands

Dominance and Submissiveness

Despite the higher economic status of Chinese men, the encounters of men and women in trans-border love and sex games and the cultural politics displayed in such interaction cannot be sufficiently explained by rigidly applying the concepts of male dominance and female submissiveness. To do this risks losing sight of the more diverse social dynamics of gender relationships in the borderlands. Both the Chinese men and the Vietnamese women have taken the initiative to venture into the trans-border sex and love adventures, and have made use of their different capitals to play such games (Bourdieu, 1977). While Chinese men make use of their economic power (to buy gifts and pay for the women), Vietnamese women make use of their physical and sexual appeal. The big guys of the Hekou tourism industry might have been commanding a more dominant position over the Vietnamese tourism workers. The Chinese men who engaged in flirting and sexual games with Vietnamese women were, however, not always playing the dominant role. On the contrary, some of them were being ordered around by their Vietnamese lovers, and made to spend for them.

Some of these Vietnamese sweet-hearts were skilful in utilizing their physical capital, and were good at manipulating their relationships with Chinese lovers for personal gain. They knew well that a good-looking face and a good body were their primary capital. Sweet smiles and a gentle voice always helped in seducing men. Feminine subservient attitudes and innocence, rather than being the essence of the virtues of Vietnamese women, were used for strategic display to solicit the favours of Chinese men. Impetuous SMS love messages and love letters with different narrative styles and choices of words also helped keep a variety of trans-border lovers and potential lovers.

The many flirting games that occur between Chinese men and Vietnamese women at the borderlands have indeed become a source of fun for both men and women. I argue that the trans-border gender relationship examined here, instead of fitting into a dogmatic model of male dominance and female subordination, is actually a transnational geo-cultural locus addressing and accommodating the desires, whether sexual or economic, of both Vietnamese women and Chinese men. Such a site of desires is created within the new trans-border political economy of the reopened border. It has bred particular courtship and flirting rituals: making new acquaintances, obtaining contact numbers, sending short SMS messages on the phone and writing love letters, and has opened new niches for women to extend their personal spaces. Without such cross-border connections, life might have been open to fewer choices, particularly for the Vietnamese women who were eager to find quick ways to enhance their economic status.

To these young women, the traditional feminine images of self-sacrifice and sub-missiveness, and the 'bitter' discourses that dominate Vietnamese women's daily experiences no longer make sense to them. They have been taking initiatives in extending personal space and linkages across the border. While transgressing the

Vietnamese–Chinese borderline to connect to and access Chinese riches, these women are at the same time transgressing the old tales of the tragic Vietnamese heroine and the 'bitter' discourses that overshadow Vietnamese women's wretched fate.

The Dialectics of Sex Gossip

Vietnamese social morality generally disapproves of the promiscuous behaviour of women. In fact, the deeds of the women who solicit material benefits through their intimacy with tourists and men across the border have created gossip and rumours within tourism social circles. The idle talk in these social circles was filled with gossip-sharing and stories about the 'misdeeds' of others, especially women. Common topics included identifying women who had promiscuous relationships with Chinese men; estimating how much these women earned from their sexual transactions; commenting on the new necklaces or handbags of these women. One female tour guide said, 'Look at that woman, her purse is always full of millions of *VND*. She likes to show off. I hate looking at her face.' Having said that, this tour guide assured me that she would not show her disaffection directly to the woman. 'When we meet each other, we still say hello to each other. We never go out together, but there is no conflict on the surface.'

Since no one was going to prove all the gossip and rumours, they remained in the social space of idle talk, providing juicy and imaginative details of the lives of others. On the one hand, it was an autonomous space for people to channel discontent against the disruption of social morals. On the other hand, it allowed much free space for people to work on the stories over time. In some cases, creative versions and sympathetic views were produced. In a later period of my field research, I began to hear some of these. One of them was like this. She [the female manager of a travel agency] was a beautiful woman and had married a young local official. She had been a good wife and a role model for other young women, until her husband became more and more violent and often beat her up when he was drunk. The woman finally divorced the man and her character had since changed. She was good-looking, so many Chinese men liked her.

A number of anthropologists have analyzed the social roles and functions of gossip. Gluckman (1963) sees in gossip a mode of integrating social groups by suppressing conflicts, asserting social values and creating bonds and boundaries. Firth (1967: 142) stresses that gossip and rumour have not just negative social functions, but serve 'as a social instrument, helping groups or individuals to gain their ends'. Handelman (1973) sees gossip as information management, and Campbell (1964) asserts that it contains social realities and helps people to form particular worldviews. Both Merry (1984: 295) and Bergmann (1993) argue that gossip is a form of social control; Bergmann specifically highlights the paradoxical structure of gossip as a social form of 'discreet indiscretion'. Turner's (1993) study of urban rumour finds that it can be a form of political resistance used by weaker groups. White (2000) distinguishes historical memory from gossip. Farrer (2002) analyzes the functions of idle talk in a Shanghai old neighborhood and finds that gossip contains information of different sorts as well as the standards and the expectations of sexual morality, particularly those of young women. In a recent article, Amster analyzes the relationship between gossip and social interaction among the Kelabit of Sarawak, and finds that gossip and discourses about gossip are critical factors in understanding 'Kelabit experiences of sociocultural change and engagements with modernity' (2004: 98). Stewart and Strathern (2004: 29; 203) treat gossip and rumour as a kind of witchcraft causing people harm. Although gossip and rumours operate outside the formal mechanisms of social control, they are significant elements of social processes and their source of power lies in the network of informal communication that runs parallel to formal social structures; and thus should be a focus of social and political analysis.

In the borderlands of Vietnam, gossip acts as a social thermometer to judge misdeeds and sieve discontent at improper behaviour. However, gossip and rumour are not static. Through time they undergo metamorphosis and different gossip versions can be generated. The social space of gossip is indeed an elastic space containing the impacts of corrupt behaviour within processes of accelerating economic aspiration and social change. As the re-opened border has raised people's expectations for economic betterment, both men and women alike take this space as a channel for promoting their economic status. The sexual strategies used by some women in attaining such goals, though they play havoc with Vietnamese feminine morality and gender ideologies, are not hard to understand. The clash between moral expectations and economic pragmatism is further down-played within the elastic space of idle talk with creative versions of rumour and sympathetic views. In other words, the dialectical space of gossip helps bridge the social and moral dilemmas caused by current cross-border gender encounters.

Conclusion: Accessible Modernity and Distanced Dreams

One evening, I was with Linh in Hekou, waiting to meet other friends in the town for a night drink. Linh told me that she and her colleagues once in a while talked about the possibility of marrying Chinese men. To them, China represents a brighter and richer future. While strolling aimlessly with me on the well-lit road along the bank of the border river, Linh said, 'Chinese women are more confident and happier than Vietnamese women. They do not work as much as women in Vietnam. Many of them just play mahjong all day long, their husbands cook for them. In China [she means Hekou], lights are brighter, streets are wider, people seem happier.' Hekou was the only place in China that Linh had been to; her experiences in Hekou fed and summarized her images of China as well as modernity. Like Linh, Phuong and Ha were also among those who saw China and Chinese men as channels to link them to a more modern life. Ha once said, 'Although I love my country, China is a better place to live. China is more developed than Vietnam and has a higher and better social culture. Vietnamese men are not good. They like to drink alcohol and beat their wives. Chinese men are gentler, but they like to have a few wives. Chinese women are rude and talk loudly . . . but they are happier than Vietnamese women.'

Modernity is not a static concept, nor can it be represented by the experiences of modernized and developed countries, especially those of the West. While different Asian places are now carrying out their modernization trajectories, the notions of modernity are often subject to an on-going negotiation of the local people within their globalizing social contexts, and to myriad experiences and discourses, including gender discourses, locally articulated. A number of theorists have argued for the study of alternative forms of and the diversity of modernity (Kahn, 2001; Appadurai, 1996; Breckenridge, 1994; Featherstone, Lash and Robertson, 1995; Miller, 1995; Parameshwar-Gaonkar, 1999). Rather than opting for universal principles and notions of modernity, these scholars stress the particularity of modern experiences. As Kahn argues, the modernity of a place is inevitably 'contaminated' by its cultural and historical conditions, and the meanings of the modern are particularistic (2001: 658).

The aspirations for modernity and a better material life which have emerged among young women in the borderlands and the changing trans-border gender relationships mentioned above are the result of a ten-year development process since the revival of trans-border contacts and in the context of economic differences between post-reform China and Vietnam. While trans-border marriage and romantic affairs are not new to the residents of the border regions, the present trans-border love- and sex-games have been particularly invested with local people's desire for economic gain and their imagination of development and a modern life, as some Vietnamese women see Chinese men as a channel to cross over the borders of poverty into an imagined land of prosperity. These games also involve more long-distance communication through mobile phone technology. For these women, China is just across the border river, accessible in a couple of minutes, but the traditional model of the ideal woman has become a distanced dream. Not only is it hardly achievable, it is also against the will and life choices of many young urban women who find the 'bitter' life of a submissive woman highly undesirable.

I have characterized the revival of contacts and interaction in the Vietnamese–Chinese borderlands in terms of the sexualization and sensualization of the border. Due to the economic differences between Chinese men and Vietnamese women, not only are there a number of Vietnamese women working as prostitutes catering to Chinese men, but the re-opened border has also created a new niche for these men and women to engage voluntarily in cross-border love and sex games. Border tourism and trans-border connections have therefore enshrined different sites and provided a means for the realization of the desires of both Chinese men and Vietnamese women.

Notes

1 The theme of domestic violence is commonplace in Vietnam (see Le, 1996; Johnson, 1996).

2 One US dollar is roughly equivalent to fifteen thousand Vietnamese dong (VND).

11

Romance and Sex Tourism

Heidi Dahles

Introduction

'It is surprising', writes Hu Ching-Fang in a review in the *Far Eastern Economic Review* (2005: 67), 'that in 2005 a Western writer can still write a 420-page book entitled *The Asian Mystique* in which Asia is depicted as nothing but a reflection of Western male sexual fantasies, or, to be more accurate, as the female object of Western male desire.' Hu's arrows of criticism target the suggestion that Asian women – much more than any other women in the world – are most happy to prostitute themselves to Western men 'because of their passports, penis size and wealth' and that 'this phenomenon is regionally specific' (Hu, 2005: 68). Hu is right in pointing out that sex sells almost everything everywhere in the world and that prostitution is not specific for a region that in *The Asian Mystique* (Prasso, 2005) extends from Thailand, the Philippines and Hong Kong to Taiwan and Japan. However, as the Orient has been and still is an integral part of Western civilization and culture (cf. Said, 1978), Western men travelling to Southeast Asia still consume the fantasies of an eroticized Orient. Therefore, the dominant discourse on sex tourism in this region is almost exclusively about Western males as consumers and Asian females as the objects of their desires (Law, 2000; Bauer and McKercher, 2003).

Another interesting point Hu makes is that 'amidst all the descriptions of lust, power and money, white women are missing' (Hu, 2005: 68). White women have been missing in popular and academic literature addressing sex tourism in Southeast Asia for a long time and have only recently attracted some attention. While it is true that 'the masculine Orient is to a large extent yet to be discovered in the West' (Hottola, 1999: 3), it is also true that prostitution and sex tourism have not been regarded as a field of serious academic study. This marginalization is partly due to a blunt rejection of 'frivolous' themes in academia which for decades negatively affected the position of tourism and leisure studies in general. Ironically, these multidisciplinary fields in their turn generated hierarchies of themes in an attempt to obtain academic recognition, allocating the bottom of this hierarchy to sex tourism. However, it cannot be denied that the marginalization of this theme also has to be blamed on the dubious quality of the research in this sub-field. Many publications are based on impressions and anecdotes that transpired from vacation trips instead of in-depth research. Attempts at serious academic research have to deal with restrictions posed by the opaqueness and inaccessibility of this sub-field. As Michael Hall (1996: 267) pointed out about a decade ago, there is a 'lack of systematic research on sex tourism as it is often informal and illegal and police, government authorities and politicians are unwilling to acknowledge its existence. It is extremely difficult to measure the scale of sex tourism at any given location and obtain interviews with prostitutes and other sex industry workers and their customers.'

This chapter will review the literature on male and female tourism-related prostitution and sex tourism in Southeast Asia. Two discursive pathways will be distinguished in the literature. First, the focus will be on the dominant discourse in which academic researchers analyse local women providing sex services to predominantly Western male tourists. Second, an emergent discourse will be identified in which local male actors provide services of a sexual and romantic nature to Western female tourists. The aim of this review is to distinguish the similarities and differences in which academic researchers interpret the involvement of local men and women with male and female tourists and of the role these involvements play in local livelihood strategies.

Sex versus Romance: A Gendered Dichotomy

Tourism literature suggests that tourism and prostitution are closely related. Where the main purpose or motivation of (male and female) tourists is to consummate commercial sex relations and where local people (male and female) meet this demand, the concept of sex tourism applies (after Graburn, 1983b). In many exotic destination areas female prostitution is common (Graburn, 1983b; Hall, 1992; Shaw and Williams, 1994; Kruhse-Mount Burton, 1995). It has been reported in Africa (Crush and Wellings, 1983) and Latin America and the Caribbean (Roebuck and McNamara, 1973; Van Broeck, 2002). The same applies to (Southeast) Asia. With the exception of scattered publications on new consumers of sex tourism, such as gay and lesbian people (*FEER*, 2004) and paedophiles, and new locations of sexual exploitation of both women and children (Hanson, 1998), such as Cambodia (Dahles and Zwart, 2003) and Vietnam (Son, 1995), the mainstream literature in this field focuses on male-dominated sex tourism in Southeast Asian countries (Cohen, 1982a; 1986; 1993; Graburn, 1983b; O'Malley, 1988; Truong, 1983; 1990; Urry, 1990; Lee, 1991; Hall, 1992; 1994; Shaw and Williams, 1994; Kruhse-Mount Burton, 1995; Leheny, 1995; Wilkinson and Pratiwi, 1994; Ghimire, 2001). As Oppermann (1998: 3) argues, most of these writings emphasize male sex tourist flows from developed (both Western countries and Japan) to developing countries, reflecting the image of masculine penetration of the female as metaphor. In the Asia–Pacific region, demand by Japanese and other Asian visitors generally exceeds demand by Western tourists (Oppermann, 1998: 1). The majority of sex tourists in infamous Thailand are from neighbouring developing countries (Mings and Chulikpongse, 1994). Moreover, a considerable number of Western sex tourists are paedophiles, while gay sex tourism is quite prominent in many Asian mass-tourist destinations (*FEER*, 2004). More recently, with AIDS/HIV affecting many communities in developing countries, a new style of discourse has entered the debates on sex tourism affecting popular stereotypes on sex workers, their clients and the organization of the industry (Law, 2000) and marking a shift from voyeuristic and moralizing to medical- and aid-based approaches.

During the last decade, an increasing number of studies have come to devote their attention to tourism-related male prostitution and to female tourists seeking both romantic and sexual encounters. One of the first documented cases is the West African country of The Gambia which has successfully been marketed in Scandinavia encouraging middle-aged Scandinavian women to openly solicit (Harrell-Bond, 1978; Wagner, 1977; Wagner and Yamba, 1986). Other evidence of Western female tourists getting involved with local men is from Barbados (Karch and Dann, 1981) and other Caribbean islands (Momsen, 1994; Herold, Garcia and DeMoya, 2001), Costa Rica (Van Schaardenburgh, 2002), Ecuador (Meisch, 1995), Israel (Bowman, 1989; 1996), Sri Lanka (Crick, 1992), Bali (Mabbett, 1987; McCarthy, 1994, Vickers, 1989), and other parts of Indonesia (Dahles, 1996; 1998; 2001; 2002; Dahles and Bras, 1999a; 1999b; Bras 2000). An interesting addition to the focus on Western women is the phenomenon of Japanese 'brides' heading for Bali to find a husband (Yamashita, 2003a). With so much attention directed at the consumers of sex and romance, one may wonder what new insights into this matter may emerge when the focus shifts to the objects of the tourists' (both male and female) desires. Cohen (1971) was among the first to examine the motives of Arab boys making sexual overtures to female tourists as early as the 1960s, and Bowman and Dahles and Bras (1999a; 1999b) analysed such cross-cultural encounters also from the perspective of the local men. In addition, attention has been drawn to the phenomenon of rastamen as a major attraction for white female tourists not only in the Caribbean (Sutherland, 1986; Pruitt, 1993; Pruitt and LaFont, 1995; Van Schaardenburgh, 2002), but also in other tourist areas such as Southeast Asia where the rastaman has become a role model which young men of non-African background attempt to emulate (Mabbett, 1987; Wolf, 1993; Dahles, 1997; 2001; 2002; Dahles and Bras, 1999a).

Since the publication of the state-of-art volume *Tourism in South-East Asia* (Hitchcock, King and Parnwell, 1993) there has been a shift of focus in the domain of sex tourism research from the dominant discourse of 'white Western males looking for sexual satisfaction with Asian women' to 'white Western females looking for . . .' – what? Strikingly, the literature on female sex tourism debates whether 'sex' is the only motivation, even a motivation at all, for women to get involved with local men. Love, affection, romance, attention, courtship, marriage and even conception of a child, instead of only sex, seem to be the ingredients of the female quest for the exotic. Comparing the literature on male and female 'sex tourism', a dichotomy is emerging: the concept of sex tourism seems to be applicable only to Western and Japanese men going to Thailand (and to South Korea, Taiwan, the Philippines, Cambodia and Vietnam), while 'romance tourism' appears to be more appropriate a concept to describe the travel motivation of Western and Japanese women going to Sri Lanka, Bali and other Indonesian islands. The majority of authors seem to agree that, in the case of female tourists looking for local encounters, the balance is in favour of romance instead of only sex (Kleiber and Wilke, 1995; Pruitt and LaFont, 1997).

In contrast with this conventional approach, Guenther (1998) argues that the difference between male sex tourism and female romance tourism is minimal, as men also often look for 'more than simple physical release and view the exchange of money for sex as unimportant'. This observation is supported by Cohen's (2003) findings among Thai prostitutes and their Western customers. His work (1982; 1986; 1993; 2003) indicates that these encounters fit in with established Thai *and* Western cultural norms: weak young woman depends on older and more powerful man. As far as the sexual involvement of local men with western female tourists is concerned, the Thai model simply seems to be reversed: poor local young men 'prostitute' themselves to rich white women older than themselves. However, as Cohen (1971; 1982; 1986; 1993) and Crick (1992) have observed in various cultural contexts, the concept of prostitution does not adequately convey the meaning of the relationships emerging from sexual encounters between tourists and locals *in general*. Cohen (1993) suggests applying the concept of 'open-ended' prostitution to characterize a kind of relationship between a prostitute and her customer which, though it may start as a specific neutral service, rendered more or less indiscriminately to any customer, may be extended into a more protracted, diffused and personalized liaison, involving both emotional attachment and economic interest. Sex, then, may not be the only motivation for Western men to meet Thai prostitutes. Some of them are looking for a bride in Bangkok (Cohen, 2003), while others return to the same prostitute every year (Cohen, 1993a).

If prostitution is not the right concept to characterize these relationships, love is not the right concept either. It is true that the male and female prostitutes underplay the commercial side of the relationship from the beginning, stage affection, change their identity and – if necessary – hide other emotional or even marital obligations. However, as I (1996; 1997; 1998a; 2001; 2002) have previously observed, the 'romantic' relationships emerging between young local men in Indonesia and Western female tourists are not characterized by such a phasing. These young men apply the strategy of risk-taking small-scale entrepreneurs who have to seize their opportunities under pressing limits of time and fierce competition from their peers. They offer companionship, entertainment and sex and, in return, they expect to experience a white woman which they regard as a meaningful opportunity to 'capture the love and money they desire' (Pruitt and Lafont, 1995: 428). Therefore, I have suggested that their sexual overtures have to be understood as entrepreneurship embedded in subsistence strategies.

The dichotomous interpretation of male-based sex tourism and female prostitution versus female-based romance tourism and male 'romantic entrepreneurship' invites a critical reflection on the concepts used. This dichotomy seems to suggest that the former outlines commercial and exploitative sex tourism, while the latter denotes non-commercial and consensual encounters. As Bauer and McKercher (2003) argue, this dichotomous understanding of the relationship between tourism and sex is highly misleading. A more appropriate approach would be to identify gender differences, commerce and power-relations as dimensions of the encounters between tourists and local people. In the next sections, first the dominant discourse on sex tourism and second an emergent discourse on sexual entrepreneurship will be de-constructed in terms of these three dimensions.

The Dominant Discourse: Men go to Thailand. . .

In writings on tourism-related prostitution, the asymmetrical, commercial and exploitative character of the sexual encounters between male tourists and female prostitutes has been widely acknowledged. In the 1980s, estimates were that 70–80 per cent of male tourists travelling from Japan, the United States, Australia and Western Europe to Asia did so solely for purposes of sexual entertainment [after Gay (1985), quoted in Hall (1996: 266)]. Positioned against the background of Western capitalism and the demonstration effect of Western consumer culture (Lea, 1988: 66), the economic significance of sex tourism has been defined in terms of foreign exchange earnings for developing countries. The statement that sex tourism is Thailand's largest single source of foreign exchange has become a trope in the literature, a trope which is generally followed by an analysis of the costs involved for societies capitalizing on this kind of tourism. These costs may involve immediate health problems such as the spread of venereal disease and the advent of AIDS, forced migration of rural women, child prostitution, the trafficking of women, widespread corruption and the expansion of related criminal activities including drug dealing.

However, blaming tourism for all problems in developing countries turned out to be too easy. As early as the 1980s, John Lea cautioned: 'It is wrong to make tourism the scapegoat for changes accompanying increasing modernization unless they are directly attributable to the industry' (1988: 69). Positioning tourism among the vehicles of modernization, tourism-related prostitution could be equalled with female industrial labour or – in Aiwa Ong's eloquent words (1996), the new trade in the labour and bodies of Asian women in the new international division of labour. 'When women move into the labour force their work is often of a highly exploitative nature, whether in a multinational-owned factory or brothel', writes Hall (1996: 270) in a paraphrase of Ong's argument. Cohen (1993) contends that rural to urban migration in Thailand entails changing female labour from industrial employment to street peddling and finally to tourism-related prostitution (see also Enloe, 1989). Tracing the roots of the problems associated with sex tourism in Southeast Asia in general and Thailand in particular shifted the focus away from the detrimental effects of cheap mass travel emanating from Western countries to the social and economic conditions of the receiving countries. Writings came to address the role of the nation state and of local society, in particular the history of patriarchal relations and women abuse in Southeast Asia. Western feminists blamed the economic and social problems of Asian women in general and prostitution in particular on the patriarchal nature of national and local cultures (Hall, 1996: 269).

As has been widely acknowledged, prostitution existed in Southeast Asia before the advent of tourism. For countries in East and Southeast Asia, Hall (1992: 68) suggests four distinct stages in the development of sex tourism. Based on local, indigenous forms of sexual exploitation of women (the first stage), prostitution becomes a formalized means of meeting the sexual needs of occupation forces under economic colonialism and militarization (the second stage). Both Japanese colonialism and American military interests in the region fuelled the growth of prostitution. After decolonization both international tourist flows (the third stage) and the growth of consumerism (the fourth stage) become powerful forces in the maintenance of the sex tourism industry. However, this should not conceal the fact that there is a local market for the sex trade which is widely overlooked by both researchers and authorities in tourist destinations (Cohen, 1993a; Hall 1992; 1994). The sex trade may not be the main purpose of travel for male domestic tourists, but the availability of prostitutes offers an additional attraction at sites as diverse as temples in Thailand and India to beach resorts in Indonesia (Ghimire, 2001: 19).

The growth of sex tourism in East and Southeast Asian countries has been encouraged by the national governments in the region. The most dominant form of government-supported sex tourism is the *kisaeng* tour specifically geared to Japanese businessmen as many Japanese companies reward their male staff with tours of *kisaeng* brothels (Urry, 1990: 62). As Hall (1992: 74) points out, 'Japanese travel agents have organised these trips to Asia and not to other countries only because Asian countries allow it.' Until the end of the 1980s the Thai government openly promoted sex tourism as a means to foreign exchange and job creation (Hall, 1996: 274). Asian governments seem to be proud of their achievements in the sex industry. As Urry (1990: 62) relates: 'South Korean ministers have congratulated the "girls" for their contribution to their country's economic development. Other countries with a similarly thriving sex industry are the Philippines and Thailand. In the case of the former the state encourages the use of "hospitality girls" in tourism, and various brothels are recommended by the Ministry of Tourism.'

Prostitution as an established but ambiguously valued economic sector in Southeast Asia is characterized by occupational hierarchies. Women catering to local markets take a low position in this hierarchy, while women providing services for businessmen in the national and international corporate sector constitute the top. As Cohen argues (1993: 164), Thai prostitutes offering their services to international tourists are among the elite of this sector. The prostitutes themselves avoid any reference to sex and prostitution and prefer to describe their activities in terms of 'working with foreigners'. Oppermann (1998: 7) observes that in many Southeast Asian countries prostitutes working in the tourism sector are often independent or attached to a bar where the customer pays to take the prostitute out. The prostitutes negotiate their own price with the customer directly and, therefore, are able to retain most of their income. In contrast to many developed countries, pimps are rare in Southeast Asia. This observation has not led researchers to develop a perspective on tourism-related prostitution in terms of entrepreneurship. In the development literature, the women are victimized in terms of their position in their own society and in Western capitalism. Most of the literature is *about* prostitutes; only a few authors are writing from the point of view of the prostitutes, unravelling their systems of meaning, their experiences and dreams. Cohen comes close to such a perspective when emphasizing the risk and playful element of open-ended prostitution as a 'serious gamble' (1993: 193). This description evokes images of the risk-taking entrepreneur in a Schumpeterian sense, but fails to address other aspects of entrepreneurship such as tactical manoeuvring and subsistence strategies that would lift prostitution from the domain of leisure to the domain of economic venture. It is striking that no research has been done in to the thin line between prostitution and other economic activities in the tourism sector, such as street peddling, despite the structural similarity between souvenir selling/shopping and body shopping/selling.

The Emergent Discourse: . . . and Where do Women Go?

One of the first anthropologists to write about Western female tourists soliciting sexual favours by local men is the Swedish anthropologist Ulla Wagner who analysed female-based Scandinavian tourism in The Gambia (West Africa) in the 1970s. Wagner argued that the sexual encounters between Scandinavian females and local Gambian men represented an inversion of the established norms ruling gender relations in many Western and non-Western societies. Wagner detects a destructive potential in these relationships: '(. . .) what to the tourist is a pleasant and refreshing interlude where the disregarding of norms in no way threatens the structures pervading in their home society, could result in the destruction of one of the very foundations of local social structure, that of ordering social life according to age and generation differences' (1977). What remains unclear is whether this diagnosis is based on an analysis of local gender relations or rather on the author's morals. The fact that the local boys 'sleep with women of their mothers' generation' – as Wagner laments – may bother a Western female academic, but may have a rather different meaning in the lives of the men involved.

Almost three decades later, this moralistic view of such encounters was echoed by an Australian journalist commenting on the subculture of male youth in Bali – the so-called 'bad boys', 'Kuta cowboys', 'gigolos' (by other people), or 'guides' (their own term), 'whose peripheral yet lasting flirtation with the West has left them with a taste for drugs, alcohol, and one night/one month relationships with tourist girls. (. . .) Maybe a life of shallow, temporary relationships, on the fringes of the tourists' largesse is better than the alternatives' (Wolf, 1993). These alternatives entail leading the life of a rice-cultivating peasant, a factory worker and the head of a large family in a situation of dire poverty. The 'Kuta cowboys' emerged with surfing, the sport that created a new lifestyle for tourists and new livelihoods for Balinese youngsters from the 1970s onwards. Besides becoming excellent surfers themselves, young Balinese men came to Kuta to make money accepting casual work in the tourism industry, collecting commissions by selling jewellery, carvings or paintings, and picking up tourist girls 'who would pay for everything' (Mabbett, 1987).

In the heyday of tourism in Bali – before the bombings in the aftermath of 9/11 – the 'Kuta cowboys' hung around tourist spaces – beaches, bars, restaurants and accommodations (McCarthy, 1994). Their trademark was their *gondrong*, i.e. 'cool and dreadly', appearance: they usually wore tight black jeans, loose shirts unbuttoned to the belly, long black hair and dark sunglasses that reflected beach life. They played guitar like Hendrix, sang Marley's songs and danced like Michael Jackson. 'You look happy' was their favourite mode of addressing tourist women while exhibiting the 'don't-worry-be-happy-attitude'. Their self-image was intertwined with outspoken ideas about masculinity. In a series of articles in an Indonesian newsmagazine, Kuta beach boys expressed their conviction that Western women come to Bali to conceive a child from a local man as they dispose of 'better seed' than Western males (Suardika, 1996a; 1996b). They achieve status amongst their male friends through sleeping with as many female tourists as possible. In the short term their aim is to pick up an endless stream of white girlfriends, but in the long run most of them strive for a steady relationship with a woman who will take them off to her country for a better life in the West (McCarthy, 1994; Vickers, 1989).

It seemed that a lifestyle copied from the Kuta cowboys exerted an enormous attraction on the male youth in other tourist areas in Indonesia. At night, the pubs, restaurants and discotheques of tourist towns and beach areas in other parts of Bali and other Indonesian islands were crowded with guides, drinking beer, smoking weed and flirting with female tourists. Their lifestyle was an imitation – not of western tourists – but of the Kuta cowboys, who led the fashion in the world of unlicensed guides and beach boys. Many young men boasted of having visited Kuta to see both the 'bare breasts' on the beach as well as the Kuta cowboys. Young men inspired by their Bali counterparts aspired to a career as musician in a local (reggae-)band, which supposedly was a life of sex, drugs and rock'n'roll. Apparently, the ever-present chance to enter into a sexual relationship with a tourist added glamour to this lifestyle. Regarding the strict cultural codes for the public behaviour of women – Indonesia is a Muslim country after all – females offering their services as guides or friends were immediately associated with prostitution. Only a small number of the guides were females, and most of the women working as guides actually were prostitutes catering also to local men. On the other hand, offering sexual services to female (and male) travellers was quite common among male guides.

As I have argued elsewhere (Dahles, 1997), those males have been labelled as gigolos, i.e., men living on the money paid by women for their sexual services; in other words, male prostitutes. In many cultures, men supported by women are regarded as deviant as their behaviour violates 'traditional' gender relations. Instead of looking at the sexual overtures of local males toward female tourists in terms of prostitution and the supposed detrimental impacts on social life, I argued that this behaviour should be analysed from the perspective of the everyday life of these men. To understand why young local men desire sexual relationships with female tourists, one needs to position these sexual relationships in the context of the livelihood strategies of the young men. Much of the employment generated by tourism in Indonesia is in the form of self-employed, small-scale entrepreneurs. They can be defined in terms of petty producers of cheap goods and services, making a living on their wits from day to day and creating new opportunities in an already crowded environment. Public space being their domain, street guides and beach boys grasp occasions for gain as they fitfully and spontaneously arise, benefiting in every possible way from the diffuse flow of individual tourists passing by. With tourists around, the chances of making a quick windfall are bigger, but the stakes are higher – not only economically. Doing business with tourists involves selling goods and (sexual) services and strategically exploiting personal networks – as is characteristic of small-scale entrepreneurs in the informal sector (Geertz, 1963a; Crick, 1992). The small entrepreneurs we are dealing with here distinguish themselves by strategically operating networks instead of land, equipment, or funds. Instead, they operate by their wits and act as intermediaries by managing sources and flows of information. They put people in touch with each other directly or indirectly for profit and bridge gaps in communication between people. They capitalize on their personal networks, their communication channels and their role relations, which are ruled by notions of reciprocity and transaction. In the next section I discuss the strategies of local males operating in a popular tourist destination in Java in terms of small entrepreneurs. This approach shows that 'romance tourism', instead of being a force undermining social structure, is embedded in the tourism industry of the local community.

Romantic Entrepreneurs

Small entrepreneurs form an integral part of the tourism industry of both developed and developing countries. Small-scale entrepreneurs are neither representatives of a traditional, informal, 'involuted' economy (cf. Geertz, 1963a), nor do they fit definitions of the completely modern, formal, capitalist sector. They participate in both economies. Depending on the kind of resources, some (those who rely predominantly on private property) operate more in the formal sector, others (those who rely predominantly on personal networks) participate more in the informal sector. The relations between the formal and informal spheres are complex. Owners of tourist businesses depend on intermediaries or, as Boissevain (1974) dubbed them, 'brokers' for the advertising and marketing of their accommodation, restaurant or shop. Brokers, in turn, depend on these owners for their commission and access to tourists. Business and brokerage constitute a safety belt that allows small entrepreneurs to operate in a rather flexible manner. Both businessmen and brokers depend heavily on networks based on personal friendships, business transactions, family relations, marriage and ethnic, and religious bonds. These networks often constitute more meaningful units than formal organizations and state-controlled associations.

Although economic considerations are the basis for much of the cooperative efforts, personal networks, family obligations and friendship are necessary for mutual support. This is where local brokers are integrated into the local tourism industry. Turning to unlicensed guides in particular, these locals who get involved in tourism without owning any other assets than their social network and wits seem to have a weak position. As one of their main resources, the tourist, is accessible only for a limited span of time, many brokers are pressed to benefit as much and as quickly as possible from the tourists. They are perpetually looking for a chance to make a smaller or larger killing, not being able to build up a stable clientele or a steadily growing business. If large-scale tourism development implies the formalization of the tourism industry, these local brokers will be pushed further into marginality. However, within the local tourism business, the role of some individuals can become rather prominent, provided they possess considerable amounts of flexibility in terms of time, space and social contacts.

Local businessmen suffer from the same fluctuating customer–provider relationships as brokers do, as tourism flows are irregular and unpredictable. While most businessmen have only limited opportunities to control these flows, brokers are in the middle of the action. They have free access to tourists and they are informed about where and when tourists arrive, where and how long they stay, where they will go next, their activity patterns, their expectations and needs, and their spending power (Dahles, 1989a; 1998b). Moreover, they are familiar with the local market and the opportunities to match demand with supply in a way that enables them to make a profit. That is why local businesses often rely on brokers to provide them with tourists. Taxi- and bus-drivers, touts and informal guides are paid a commission to re-direct the tourist flows to small accommodations and restaurants in back alleys; bell-boys, waiters and shop assistants are instructed to pick tourists from the street and direct them to a restaurant or souvenir shop. The case study below, which is based on my anthropological fieldwork in the mid-1990s among the unlicensed guides of Yogyakarta, may illustrate the role that unlicensed guides played in the tourism industry of this then popular tourist destination – 'romantic entrepreneurship' being one among many economic strategies, though the most desirable one.

Unlicensed Guides in Yogyakarta

The streets of Yogyakarta swarm with young men offering their services to passing tourists. According to government authorities and managers of the star-rated hotels, these men represent the 'unqualified', 'unorganized', and permanently 'unemployed' people who constitute the informal sector of the tourist industry. They are referred to as 'unlicensed guides', 'informal guides', 'street guides', 'batik guides', and *'guide liar'* (*liar* is the Indonesian word for 'wild'). Other less favourable names are guide liar ('guides that lie'), nuisances and criminals. The young men call themselves 'friends'. Some of them operate in small, loosely structured groups of friends sharing and controlling a hangout, but many operate on their own, only sharing the hangout with colleagues. The hangouts may be organized according to a shared ethnic and/or geographical background, having been at the same school or college, or being relatives. The best hangouts – the ones along Malioboro Street – are controlled by men from Yogyakarta families, their relatives or in-laws. Being engaged or married to a girl working as a shop assistant or being related to the security or parking-lot man enhances one's opportunities to be tolerated at the doorstep. A newcomer requires the introduction of an already established friend or relative, otherwise he will not be accepted at a hangout. Being born and raised in Yogyakarta facilitates the access to these hangouts; men from outside town find it difficult to be admitted into such a group.

Within a group there is a loosely structured division of tasks. Success in the 'tourist hunt' is largely dependent on communicative abilities, outward appearance and mastery of foreign languages. Group members scoring high on these criteria usually take the initiative of approaching tourists. If they are successful, they receive the biggest share of the profit. If they fail, other group members try to take over. While the tourist experiences a series of approaches by different young men during her city walk, these men often belong to the same group. If one of the group 'has a bite', the others follow him and his guest at a distance, observing which restaurants or shops are visited, what souvenirs are bought and how much money is spent. After the tourist and her 'guide' have left, group members enter the shop or restaurant to collect the commission, which will be divided amongst the group. But the smart and handsome guides break away from the group when they turn out to be successful. In that case they prefer working for themselves.

The most marked aspect of the guides' work, i.e. accompanying tourists, is only a strategy to earn money. The guiding as such does not provide a substantial income. They have to be satisfied with a tip that tourists give them voluntarily, a meal, a drink or cigarettes. If they are lucky they receive gifts of some value: western consumer goods like wrist watches, walkmans, radios, leather jackets. Street guides do not ask for money straight away. If a tourist is reluctant to buy souvenirs, the guide starts talking about 'problems': his poor family being unable to pay for his expensive education, his old mother requiring medical treatment, his young children going hungry, him being an orphan. If the tourist does not or pretends not to understand, then the street guide has no other choice than turn and walk away, as he has no right to ask for a fee. The guides' income consists substantially of the commission they receive for taking customers to the small hotels, the souvenir shops and restaurants that the city has in abundance. The commission is a percentage of the selling price of the products and services purchased by tourists. In Yogyakarta small business proprietors usually hand over about ten per cent (but sometimes even 50 to 60 per cent) of the selling price to intermediaries, street guides and other touts. This applies to the numerous small enterprises and budget accommodations in the narrow alleys of the tourist areas and the shops and factories at the outskirts of the city; it does not apply to the big stores and star-rated hotels in the main shopping area.

Unlicensed guides have to attend to several jobs all the time. They usually combine the guiding of tourists with different kinds of economic activities. Some of them do odd jobs for (souvenir) shops, boutiques or small workplaces where batik, masks, *wayang* puppets or wood carvings are manufactured. They always work as touts for several shops on a commission basis. Some sell toys, ice cream, or cold drinks on the street; others work occasionally as barkeepers, waiters, security men, or bellboys in hotels. Sometimes they invest money in bulk buying goods to sell with a profit. At other times they walk the streets with samples of fake Rolex watches or perfume, trying to sell these products on a commission basis. Most of the time, they do all these things. Working as a street guide on occasion is popular with schoolboys, students, truants and dropouts. In the afternoon, after the lectures and lessons in the countless institutions for vocational and professional training are finished, the number of street guides increases significantly in the streets of Yogyakarta. Many students (and those who claim to be students) try to make some extra money by taking tourists to shops and restaurants. Some are so attracted by the money and glamour associated with tourism that they discontinue their studies to focus completely on petty jobs in the tourism sector.

We are dealing here with a rather differentiated group characterized by striking differences in their style of doing business and their future perspectives. For many young males, taking advantage of passing tourists represents an additional, though irregular, source of income and excitement. They leave their jobs temporarily and at short notice to earn some money by taking tourists to shops. People operating on this ad hoc basis can be found among the hotel and restaurant staff, shop-keepers, office clerks, workshop employees, museum staff, and travel agents. I call them 'occasional touts'. Individuals constituting this category are more or less permanently employed and are tied down to a specific locality to perform their jobs. Those who deal with tourists directly, like receptionists, waiters and bar-tenders, have a privileged position. A second category that I call 'odd-jobbers' is constituted by individuals with occasional employment that requires considerable mobility, like taxi-drivers, street vendors and lottery and ticket sellers. These people have all kinds of jobs and businesses that are often tourism-related and that can easily be left behind for a while to engage in more lucrative deals with tourists. Commissions, tips and gifts, and perhaps long-time financial and personal commitments from tourists are important sources of income for the 'odd-jobbers'. Finally, there are young men who maintain an almost professional outlook on street guiding. I call them 'professional friends'. They regard guiding as their profession and tune their lives to dealing with tourists in a way that generates a reasonable income. Most of them operate in small groups and concentrate on taking tourists to the shops as directly as possible. Others work individually and conduct informally arranged guiding tours. Like the odd-jobbers both the group-based and the individual 'friends' depend on commissions, tips, gifts and the particular commitments of tourists, but unlike the odd-jobbers professional *guide liar* do not have additional sources of income. A characteristic of all these young men is their keen interest in romantic and sexual encounters with female tourists. The concept of 'romantic entrepreneur' adequately describes (young) men putting much effort into the establishment of romantic relationships with female tourists, with the aim of being supported by these women or of acquiring a ticket to follow them to their home country.

Conclusions

There have been important changes in the academic embedding of both tourism studies and research on sex tourism emanating from a 'happy marriage' of two multidisciplinary fields, i.e., tourism studies and regional studies (in particular Asian studies) starting in the early 1990s. Scholars who worked in Southeast Asia on (tourism-related) developmental issues turned their attention to the ways in which international tourism affected the communities under study. An *emic* perspective – an approach from the everyday life of local people – coupled with a situational analysis rendered surprising new insights into local strategies and meanings given to sex tourism which went beyond the moralising tenor of many writings by looking at this phenomenon from an *etic* point of view. A methodology that approached sex tourism not as an isolated phenomenon but as part and parcel of the livelihood strategies of local people gave rise to a new conceptual framework within which tourism-related prostitution came to be analysed. Instead of victimizing local people as objects of neo-colonial exploitation by

Western sex-consumers, this new approach acknowledges their active role in terms of entrepreneurship. A combination of community-based and actor-centred approaches allows for developing a more appropriate gender perspective on sex tourism, including both female and male actors, and other forms of sex tourism that may locally be of great importance. However, this new perspective is still unbalanced. There are striking differences in the ways in which academic researchers interpret the involvement of local men and women with male and female tourists and the role these involvements play in local livelihood strategies. By way of conclusion, I summarize these differences below in terms of themes for future research.

Research on the *feminine Orient* needs to develop an actor-centred approach. Scholarly perspectives have changed from victimization to agency, but an embedding of prostitution in entrepreneurial and livelihood strategies is still to be accomplished. This applies in particular to the intertwining of sex services with other economic activities. There is reason to believe that full-time prostitution is only one of the many ways in which sex services are deployed as a livelihood strategy, the more so as tourism shows seasonal variations. Moreover, research on both the *feminine and masculine Orient* requires a more balanced geographical distribution. Available literature focuses on Thailand for the female actors and on Indonesia for the male actors. The question has to be raised whether this focus is due to the researchers' random choice of fieldwork location or, instead, to local gender-relations which either facilitate or prohibit male or female involvement with foreigners or with extra-marital sex. Finally, future research also will have to address the diversifying supply of sex services. There is little to no academic literature available about tourism-related gay/lesbian and child prostitution in Southeast Asia. While NGOs and national governments in both Asia and the West have issued measures against the consumers of these services offered by children, there is a lack of knowledge of the ways in which child prostitution is organized and sustained.

Conversely, there is a void in the literature regarding insights into the backgrounds, motives, desires, dreams and behavioural patterns of the sex tourists, both male and female. This is striking given the attention paid to the consumers in tourism literature in general. There is a lack of research on male tourists both heterosexual and homosexual. While these men are also victimized as pathetic losers in popular writings, there are indications that some of these tourists travel to Southeast Asia not only for sex but also for finding a bride or partner or seeking some affection. In a similar vein, female tourists getting involved with local men in Southeast Asia are 'mysterious beings' as there is only cursory reference to their backgrounds, motives, hopes and prospects in the literature. As is the case with male sex tourists, these women are depicted as lacking prospects in the dating scene at home because of age and physical appearance, which is clearly too simplistic.

On balance then, there is more knowledge about the supply side of sex tourism in Southeast Asia than about the demand side. Future research should explore individual actors against the background of changing gender identities and shifting power relations between nation states and regions in the global tourism industry.

12

A Political Ecology of Sustainable Tourism in Southeast Asia

Michael Parnwell

Introduction

Some say the tourism industry is sowing the seeds of its own destruction, because it has taken so long for popular interest in sustainable development to permeate the tourism sector (Berno and Bricker, 2001). Yet despite such concerns the industry has continued to boom: international tourism arrivals worldwide grew from 457 million in 1990 to 698 million in 2000 (an increase of 53 per cent), and 808 million (77 per cent up on 1990) in 2005 despite some quite rocky recent times (WTO, 2006). Similarly for Southeast Asia: despite a series of major external and internal shocks (e.g. the World Trade Center attacks in 2001, the Bali bombings in 2002 and 2005, the SARS crisis in 2003 and the Asian tsunami in 2004), growth in international tourist arrivals within Pacific Asia was 7 per cent in 2005, and in some countries was nothing short of spectacular: Cambodia (35 per cent, January to November), Laos (27 per cent January to September), Vietnam (18 per cent) and the Philippines (14 per cent) (WTO, 2006). The future prognosis is also bright: for example, international tourism to the Greater Mekong Subregion is projected to increase from 14.6 to 50.2 million (306 per cent) between 2004 and 2015 (Asian Development Bank, 2005). The fastest growth is thus occurring in relatively new destinations – locations that are generally least well-equipped to cope with tourism's pernicious impacts. Sustainability is under threat, but the industry is belatedly starting to respond.

Since the mid-1990s 'sustainable tourism development' has become a central preoccupation of stakeholders across the industry's spectrum, from the local to the global, and among tourism analysts, academics and practitioners (see e.g. Weaver, 2006; Elliot-White and Lewis, 2004; Mowforth and Munt, 2003; Sofield, 2003; Harris, Griffin and Williams, 2002; Aronsson, 2000; Holden, 2000; Cater, 1999; Hall and Lew, 1998; France, 1997). A *Journal of Sustainable Tourism* was launched in 1993, aiming to provide a 'critical but constructive review of approaches which seek to balance the requirements of tourism and its host communities and habitats' (www.multilingual-matters.com/multi/journals/journals_jst.asp). But in reality, the literature on sustainable tourism has tended to split between, on one side, a constructive dialogue about the tools of policy, management and mitigation needed to maintain the industry's healthy growth and expansion, and, on the other, a fundamental critique of tourism's consumptive processes and deleterious impacts. How do we account for this seeming discrepancy between a theory of inevitable decline and an apparent empirical reality of inexhaustible boom?

Answering this question requires a close assessment of what exactly we are trying to sustain, and thus what 'sustainable tourism development' actually means and involves. A widely-used definition, promoted by the UN World Tourism Organization and matching the popularly held definition of sustainable development (World Commission on Environment and Development, 1987: 43), is: 'tourism development that meets the needs of present tourists and host regions while protecting and enhancing opportunities for the future. It is envisaged as leading to the management of all resources in such a way that economic, social and aesthetic needs can be fulfilled while maintaining cultural integrity, essential ecological processes, biological diversity, and life support systems' (WTO, 1998: 21). By way of contrast, the definition employed by the Dutch development agency SNV (www.snv.org.vn) states that the sustainable development of tourism involves:

> . . . a balanced target group oriented development strategy involving:
> - socio-economic development and economic empowerment;
> - local participation, social and political empowerment;
> - economic sustainability;
> - ecological sustainability;
> - socio-cultural consciousness;
> - improving gender equality.

These two definitions appear to have somewhat different emphases. The former adopts a development-centric perspective which recognizes that tourists, as key actors, have to be satisfied by the quality of the resources available to them, and that this is crucial to the maintenance (i.e. sustainability) of development returns to host communities and the loci of these resources. A balance has to be struck between the developmental imperatives of the present and the saving of resources for the developmental benefits of future generations.

The latter adopts a much more community-centric viewpoint which, whilst recognizing the importance of developmental gains, emphasizes empowerment and conscientization to ensure community involvement in decision-making and control, the minimization of negative impacts and the distribution of benefits to those in greatest developmental need. Although there is apparent consensus on the nature of the problem, there is scope for significant variation of emphasis as to the relative priority that is given to developmental and sustainability considerations and how we might move towards an effective solution to the challenges posed by the tourism boom.

Degrees of Sustainability

The issue boils down to a question of what is to be sustained, tourism or the resources upon which tourism is built, or more accurately the relative importance of one or the other, notwithstanding their longer-term inseparability. Where should action be placed on the pendulum between 'weak' (anthropocentric) or 'strong' (ecocentric) sustainability (Fennell and Ebert, 2004: 417)? 'Weak sustainability' gives priority to numbers, and seen from this perspective there is little need for urgent and radical action because the future prognosis for the industry is very optimistic. The notion of a *'tourism iceberg'* supports this view. Ever since steamships started sailing the seas with early, élite tourists the industry has grown exponentially as more people have enjoyed more disposable income, more leisure time, a greater inclination to travel, a removal of barriers to travel, improved means and more favourable real costs of travel. Over time a greater array of social groups has joined the expanding throng of travellers and visitors. Recent changes in the make-up of the tourism sector in Southeast Asia support this view, with a shift from predominantly western, to predominantly Asian, to predominantly domestic tourists underpinning a healthy expansion in tourist visits to a steadily growing array of destinations, activities and attractions. This trend seems likely to continue as modernization and development provide more means, opportunity and inclination to travel. The iceberg analogy suggests there is more to come than is immediately visible, and thus the industry's overall sustainability seems assured, even while local life cycles see particular tourist destinations wax and wane.

The critical perspective, advocating 'strong sustainability', argues that a numbers approach to sustainability is neither adequate nor appropriate; it misses the point. The literature over the last 20 years or more is replete with illustrations of the serious damage, disadvantage and disequilibrium that the tourism industry is leaving in its wake: cultural erosion and dislocation, damage to fragile coastal and mountain ecosystems, exploitation and exclusion of local populations, inflation and conspicuous consumption, pollution and resource shortages, fickleness and insecurity. The critical perspective challenges the notion of tourism as an 'industry without chimneys' (World Land Trust, 1997), and advocates a radical reappraisal of the priorities, procedures and patterns of tourism development in a way that prioritizes saving, conserving and rebuilding, and the delivering of genuine developmental benefits to those in greatest need.

We thus have a 'continuum of consternation', ranging from *ostrichism* (heads buried in the sand, refusing to accept that anything is fundamentally wrong with the status quo, or arguing that the positives outweigh the negatives), through *reformism* (a recognition that change is necessary, but in a gradual and evolutionary manner which leads from the status quo) and *revisionism* (diverging from the status quo into new forms of tourism which are based upon fundamentally different sets of principles and practices), to *radicalism* (an anti-development perspective where the only sustainable form of tourism is no tourism). Where one is placed along this continuum, and where the solutions to tourism's pernicious effects are seen to lie, rests with individuals and institutions, their priorities and ideologies, their positions and perspectives. Different actors and different interest groups have different viewpoints on sustainable tourism development, which thereby becomes a contested domain and a fundamentally political issue, albeit socially and culturally framed and determined. The relative emphasis given to human and environmental needs ultimately boils down to the nature, balance and dynamics of power: the power to decide, the power to act, the power to resist, the power to elicit change and the power to represent.

The Political Ecology of Sustainable Tourism

The political ecology of sustainable tourism provides a framework within which to explore the political dimensions and implications of contestation over access to, use of and the impacts resulting from (human, physical, cultural, heritage) resource use in support of tourism development. Political ecology is rooted in the discipline of geography, and centres on the political dimensions of the discipline's traditional concern for human–environment interaction. Political ecology leans towards radical and ecocentric challenges to the developmental status quo (Atkinson, 1991: 13), and is quite dismissive of attempts to confront the environmental crisis through reformist or technocratic processes, or of the compromise position of 'sustainable development' (Bryant and Bailey, 1997: 5; 19).

Political ecology is concerned with the study of political struggles for control over natural resources (Greenberg and Park, 1994), and is 'an attempt to understand the political sources, conditions and ramifications of environmental change' (Bryant, 1992: 13). Environmental outcomes from tourism development are not simply the consequence of failures of policy or the market, but of conscious choices made by influential actors. These choices are codified, defined, negotiated, promoted, resisted, challenged and reformulated through the everyday politics of development. Thus political structures, institutions, practices and processes all lie behind these policy and market failures and their environmental outcomes (Bryant and Bailey, 1997:

2), and it is in the political realm that we might find solutions to currently pressing ecological issues. Conversely, social choices and political actions emerge from environmental change, through conscientization, realization and empowerment, and through changes in the local (e.g. neo-localism, post-developmentalism) through to global (e.g. neo-liberalism, post-structuralism, environmentalism) context. Thus the political ecology of sustainable tourism is constantly being moulded and negotiated; the politics of the environment are in a constant state of flux.

At the core of political ecology are 'different actors [who] contribute to, are affected by, or seek to resolve, environmental problems at different scales' (Bryant and Bailey, 1997: 33). These different scales, ranging from the local to the global, and imbued with relations of power, are complexly linked together through the political relations of tourism development (Stonich, 1998: 29). The following discussion attempts to operationalize these actor-centred relations of power at the two ends of the 'continuum of consternation' in relation to sustainable tourism development: business as usual, and radical change. The two schematic diagrams outlined below suggest the structure, balance and directionalities of power and influence within orthodox and alternative tourism frameworks.

The Balance of Influence in Orthodox and Alternative Tourism

Schema 1. Figure 12.1 presents a schematic summary of the relative influence of the key stakeholders within an orthodox tourism framework – i.e. that which broadly prevailed until concern for sustainable tourism development emerged in the early 1990s. The diagram approximates the relative influence of these actors in controlling the pattern and process of tourism development, and as a consequence its various impacts. The schema posits multinational tourism businesses as exerting a significant degree of domination and control over a major segment of the tourism sector. The penetration of domestic economies by international tourism actors is facilitated by what we might call 'conduits of capitalism' – gatekeepers and go-betweens in positions of influence and authority (e.g. business and political élites) who create space and opportunity for international and multinational firms to access domestic markets and resources, and to promote a pro-development paradigm. The three layers of the domestic tourism economy – national, local and petty – are posited to mould themselves according to the prevailing orthodoxy, driven in the main by the imperative of growth and the development benefits that this will bring. Government agencies are placed in a cleft stick position within the tourism business world – struggling to rationalize the twin responsibilities of regulation *for* development (managing the domestic business environment in order to maximize the potential contribution that tourism can make to the national economy) and the regulation *of* development (imposing and implementing controls to ensure that such development does not have deleterious impacts on resources, societies, cultures, heritage and security). The schema suggests that, with orthodox development, regulation *for* tended to supersede regulation *of*: a grow now, clean up later philosophy prevailed which was driven by the need and desire to achieve the fastest possible mobilization of tourism potential as a means of strengthening, speeding up and extending the process of development. Thus the lines which signify the regulatory influence of government on both domestic and international business are much weaker than in the case for the promotion of mainstream development.

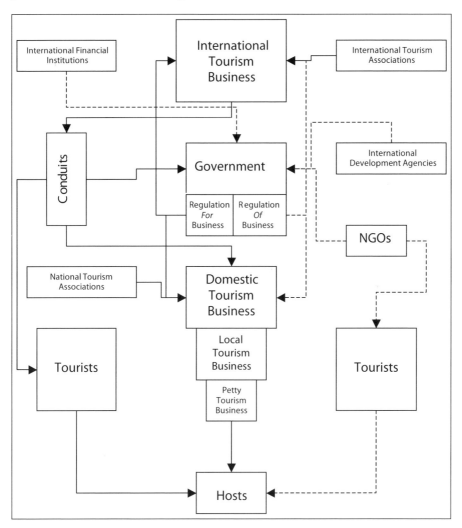

Figure 12.1: Schema 1 – Schematic representation of the relative balance of influence in orthodox tourism

Although international financial institutions and international development agencies are clearly important in the promotion and support of development in regions such as Southeast Asia, their influence in the field of tourism before the early- to mid-1990s was relatively limited, hence their connections with host governments are here indicated to be quite weak. The non-governmental sector, which we later show to have been influential in first promoting and then facilitating alternative approaches to and philosophies of tourism development, is also, within the orthodox framework, shown to have a relatively minor influence on development patterns, processes and outcomes. Its approach has mainly focused on influencing government policy and practice by raising awareness of the pernicious impacts of under-regulated tourism development. NGOs are also suggested as a potential means of influencing the behaviour and attitudes of tourists, but they are fighting an unequal battle with those who promote, market and facilitate mainstream tourism. Finally, hosts are presented as stakeholders with relatively limited influence over their developmental destinies or control over the multifarious impacts of tourism.

Schema 2. The suggestion is that the above development model has been principally responsible for the challenges to sustainable tourism. Advocates of sustainability argue for a change in the balance of stakeholder power and the direction of influence if some of the harmful effects of tourism are to be controlled and its development potential better managed. Figure 12.2 presents an idealized alternative structure of power and influence within the tourism industry which should be a precursor to more sustainable patterns, processes and practices. How we reach this point is a bone of contention: some advocate that it can only be achieved through a radical re-adjustment of the balance of power, while others argue that change in an appropriate direction is already happening within the orthodox development framework. Clarke (1997) also reminds us not to polarize mainstream and sustainable tourism, but to think of sustainability as movement in the 'right' direction. She also suggests that radical change may be neither realistic nor essential, given an on-going process of stakeholder convergence around a broad vision of sustainable tourism.

A challenge to the status quo requires a shift in the balance of power and major changes in the directionalities of influence (Bryant and Bailey, 1997: 5, 28; Berno and Bricker, 2001). Host communities require empowerment in order to have more say in the nature of tourism development and, in the form of grassroots business, to derive a much greater and more direct share in the industry's spoils. The process of empowerment and conscientization may be promoted and facilitated by the non-governmental sector, and civil society more generally, which, as democratic space has opened up in Southeast Asia, has grown in size and influence. NGOs are also increasingly seeking to influence the awareness and behaviour of tourists as discerning consumers, encouraging their participation in more responsible forms of tourism activity.

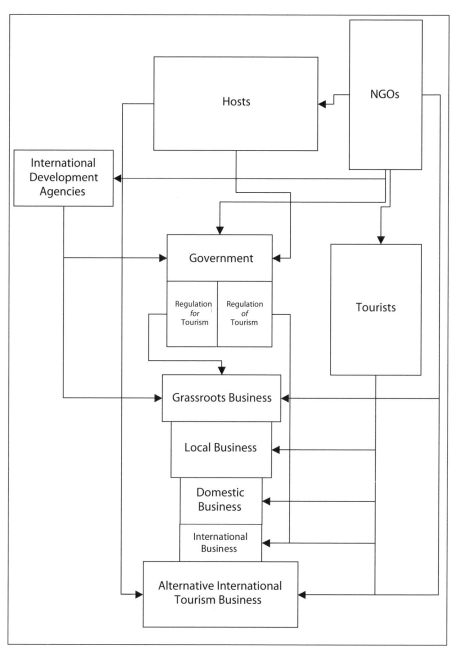

Figure 12.2: Schema 2 – Schematic representation of the relative balance of influence in alternative tourism

The NGO sector, influenced by the changing balance of state power and a growing role for civil society, is posited to have some scope for influencing government policy and action, initially by standing in opposition to government in order to place the adverse effects of tourism development on the policy agenda, but latterly by working in tandem with government (and receptive business actors) to facilitate the transition to sustainable tourism development. Government support for tourism development becomes more directly oriented towards tourism micro-business. Meanwhile, the government's role in the regulation *of* tourism development is also given greater prominence and support. Finally, the international development agencies, having become much more involved in the tourism sector during the era of sustainability, and perhaps influenced by the advocacy work of the NGO sector, can also, through the financial and technical resources at their disposal, become highly influential actors in the field of sustainable tourism.

Whilst in an idealized sense the second schema is a radical departure from the first, the respective virtues of the two models are subject to on-going debate. Political ecology asks (a) whether one model is intrinsically better than the other, or whether radical change is necessarily superior to evolutionary reform whereby a sustainable tourism agenda becomes suffused within the orthodox tourism framework, and (b) just how, in a realist political economic situation, the political baseline can shift from one framework to another. Another important question (c) concerns the dynamics of change – what processes and power shifts can take us from 'orthodox' to 'alternative', and what forms might resistance to such a shift take? What has placed sustainable tourism development higher on the policy, planning and development agendas? We might posit that environmentalism and democratization have been particularly influential in adjusting the relative prominence of environment *vis à vis* development within the global capitalist system, and also in shifting the power relations that underpin sustainability, poverty reduction and distributive justice outcomes. Schema 2 posits the non-governmental sector – as both an agent in, and a manifestation of, the environmentalism and democratization movements – as having been particularly influential in bringing about change (Smillie, 1997: 564). However, the following discussion reveals how international development organizations have, since coming very late in the day to the tourism sector, placed themselves firmly in the driving seat of the sustainability agenda.

Moving Towards Sustainable Tourism Development in Southeast Asia

Considerable progress has been made in the direction of sustainable tourism development over the last decade or so. The following discussion will outline some of the areas where movement has taken place, seen from the perspective both of the actors involved and the actions they have taken.

244

One of the most influential sets of actors in recent years has been the international development organizations (IDOs: a generic term which includes international financial institutions (IFIs), multilateral and bilateral development agencies). Historically, their involvement in the tourism sector had been minimal because it was seen as a luxury sector with little need for development assistance. The World Bank, for instance, supported only 17 tourism-specific activities out of 1,555 projects between 1997 and 2002 (Markandya, Taylor and Pedroso, 2005). But the global importance of tourism and its potential to generate growth and employment in peripheral and economically marginal areas has seen IDOs focus much more on its value as a target of international development assistance in recent years. Nonetheless, the principal strategy until quite recently has been growth-oriented, seeking to mobilize tourism resources through infrastructure development to facilitate tourist access to more remote areas. Much less concern was paid to the environmental and social impacts of tourism (UNEP, 2001).

Since the Rio Earth Summit in 1992, and the adoption of Agenda 21, more emphasis has been placed by IDOs on sustainability issues, and this has been reflected in tourism-related lending or assistance. The United Nations General Assembly in 1997 drew special attention to the importance of tourism in the implementation of Agenda 21, and commissioned an action plan specific to tourism development. One particular concern – with implications for the political ecology of sustainable tourism – had been the way that the different stakeholders in the tourism industry tended to act and make decisions in a mutually exclusive, even competitive fashion, with conflicting interests and few channels for consultation and collaboration (Berno and Bricker, 2001). One of the most important developments in recent years has been the formation of complementary stakeholder partnerships in order to promote sustainable tourism.

Public–private partnerships (PPP) are one such partnership approach. Governments take the lead by providing the legal, policy and institutional framework within which sustainable tourism can be achieved, and local governments translate these principles into effective action at the grassroots level. NGOs act on behalf of local communities to raise the consciousness of tourism issues and challenges, and serve as mediators or consensus-builders between various public and private sector stakeholders. They can act simultaneously as the facilitators of change for private sector interests, sharing the intelligence and experience that they have gained from working with local communities and institutions, whilst acting as a 'nagging conscience' to draw attention to weaknesses of action and approach, and to monitor performance and compliance with sustainability criteria (De Lacy et al., 2002: 6–8). The private sector, at various levels and scales, is able to take advantage of the resources, support and infrastructure that are provided by the other stakeholders, in the process gaining in efficiency while delivering a stronger commitment to sustainability, delivered in a ethically responsible and self-regulatory manner according to negotiated and agreed indicators and standards, such as through the co-management of protected areas (De Lacy et al., 2002: 8).

Following the 2002 World Ecotourism Summit, the donor community was asked to support capacity-building for national and local policy-making and implementation for ecotourism development. The United Nations Environment Programme introduced a set of principles intended to promote the integration of tourism within countries' overall strategies for sustainable development. These included the formulation of integrated national tourism strategies which prioritized the preservation of environmental and biodiversity resources, and which required different agencies and stakeholders to coordinate their activities and jurisdictions around a single sustainability agenda. Inasmuch as IDOs are influential because of the resources they can mobilize and the sway they thus hold over national governments and non-governmental organizations, their promotion of a sustainability agenda, and of collective and collaborative stakeholder responsibility, augurs well for the future.

The Greater Mekong Subregion (GMS) Tourism Development Project (TDP) provides a good illustration of multi-stakeholder coordination in pursuit of sustainable tourism development. The GMS programme commenced in 1992, seeking the 'peace dividend' of regional integration in post-Cold War mainland Southeast Asia, with the Asian Development Bank (www.adb.org/gms) as the lead agency investing in infrastructural improvement. Tourism was introduced as a key sector within the GMS framework in 1993, with the sub-region promoted as a single tourism destination as a means of contributing to poverty reduction and sustainable development (Asian Development Bank, 2005). $440 million is being invested in the GMS TDP from 2006 to 2010, co-funded by national governments, development agencies, IFIs and the private sector. The GMS Tourism Working Group brings together several IDOs (e.g. ADB, UNESCAP, UNESCO, UNWTO, SNV), the Pacific Asia Travel Association (a non-profit private sector tourism trade association) and the national tourism organizations of the six participating Mekong states. The IDOs, in turn, have various codified networks with both the private and non-governmental sectors: e.g. the ADB has had a formal policy for cooperation with NGOs since 1998 (www.adb.org/NGOs/). The GMS thus provides a strong example of multi-agency cooperation in tourism development.

The Dutch bilateral development agency SNV has also been active in promoting sustainable tourism development in the Lower Mekong Basin. In Laos it has developed a SNV–Lao National Ecotourism Advisory Programme (www.snv.org/la), providing the national government with advice on policy, strategy, management and tourism product development. In Vietnam SNV (www.snv.org.vn/) has been working in conjunction with the IUCN to support sustainable tourism with a pro-poor emphasis within its National Sustainable Tourism Project, which commenced in 1998. The Project had a strong conservation focus, with ecotourism as the principal driver, but also includes community-centred tourism initiatives. An example is in the northern tourism hotspot of Sa Pa, where local villagers had largely been excluded from the spoils of tourism development by tour operators, and had hardly any involvement in the planning and management of protected areas. The SNV/IUCN initiative, in conjunction with the Sa Pa District People's Committee, became the first community-based sustainable tourism project for Vietnam, and is being used as a pilot for a new approach to integrated local tourism planning and development. The initiative is also working with the Vietnam National Administration of Tourism (VNAT) to draft legislation to support community and poor people's participation in tourism development.

The development side of sustainable tourism development has not been neglected. Another priority of IDOs has been a major initiative on pro-poor tourism (PPT) with a strong community focus (see also Chapter 8 by Harrison and Schipani). The UK's Department for International Development (DfID, 1999a) has been a leading advocate of pro-poor sustainable tourism development (DfID, 1999b), seeking to mainstream a holistic poverty alleviation agenda within the conventional tourism sector, rather than creating a niche sector – a good example of reformism obviating the need for a more radical alternative tourism approach. It addresses the barriers to full participation in the process of tourism development among poor and peripheral communities, such as elite capture, physical isolation, social exclusion, adverse policy and regulatory frameworks, capital scarcity, knowledge and skills deficiencies. IDOs often work through NGOs to raise awareness of poverty issues within public sector institutions and private sector businesses. The objective is to mainstream a bottom-up approach by getting the public sector to include pro-poor strategies in tourism policy, and the private sector to contribute expertise, marketing and support to facilitate a more inclusive form of tourism development. The GMS Tourism Sector Strategy (Asian Development Bank, 2005) now has a strong pro-poor focus, with village-based tourism a primary model. The following statement from the Tourism Sector Strategy (Asian Development Bank, 2005: 45) illustrates how far the pendulum has swung from the orthodox framework depicted in Figure 12.1: 'Poor local communities will be the primary beneficiaries in planning and owning their future in tourism development with the private sector, development partners, and nongovernmental organizations providing policy, technical assistance, capacity building, and financial support.'

The discussion so far has mainly focused on the catalytic role that IDOs have played in promoting a tourism development agenda that is more conducive to both sustainability and poverty reduction, and in shifting the balance of power among the industry's stakeholders. However, it is the private sector that must take this agenda forward. The following discussion looks briefly at how the private sector has responded to the changing policy environment, using the example of trade associations[1] which influence how the private sector functions in terms of compliance with national regulatory environments and in terms of self-regulation according to sustainability criteria.

In 2001 the Pacific Asia Travel Association (PATA), in conjunction with APEC,[2] adopted a Code for Sustainable Tourism, followed in 2002 by a PATA Traveller's

Code. About the same time PATA also established a Sustainable Tourism Committee to guide the Association's strategy for responsible and sustainable tourism, including the incorporation of pro-poor principles. The Code for Sustainable Tourism encourages tourism to be used as a means of conserving habitats and the rectification of past damage. It requests that members identify areas of environmental, social and heritage sensitivity and plan levels and forms of tourism appropriately, informed by local conditions, priorities and values. It advocates full participation of local communities in tourism planning and implementation, and full compliance with local policies and regulations (www.pata.org). On paper the Code suggests that PATA and APEC are not only moving in the direction of sustainable tourism development, but are also exerting influence on the industry practices of its member countries and firms. However, in reality the voluntary Code has no enforcement or regulatory power, raising the risk that it mainly serves a public relations function that camouflages a business-as-usual pro-growth approach: in other words 'greenwash':

> The tourism industry and tourism destinations have many sophisticated techniques and an enviable track record, often with successful marketing initiatives, to influence consumer behaviour. Clever marketing and image creation can easily present a façade of environmental and cultural sensitivity and responsibility, which will appeal to an increasingly eco-sensitive marketplace . . . One of the greatest dangers is where the tourism industry starts to believe its own pro-environment rhetoric. The marketing spin needs to be positive and enticing but care and understanding need to be exercised in doing so.
>
> (Worboys et al., 2001: 38)

Ultimately, as markets increasingly liberalize, private business holds the key to sustainable tourism development. Their historical priority has been profit maximization and the need to maintain a competitive position in the marketplace, and they have largely escaped accountability for the industry's impact on local ecosystems, cultures and societies. With a gradual shift in the balance of power, more public scrutiny of business practice, and firms' growing sensitivity about their public image, concepts such as 'fair trade tourism' (Tourism Concern, 2000) and 'caring capitalism' (Glassman, 2000; Ayres, 1998), ethical business, social accountability and corporate social responsibility (CSR) are becoming much more commonplace. The advocacy group TourismConcern (2000) has identified some of the principles of CSR and ethical business practice: transparency and accountability in business operations; environmental and social audits to ascertain actual and potential impacts; participatory and equitable processes of consultation and negotiation in tourism development; enhanced local employment, and training for local occupational mobility; use of local products and services, and fair prices negotiated with local producers; fair competition and fairly shared revenues between extra-local and local businesses or actors; adherence to local environmental and taxation regulations. The challenge is to find ways of promoting these sound principles without jeopardizing the very real economic and social benefits that tourism brings to local areas and communities. But once again, the fact that such principles are even being promoted and taken seriously suggests how much the political ecology of tourism in Southeast Asia has changed in recent years.

The tourist has an important potential role to play in the promotion of CSR. As increasingly discerning and concerned consumers, pressure is placed on the corporate sector to deliver more appropriate business packages. Over the last decade or so certification schemes have increasingly been used to benchmark products that match consumer preference for more sustainable tourism activities. Tourism products and services are vetted by an accreditation body – such as Green Globe, Blue Flag, Voluntary Initiative for Sustainable Tourism (see also Chapter 13 by Cochrane) – according to sustainability criteria and standards, and these may then be marketed as sustainability compliant. Not only does this create a sustainability niche market that, with sufficient consumer demand, enterprises might end up competing to serve, but firms can increasingly compete on the basis of reputation and public image. Nonetheless, a Worldwide Fund for Nature report found that certification schemes seldom live up to expectations as a means of promoting sustainable tourism (WWF, 2000), claiming that only 60 out of 500 Green Globe 21 companies actually meet the requirements for usage of the certification logo. Less than one per cent of tourism businesses worldwide have joined up to certification schemes. Also, with the rapid emergence of niche markets like ecotourism there has been a recent proliferation of certification schemes (there are more than 260 worldwide), with no supranational accreditation body to monitor compliance and set global certification standards. The vast majority of certified tourism products today are found in the advanced industrial countries, with very few in regions such as Southeast Asia. The associated assumption that tourists are becoming ethical consumers also appears to have little supporting substance. Dodds and Joppe (2005: 15) found that price rather than ethical principle still provides the overwhelming criterion in guiding consumption choices: 'Sustainability issues are (. . .) not perceived to be a key factor in the tourist decision making process (. . .). Surveys have been unable to conclude that environmental, social or sustainability criteria are a key concern in holiday decision-making by tourists – even so-called ecotourists are not often motivated to travel because of interest in being "responsible" or "environmentally concerned".'

The use of tourism as a positive force in environmental conservation provides a further illustration of some of the progress that has been made towards sustainable tourism development in Southeast Asia in recent years. There are 319 protected areas in Thailand, accounting for some 21 per cent of the land area, including 145 terrestrial and marine national parks, 53 wildlife sanctuaries, 52 non-hunting areas and 69 forest parks (Dachanee and Surachet, n.d.: 2). There is a growing concern in Thailand for the sustainable management of protected areas, and growing media attention is given to failures to manage these areas effectively. But media attention is also raising awareness of the presence and attractions of protected areas, which are increasingly becoming used for the purposes of tourism. This exploitation–conservation dilemma lies at the heart of the current challenges facing sustainable tourism development.

A good illustration of participation and partnership in protected area management in Thailand can be found in Phuket, where two by now quite well-known companies – Sea Canoe and Siam Safari – have managed to contribute to the needs of conservation whilst maintaining a profile as viable ecotourism businesses. Research by Kontogeorgopoulos (2004; 2005) has shown how these two companies have managed to promote some of the purer principles of ecotourism within a mass tourism context. A strong emphasis is placed on the education and training of both employees and tourists in order to raise awareness of ecosystem sensitivity and individual behavioural responsibility (Kontogeorgopoulos, 2004: 4). The businesses also raise funds for conservation (Kontogeorgopoulos, 2005), and a strong emphasis is placed on supporting local communities, in part by ensuring that staff are mainly drawn from the vicinity, and that up to 98 per cent of materials and services are sourced locally (Kontogeorgopoulos, 2004: 5). Tourists pay more for their experience with Sea Canoe, but most understand that the principles of sustainability that the company seeks to promote come at an additional cost, and most seem willing to pay that little bit extra.

Sea Canoe's operations are tailored to match the carrying capacity of the marine areas where their kayaking activities take place, in part to minimize the impact of tourism on the ecosystem itself, but also as a way of preserving the sense of isolation and wilderness which is an important part of the experience for participating tourists (Kontogeorgopoulos, 2004: 4). However, a lack of regulatory control and enforcement by the national park authorities has allowed other companies, which do not follow the same principles of sustainability, to expand and compete with Sea Canoe, in the process adding massively to the numbers of tourists visiting a very sensitive ecosystem. Gradually, mass tourism has competed with, and eventually threatens to swamp, an established and sustainable ecotourism operation (Shepherd, 2002a), principally because prices are lower because environmental and social overheads are absent, and most tourists continue to make their activity decisions based first and foremost on cost.

Sea Canoe seeks not only to protect nature but also to enhance the quality of life of local communities through community-based ecotourism development – something akin to 'fair trade tourism' (Kontogeorgopoulos, 2005). This model has been promoted elsewhere in Thailand by the Thai NGO REST (Responsible Ecotourism Social Tours). REST has been involved in the participatory development of community-based ecotourism in 15 rural communities across Thailand, some in protected areas and adjacent buffer zones (www.rest.or.th). Its role is to raise local awareness of the potential for and associated pitfalls of tourism development. The NGO seeks to build a bridge between communities and the tourism sector, and as such acts as a conduit between local populations, private businesses and local governments – three important stakeholders identified in Figure 12.2. REST ensures the full participation of local communities (especially women and youth) at the inception, planning, development and evaluation stages of tourism development in order that the benefits of tourism remain locally rooted. Young people are engaged to undertake fauna and flora mapping, the idea being that future generations will regain an interest in and knowledge about the ecosystems from which they derive an important part of their livelihoods.

REST promotes and markets tourism on behalf of communities during the early stage of development. It also promotes community-based ecotourism as a model across the country through its Community-Based Tourism Learning Centres. REST has also been lobbying the government, and the national industry association the Tourism Authority of Thailand (TAT), to give greater scope for community-driven ecotourism initiatives (REST, 2003: 3). One constraint that REST has encountered is the limited number of 'alternative tourists', their target group, who are interested in 'cultural and environmental discovery' and thus community-centred tourism activities, and thus most of the participants were drawn from the mass tourism market. Nonetheless the number of 'alternative tourists' is growing: 'Information about the negative consequences of tourism has become more readily available and many more tourists now wish to understand and avoid the hidden environmental and social consequences of their escape to paradise' (REST, 2003: 7–8).

A final illustration, which epitomizes the progress that has been made towards sustainable tourism development in recent years, concerns a pilot community-based ecotourism programme in the Lao PDR (see also Harrison and Schipani in this volume). The Nam Ha Ecotourism Project (NHEP), in the northwestern province of Luang Namtha, was launched in 1999, and is a joint initiative involving UNESCO, the Lao National Tourism Authority (as well as several Lao government departments), the New Zealand International Aid and Development Agency, the International Finance Corporation, SNV, the German aid agency GTZ and the European Union. A sustainable nature and culture based tourism industry is one of eight priority areas for the Lao government's national economic development and poverty alleviation programme. It also dovetails centrally with the ADB's GMS TDP, for which it is being used as a pilot programme to assess and demonstrate the potential for community-based pro-poor ecotourism in protected areas. It is also being used as a national demonstration project in order to build capacity for both mobilizing resources for ecotourism development and simultaneously conserving what has been described as 'the most intact natural environment in Southeast Asia' (UNESCO, 2004: 6). The NHEP is located in the Nam Ha National Protected Area (established in 1993), which consists mainly of mixed deciduous forest and some dry evergreen forest, and contains significant mammals such as the clouded leopard, leopard, tiger, guar, sun bear and Asian elephants. The NHEP focuses on locally managed community-based culture and nature tourism which is intended as a tool in heritage conservation and rural development (UNESCO, 2004: 4).

Tourism activity centres on trekking trails and river trips, with overnight stops in (mainly ethnic minority) village homestays. Strong community participation is encouraged in decision-making and the subsequent development, management, regulation and monitoring of tourism development. Tourism is intended to relieve economic pressure on natural resources in the protected area by giving local communities a livelihood alternative to shifting cultivation, the collection of non-timber forest products and the hunting of wildlife. Tourism is also intended to help protect the cultural rights of 30 indigenous ethnic groups in the project area. Local communities are allowed to set the rules with which tourists must comply (they must attend an obligatory cultural and safety orientation the night before their trek commences), and also identify local carrying capacity (Schipani and Marris, n.d.). Only locally-produced food and other products are available to the trekkers. Villagers act as guides, both for the treks and to introduce tourists to local landscapes, fauna and flora, and traditional practices such as herbal healing and hunting techniques. Money from trekking permits goes to the Nam Ha National Protected Area Management Unit and is used for trail maintenance, conservation activities and biodiversity threat monitoring. Receipts from lodging go to a communal fund which can be used for further ecotourism development or to support local small-scale development projects. A small tax on ecotourism revenues is used to finance monitoring activities in which the ecotourists, as sensitive observers of environmental conditions, play an active role as assessors of the impact of ecotourism on the destination areas (Schipani and Marris, n.d.: 4).

Conclusion

The NHEP, which was given the prestigious United Nations Development Award in 2001 for 'outstanding achievements in the area of sustainable human development and alleviation of poverty in the Lao PDR', provides a strong illustration of the innovative forms of tourism development that have recently emerged in Southeast Asia from the operationalization of the sustainability concept. It involves multiple stakeholder collaboration with a pronounced community and pro-poor focus, with local empowerment and capacity-building, concientization among locals and tourists alike, and a strong conservation emphasis. It demonstrates the progress that has been made, on paper at least, in the direction of sustainable tourism development in Southeast Asia over the last decade or so. Issues such as community participation, poverty amelioration, environmental mitigation, stakeholder collaboration, cultural preservation, ecological conservation and integrated planning, which were only just appearing on the radar screen at the time of our earlier publication (Hitchcock, King and Parnwell, 1993), appear to have become normative concerns. There has been some difficulty and delay in turning principle into practice, as some of the illustrations above have suggested, but the fact that sustainability is now quite high up the agenda, and various sets of quite influential stakeholders appear committed to keeping it there, is an obvious source of future optimism.

From the perspective of political ecology, the discussion has shown how different actors have either driven or deepened the sustainability agenda in a manner which includes some combination of reformism and revisionism. Ostrichism is no longer an option, it would seem, and, arguably, sufficient progress is now being made on both the sustainability and development fronts for radical, anti-developmental measures to be both unrealistic and unnecessary. A shift in the balance of power has occurred within the tourism sector: it approximates much more closely to the latter of the two schemas that were discussed earlier. Although the private sector at various levels clearly remains in the driving seat, the regulatory and ethical environment within which it operates has changed. There is more awareness of the harmful effects that unbridled tourism has on people, cultures and environments, there is less tolerance of these negative impacts than in the past, and there is a panoply of mitigation and management measures which can be deployed to combat or prevent the industry's deleterious outcomes and, as we have seen, to enhance its local developmental potential.

This chapter has suggested that a gradual power shift among actors and stake-holders has been instigated from above and from below: IDOs, having arrived late on the tourism scene, have been very influential in both promoting and supporting the sustainability agenda, whilst the non-governmental sector, with its creeping tentacles at the grassroots level, has been in a strong position to match local intelligence and experience to the community-focused imperatives of sustainable tourism development. Governments' regulatory emphases appear to be shifting towards an appropriate balance between regulation *for* and the regulation *of* development, and the private sector seems increasingly receptive to adopting ethical principles in its local tourism business practices, although of course 'business as usual' and 'growth at any cost' are still quite widespread philosophies in the private and public sectors. Much more work nonetheless remains to be done, not least in convincing tourists to act as ethical consumers who can potentially wield immense power over the future direction of sustainable tourism development in Southeast Asia.

Notes

1 Members of tourism trade associations typically consist of: national tourism organizations; national, provincial and municipal tourism departments; air and cruise lines; major tourism companies;` and individual firms.

2 Asia–Pacific Economic Cooperation: a 21-country multilateral forum for the promotion of economic and business development and trade/investment liberalisation in the Asia–Pacific region.

13

New Directions in Indonesian Ecotourism

Janet Cochrane

Introduction

The Declaration on Ecotourism prepared at the World Ecotourism Summit in 2002 recognized the travelling public's growing interest in visiting natural areas (WES, 2002). Governments and private companies are benefiting from the competitive advantages offered by the natural environment of their countries by capitalizing on this trend, sometimes so successfully that tourism to natural areas has become the cornerstone of their industry. In other places, nature-based tourism is just one of a range of opportunities, such as in Indonesia, with its strong beach, cultural and shopping tourism sectors. Yet the volume of tourism to Indonesia, at 5.1 million in 2005, makes even the minority activity of ecotourism significant, while the effects can be considerable in relation to the sometimes fragile environments, cultures and economies where it often takes place.

Any appraisal of ecotourism will cover not just product and market-related factors but also the context of the industry and the discourses which shape its development. This broader context encompasses domestic policy decisions on ecotourism and the social, political and cultural influences on these, and the international trends and issues which shape demand. Discourses affecting ecotourism include attitudes to natural resource management within the Indonesian polity, public opinion and actions on environmental conservation, the poverty alleviation agenda, dilemmas over the use of protected areas, and whether ecotourism – which is sometimes conflated with sustainable tourism – can, in fact, be recognized as making a genuine contribution to sustainability.

It is now largely accepted that ecotourism is no longer situated within the spectrum of 'alternative' tourism (as opposed to 'conventional' tourism) where it was placed in the early 1990s (for example Cater, 1994). Its integration into mainstream tourism and the difficulty of disaggregating its impacts and practices from other forms of tourism are now widely recognized. In Europe, for instance, forms of tourism which would be labelled 'ecotourism' in developing countries are termed 'agritourism' or 'rural tourism', while Kontogeorgopolos (2003a) points out that ecotourism does not always occur in spatial isolation from conventional tourism. He and other authors (e.g. Weaver, 2002; Sofield and Li, 2003) have remarked on the emergence, especially in Asia, of mass ecotourism, in other words tourism and other recreational activities which share many of the attributes of conventional tourism but which are located in natural areas. The high volume of visitors to natural areas in Southeast Asia was already noted by Cochrane (1993a) in an earlier assessment of ecotourism in Southeast Asia, and numbers have increased substantially since then. Purists may argue that the concept of mass ecotourism has too many internal contradictions to be valid, but its undeniable existence means that not only the tourism industry but also conservation planners and development policy-makers must take it seriously.

These three groups are the actors most closely involved in stimulating or managing ecotourism, but they often interpret ecotourism in different ways. For the industry, using the term to describe tours can reflect a marketing construct rather than a management philosophy, leading to accusations of 'greenwash' (although there are many sincere companies which adhere strictly to low-impact policies). For development workers, an idealized, product-focused approach can mean that market and commercial considerations are neglected, while both this group and conservationists have only recently begun to grapple with the fact that the benefits initially promised by ecotourism to marginalized communities and biodiversity conservation have rarely been realised. Blamey (2001) concludes that different definitions are useful according to different circumstances and different perspectives. In this chapter, the understanding of ecotourism that is used gives equal prominence to three different aspects: successful ecotourism is commercially viable tourism in natural areas which contributes to environmental conservation and improves the welfare of local people. At the same time, the difficulty of distinguishing between conventional tourism and ecotourism in its Asian form is recognized.

To set the background for ecotourism in Indonesia an overview of the Indonesian tourism industry generally is given, particularly over the last fifteen years, followed by an assessment of how ecotourism has developed over the same period. The discussion is informed by market-orientated insights and by a reflection on the opportunities for further development, and by a consideration of the economic impacts and benefits of ecotourism in the local context. The obstacles to success cannot be ignored, and attempts to overcome these are evaluated: recent strategies based on the sustainable livelihoods approach appear to offer some hope for the future.

Indonesian Tourism: Stagnation and Change

In the 1990s it was apparent that both the Indonesian government and tourism industry concurred with the widely-held international view that ecotourism was a minority, 'alternative' form of tourism and, as such, was unlikely to generate much economic reward for either public or private sector. The emphasis was then on fostering the growth of a 'beach-with-cultural-overtones' model of tourism. This policy worked well in the late 1980s and early 1990s when Indonesia's apparent political stability and economic strength coincided with new demand from generating countries. The result was that visitor arrivals grew more than five-fold from 825,035 in 1986 to 5,034,472 in 1996 (Table 13.1: the per cent change column displays the year-on-year growth in tourism, and reveals steady to spectacular growth in tourism numbers during this period; the final column highlights even more spectacular growth in foreign exchange earnings from tourism over an even greater period). Since then, however, the situation has changed considerably, with international tourism having stagnated or declined. The reasons for this are well-rehearsed: major markets were affected by the Asian recession of the late 1990s and by several years of economic, political and social instability surrounding the ending of the Suharto regime in 1998, and then by the bombing of tourism targets in Bali in 2002 and 2005. The result is that by 2005 arrivals had barely climbed back to their level of a decade earlier, with 5.1 million international visitors.

It is notable, however, that even though tourism to Indonesia was badly hit by terrorism and other destabilizing factors, the industry has not only survived but experienced relatively short periods of actual decline. This is partly because of steps taken by the authorities – especially in Bali – to manage the various crises. During the late 1990s the Balinese distanced themselves through promotional positioning from the rest of Indonesia in order to continue to attract their traditional core markets, and although the island's peaceful image was shattered by the bombing of the nightclubs in Kuta in October 2002, a potentially volatile situation was contained through well-publicized religious ceremonies offering spiritual healing and through using the system of village banjars to ensure that no retaliation was taken against the Javanese Muslim community, from amongst which the bombers were quickly known to have come (Hitchcock and Darma Putra, 2005). Meanwhile, the Indonesian security services acted swiftly to apprehend the bombers and tackle sources of terrorism generally in the country (Brown and Junek, 2004). After the first bombings the crisis management process was supported by the PATA-led Bali Recovery Plan (PATA, 2003) and after the second by the creation of a stronger public-private sector partnership within the Bali Tourism Board (WTO, 2005c).

Industry leaders appealed to other Asians to visit in greater numbers to support jobs and the tourism infrastructure (Sukamdani, 2003), and a further demand recovery factor was the increasing desire and ability on the part of Indonesians to explore their own country. Within Indonesia's large population (225 million in 2005), is a substantial and growing middle-class whose travel and leisure patterns are changing: private car ownership is growing, and an increasing proportion of people are less inclined to go on excursions in large groups of neighbours or work colleagues, instead preferring to holiday with their extended nuclear family or smaller groups of friends. Civil servants no longer work 6 short days per week but five longer ones, giving a vast category of people with stable incomes the available time for weekend travel. Domestic tourism had anyway been a significant feature of the Indonesian industry since at least the mid-1970s, and had long been encouraged by the government as a way of fostering national integration, redistributing income from urban to rural areas, and discouraging people from travelling abroad to spend their disposable income (Spillane, 1987; Hadmoko, 1998). Now, it was recognized that the domestic market was more stable than the international one (Martana, 2003), while people were encouraged to travel as a form of patriotic duty in order to bolster the industry (Handoyo, 2002).

The result has been a huge growth in domestic tourism, with its concomitant possibilities for wealth redistribution. This is indicated in a 66 per cent increase in domestic hotel nights over the period 1999–2003 from 21,700,005 to 36,060,233 (BPS, 2005), while domestic tourism expenditure in 2001 was calculated at $7.7 billion (budpar.com). These huge movements of domestic tourists are of great significance for ecotourism, as will be seen below.

Ecotourism Opportunities in Indonesia

The broad-brush picture of annual visitor totals masks considerable changes and trends within the composition of arrivals and tourism flows around Indonesia, and it is the more detailed picture which is relevant to ecotourism. When tourism to Indonesia began to be encouraged in the early 1980s as part of an export-oriented growth and diversification strategy, the markets targeted were traditional ones from Europe and Australia, and the emerging markets of East Asia. By the late 1980s tourists from Asia surpassed arrivals from Europe, but European arrivals continued to increase, many of them travelling with the specialist nature, culture and adventure tourism companies which by then were well-established. These included, for example, the British companies Exodus (founded 1974), Explore (1980) and Naturetrek (early 1980s), and the Dutch companies Koning Aap (1980), Sawadee (1983), and Djoser (1985).

The number of specialist tour operators set up in the 1970s and 1980s indicates the growing sophistication and diversity of more established tourism markets. The companies were often run by people who had come to know certain destinations through

Table 13.1: Tourism Arrivals to Indonesia 1969–2004

Year	Visitors	% Change	Foreign Exchange (US$ Million)	% Change
1969	86,100		10.8	
1970	129,319	50	16.2	50
1971	178,781	38	22.6	40
1972	221,195	24	27.6	22
1973	270,303	22	40.9	49
1974	313,452	16	54.4	33
1975	366,293	17	62.3	15
1976	401,237	9	70.6	13
1977	433,393	8	81.3	15
1978	468,514	8	94.3	16
1979	501,430	7	188.0	99
1980	561,178	12	289.0	54
1981	600,151	7	309.1	7
1982	592,046	(–2)	358.8	16
1983	638,885	8	439.5	23
1984	700,910	10	519.7	18
1985	749,351	7	525.3	1
1986	825,035	10	590.5	12
1987	1,060,347	29	837.7	42
1988	1,301,049	23	1,027.8	23
1989	1,625,965	18	1,284.5	25
1990	2,177,566	34	2,105.2	64
1991	2,569,870	18	2,522.0	20
1992	3,064,161	19	3,278.2	30
1993	3,403,000	11	3,987.6	22
1994	4,006,312	18	4,785.3	20
1995	4,324,229	8	5,228.3	9
1996	5,034,472	16	6,307.7	21
1997	5,185,243	3	5,321.5	(–16)
1998	4,606,416	(–11)	4,331.1	(–19)
1999	4,727,520	3	4,710.2	9
2000	5,064,217	7	5,748.8	22
2001	5,153,620	2	5,400.0	(–6)
2002	5,033,400	(–3)	4,300.0	(–20)
2003	4,467,021	(–11)		
2004	5,321,165	19	4,800.0	
2005	5,006,797	6		

Sources: Directorate General of Tourism, Jakarta; Biro Pusat Statistik, Jakarta; Ministry of Tourism and Culture, Jakarta.

travelling there themselves, while their customers sought a channel for their aspirations to understand more of the world, were experienced enough at travelling to short-haul destinations to venture further afield, and had sufficient disposable income to indulge their interests. It is no coincidence that the term 'ecotourism' was coined in the mid-1980s (Orams, 2001): its encapsulation not just of tourism in ecologically interesting areas but also of a broader concern for environmental issues led to its rapid adoption.

This favourable market environment meant that developing countries with a relatively unaltered natural environment and substantial assets in the form of scenery or wildlife were well placed to exploit these opportunities. Some were highly successful at doing so, including Nepal, where the trekking industry became its largest source of foreign exchange; Costa Rica, where a small number of well-organized national parks became the focus of an important industry; and, most obviously, the more stable countries of eastern and southern Africa, with their charismatic megafauna and local entrepreneurs able to penetrate and exploit suitable markets.

Indonesia, too, has a number of features which should give it competitive advantage in this market. It has a huge variety of beautiful landscapes, large tracts of which remain relatively undisturbed; many species of unique wildlife, including some with popular appeal (or at least recognition) such as the orang-utan and the Javan rhinoceros; an extensive network of protected areas; and an improving infrastructure of transportation, accommodation and experienced tourism industry personnel. The country also has several 'unique selling propositions', including internationally-known landscape formations, colourful cultural elements in its diverse ethnic groups, and the renown (or notoriety) of some of its islands, tinged with mystique, adventure and even danger. For instance, King Kong was discovered terrorising an island in uncharted waters off Sumatra, the plot of a Sherlock Holmes novel hinges on the Giant Rat of Sumatra, and the heroes and anti-heroes of Conrad's novels plied pirate-infested waters around Borneo. More reliably, the catastrophic 1883 eruption of Krakatau was well documented and the residual Krakatau islands are a considerable tourist attraction, despite the obvious geological hazard they signify (tragically confirmed by the 2004 tsunami).

State-sponsored promotion of tourism in Indonesia has paid little attention to historical or literary references or even to natural history, however, preferring to concentrate on the mainstream and more immediately profitable beach and cultural sectors. Despite this, by the late 1980s the international ecotourism market was beginning to show some promise, particularly two specialist sectors and a more general interest one. The most significant specialist area (if we exclude surfing tourism as a non-specialist tourism undertaking) is sub-aqua diving. The rich coral reefs around the archipelago attract a substantial clientele and localized facilities have grown up to provide for (and profit from) them. In 1992, for instance, the diving industry around the Bunaken Marine National Park, in North Sulawesi, already employed at least 150 people as dive guides and buddies, boat-drivers, maintenance men and hotel staff (Cochrane, 1993b), and by 2005 there were other major diving centres around the islands of the Komodo National Park, on the reefs off the south coast of Flores near Maumere, and around the Togian and Tukang Besi groups of islands off Sulawesi. Diving is also important in the Thousand Island archipelago north of Jakarta and around Bali because of its accessibility to nearby markets, although reefs here often suffer damage from pollution and destructive fishing methods.

The second specialist market is bird-watching. Indonesia has over 1500 species of bird, representing 17 per cent of the global tally (Jepson, 1997). Birders often demonstrate an enthusiasm bordering on obsession for their hobby and are famously price-insensitive, ready to put up with uncomfortable travel and basic facilities if the bird-watching is of high quality. From the late 1970s a few tenacious foreign bird-watchers based in Indonesia, supplemented by visiting birders, ventured to remote corners of the country and documented the extraordinarily rich avifauna, and in certain areas (for instance Central and North Sulawesi and Halmahera) a locally significant tourism sector evolved around this market. Although lucrative on a per capita basis, however, this market is only ever likely to remain small.

Tapping into less specialized markets, a few general interest companies brought tour groups to the more accessible and better-organized national parks and nature reserves where a degree of comfort could be assured, and where wildlife viewing was easier because of the more open habitat or through habituation of wildlife. Such places included the orang-utan centres at Bohorok (North Sumatra) and Tanjung Puting (South Kalimantan), where formerly captive orang-utans were reintroduced to the wild; the Komodo National Park, where the 'dragons' were baited with freshly-slaughtered goats (until the practice was banned in the early 1990s as interfering with the giant lizards' natural behaviour); and the Baluran and Ujung Kulon National Parks in Java, where open areas of grassland facilitated the viewing of species such as banteng (wild cattle), deer, wild boar and peacocks. In some cases people's knowledge-seeking aspirations could be satisfied through the interpretation of local cultural and environmental features, and a degree of communicative staging was often essential: for instance although Ujung Kulon shelters the world's last viable population of the Javan rhino, it is extremely unlikely that casual tourists will spot one, but the knowledge of its presence – ideally confirmed by footprints or piles of dung – adds cognitive value to their stay.

Although visitor numbers to Indonesia in the last few years have been uninspiring, belief in a latent demand for Indonesian tourism generally and for more specialist forms in particular has meant that the commercial infrastructure has grown much more sophisticated. This has been facilitated by the more liberal business environment since the change in regime which has made it easier for foreigners to set up businesses and because young Indonesian entrepreneurs have built on their enthusiasm for the country's wild places to develop adventure tourism and ground handling operations. Meanwhile, the market for ecotourism has greatly expanded, with increased demand both from tour operators based in generating countries for new, off-the-beaten-track products, and from an ever-expanding cohort of individual tourists experienced in long-haul travel and enfranchised by the Internet.

As with conventional tourism in Indonesia, however, the major general interest market for ecotourism comes from local tourists. A significant feature of domestic tourism throughout Asia is the popularity of natural attractions such as beaches and mountains, and Indonesia is no exception. In Thailand natural attractions such as the seaside and mountains were found to rank highest amongst domestic tourists' favourite destinations (Kaosa-ard, Bezic and White, 2001), in Malaysia large numbers of urban-dwellers visit natural areas at weekends (Hamzah, Khalifah, Dahlan and Kechik, 2003), and for China, Sofield and Li (2003) remark on the vast demand for leisure attractions in the countryside. Tourism to natural areas in Asia is not only high volume but also growing at a rapid rate: for instance visitors to Khao Yai National Park, in Thailand, increased from 401,661 tourists in 1987 (TDRI, 1995) to 4.8 million in 2002 (Ross 2003), and from 91,891 in 1991 at Bromo Tengger Semeru National Park, Indonesia, to 900,483 in 2004 (DepHut, 1996; 2005). This large and ready market has given rise to spontaneous entrepreneurial responses, the challenges of which are discussed in a later section of this chapter.

Ecotourism and Local Economies

Another feature of ecotourism is that the sector is sometimes subject to 'over-planning' in the form of an externally-generated agenda applied by development and conservation NGOs. By the late 1980s, this sector had begun to seize on the opportunities of ecotourism as a means of achieving conservation and development objectives in the face of countervailing social, cultural and economic influences, and there are numerous examples of NGOs and other development agencies implementing feasibility studies and setting up ecotourism and other income-generating ventures associated with national parks. This strategy has been successful in some cases. In Nepal, the Annapurna Conservation Area Project demonstrates that tourism's impacts can be successfully managed while providing an improved standard of living for local people (MacLellan, Dieke and Thapa, 2000; Holden and Ewen, 2004), and in Namibia community-based wildlife tourism initiatives appear to be able to generate income from wildlife while resolving disputes over access to resources (Schalken, 1999; Ashley, 2000).

In the Annapurna area, at least, impact mitigation measures were overlaid on to a pre-existing tourism industry, but in other places process-led initiatives have been based on weaker foundations and ventures have sometimes failed to flourish. For instance in Indonesia, community-run guest-houses have been set up in the

Halimun National Park and at Taman Jaya, on the border of Ujung Kulon (both in West Java), and at Pamah Simelir, on the edge of the Leuser National Park (North Sumatra). At Halimun, a consortium of ecologists, entrepreneurs and development agencies established several village guesthouses, handing over ownership to local communities in 1998. Villagers were trained in tourism services and management, but by 2004 the project was still not attracting enough visitors to make it economically viable (although limited ecotourism activities do take place). A combination of indigenous and exogenous circumstances seems to have been responsible, including the construction of a better-quality guesthouse nearby, the lack of modern methods of communication, and difficulties with maintaining the partnership between the funding agency, the project managers, and the local community (Joy, 1997; Fauzi, 2001; Hartono, 2005). Some of these problems were symptomatic of the absence of the market orientation which is essential to any tourism venture. Ecotourism of this small-scale, project-driven type was anyway a tiny sector and in addition, the timing of the scheme was unfortunate in that it was launched as Indonesia began to suffer from poor publicity and declining tourism numbers from the late 1990s.

Within Indonesian tourism generally, hotel occupancy levels after the 2002 Bali bombings plummeted and growth projections were nullified, affecting stakeholders from larger investors to individual employees. Employment in tourism had alleviated pressure on natural resources, but individuals were now forced to rely on these to survive. An illustration of this came from an encounter by the author with a land-worker in the northern Sumatra rainforest in early 1998, when the monetary crisis was at its most severe and tourists were deterred by political and social instability. Until recently this man had worked as a cook at a four-star hotel, but he had lost his job when the tourists stopped coming. He was now planning to clear a patch of forest to plant a cash crop for income to feed his family. A second example comes from the Bromo Tengger Semeru National Park, in East Java. When tourism was at its height in the mid-1990s, villagers able to diversify their livelihood strategies to include tourism as well as agriculture were less likely to collect fuelwood from the adjacent protected area than people living in similar villages who relied solely on farming. In 2005, however, after several years of decline and change in tourism, it was found that some families who had previously used alternative fuels (especially kerosene) had reverted to using wood from the protected area as a 'free' resource to supplement the household economy (author's research).

This kind of direct link between tourism and the use (or non-use) of natural resources indicates that the fall-back position for many low-paid Indonesian workers in times of recession is to return to agricultural or forest-based forms of cash-generation. Research in Bromo Tengger Semeru and other studies (for example Brandon and Wells, 1992) suggests that many Indonesian and other peasant workers in any case use tourism as part of a spectrum of income-earning opportunities. This, again, makes it difficult to place a clear dividing line between conventional tourism and ecotourism, since employment in conventional tourism may reduce pressure on natural resources as much as working in ecotourism – a factor perhaps overlooked by commentators from industrialized countries where the alternative to working in tourism is employment in another service or manufacturing sector, or support from the social welfare services.

Addressing Challenges

A related aspect is that when a natural area becomes a popular destination, entrepreneurs will be drawn in from outside to supply the necessary services. These people may increase pressure on the natural environment through their own needs and may begin to exclude local residents through better access to capital or skills. This is part of the seemingly inexorable progression of tourism illustrated by Butler's 1981 model of the Tourist Area Life-Cycle. A classic example of this is offered by Bohorok, in North Sumatra, referred to earlier as one of the few places where wildlife can be easily seen.

Here, a centre for reintroducing formerly captive orang-utans to the wild was set up in the early 1970s on the edge of a river in the rainforest several hours' drive from the nearest city, Medan. For many years it received few visitors, and those who came were prepared to put up with primitive facilities. By 1989 three guest-houses had appeared to cater to the trickle of tourists, and four years later there were fourteen, by which time road communications from Medan had improved so that the journey took less than three hours. Just two years later the tourism infrastructure had swelled to 32 hotels and guest-houses with 268 stalls selling food, clothing and souvenirs, and by 1998 there were too many hotels and stalls to count in a three-day visit – and as almost all were unlicensed the authorities also had no idea how many there were. The majority of tourists were domestic visitors from the city, seeking refreshment from the polluted urban environment. Despite its location on the edge of a national park, there were no constraints on developments, with more and bigger ones even planned; all the stakeholders (except the orang-utans) had an interest in allowing as many tourists as possible to arrive.[1]

Because of over-development and over-crowding, Bohorok was fast acquiring a bad reputation amongst foreign tourists. Whereas for about a decade it had been a popular stop-over point on the standard backpackers' route through Southeast Asia, those 'in the know' were now shunning the place. The messy reality of tourism at Bohorok, with its inadequate waste and sewage disposal facilities, unchecked building and commercial development, loud music, hustlers and poor environmental and species management is an example of how private and commercial interests are likely to override the public good in the absence of a strong institutional framework.[2] This, unfortunately, is an all-too-frequent, 'tragedy of the commons' scenario in Indonesia: when tourism flourishes, private interests tend to prevail over the public good.

By comparison, the technological means to mitigate the environmental impacts of ecotourism are straightforward, for instance through improvements to the micro-infrastructure of visitor facilities such as installing surfaced walking trails or board-walks, the creation of 'honeypot' attractions in more robust areas, measures to steer crowds away from more fragile areas or limit visitor numbers generally, or through educational schemes aimed at modifying visitor behaviour. These techniques are well understood and have been tried and tested in a number of locations.

Technological means can also be used – although less successfully – to address the product-related barriers to ecotourism constituted by the nature of the wildlife. Except in the case of the coral reefs, avifauna and a few attractive and easily-viewed larger species, Southeast Asian wildlife is solitary, shy and difficult to see. Far more could be done than at present to ensure that visitors who wish to learn more about the tropical environment can do so, for instance through the habituation of more compliant species of animal, the provision of good-quality interpretation centres, or arranging early morning or night-time walks with knowledgeable guides.

More testing are the challenges presented by the governance of natural resources, and it is the weakness of this institutional and political context which means that the economic opportunities of Indonesian ecotourism are not being fully realized. Two constraints of this type were already identified in the 1993 assessment of ecotourism in Indonesia mentioned above (Cochrane, 1993a), and it is interesting to review them in the light of industry developments over the last fifteen years.

First, a mismatch between the expectations and reality of tourism in protected areas was noted, in that the knowledge-seeking objectives of Western tourists, shaped by television documentaries and previous travel experiences, were at odds with the more hedonistic, leisure-seeking aspirations of domestic tourists who already crowded the more accessible protected areas during weekends and holidays. The failure to under-stand the aspirations of different markets is largely due to the way that Indonesian national parks were originally set up in the 1970s and 80s, and continued to be insufficiently addressed right up to the early years of the twenty-first century.

Although tourism was nominally part of the rationale for the core network of national parks when they were established (FAO, 1982), park planners and advisers were foresters or ecologists without expertise in tourism or development issues, and little attention was paid to market needs or characteristics or even to the wider tourism infrastructure in terms of handling agents, linkages with other attractions in the vicinity, or the capacity of local communities to provide tourism services. This meant that appropriate markets were often unaware of Indonesian nature products, while higher-income groups were unlikely to visit the parks because they lacked appropriate facilities. Western tourists with an orientation towards a self-conscious enjoyment of the unaltered natural environment were deterred by leisure facilities such as shops and the plethora of eating venues which appeared at locations popular with domestic tourists.

In the event, the various needs of different market segments have been partly resolved by the spatial separation of international visitors from mass-market local tourists through market mechanisms which take foreigners to the more remote – and expensively accessed – places, while locations close to urban centres continue to be popular with domestic visitors. The requirement for different types of facility could be further overcome by interpretive means of the kind described above.

A second inhibiting factor to ecotourism development noted in the earlier assessment relates to the institutional characteristics of the governing bodies responsible for the national parks. Neither the Indonesian authorities nor their international advisers knew much about tourism during at least the first couple of decades that the parks were in existence, and because of the preservationist philosophy of protected areas management which then prevailed, they were often reluctant to countenance any economic activity in them – even low impact forms of tourism or sustainable use of forest products. Furthermore, protected areas were under the jurisdiction of the Ministry of Forestry and were institutionally impervious to influence by the tourism authorities, since the hierarchical nature of the Indonesian bureaucracy militates against cross-sectoral co-operation (Timothy, 1998).

Institutional arrangements also meant that there was little financial incentive for national park managers to attempt to integrate tourism and conservation: entry fees were at first non-existent or set locally, with little accountability, and once a national fee system was introduced in 1992 the monies were returned to national or regional treasuries (PHPA, 1992). At the same time, the generally lax attitude to public accountability amongst civil servants in Indonesia meant that where tour operators and individual tourists did overcome the lack of information and infrastructure to reach the national parks, staff were quick to seize the opportunity to make money from them through semi-official fees for guiding or other services such as driving boats or, more dubiously, through simply pocketing cash from entry fees or abusing their position to profit from tourist expenditure. For instance, the head ranger at the Bromo Tengger Semeru National Park built a hotel on national park land in a prime position overlooking the view of volcanoes, mountains and lava flows which was the primary element of the tourist 'gaze'. Having started out in 1996 as a small lodge, by 2005 the hotel was a substantial installation of over 40 rooms (author's research).

It is generally accepted in Indonesia that 'corruption is the prerogative of the élite' (Vatikiotis, 1993: 54), with 'élite' groups at various levels of society profiting by larger or smaller amounts. For most of the post-Independence era, Indonesians have enjoyed considerable scope to ignore regulations designed to cover civil aspects of society such as health and safety, the just and proper management of the nation's finances, and protection of the environment. The neglect of these areas applies equally to those who are supposed to abide by the regulations and to people who are supposed to enforce them, and these institutional weaknesses are compounded by the lack of political will to enforce sustainable management of natural resources. Conservationists fear that conflicts between individuals and between private and public interests over resource use have become more marked under decentralization measures since the fall of Suharto in 1998, with 'the old central government kleptocracy' having been replaced by 'a plethora of district-level kleptocracies' (Jarvie, Kanaan, Malley, Roule and Thomson, 2003).

Nevertheless, there are signs that some measures are being taken to redress the balance of resource management in favour of the public interest. These are occurring in the context of a global policy shift away from 'government' towards 'governance', in which civil society plays a more prominent role in managing collective affairs, rather than allocating decision-making to the public sector, and in the case of protected areas, this shift is reflected in the more pragmatic approach to management being applied by development and conservation agencies.

Co-Management: Integrating Conservation and Tourism

The latest policies build on steps already introduced in the early 1990s to make protected areas more economically productive. The concept of ICDPs (Integrated Conservation and Development Projects) had by then been used in a number of places, resulting in some of the well-meant but flawed projects of the type described at Halimun. By the beginning of this century a desire to ensure that protected areas addressed objectives of social justice as well as biodiversity conservation, coupled with a more sophisticated understanding of the processes of resource utilization, had generated a more complex management approach. This centred on marrying market mechanisms with the concept of sustainable livelihoods, which encompasses micro and macro levels of human use of natural resources, and recognizes that change can only take place at village level if actions are linked to a broader enabling environment of policy, advocacy and capacity-building (Conway, Moser, Norton and Farrington, 2002; Worah, 2002).

In the field of natural resource management this discourse has taken expression in collaborative management, or co-management, initiatives. The approach was pioneered in social forestry and protected areas management and acknowledges that the support of all affected parties will only be achieved through involving people at all stages of planning and management (Jamal and Getz, 1995) and through creating institutional structures which facilitate genuine, active and representational participation by stakeholders. In essence, co-management uses horizontal and vertical networks of stakeholders as social partners who agree to share and manage resources through a process of negotiation, continual learning and adaptive management (Borrini-Feyerabend, Farvar, Nguinguiri and Ndangang, 2000; Berkers, 2004; CGIAR, 2005).

In Indonesia, collaborative management of national parks was introduced in the late 1990s and the early years of this century under several aid and development programmes, for instance at the Bunaken Marine National Park (North Sulawesi), at Komodo National Park (Nusa Tenggara), and at Kayan Mentarang National Park

(Kalimantan). In a typical structure, the park at Bunaken is managed by an advisory board representing dive operators, environmental organizations, universities, government departments and resident communities. The arrangements were designed to address resentment felt by park residents that they were being excluded from the benefits of tourism. Most of the revenue from dive tourism is used to fund conservation and community development programmes within the park, with the remainder split between different levels of government (Cochrane and Tapper, 2006).

The benefits of collaborative management for all sides seem clear. The government's administrative burden is reduced, the interests of local communities are addressed, conservation objectives are more likely to be achieved, and tourism has a better chance of commercial success since the private sector has more capacity to address market aspects such as creating attractive products, understanding market segments, communicating with target markets, and delivering better service. The Indonesian government showed its recognition of these advantages by issuing a decree on collaborative management for protected areas in 2004, cautiously welcomed by conservation groups (Purnomo and Lee, 2004).

Of course, co-management initiatives have drawbacks: they rely on a positive enabling environment, on a strong institutional framework and good, transparent leadership to resolve conflicts and ensure that more powerful groups do not gain disproportionate access to resources, and on a source of funds which can be used for community development and management interventions. Not all protected areas can generate funds through tourism, and in all but a very few cases the level of tourism-generated revenues is tiny compared to the cost of management. There may also be reluctance on the part of stakeholders representing the interests of the environment to permit mass ecotourism, even though this is likely to become the established model for the majority of Asian ecotourism activities – and, carefully managed, could generate substantial funds for conservation and community development. This, again, comes back to the need for institutional management able to plan for tourism, to ensure that private sector interests do not over-ride the public good as in the case of Bohorok.

Conclusion

Many of Indonesia's most outstanding natural assets are protected in national parks, and these accordingly offer the most obvious focus for partnership approaches to ecotourism. It is too early to tell whether collaborative management schemes will always be successful in funnelling tourism revenues into biodiversity conservation and poverty alleviation, but the indications from the few schemes which exist so far are promising: they offer a way of combining the institutional strength of the public sector and the entrepreneurial expertise of the private sector, while incorporating the needs of marginalized indigenous communities whose participation in tourism is often hard to achieve.

In addition, there are many enterprises and initiatives outside protected areas which are founded on the principles of ecotourism as defined at the beginning of this chapter: that tourism should support environmental and human welfare while being commercially viable. Such enterprises include the boutique resort of Nihiwatu, in Sumba, where foreign investors have partnered with the local community to run up-market activity holidays; a group of eco-lodges in Bali, Flores, Kalimantan and Java which have won recognition of their high environmental management standards under the Green Globe 21 accreditation system (see also Chapter 12 by Parnwell); and Kaliandra, in East Java, where a local philanthropist has provided seedcorn funding for lodges in the uplands above Surabaya, and an environmental activist-turned-entrepreneur trains local people for employment in nature-based tourism products. Kaliandra runs team-building and incentive programmes for businesses from the industrialized hinterland of Surabaya, with a through-put of thousands of participants each month, in addition to white-water rafting excursions aimed at domestic thrill-seekers and hiking, pony-trekking and village-based programmes which target Western tourists.

For all of these, the label 'eco' seems to be justified in that nature tourism is at the core of the product, and efforts are made to minimise environmental impacts and to share economic benefits with local people. In all three cases there has been an element of altruism in that the entrepreneurs concerned have been motivated partly by a desire to increase community participation in ecotourism, but in each case market considerations have been central to product development, and all attract visitors on a commercial basis and in competition with other enterprises. This approach is undoubtedly the key to achieving a long-term market presence, a lesson which development and conservation agencies have now learned and are applying in co-management schemes.

The ideal ecotourist for many is the environmentally-aware, well-off bird-watcher or scuba diver, but the reality is that the majority of tourists to natural areas in Indonesia are domestic or regional tourists. As far as mass ecotourism is concerned, commercial viability seems to be readily achieved, but the picture is less clear regarding the other two principles of ecotourism. Local entrepreneurs can make money if their skills facilitate entry into the industry, but outside entrepreneurs are likely to be drawn in because of the income-earning opportunities. Although in some cases involvement in tourism reduces direct and destructive exploitation of natural resources, there is insufficient evidence to show that pressure on the natural environment is reduced overall. On balance, the impacts are likely to be significant because the presence of tourists means a greater demand for water, waste disposal, souvenirs which may be based on wildlife products, and habitat loss to tourism installations. This is especially true in Asia because much tourism in natural areas here shares features with conventional tourism, especially a focus on artificial leisure facilities such as shops, eating venues and entertainment opportunities, rather than an orientation towards a self-conscious enjoyment of the unaltered natural environment.

On the other hand, mass ecotourism does offer opportunities for ensuring that economic benefits flow in several directions. The direct, indirect and induced income from tourism expenditure creates five principal beneficiary groups: governments, the tourism industry, tourists, host communities, and the environment. While all five of these are affected in some way by any kind of tourism, the difference between conventional tourism and ecotourism is that, according to the definition established earlier in this chapter, the latter is supposed specifically to support protective measures for the environment in order to foster biodiversity, and to address social inequality through targeting poorer groups in society. Whether it does so or not depends on the wider context of governance and the enabling environment, and on the commitment to ecotourism by the stakeholders most able to influence it: the tourism industry, local government bodies and the community.

All too often, however, the commitment to genuine ecotourism from these is lacking, mainly because private interests tend to prevail over the public good. In general, the interplay of market forces means that the most profitable enterprises will predominate, regardless of any negative social and environmental consequences, unless trammelled by a robust regulatory framework supported by strong political will; thus far, such a framework has not been created in Indonesia. Furthermore, it is known that self-regulation in the tourism industry is a weak instrument for achieving sustainability, despite moves by some tourism companies and associations to apply environmental management systems in the fulfilment of their corporate social and environmental responsibilities.

Nevertheless, as standards of governance improve under a more open and accountable governance system in Indonesia and as awareness of the need for prudent management of natural resources grows, it is possible that large-scale occurrences of ecotourism will be managed on a sustainable basis, either through public-private sector partnerships of the kind seen in collaborative management initiatives, or through the vision of individual entrepreneurs and altruists in the private sector. If entrepreneurs and the public sector continue to respond to market conditions, then both mass ecotourism and more specialized forms will offer Indonesia a substantial opportunity to improve its international image and generate benefits for a number of beneficiaries, including the environment, while ensuring that the recreational needs of the domestic population and of neighbouring countries are addressed.

Notes

1 Information gained from six extended visits to Bohorok between 1985 and 1998, with additional material from local government bodies, foreign consultants and NGO newsletters.

2 Tourism at Bohorok was abruptly halted by a flash flood in 2003 which swept away much of the tourist village. There are attempts to rebuild it on more sustainable lines, although some reports suggest that environmental controls are again being flouted.

14

Dragon Tourism Revisited: The Sustainability of Tourism Development in Komodo National Park

Henning Borchers

Introduction

One of the most significant developments in global conservation efforts over the past decades has been the increasing emphasis on socio-economic development as an integral part of biodiversity conservation. This feature can be explained in two parts. For one, nature conservation for nature's sake alone denies the basic reality of livelihood needs of local residents in densely populated and often poverty-stricken parts of the South. At the same time, government spending on biodiversity conservation is hardly sufficient to assure sustained protection and conservation of the world's natural resources. Ultimately, conservation areas need to generate revenue in order to demonstrate their profitability and their prospects for survival.

Indonesia is a telling example. The country's natural resources have suffered tremendous degradation during the past decades. Mismanagement, commercial exploitation through illegal logging and fishing, and natural disasters, drought and forest fires have caused widespread devastation. However, despite large-scale resource exploitation at multiple levels, local communities are often singled out as the main perpetrators (Campbell, 2002: 30; Escobar, 1998). In Indonesia, this phenomenon has been amplified by the Asian financial crisis, which further marginalized already disadvantaged communities. Also, the government's budget for conservation spending – insufficient at the best of times – dropped substantially. Watched over by under-paid and ill-equipped park rangers, national parks and other protected areas were thus at the mercy of commercial enterprises as well as deprived communities, who had to rely increasingly on resource extraction as the cash economy failed to meet their needs.

Ecotourism

Acknowledging that the livelihoods of local resource users have to be met to guarantee conservation success, most conservation programmes feature a socio-economic development component. The provision of alternative livelihoods aims at minimizing pressure on natural resources, while creating sustainable economic alternatives for local communities. Moreover, a long-term purpose is to make conservation self-financing, by generating sufficient revenue to cover operational and managerial costs in national parks and other protected areas. Therefore, conservation has become a platform for economic development. The most prominent alternative is the development of ecotourism, considered the most sustainable and profitable option for resource use (Spergel, 2001; Walpole et al., 2001; Brandon, 1996; see also Chapter 13 by Cochrane in this volume).

Although ecotourism has been a significant instrument in conservation and development for the past two decades, it remains a concept that lacks clarity. It can range from nature-based adventure tourism with little to no contact with local residents to community-based programmes providing cultural experiences to tourists and a livelihood to communities. Indeed, the terms 'ecotourism' and 'nature tourism' are often used interchangeably and ecotourism programmes do not always imply all the features that the concept is said to entail (Brandon, 1996: ii).

As part of a revenue-generating scheme for the financing of national parks, ecotourism is understood actively to involve, empower and benefit local communities (Scheyvens, 1999). This has been acknowledged by the global conservation community and is reflected in project designs around the world. Yet, many ecotourism projects which propose the provision of economic benefits to local communities are often hampered by ecological, social, cultural and institutional factors. The growing perception of a global biodiversity crisis continues to outweigh concerns for community development in favour of ecological priority-setting (Wilshusen et al., 2002). Also, proponents of nature tourism tend to idealize a wilderness not disturbed by human presence, an ideology that stands in stark contrast to the populated conservation areas of the South (Borchers, 2004: 30/31). These populations, moreover, are not homogeneous. Ecotourism project designs rarely take into account social hierarchies and power relations at the community or village level. These in turn are likely to affect access to ecotourism projects. Ultimately, it may be the powerful who benefit from ecotourism development, while the poor are further marginalized. The conservation discourse has been largely depoliticized, which denies the reality of complex local, national and global issues that may conflict within any conservation landscape.

The Komodo National Park

The Komodo National Park in Eastern Indonesia, the subject of Hitchcock's chapter in this book's 1993 predecessor, provides us with one such scenario. One of the biologically most diverse ecosystems in Indonesia, the park has been subject to continued resource exploitation, which necessitated urgent measures to halt the rampant destruction. Alongside increased protection and plans to provide alternative livelihood strategies to communities within and surrounding the Park, the development of ecotourism is the main pillar of a scheme that aims at making the Park self-financing by 2012.

In order to achieve this goal, a joint venture between The Nature Conservancy, an American environmental organization, and P. T. Jaytasha Putrindo Utama, an Indonesian tourism operator, applied for a concession to manage tourism and other aspects of park management for thirty years. After several years of fierce debate for and against the concession both at the local and national level, it was finally granted in 2005. Effectively, Komodo National Park, flagship of Indonesia's natural heritage, has been privatized. The decision is being applauded as an innovative concept that could point to the future of conservation financing. However, the concession as well as the current management initiative also continue to be strongly opposed by local organizations and fishing communities, who claim that new regulations infringe their rights to access and harvest marine resources. Moreover, tourism operators in Labuan Bajo and Bali fear that tourism in the park may be monopolized under the management of a profit-oriented joint venture. A review of the development of tourism in and management of Komodo National Park to date indicates how the scheme could impact on the future livelihoods of local communities within and around the park.

Conservation and tourism development in Komodo not only bear the question of sustainability from an ecological perspective. Only a balanced approach that also considers local economic, social and cultural aspects can guarantee overall success. An analysis of the current status of Komodo National Park presents a timely opportunity to re-study the locality after almost two decades, during which the park underwent major changes. Interestingly, the question of whether the priorities of wildlife conservation and national development can accommodate the needs of local communities is as relevant now as it was in the early 1990s. Ecotourism may be the optimal strategy to secure sustainability of the park's natural resources through innovative financing schemes. Will its virtues, however, also benefit the communities in and around the park?

The Locality: Now and Then

At first impression, Komodo National Park seems barren and desolate – a fitting environment for the world's largest lizard, one may think. The Komodo dragon is still the best-known attraction of the park. However, the seas surrounding the park are said to be among the richest in the world (PKA and TNC, 2000a: 5). Here, one can find several hundreds of species of coral and fish, along with sea turtles and an impressive array of sea mammals, which has put Komodo National Park on the map of the region's hot-spots for scuba-diving and other recreational marine-based activities.

Since the 1980s there has been a steady and increasing flow of tourists into the park and surrounding areas. Visitor numbers peaked in the 1996/97 financial year with more than 30,000. Tourism had a considerable impact on the regional economy, although many tourists arrived on pre-organized package and cruise ship tours, and thus spent comparatively little time in the actual locality. The local economic impact of tourism continues to be highest in Labuan Bajo, Western Flores, where most hotels, restaurants and dive operators are based. However, most tourism revenue has thus far been generated outside the local economy, by tour and cruise ship operators in Lombok, Bali, Java, and overseas (Walpole and Goodwin, 2000: 570).

Beside four villages located within the park, there is still little in terms of tourism infrastructure. Loh Liang and Loh Buaya, the tourism villages on Komodo Island and

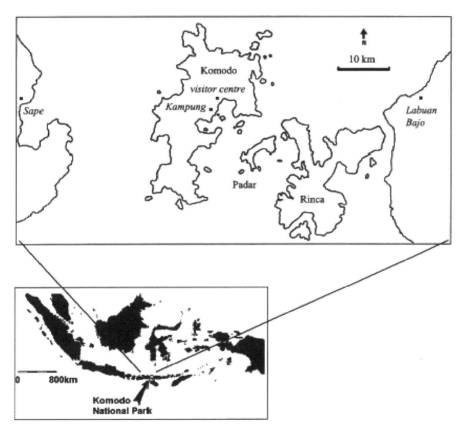

Figure 14.1: Komodo National Park. Source: Walpole and Goodwin, 2000: 562.

Rinca Island respectively, are the sole such facilities, providing basic accommodation and food. Loh Liang and Loh Buaya are maintained and operated by staff of the national park authority, who thereby obtain an attractive extra income alongside their meagre salaries. Upon my first visit in 1998, the facilities in Loh Liang were in a poor condition, and food in the attached restaurant was limited to a handful of items on the menu. More revealing was the situation in Komodo Village, an hour's walk from Loh Liang. Many houses were in a state of disrepair and most residents were decidedly poor.

Despite the proximity of local communities, there did not appear to be a significant link between villagers and the tourism industry. Although tourism had been a growing regional industry at least up until 1997, communities within the park have historically been largely unaffected. Indeed, in their detailed study of economic impacts of tourism in and surrounding Komodo National Park, Walpole and Goodwin (2000) noted that only 24 (7 per cent) tourism-related full-time jobs were found to be within the park, with the majority (74 per cent) in Labuan Bajo and 17 per cent in Sape, gateway town to the park in neighbouring Sumbawa.

I returned to Komodo National Park in 2002 on a research trip funded by New Zealand's Official Development Assistance (NZODA). The subject of enquiry was the process of park management, the nature of ecotourism development and its impact on the empowerment and the livelihoods of local communities. My initial approach was informed both by impressions from my previous visit and the by then wide availability of secondary literature, mostly commissioned by The Nature Conservancy and associated bodies.[1] In Komodo Village and Labuan Bajo, I interviewed staff members of the national park authority, private operators, staff of local NGOs, village officials and villagers/fishermen, who are most affected by current regulations. Most interviews were in Indonesian, while some were in English and Indonesian. I had also been in contact with TNC staff in Labuan Bajo, but experienced difficulty in obtaining consent for an interview with a leading staff member. I thus decided to rely on publicly available material, which does reflect informal discussions I had with TNC staff.

In 2002, the number of tourism-related jobs in and around the park had changed to the disadvantage of Komodo. According to villagers, only one wood-carver was able to make a living from tourism alone. Other villagers involved in the industry as wood-carvers, guides, boatmen and hawkers had also to rely on marine resource extraction to make ends meet. To a great extent, this had to be blamed on the drop in visitor numbers following the Asian financial crisis and other global events that initiated unrest in many parts of the archipelago. The cruise ship segment, historically a constant and significant component of regional tourism, suffered the severest setback, while backpackers and independent travellers continued to arrive, albeit in smaller numbers.

The facilities in Loh Liang, on Komodo Island, had been upgraded, with a new, attractive restaurant and a basic 'museum' as part of the locality. The presence of the facilities, however, continues to be questioned. A staff member of a Labuan Bajo-based NGO asked why no facilities were allowed in the villages: 'Very few people go to Komodo, not so many. Why do they move to Loh Liang, why? It's better they can make an office in Kampung Komodo, and then tourists come. They don't need to build a restaurant [in Loh Liang]. People own it, they can make a restaurant.'

Hawkers from Komodo Village sold woodcarvings and other handicrafts from stalls set up near the boat landing. The park authority generally provides guides, who are trained in conservation and monitoring and who often profess some level of English language skills. When tourist numbers are high, locals are engaged as additional guides. However, due to low visitor numbers since the late 1990s – the last few years saw between 12,000 and 15,000 visitors at the most – there is little opportunity for residents to become involved. According to one local NGO staff, it is 'a pity that the national park [authority] don't ask the people, or empower the people to work together'. Many villagers in Komodo Village also voiced their aspiration to be provided with the necessary training and English language instruction to enter the tourism industry. To date, several villagers have received training in guiding, diving, woodcarving and handicrafts, yet access to the industry remains limited and beneficiaries tend to be from better-off families who can afford to send family members on training programmes. Poor community members need every family member's contribution to fill the food basket.

Moreover, those villagers formerly operating as boatmen on the shuttle, picking up passengers from the Sape–Labuan Bajo ferry, which used to stop off briefly at the islands, lost this opportunity when the ferry discontinued its unofficial stop-over. Villagers were not given a reason for this change of schedule, but suspect that Labuan Bajo-based boat owners wanted to monopolize transport into and within the park. Indeed, boat owners in Labuan Bajo now dominate this comparatively profitable business and sell return trips to and from the park on often insufficiently equipped boats. Park residents no longer have access to this potential source of revenue. It has to be said, however, that boat owners within the park are among the better off.

Overall living conditions of villagers are dire. The four settlements inside the park accommodate approximately 4,000 residents of diverse ethnic affiliation. There remains an almost indistinguishable minority of original residents on Komodo Island. The Ata Modo are distinguished by language and custom (Goodwin et al., 1997: 14; Hitchcock, 1993: 307–308). The majority of residents, however, originate from neighbouring Bima province on Sumbawa, Western Flores and from the sea-faring Bajo and Buginese.

Due to their low level of education, residents have few opportunities to find employment beyond the park's boundaries. Extraction of marine resources is the mainstay of the local economy, and the large majority (97 per cent) of people living within the park live off the sea (PKA and TNC, 2000a: 15).[2] Alongside park residents, fishing communities living around the park also rely heavily on the park's resources. Until recently, even fishing communities and enterprises from as far away as Sulawesi frequently used to exploit the fishing grounds of Komodo National Park. Outsiders in particular put great pressure on resources by indiscriminately using destructive fishing techniques such as dynamite and cyanide fishing (PKA and TNC, 2000a: 22). Among communities within the park, few groups have been proved to employ destructive methods. Only one community was singled out as harbouring groups responsible for destructive use.

The strong presence of outsiders comes as no surprise. Komodo National Park is widely known to contain a wealth of resources, and its popularity with fishermen is also due to the conservation status bestowed upon the area. The fact that the area has been protected – with varying levels of efficiency – since it was designated a national park in 1980 meant that it was spared the early exhaustion of resources experienced in most other parts of Indonesia. Most locals see the need for conservation in the park and welcome efforts to reduce the presence and impact of outsiders within park boundaries. Moreover, both under old and new management regulations, some level of customary resource use is granted to park residents. This has led to a surge in migration to the park, largely from neighbouring Sumbawa. Komodo residents, in particular, are strongly linked to coastal communities from Sumbawa. Intermarriages are common, and often lead to resettlement into the park, where special regulations on resource use are in place that are not enjoyed by communities surrounding the park.

Conservation Efforts

Subject to unrestrained resource exploitation and the lack of the financial as well as technical and managerial capacity to respond to the crisis on the part of the Indonesian government, Komodo National Park's very survival was at risk. The park's coral reefs, in particular, fell prey to unrestrained cyanide and dynamite fishing. In 1995, the park authority – representing the national conservation agency PKA[3] – started receiving support from The Nature Conservancy. TNC's managerial expertise and financial assets were urgently needed to halt the on-going destruction of Komodo National Park. This reflects an increasing trend in conservation efforts worldwide. Global environmental NGOs, such as TNC, WWF (World Wide Fund for Nature) and Conservation International, are among the main actors involved in the conservation and protection of biological diversity, thereby 'addressing the problems of a shrinking and environmentally threatened global commons' (Meyer, 1997: 123).

The collaboration between the PHKA and TNC led to the planning and design of a 25-year management plan that was completed and implemented in 2000 (PKA and TNC, 2000a). Management strategies as articulated in the plan have, however, already been enforced almost since the presence of TNC. The planning process initiated a revision of the park's zonation along with new resource use regulations and the establishment of an effective enforcement regime, to ward off the destructive impact of illegal fishing techniques.

Some forms of resource use, such as the collection of marine biota on the reef flats at low tide (*meting*), has been completely prohibited. However, during low season for liftnet fishing, the mainstay of the local economy, *meting* is the main source of livelihood for poor community members, most of whom do not own boats. The information that influenced decisions on marine resource use may have been based on scientific facts, or the interpretation of ecological indicators. Many fishermen, however, maintained that when *meting* was outlawed, life became much harder for the *masyarakat kecil*, the small, or poor, people.

Also, cultivation, animal husbandry, hunting and the collection of woodland products, all part of the local economy at the time of Hitchcock's visit in the 1980s, have been largely restricted or prohibited under the new management regime. Not all villagers agree with the new regulations, and refer both to a lack of clarity as to regulations and zonation, as well as a lack of alternatives as the main shortcomings of the new management regime. The management authority often cites scarcity of water as a main reason for the prohibition of any form of agriculture within the park. Residents consider this as overly rigid, as water supplies during the wet season would allow for limited agriculture. As it is, most food items now have to be imported from neighbouring islands. During the dry season there is little fresh water available and those who can afford it import potable water from neighbouring islands. Not everyone can, though, and a cholera outbreak in Komodo Village hospitalized 100 people and claimed four lives in March 2001 (Ruitenbeek and Cartier, 2001: 19).

Access to fresh water has in fact been a contentious issue on the island. The spring that provided Komodo Village with fresh water throughout the years now supplies the tourist village in Loh Liang. There have been several acts of sabotage to destroy the pipeline feeding the tourist village, but the issue continues to be unresolved. Pleas by villagers to install fresh water tanks are yet to be addressed.

New rules restrict further in-migration. Indeed, the human carrying capacity within the park may well have been exceeded, yet a prohibition on the resettlement of outside family members into the park was not well received by local residents. One significant side effect of the continuous influx of migrants is the changing constitution of resident communities. With a growing population of mostly recent migrants and intermarriage, the indigenous people of Komodo, the Ata Modo, have progressively been marginalized. This phenomenon carries particular weight when customary access to resource use is argued on the basis of customary rights bestowed upon 'original' inhabitants.

The data collected by the national park authority and TNC stipulate that 'there are no *pure blood* people left and their culture and language is slowly being integrated with the recent migrants' (PKA and TNC, 2000b: 57, emphasis added). This argument could imply that as part of a dominant culture of recent migrants, no one group within the park should be granted special resource use privileges based on customary rights. The question of the rights of indigenous or local people is not one limited to Komodo, Indonesia, or even the context of conservation. Yet for those communities whose basic survival depends on the same resources that are the subject of global conservation efforts, the matter appears to pitch one against the other, while the solution must be found in a combination of the two.

Thus, the national park authority together with TNC initiated several alternative livelihood programmes as part of the overall management strategy. Accordingly, through a co-operative management approach, the needs and aspirations of local residents, park managers and conservationists are considered as a means of facilitating collaboration and thereby negotiating a consensus upon which a feasible and legitimate conservation strategy can be established (PKA and TNC, 2000a: 63). Based on these premises, education and the provision of alternative livelihood strategies for the park's inhabitants and communities surrounding the protected area aim at meeting the overall objective of conservation and biodiversity protection. However, living conditions in villages inside the park are yet to improve considerably. Many park residents continue to live in poverty.

Ironically, most communities targeted by alternative livelihood programmes are located outside the park, as they are held responsible for having employed destructive fishing techniques (PKA and TNC, 2000a: 33). Only one park community, which was known to harbour groups that made use of destructive fishing techniques, participated in one such programme to a significant extent. The logic behind this strategy is well in line with current conservation thought: to prevent resource users from devastating resources, alternatives need to be provided. Unfortunately, however, most communities within the park have seen few such alternatives, while they are the ones most affected by current restrictions.

A pilot project to establish a fish hatchery has been struggling to succeed for years, hampered by the fact that the necessary equipment was not affordable for most fishers. The installation of fish aggregating devices[4] in deep water for pelagic fishing failed to attract fishing communities from within the park as travelling to and from the devices was not economical. Moreover, boats were not seaworthy for deep-sea fishing, and fishermen felt uncomfortable in the open sea as their fishing activities are traditionally based in shallow waters. Only a seaweed project proved to be moderately successful with one community within the park and several coastal communities in Sumbawa, though fishers have difficulties marketing their produce.

To date, restrictions have not been matched by adequate alternatives. Local fishing communities maintain that the needs of the stomach must take priority over other needs. Most park residents see the need for conservation of resources they rely upon for a livelihood. Also, they confirm that most damage to marine and terrestrial resources originates from outsiders. They do not understand, however, why they suffer most under resource use restrictions. '*Orang asli Komodo bisa terbatas*', locals from Komodo can be restricted; but it is more difficult to restrict outsiders, who can enter the park, harvest resources, and disappear without fearing permanent repercussions.

As long as these restrictions are not altered in order to enable park residents to meet their most substantial needs, the provision of economic alternatives is of the utmost urgency. While the management plan entails several alternatives, such as the above-mentioned marine culture programmes, the most obvious opportunity for the development of compatible enterprises has been identified in the field of ecotourism (PKA and TNC, 2000a: 68). Ecotourism is considered 'perhaps the most obvious sustainable use of the Park's resources' (PKA and TNC, 2000a: 57). To date, however, involvement of park residents in tourism has been small, and it is acknowledged that '[f]ew of the revenues generated by tourism actually trickle down to the local villages' (PKA and TNC, 2000a: 17).

Tourism Development Under the New Management Initiative

The management plan aims at meeting the objectives of nature protection and sustainable development (PKA and TNC, 2000a: 11) through community participation, partnerships between several stakeholders, a co-management approach to natural resource management, and the optimization of local benefits (PKA and TNC, 2000a: 53).

The establishment of a tourism concession, held by a joint venture between TNC and an Indonesian tourism operator, was a central proposition of the plan. With TNC providing the scientific expertise informing conservation management, the tourism operator is meant to help develop and market Komodo National Park as a world-class tourism destination in the same league as Galapagos National Park in Ecuador, another World Heritage Site and home to unique species. According to the authors, the tourism concession is responsible for financial management, investments, infrastructure development, marketing and the distribution of funds to finance several aspects of park management, including the development of alternative livelihoods. Moreover, the tourism concession 'should have the authority to set and collect gate fees, set entry capacity limits, arrange and facilitate enforcement, set environmental standards, select and deselect seconded Park staff, set staff performance and expertise differentials, and implement a licensing system for tourism operations' (PKA and TNC, 2000a: 78).

Effectively, the authors suggest that the concession covers most aspects of park management, which undoubtedly also impacts significantly on the communities reliant on the park's resources. Not surprisingly, the proposition initiated a lengthy and heated debate between numerous stakeholders that would dominate the local media for years and occasionally emerge on a national and global level (Borchers, 2004; Dhume, 2002; Leiman, 2002). The concession was eventually granted in 2005, despite strong opposition by local stakeholders. Komodo National Park thus became a pilot site to test new park financing mechanisms through the privatization of tourism and national park management.

Ecotourism, according to the management plan, 'is defined as visiting natural areas to view and enjoy the plant and animal life with minimal or no impact on the environment' (PKA and TNC, 2000a: 68). The attractions that make ecotourism an ideal option in Komodo are its scenery and marine biodiversity, which offer world-class diving, snorkelling, sea kayaking, sailing, bird watching and blue water catch-and-release fishing (PKA and TNC, 2000a: 69). The concession would serve the goal of protecting the park's biodiversity by generating revenues required for the park in a way that is environmentally sound, socially responsible and economically viable (Leiman, 2002: 7). Accordingly, TNC proposes to commit itself to working with local communities in order to develop environmentally and culturally sustainable sources of income by creating a 'vibrant, environmentally compatible tourism industry' (Leiman, 2002: 8). The strategy for the development of ecotourism should thus focus on the involvement of local people and the provision of benefits to the local economy (PKA and TNC, 2000: 57).

Studies undertaken among the park's communities indicate that the residents of Komodo village would indeed welcome increased participation in ecotourism development and that attitudes towards tourism development are very positive (Borchers, 2004: 72; Walpole and Goodwin, 2001; PKA and TNC, 2000: 69). Until the late 1990s, tourism had been an increasingly stable and successful generator of revenue and foreign exchange in the regional economy. A higher standard of living in the gateway towns further acts as an incentive for local communities to become more involved in tourism ventures as a perceived opportunity to enhance their welfare.

To date the park authority and TNC have involved several villagers in alternative livelihood programmes aimed at an increased involvement in the tourism industry, such as woodcarving, sewing, weaving and embroidery. Yet these efforts have been marginal, and among those involved in the tourism industry there are few who can make a living from it alone. Certainly, one of the reasons is the low number of visitors to the park, for which park management cannot be blamed. At the same time, few efforts had been undertaken in the past to encourage the involvement of villagers in any significant way. Consequently, there is little evidence that park residents derive any meaningful direct benefits from their proximity to one of Indonesia's most prominent natural tourist attractions.

Marine resource use is expected to remain the foundation of the local economy. Some villagers continue to voice their aspirations to become more involved in tourism, and ask for the provision of basic training in English and related skills, the lack of which constitutes a main barrier to increased participation. A number of people suggested providing food and accommodation in the villages inside the park. However, ecotourism '[f]acilities development (. . .) will be restricted to outside the Park boundaries' (PKA and TNC, 2000a: 57). Loh Liang and Loh Buaya will remain, yet under the operational management of national park staff, who will continue to receive the benefits. There appears to be little opportunity for park residents to become involved beyond the present level. As Hitchcock (1993: 313) has already pointed out, tourism has been a mixed blessing for Komodo islanders – as well as for the other three settlements inside the park. Most benefits at the local level have thus far accrued to people resident in Labuan Bajo and, to a lesser extent, Sape. Local villagers also fear that in the future they will only be by-standers in regional tourism development.

More notably, the lack of meaningful community participation and resulting management decisions and developments has led to an on-going conflict between local communities and the management body. This is reflected in the on-going dispute around customary resource use and the regulations and restrictions imposed under the new management plan. One community leader summarized the most basic needs of residents of Komodo Village: community involvement in decision-making as well as the provision of clean water and alternative livelihood strategies were the most urgent issues that need to be addressed to alleviate the current status of underdevelopment in the park.

Yet, reflecting a common shortcoming of conservation interventions in Indonesia and beyond, ecological indicators and priorities to date prevail over the needs and aspirations of local communities for underpinning their cultural and economic survival (Campbell, 2002: 38; Wilshusen et al., 2002; Ministry of Forestry, 2001: 9). In Komodo, certain forms of customary resource use are either restricted or prohibited. While boat owners are considerably well-off, poor villagers – many of whom are indebted to local skippers – have to rely on often restricted or prohibited forms of resource use. They have not yet been provided with viable livelihood alternatives. In a sad irony, with their resource use practices criminalized under current regulations, these community members are often forced to further infringe prohibitions in order to survive. The survival of Komodo National Park has thus been pitched against the survival of its human inhabitants.

The Future of Tourism in Komodo National Park

Goodwin (1998: 3) argues that while tourists are often enjoined to 'leave only footprints' in order to minimize adverse environmental effects, the greater challenge is to find ways of leaving a significant economic impact in the local economy by increasing local tourist spending. This is likely to be achieved through activities that build on the cultural and resource base of the community and the region for further development, and thus depends heavily on local involvement in design and implementation.

For tourism to be a viable strategy of sustainable development, Goodwin (1998: 4) further suggests that there is a strong case for intervention at a local level in tourist destination areas. By facilitating the access of local communities to the tourism market leakages from the local economy can be minimized. Socio-cultural sustainability could be assured by building on and complementing existing livelihood strategies through employment and small enterprise development as a linkage between the local economy and the tourism industry. Tourism projects should be evaluated for their contribution to local economic development, while at the same time ensuring the maintenance of natural and cultural assets and controlling negative social impacts.

In the case of Komodo National Park, ecotourism is not an end in itself, but rather a means of securing the viability and sustainability of the park. Also, the role of tourism is to generate revenue to finance other aspects of park management, including alternative livelihood programmes for local communities. The joint venture aims at developing infrastructure in and around the park to create a world-class nature tourism destination. To date, most hotels and restaurants are basic, mainly catering to budget travellers. Currently, available facilities are unsuitable for the top-end market segment targeted by the joint venture. There has been heavy private investment in buying coastal property in Flores, which will be developed in order to provide star-rated facilities for higher-end tourism. With enhanced infrastructure and an improved and secured status of the ecosystem, the joint venture plans to raise entrance fees from the current low figure of US$2 to around US$50. Additional fees will be charged for activities such as diving and snorkelling, as well as for concessions for tourism operators (Environment North and Associated Consultants, 2001: 105). This in itself is necessary to emphasize the fact that tourists and operators present in the park will need to contribute to the management of Komodo. Yet it has also caused dismay among dive operators in Bali and Labuan Bajo, who fear for their access rights to the park. The authority to grant access now ultimately lies with the joint venture, yet there have been no concrete agreements with most other tourism operators.

According to the charter of the joint venture, any profits and revenue earned through user fees and concessions will be reinvested in conservation and park management (TNC et al., 2002: 3). Moreover, '[i]f successful, the concession could lay the foundation for expanding management activities to include additional aspects of Park management such as enforcement and sustainable community development projects' (PKA and TNC, 2000a: 78). This would imply that enforcement and sustainable community development projects are not necessarily part of the initial project phase. Rather, they are suggested as complementary aspects of park management depending on the success of the concession scheme.

In fact, both enforcement and community development projects have already been initiated. Enforcement has been particularly efficient, as park management succeeded in halting destructive fishing techniques. Coral reef cover in the park is said to have increased again, suggesting that the national park authority and TNC can indeed be applauded for having achieved considerable success in protecting and enhancing the marine environment of Komodo National Park.

As mentioned above, community development projects have been less successful to date. This is the main shortcoming of the current management body that appears to deny the socio-economic reality of fishing communities living within and surrounding the park. Admittedly, the deteriorating status of the Komodo ecosystem required urgent measures to assure its survival. The measures taken were successful thus far, in that the incidence of destructive fishing has been minimized. They were not well received by local residents, however, and the inadequate provision of alternative livelihoods has only aggravated the perception that local communities were indeed marginalized for the sake of nature.

This negligence has now created a conflict that is anything but conducive to successful park management and tourism development in the long term. At what cost should ecological sustainability be bought? Many residents feel abandoned and left with few options. Several offenders against park regulations have been resettled out of the park. This, in itself, may appear a harsh penalty, but one that is hard to ignore for any potential future offenders. At the same time, however, many poor park residents are in the precarious situation that without any adequate livelihood alternatives in place, they cannot but break the rules. Indeed, a number of villagers voiced the fear of having to resettle to neighbouring islands outside the park, since, as they maintain, it has become increasingly more difficult to sustain a living in Komodo National Park.

This scenario may not be too far-fetched. It is in fact a stated objective of the management initiative to develop 'incentives' for the communities within the park to move to other islands, thus promoting 'voluntary resettlement' (PKA and TNC, 2000b: 66). While population pressure inside the park is a serious issue that needs to be addressed, it has to be questioned whether resettlement is the most suitable answer to this problem. Hitchcock (1993: 313) criticized this consideration, as resettlement would simply relocate poor populations between equally economically depressed regions. It would thus not solve the problem, but transfer it, and thereby remove it from the responsibility of park management.

It is by now common knowledge in the conservation community that the paradigm of 'parks without people' should be a thing of the past, although the idea again attracts proponents among conservation practitioners (Terborgh and Peres, 2002; Wilshusen et al., 2002). National parks and other protected areas in countries like Indonesia tend to be inhabited, many of them by communities who for hundreds of years may have sustained a living in those environments. Relocating these communities to create a pristine conservation area would only aggravate the human-nature dichotomy that has historically influenced Western exclusionary notions of conservation. Moreover, it would likely create the foundation for lasting conflicts over resource access and use as they already are in place today.

Resettlement should thus not be an option. On the other hand, it is important actively to involve resident communities in activities and decisions pertaining to park management and economic development. Progress to date suggests that despite efforts to consult with local people and consider their perspectives and ideas, little of that information has influenced final decision-making. What appears to have happened is that consultation and socialization efforts were merely a means of assuring predetermined conservation objectives. Consequently, efforts at providing alternative livelihood strategies have not yet met their objectives. As long as strict regulations remain in place, villagers find themselves between a rock and a hard place in their efforts to sustain a living in Komodo National Park.

An increased involvement of local communities in the tourism industry in Komodo is desirable. Most villagers feel estranged from an industry that for the past two decades has barely acknowledged their existence. The groups that briefly visit Komodo Village to buy woodcarvings and ponder on the simplicity of life in Jurassic Park do not spend enough time in the village to strengthen ties between tourists and locals, which would undoubtedly improve mutual understanding. Although prohibited to date, it should be considered whether limited infrastructure development within or near village enclaves may be an option – after all, infrastructure within the park is not a problem *per se*, as the presence of tourism villages confirms. Such facilities need not be, in fact should not be, star-rated hotels. Tourism infrastructure should not run the risk of further marginalizing communities by creating an evident wealth gap between hosts and guests. Basic infrastructure could still provide for increased contact and, more importantly, direct benefits at the local level. Many localities in Indonesia could serve as an example for this development. The value of conservation needs to be made more tangible for resident communities.

Thus far, however, one of the tenets of ecotourism, the provision of benefits to local communities, is not sufficiently evident in Komodo. The high-end market segment targeted by the joint venture is unlikely to increase benefits at the local level to any extent. Few locals will gain access to employment opportunities which often require a basic education and language skills, none of which is accessible to park residents. It is more likely that the opportunities generated through future tourism development will mostly benefit residents in Labuan Bajo, which to date has been the regional hub for foreign and domestic tourists, as well as better-educated people from Bali and Java.

For the inhabitants of Komodo National Park, tourism is likely to remain a mixed blessing. Indeed Environment North and Associated Consultants note in their tourism study of Komodo National Park that

> . . . it is highly likely that the major benefits will accrue to land developers and tour operators (largely from outside the region) and many of the costs will be borne by local communities. There will be some winners amongst local entrepreneurs (such as woodcarvers) but distribution of wealth is likely to remain uneven. Such an outcome is not in line with accepted ecotourism principles.
>
> (2001: 49)

The overall sustainability of current developments in Komodo National Park thus has to be questioned as long as the needs of local communities are not adequately addressed. Tourism as an industry is highly susceptible to external factors on a national, regional and global scale, as recent events have demonstrated. Although an increased involvement of park residents is desirable, tourism should at the most constitute a complementary feature of the local economy. Instead, one can only reiterate Hitchcock's (1993: 315) suggestion of diversifying the local economy based on active participation of villagers in planning, design and implementation.

The provisions in the management plan arguably entail considerations for accommodating the socio-economic needs of resident communities. It has to be noted, however, that the plan is yet to be fully enforced, in that thus far there has been a disproportionate emphasis on meeting the goals of resource protection, conservation and the development of nature tourism, to the disadvantage of the livelihood needs of local communities. According to the current conceptualization of ecotourism, there will be little direct benefit to communities inside the park. Tourism as such will thus be rather more nature-based than community-based. The tourism concession and management structure of Komodo National Park remain controversial. The future will show whether or not local concerns were well-founded.

Notes

1 Among others, the Joint Venture's project, the Komodo Collaborative Management Initiative, receives funding from the Global Environmental Facility through the International Finance Corporation.

2 The PKA/Direktorat Jenderal Perlindungan dan Konservasi Alam (Directorate General of Nature Protection and Conservation) is the portfolio within the Department of Forestry responsible for nature conservation, in particular the administration of national parks and other protected areas. It is now known as the PHKA/Direktorat Jenderal Perlindungan Hutan dan Konservasi Alam, the Directorate General of Forest Protection and Nature Conservation.

3 Now PHKA.

4 A floating device that attracts pelagic fish, such as tuna, which tend to gather near natural floating objects.

15

Is the Beach Party Over? Tourism and the Environment in Small Islands: A Case Study of Gili Trawangan, Lombok, Indonesia

Mark Hampton and Joanna Hampton

Introduction: Tourism, Development and Small Islands

Many small islands[1] around the world host sizeable tourism industries (Wilkinson, 1989; Ioannides et al., 2001; McElroy, 2002) and have become highly dependent on tourism. The Bahamas, Barbados and the Maldives are now so reliant upon tourism that it generates over 50 per cent of their export earnings (Commonwealth Secretariat, 1997). Places such as Mauritius or Fiji conjure stereotypical images of idyllic tropical islands with coconut palms and white sand beaches. This image is a powerful marketing tool both for the travel industry and tourism departments in many less developed countries (LDCs) where tourism is seen as crucial for economic growth. As the tourism development process begins to be better understood, environmental impacts are beginning to attract increasing attention, especially for small places.

Small islands have been seen by some writers as 'vulnerable', not just economically (Briguglio, 1995; Prassad, 2003), but also environmentally (Commonwealth Secretariat, 1997; Royle, 2002). As small places surrounded by the sea (by definition), arguably the entire island is a coastal zone, that is the boundary between a marine environment and a terrestrial environment (de Albuquerque and McElroy, 1992). Other writers have suggested that the ecologies of small islands are in fact highly 'complex systems' (Ratter, 1997).

Since the beginnings of mass international tourism in the 1960s facilitated by wide-bodied aircraft, tourism's effect on LDC economic development has been increasingly debated. Initially, in the 1960s the broadly positive view of tourism as a vehicle for economic growth was exemplified by the enthusiasm of the World Bank and OECD (1967) as well as individual countries. However, from the late-1960s the emerging school of underdevelopment and dependency theorists such as Andre Gunder Frank (1971) began to question orthodox economic development theory. This critique was extended to tourism by Turner and Ash (1975) who characterized LDCs as the 'Pleasure Periphery' of the industrialized countries. Britton (1991) analysed international tourism in the light of dependency theories, arguing that it was a new form of the old colonial patterns and relationships, and Weaver (1990) proposed more specifically that international tourism activities in Caribbean islands could be seen as the 'new plantations'.

From the late 1980s the notion of 'sustainable development' became increasingly current and was further popularized in the aftermath of the 1992 Rio Earth Summit. The concept of sustainability was then increasingly attached to the tourism industry, although some observers argue that the notion of 'sustainable tourism' is perhaps a contradiction in terms (Gossling, 2002; Mowforth and Munt, 2003) or an industry 'greenwash' of unsustainable tourism practices. The literature on the environment and tourism, especially for islands, focuses on using environmental impact assessments for tourism (Hunter and Green, 1995); the concepts of carrying capacity and limits of acceptable change (McCool, 1994); and more recently developing tools such as trade-off analysis (Brown et al., 2001) and ecological footprint analysis (Gossling et al., 2002).

This focus on the 'sustainability' of tourism was particularly linked to the rapid growth of up-market ecotourism, what Wheeller (1994) dubbed 'ego tourism'. The 1980s also saw an increase in other types of 'new tourism' (Poon, 1993) that differed from conventional mass 'old tourism', particularly the rise of backpacker tourists. Falling real prices of long-haul air travel meant that regions such as Southeast Asia became accessible to such tourists who tended to stay in guesthouses, eat at food stalls and small restaurants and travel on local transport (Cohen, 1982b; Riley, 1988; Hampton, 1998; 2003; Scheyvens, 2002a). Backpackers can broadly be defined as tourists who tend to travel independently rather than buy package holidays, take longer trips than mass tourists, travel on limited budgets and generally – whilst comprising many occupational groups – are youthful, being under 35 years old (Pearce, 1990; Government of Australia, 1995; Loker-Murphy, 1995; Wilson, 1997; Hampton, 1998; Scheyvens, 2002a).

This chapter explores the nature of the relationship between this sub-sector of international tourism and the environment in a small tropical island. Gili Trawangan in Lombok, Indonesia, is well-known along the backpackers' route in Southeast Asia as a place for snorkelling, diving, sunbathing and as the 'party island' (Kasmsa and

Bras, 1999). Since the 1980s international tourism in Gili Trawangan has increasingly replaced agriculture and fishing as the dominant economic activity. Tourism on the island has grown in an unplanned way and generally comprises small-scale accommodation and simple beach restaurants. Conventional wisdom concerning the scale of tourism development might suggest that backpacker tourism may be less environmentally damaging – particularly on an island – than mainstream mass international tourism, given the smaller absolute numbers, and also the fact that backpackers tend to demand fairly minimal facilities such as basic accommodation without air-conditioning or hot water. This chapter begins to test this perspective on the proposed environmental friendliness of backpackers.

The chapter begins with an examination of the role of tourism in the economic development of Indonesia since the late 1960s before considering the rapid growth of tourism in Lombok's Gili islands in the eastern part of the archipelago. Then the main section of the chapter presents the results of a study of tourism and Gili Trawangan's island environment based upon two periods of field-work. Fundamental issues for the island's terrestrial environment are examined including water supply, solid waste (garbage), sewage and building materials. Tourism planning and local reactions are discussed, before a consideration of the marine environment, which utilizes a coral reef survey. Finally, the implications of the rapid growth of tourism for other small tropical islands are discussed.

Tourism in Indonesia

Tourism and National Development

President Suharto's regime (1967–1998) placed international tourism high on its development agenda. Picard (1996) argues that tourism was encouraged, not only for its perceived economic benefits to the struggling economy, but also, perhaps more significantly, to give the regime international legitimacy, and replace Indonesia's image as a violent, disturbed place, with scenes of golden beaches, holiday-makers and cultural performances. The first *Repelita* (Five Year Development Plan) for 1969/70–1973/74 outlined international tourism as part of the development of a modern, diversified economy and Indonesia obtained sizeable World Bank loans for large tourism projects in Bali from the 1970s. As Indonesia stabilized, international tourist arrivals increased from around 26,000 at the time of the 1967 upheavals to around 400,000 per year in the mid-1970s and 1.06 million by 1987. Through the 1980s the Jakarta government, and increasingly the regional governments, saw tourism as an important development strategy replacing foreign exchange earnings from declining petroleum and timber exports (Booth, 1990). In 1990, foreign visitor arrivals reached 2.17 million, and by 1995, 4.3 million. Arrivals peaked at 5.6 million in 1996 (Directorate General of Tourism, 1996).

However, the political crisis and economic troubles of 1997–1999 surrounding the fall of Suharto, combined with the large forest fires in Borneo and Sumatra saw international arrivals dip to 5.2 million in 1997, falling to an estimated 3.8 million in 1998 and 3.92 million in 1999. From 2000 there was a recovery with 5.06 million international arrivals per year in 2000, 5.15 million in 2001 and 5.03 million in 2002 (Tourism Indonesia, 2002; BPS, 2004). In 2003, tourist arrival figures fell sharply to 3.69 million (Tourism Indonesia, 2004) due to further exceptional events: the terrorist bombing of Bali in October 2002, the 2003 SARS epidemic that spread to Southeast Asia, and, to a lesser extent, a dampening of long-haul tourism demand around the time of the US-led Iraq war in March 2003. With respect specifically to Indonesia, the terrorist bombing of the Jakarta Marriott hotel in August 2003 and travel advice from several governments, including the UK and Australia, warning against non-essential (that is, leisure) travel to Indonesia, slowed recovery (BBC Online, 2003). The Boxing Day tsunami of 2004 may have also affected visitor choice for the 2005 season, despite the fact that the main Indonesian tourism destinations of Bali and Java were unaffected by the severe tidal waves, and Aceh and Northern Sumatra are not major tourist areas.

Indonesian tourism policy has targeted international mass tourism, rather than small-scale backpacker tourism. Large resorts have been developed, often with massive foreign loans and direct investment such as Nusa Dua in Bali, and Bintan island near Singapore (Wall, 1996a; Shaw and Shaw, 1999). Overall, as in many other LDCs, the backpacker sub-sector was ignored by government, or even actively discouraged in tourism planning (Richter, 1993; Pattullo, 1996). In addition, the lack of research on the economic impacts of backpackers also contributes to the somewhat prejudicial official attitudes towards these tourists (McCarthy, 1994; Wilson, 1997; Scheyvens, 2002a). However, this chapter focuses upon backpackers, as, despite the lack of attention given to this international tourism sub-sector by planners, these tourists have significant expenditure effects in many local economies across Indonesia (Hampton, 1998; 2002).

Tourism in the Gili Islands

The island of Lombok, Nusa Tenggara Barat province, eastern Indonesia, has a population of around 2.4 million and an area of 5,435 square kilometres. It is of comparable size and population with Bali, its well-known neighbour to the west. Lombok has white sand beaches and coral reefs plus some rice lands in the centre but is significantly drier than Bali. Lombok is dominated by Mount Rinjani, a live 3,720 metre volcano. Unlike Bali, Lombok is predominantly Muslim and the majority of its population are Sasak with some Balinese settlers and other groups such as Chinese and Arabs.

As Bali moved up the S-shaped resort cycle curve (Butler, 1980) and became increasingly a mass tourism destination in the 1980s, backpackers then 'discovered' Lombok, and the Gili islands became well-known backpacker destinations. The Gili islands are sometimes used as rest stops before the backpackers travel eastwards to Komodo Island and Flores. The Gili islands form part of an increasingly well-defined route across Southeast Asia from Bangkok through peninsular Malaysia, Singapore, Java, Bali and then on to Australia.

New areas with few visitors are constantly sought by such tourists (or 'travellers' as they call themselves) of which Vietnam and Laos are recent additions.

By 1991, Lombok had 56,000 annual visitors, of which approximately 80 per cent were foreign tourists, whereas Bali had 1,850,000 visitors (1990) of which 60 per cent were foreign tourists (Wall, 1996a: 9). It is unknown what proportion of these international tourists were backpackers. The only major study of backpacker tourism, from Australia, shows backpackers comprising 6.5 per cent of international visitors to Australia (Government of Australia, 1995). With the exception of Bali, existing data are scarce on tourism in eastern Indonesia. Research is particularly lacking on Lombok with a very small body of literature (Wall, 1996a; Hampton, 1998; Kasmsa and Bras, 1999; Wong, 2001; and Fallon 2001). In addition, official statistics are somewhat problematic as, unlike nearby Bali, Lombok is not a province but falls within Nusa Tenggara Barat so that official statistics cover the entire province.

Lombok has three main tourist centres: Senggigi beach on the west coast, Kuta beach at the south, and the Gili islands offshore from the north-west. Senggigi is the largest resort having international mass tourism and franchised hotels including the Sheraton and Holiday Inn. Kuta is planned to be an enclave type 'integrated resort' like Nusa Dua in Bali but has seen local protest (McCarthy, 1994; Wall, 1996b; Fallon, 2001). This chapter focuses on the Gili islands as it is concerned with the effects of backpacker tourism, and the other resorts are conventional tourism developments (Figure 15.1).

Gili Trawangan, Gili Meno and Gili Air islands can only be reached by boat. The islands have basic facilities and accommodation is mainly simple chalet-type huts. Most restaurants provide Indonesian dishes, seafood and backpackers' specialities such as banana pancakes.

Gili Trawangan is approximately 6 square kilometres with a local resident population of around 400. Land use is mainly agricultural (coconut plantations, small fields of vegetables, seaweed drying racks, and some livestock) but tourism is the dominant economic activity, with July–August being the main season with smaller peaks in December, January and February.

In August 1997 we observed 280 bungalows, with two more being built. Assuming mostly twin occupancy, island bed space was estimated as between 560 and 600, figures which were confirmed by islanders. Since March 1996, an extra 110 bungalows[2] had been built, so that the island's bed capacity had increased from around 350–400 beds (Hampton, 1998). The older bungalows were usually wood-framed, with palm thatch, woven bamboo screen walls and unglazed window apertures with wooden shutters. The new bungalows were notably different, being more permanent constructions of concrete blocks with tiled roofs and glass windows. The *Lonely Planet* guidebook is typically outspoken:

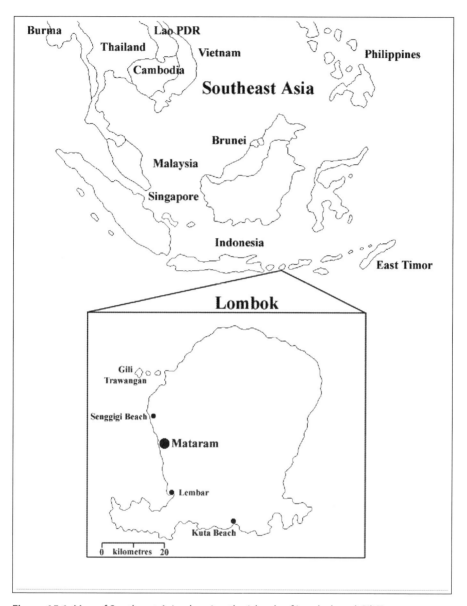

Figure 15.1: Map of Southeast Asia, showing the islands of Lombok and Gili Trawangan.

> The result is reminiscent of Kuta beach in Bali – charmless concrete boxes are cramped together as closely as possible with no sense of local architectural style and no sensitivity at all to the natural environment.
>
> (Lyon and Wheeler, 1997: 406).

Significantly, in 1997 we also observed the island's first large hotel being finished, complete with a two storey restaurant, pizza oven in the grounds, and an artificial beach with reclining sunbeds. Staff informed us that a double room would cost 80,000 Rupiah ($32 at August 1997 exchange rates[3]) compared with average backpacker accommodation costing 12,000 rupiah ($8). Clearly, the island is starting to move away from backpacker tourism. It has been suggested that backpackers form the 'advance guard' of international tourism, opening up new areas and demonstrating tourism's economic potential to investors from outside the region (McCarthy, 1994; Cochrane, 1996a). In terms of Butler's (1980) S-shaped curve to describe the resort cycle, Gili Trawangan could perhaps be seen as being between the 'exploration' and 'involvement' stages.

The main beach follows the east coast with a fringing coral reef. Island transport is basic consisting of bicycles and *cidomo* (pony traps) using unsealed dirt tracks. The island has an electricity generator and an international telecommunication office. The other two Gili islands (Gili Meno and Gili Air) are broadly similar to Trawangan, and also host backpacker tourism (Wong, 2001).

Tourism and the Island Environment

Methodology

It has been suggested that given the complexity of tourism, any analysis of its impacts should be explicitly multidisciplinary. Christensen and Royle (2002) have argued that there is now an increasing need for Integrated Impact Appraisal (IIA) for tourism that uses multidisciplinary research teams to gain insights from their different perspectives brought to the study. The research reported on in this present chapter is in effect a small-scale pilot study using an IIA-type approach as the authors of this chapter are a tourism specialist and a marine ecologist respectively.

The chapter draws on field-work in Gili Trawangan during 1996 and 1997, and a pre-field-work visit in July 1995. The first study was carried out in March 1996 and then further field-work was undertaken in August 1997. The visits were brief, with each lasting two weeks following Theis and Grady's (1991) suggested guidelines for rapid appraisals. Field-work investigated several aspects of backpacker tourism in the island, and this chapter focuses on the environmental effects. The techniques used included mapping, direct observation, a coral reef survey which was carried out at the main beach; questionnaires of the backpackers (1996, n=47; 1997 n=76); repeat interviews with key informants and semi-structured informal interviews (n=25) with guesthouse and restaurant owners, waiters, hawkers, shop-keepers, other villagers, staying tourists and day trippers.

The authors of this chapter also have previous extensive experience of tourism development in the Asia–Pacific region, and specifically in Indonesia, what Pagdin (1989: 248) terms 'pre knowledge', and have made several lengthy visits as backpackers since 1989. It is recognized that this chapter is a 'snapshot' of the resort before the continuing economic crisis in Indonesia and the terrorist bombs in Bali in 2002 and Jakarta in 2003.

Terrestrial Environmental Issues

Field-work examined several terrestrial environmental aspects of the growth of tourism in Gili Trawangan, including water supply, solid waste (garbage), sewage and building materials. As with many islands, Gili Trawangan has limited fresh water. Wells near the village supply fresh water, but elsewhere the water is brackish (salty). Water is used for three main purposes: direct consumption (drinking and cooking), washing and toilet purposes, and cleansing diving equipment.

Since most island water is brackish the *losmen* (guesthouses) and restaurants furthest from the village transport fresh water by *cidomo* across the island.[4] Apart from tea and coffee, tourists drink little local water; rather they drink cheap bottled water from Lombok (in 1996 around 50 US cents for 1.5 litres). However, disposal of the plastic water bottles creates problems which are discussed below.

The main tourist use of island water is for washing and toilet purposes. Most tourist bungalows have gravity showers or traditional *mandi* (a 'scoop and throw' technique) and baths are uncommon. Where *losmen* offer a laundry service, it is hand washed using the brackish water. In the modern bungalows western toilets were increasingly common, whilst in older huts Asian-style toilets are standard. The former use significantly more water than the latter which are flushed by tipping small containers of water down the pipes. Thus, for washing and toilet purposes, backpacker tourism appears to have a low demand for water. However, if the island continues to move up the resort cycle, as exemplified by the new hotel, it is likely that wealthier tourists will demand significantly more water for baths and western toilets which will exacerbate the island's supply problem.[5]

The island's dive schools also use water for rinsing scuba equipment. Interestingly, we observed that equipment was washed in brackish water, which is not ideal as scuba equipment should be rinsed in fresh water to minimize corrosion. If this issue was forced either by the divers or by diving organizations such as PADI, and fresh water had to be used, this would further increase demand for the island's limited supply, although it is unclear how much extra water might be needed.

The disposal of garbage or solid waste appears to be the most visible of the island's terrestrial environmental issues. Garbage disposal is a common problem in other small islands with high tourist densities such as Thailand's Koh Samui, and in the Turks and Caicos Islands (Parnwell, 1993; Ratter, 1997). We observed some incineration, but also recorded a noticeable increase in the amount of garbage around the island by 1997, especially plastic bottles. Other drinks containers such as glass bottles are taken off-island and recycled, whereas the large plastic drinking water bottles are not recycled and accumulate.[6] Some plastic bottles are used as fishing net floats but this only comprises a small percentage of the total. Assuming that in peak season the island has a regular staying tourist population of between 500 to 600, plus another 100 day trippers per day, that could generate around 4200 plastic bottles per week, which is a significant amount for a small island.[7] It also appears that the litter generated by the 5 or 6 boats of day trippers each day in high season is not taken off-island by them, and thus adds to the growing garbage disposal problem.

In addition, as Gili Trawangan increasingly attracts up-market and thus wealthier tourists such as divers, there is growing demand for packaged food in plastic wrappers such as biscuits and confectionery rather than local food. In 1997 we observed that even vegetables imported from Lombok markets were packed in plastic. This all adds to the garbage problem. The increasing litter was commented upon by several backpackers:

> They should do something about the garbage. Big bottel [sic] problem.
>
> (26-year-old Danish student)

> We have been here 12 years ago and since 7 times, but sincerely regret that the island (G. Trawangan) has deteriorated so much (rubbish everywhere almost).
>
> (43-year-old German director of a public relations firm)

Several litter bins had been placed in 1997 on the main path between the village and the beach, but next to the path were significant amounts of litter and plastic bottles. However, in fairness, some interview respondents noted how beautiful the island was, and compared it favourably with Kuta, Bali and Senggigi which were 'very touristical, not relaxing – so this island is fantastic' (28-year-old German student).

Concerning sewage, western toilets are replacing traditional Asian toilets in some accommodation and larger restaurants. Most *losmen* have their own sewage systems and sewage is piped to a common soak-away. We did not see any evidence of direct piping of sewage into the sea. At present the amount of sewage generated by tourists appears to be manageable and within reasonable levels. However, it is unknown whether increasing numbers of staying tourists would overload the capacity of the septic tank systems and lead to leaching into the water supplies or the sea.

Regarding the construction of tourist facilities, two points can be made about building materials. First, new bungalows, restaurants and shops are built using concrete blocks. We observed concrete blocks being hand-made and interviewed several workers. Cement was imported from Lombok but sand was obtained from the island. Given the relatively small scale of building on Gili Trawangan, the amount of sand required appears to be insignificant. However, if tourism development accelerates and building booms, then the increased demand for sand for concrete from the island's beaches might begin to be significant. Coral blocks are not used in construction.

Secondly, the island's dominant vegetation is coconut plantations and mangrove along the coastline. The latter has been used for building in some cases. We saw significant mangrove destruction, especially on the east coast, and on one occasion observed mangroves being cut and the wood used for hut construction. It was unclear, however, whether the areas of denuded mangroves had been cut for firewood by islanders or were used for tourism purposes.[8] In 1997 we observed that the new large hotel, built to the south of the main village, had an artificial beach in front of it and that further mangroves had been cleared.

In all of these terrestrial environmental issues it appears that present numbers of backpacker tourists are just about within reasonable limits, what could be seen as comprising part of the island's physical 'carrying capacity'. The lack of fresh water and the increasing amount of garbage are immediate problems, of which the latter is the most obvious to many tourists. If Gili Trawangan continues to develop however, with increasing total numbers of staying tourists, or begins to attract significant numbers of wealthier tourists there may be serious problems ahead. In either case, increased tourist demand for fresh water may exceed the local supply, necessitating the importing of water for tourists, and this may cause affordability problems for poorer islanders. Increasing tourist facilities might also create sewage problems and, if the septic tanks are overwhelmed, lead to discharge into the sea with possibly serious effects on the reef and water quality at the beaches. Finally, demand for building materials, particularly sand, is low at present. Future hotel construction could change this and might even create demand for coral blocks mined from the reef.

Tourism Planning and Local Reactions

Overall it seems that the rapid growth of small-scale tourism in Gili Trawangan since the 1980s has been effectively un-planned and 'bottom-up', although by 1997 there was increasing evidence of local government intervention and infrastructural expenditure. The Gili islands are in the Lombok Barat regency and tourist accommodation is subject to local taxes payable to the regency government. By 1997 several new developments were observed both in the island and on the mainland at Bangsal, the port for the Gili islands. In Gili Trawangan we observed a new paved area of small shops in the village and a new concrete pier. The new pier may result in declining use of traditional out-rigger boats that currently serve the island. Such vessels cannot easily dock at a conventional pier due to the lateral projection of the bamboo outriggers, so that they land on the beach and passengers disembark into the shallows. However, wealthier tourists heading to the new hotel in modern boats that can use the new pier will not get wet feet when disembarking. In addition, the new pier may alter sediment movement and current patterns. It is unknown how this may affect the coastline generally and the coral reef.

The new area of shops has also generated mixed reactions from local people. Previously, islanders built simple wooden kiosks along the foreshore (sometimes using mangrove wood), and did not pay rent. Respondents told us that the government regulations now forbid such informal structures and they have had to relocate to the permanent buildings of the new shopping area and pay rent. Several shopkeepers told us that the new area was poorly located compared with their previous beachfront sites as tourists did not naturally pass by so that business was now worse, plus they had higher overheads and rent to pay.

On the Lombok mainland, the Bangsal development consists of a new pier and a bus station. Both appear to have problems. The new pier is unfortunately unsuitable for the outrigger boats to the Gili islands which continue to launch from the shore about 10 metres further along the beach, leaving the pier to be used by occasional fishermen. Similarly, a new bus station has been built, about a kilometre inland from the boat landing. Vehicles, which previously could unload passengers near the boats, particularly backpacker tourists from minibuses, now unload at the bus station so that the tourists have to walk the kilometre with their baggage in the heat. This appears to be a classic example of top-down planning of an infrastructural project that probably seemed good on paper but has actually increased inconvenience for tourists and locals alike, what the *Lonely Planet* guide book described as 'ill conceived (. . .) [and] costly white elephants' (Lyon and Wheeler, 1997: 400).

More seriously, in both field-work periods we observed remains of tourist huts near the beach. Many respondents talked of repeated army visits during 1995 when the huts were demolished. This was confirmed in several interviews, and Kamsma and Bras (1999) also record similar enforced demolition of tourist bungalows. Local people described their land tenure problems, specifically their not being issued land ownership certificates. The regency government has published plans for a four-star resort development by the main beach and appears to have used the physical demolition of 'unauthorized' tourist accommodation to dissuade unplanned development in the area slated for the luxury resort (Kasmsa and Bras, 1999). A similar process of 'discouragement' was also documented in the 1990s around Kuta beach, south Lombok, where local villagers without land ownership certificates were forcibly removed and their homes demolished to make way for hotel development (McCarthy, 1994; Wall, 1996; IRIP, 1996a; Fallon, 2001). However, it was reported that, following negotiations, villagers in Gili Trawangan have now received 'fairly substantial compensation' from the government (IRIP, 1996: 1). In addition, the continuing economic crisis in the country may have fatally damaged such plans for up-market development of the island.

In August 1997 several islanders told us that many of them were still deeply unhappy with the political situation and the continuing uncertainty over the island's future development and that the increasing litter problem was symptomatic of many islanders' frustration with the authorities. This interpretation is difficult to validate, but may contain some truth as the lack of security of land tenure may generate feelings against the regency government on mainland Lombok. If islanders feel that they are only temporary residents on Gili Trawangan this may help explain some of their apparent lack of care for their immediate environment, and may also discourage further investment in tourism activities that might be more 'sustainable'.[9]

The continuing Indonesian economic crisis at the time of writing, with its resultant uncertainty and the disruption of foreign and local investment, may affect future possibilities of large-scale tourism developments in the Gili islands. Much depends on whether the central government can restore legitimacy and calm. Tourism may take some time to return to Indonesia given the television images of the 2002 Bali terrorist bombing, the devastation of the 2004 tsunami in Aceh, and the simmering communal violence across the archipelago including Maluku, Kalimantan, and on occasions in Java (Hill, 2000; BBC Online, 2000; 2001). Interestingly, at the time of the 1998 riots and the fall of Suharto, large hotels in Jakarta experienced extremely low occupancy rates whilst at the same time, the cheap backpacker *losmen* saw relatively high occupancy rates.[10] This suggests that backpackers were the last tourists to leave Indonesia as the political situation worsened, but also they appear to be the first to return. Given Indonesia's continuing economic troubles, backpacker expenditure in the local economies could assume real importance, especially for low income communities in Lombok and elsewhere (Hampton, 1998; 2002).

Further, after the September 2001 terrorist attacks on the USA, international tourism to Muslim countries saw decreasing visitor numbers according to the World Tourism Organization. The net effect all points to international tourism in Indonesia continuing to be under pressure (Hall, 2000; World Bank, 2002). However, despite this bleak scenario, in the medium- to long-term (assuming a return to political stability, and an international tourism up-turn) tourism should play a significant role in Indonesia's future economic development.

Marine Environmental Issues

Gili Trawangan is surrounded by a fringing coral reef, which is one of the island's main features, attracting backpackers for snorkelling and diving. The former is more common given its low cost and the ease of renting equipment. Snorkelling occurs offshore from the main beach located on the island's sheltered east coast, one kilometre from the nearest land mass (Gili Meno). The reef consists of a reef flat with a 15 to 25 metre drop-off sloping down to a sandy sea bed. The main beach coral reef was surveyed to assess its condition and begin investigating possible effects, both direct and indirect, of backpacker tourism. Observations from the 1995 pre-fieldwork visit suggested that the amount of live coral of the reef flat decreased southwards towards the harbour. Little coral grows adjacent to the harbour and this may be due to the boats churning up sediment and choking the coral polyps.[11]

In March 1996 the condition of the coral reef was investigated along the first 200 metres of the 400-metre stretch of the main beach (Figure 15.2). This site was chosen because tourism-related activities are concentrated here including snorkelling,

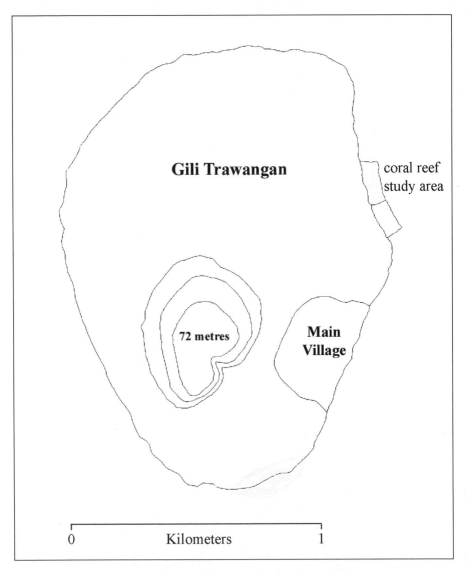

Figure 15.2: Map showing the location of the coral reef study on Gili Trawangan.

swimming and boating activities from day trippers. Due to the strong north to south longshore current estimated as reaching up to 2 knots (Muller, 1992: 143), tourists drift-snorkel the reef along the main beach. An average snorkelling trip lasts about half an hour along the 400 metre stretch. The reef survey in this study was based upon Whitten et al.'s (1987) adaptation of the method recommended by the South Pacific Commission for environmental monitoring programmes.

Our study deployed the technique of surveying the coral within circular plots of 50 square metres in each of the major reef habitats. The main reef habitat used by snorkellers is the 30 metre wide reef flat which lies between the reef drop-off and the shore. It was decided to divide this habitat into two zones: the inner reef (10 metres); and the mid-outer reef (20 metres).

Circular plots were randomly selected within the inner and outer reef at three points from the main beach, except the third point where the outer reef was surveyed only (Figure 15.3). The first point was chosen at the beginning of the northern end of the beach where the snorkellers enter the water (0 metres on Figure 15.3). Points 2 and 3 were chosen randomly at 120 metres and 200 metres respectively. Once in a zone, each 50 square metre circular plot was established by visually marking its centre and then measuring a 4 metre radius to visually mark its outer edge. The percentage cover of different substrate types (mud, sand, rubble or blocks); live coral (hard and soft coral, sponges); dead standing coral; and marine plants was recorded. In addition, the different forms of hard and soft coral and marine plants were recorded for their presence, dominance and size. The following animals, if present, were counted: mushroom coral, giant clams, sea cucumber, starfish and urchins. Visible pollution, if present, was also recorded by type and amount.

The results of the plots surveyed suggest that two opposing trends occur between the mid-outer reef and the inner reef. Cover of live hard coral of the mid to outer reef decreases towards the main village, from high (51 to 75 per cent cover at point 1) to low (6 to 30 per cent cover at point 3), whilst in the inner reef, cover increases from only 1 to 5 per cent low cover at point 1, to 51 to 75 per cent high at point 2. The result of 31 to 50 per cent dead standing coral at point 1 indicates that the inner reef has been damaged considerably. This may explain our finding of only 5 per cent live hard coral here. This location is where most snorkellers enter the reef area, and we would expect less live hard coral here on the inner reef because of trampling. In addition, this is also where many day trip boats land. We return to this later. In contrast there was only 5 per cent dead standing coral in the mid to outer reef which remains constant at this level of 5 per cent cover towards the village.

The decrease in live hard coral cover in the outer reef towards the village (that is southwards) saw a corresponding significant increase in rubble (from 5 per cent to 31 to 50 per cent) and a slight increase in sand cover (6 to 30 per cent). Increased rubble and sand cover may be explained by our observations of the circular sites of fish bomb damage in these same areas.

Although many forces affect the morphology and ecology of coral reefs over time (both directly from human actions but also from natural activity such as wave action erosion or sedimentation) here we focus upon the effects of tourism. As such, tourist damage to Gili Trawangan's coral reef can be discussed under five headings: damage from walking on the reef; from snorkelling; from diving; from boats; and from fishing activities. Interestingly, unlike Bali (and the case of Candidasa: see Knight et al., 1997) there is no evidence of coral mining for building purposes, although this

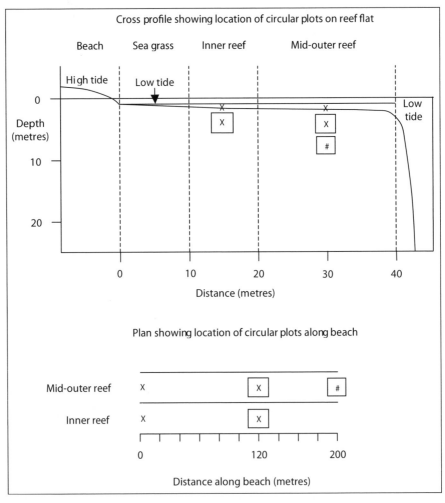

Figure 15.3: Diagram to show location of the survey plots.

happens elsewhere in Lombok. The lack of coral mining so far may be due to the small-scale nature of tourism on the island.

First, tourists were frequently observed walking on the inner reef at low tide, despite clear warnings against doing so in the popular *Lonely Planet* guidebook used by backpackers (Lyon and Wheeler, 1997: 400). Liddle and Kay (1989) discussed reef damage from human trampling, noting that initial damage from trampling appears to be the most serious, and the most vulnerable corals such as the branching types are notably affected. Hawkins and Roberts (1993) reported similar findings, although they observed a high level of re-growth of damaged corals.

Secondly, the coral appears to be being damaged by the considerable numbers of snorkellers. The inner reef is easily accessible from the main beach, lying only 4 metres offshore in places at high tide. Damage from snorkelling consisted of standing, bumping and breaking off pieces of branching corals for souvenirs (Rogers, 1988). In their research on Red Sea reefs, Hawkins and Roberts (1993) commented that the snorkelled zone 'was interesting because it exhibited intermediate levels of damage between trampled and untrampled areas. Damage was very patchy; badly damaged in parts, fairly pristine in others. This can be explained from observations of snorkellers' behaviour. Usually they float face down causing little damage. However, when snorkellers stand up, the damage caused by cumbersome, uncontrolled fins can be severe' (Hawkins and Roberts, 1993: 30). Our own observations concur that snorkellers can cause considerable damage to corals by bumping into them or standing on them whilst snorkelling, and we observed patchy damage to the corals. There were two porite species of dome-shaped coral which at low tide could be easily stood on by snorkellers and swimmers. As noted above, our findings suggest that the inner reef is showing most signs of damage from snorkellers in the northern part at the usual entry place.

Thirdly, concerning damage from scuba diving, although the island has several dive schools, this appears to be a less significant factor as this reef is visited less by divers than reefs to the north of our study area. However, the basic PADI training of the new divers takes place near the harbour, to the south of our study area, but some advanced training takes place along the drop-off. The initial training period can be a particularly vulnerable time as there is more accidental contact with coral by divers as they are unused to maintaining neutral buoyancy. Hawkins and Roberts (1993) examined Red Sea dive sites and sampled coral, finding that around 10 per cent of the coral was broken. More recently Zakai and Chadwick-Furman (2002) found four times more damaged coral than Hawkins and Roberts in an intensively dived reef near Eilat. However, our findings suggest that at present the effect of divers on this stretch of reef appears fairly minimal in relation to the effects of snorkellers, day trip boats and fish bombing.

Dixon et al. (1993) in their research in the Netherlands Antilles suggested that there was a threshold above which impacts suddenly become highly significant from diver pressure on a given reef. As Davis and Tisdell (1995) comment, this is somewhat similar to the concept of 'carrying capacity' in that how does one define this point? Zakai and Chadwick-Furman (2002) note there is an on-going controversy over carrying capacities of reefs for recreational diving, nevertheless Davis and Tisdell argue that:

> [T]here is little evidence that severe biological degradation or loss of biological diversity results from recreational scuba-diving (. . .) The caveat that applies to this conclusion is that no long-term monitoring studies have been undertaken of diver-induced impacts, even in highly dived areas. However, concerns do arise about critical threshold levels of use at particular dive sites. Beyond such thresholds biological impacts might be severe, and, ultimately, irreversible.
>
> (1995: 34–35).

Nevertheless, Tilmant and Schmal (1981), examining recreationally-used reefs in Florida, noted that natural wave action and substrate erosion accounted for the majority of coral damage. In our study it is unknown how much of the damage to the outer reef has occurred from natural wave action; however, local storms are predominantly from the north-west. Given the location of this part of the reef on the island's sheltered east coast it is reasonable to assume that direct wave action is a less significant cause of reef damage. Further, the circular nature of much of the outer reef's damage is typically associated with fish-bombing. Whatever the initial cause of coral destruction, once a fringing reef is damaged, waves break nearer the shore, their erosive power increases and more scouring occurs. We also observed that waves were breaking directly on the shore rather than on the reef which had no obvious reef lip. This also suggests that the reef is damaged. In addition, the indirect effect of the erosion from storms generates sediment which can choke coral. Thus we have to be cautious in our preliminary findings here.

Fourthly, there was damage from boats. This included the tourist day-trip boats, the effects of anchors, and the regular ferries to the island. We frequently observed 5 to 6 tourist day-trip boats arriving each day on the main beach in peak season from the large Senggigi resort. Commonly, the hulls could be seen (and heard) damaging the coral at low tide, with crew members walking on the reef to push the boat off as it grounded. Interestingly, crews were generally not islanders, and we observed that when islanders launched boats they appeared to be more careful of the reef. This appears to augment the damage associated with the snorkellers to the inner reef at the northern end of the study area, although the relative contribution to the damage to the coral originating from boats or from snorkellers is not clear at present.

Other damage originated from boats' anchors when moored for tourist fishing, snorkelling or diving. Anchor damage has been observed on coral elsewhere including the Red Sea (Hawkins and Roberts, 1994), and Sri Lanka (Rajasuriya et al., 1995). In contrast, most of the daily out-rigger ferries to Gili Trawangan were secured by large iron stakes driven into sand on the beach or tied to trees. Nevertheless, the ferry landing area was a noticeably denuded area, with evidence of mostly dead and bleached coral and sea grass.

Finally, concerning fishing, it appears that no meaningful controls exist over spear fishing. On one occasion we observed a tourist disembarking from a chartered out-rigger proudly displaying his 'catch' of inedible small angel fish. Certainly, there appears to be increasing tourist demand for large fish for the island's restaurants with snapper, grouper, shark and barracuda regularly appearing on menus. Local in-shore fishing techniques use gill nets with small mesh which are unselective and trap all fish in the net's vicinity. It is unclear what effect the removal of such numbers of the largest pelagic and reef fish predators might have on the reef's ecology. We observed few predators such as barracuda in the coral survey area, and the specimens that we saw were small. It is possible that over-fishing has contributed, as decreasing fish size is linked to the decreasing size of a proportion of adult fish so that the breeding population falls, resulting in a general decrease in the total population.

In addition, as already noted, blast fishing continues despite the official ban in Indonesia. On at least two occasions we heard recognisable loud bangs and snorkelling trips showed the typical circular damage which was clearly visible at several points on the outer reef with a low coverage of live hard coral, and significant rubble and dead coral. Bryan (2002) notes that Indonesia's continuing economic crisis has seen increasing illegal blast fishing and cyanide used to stun fish and collect them for the international aquarium trade.

Thus, our initial reef survey suggests that the inner reef is now showing some signs of damage at the northern end in terms of percentage cover of live hard coral, whereas the mid to outer reef appears to be in good condition. The opposite was seen to the south where the inner reef appeared less damaged with high coverage of live hard coral, and the mid to outer reef showed signs of damage and low percentage cover of live hard coral. We suggest that the damage to the inner reef to the north was associated with the snorkellers (and perhaps an element from day-trip boats) whilst damage to the outer reef in the south appeared to be linked to fish bombing.

Therefore, it seems that even small-scale tourism to Gili Trawangan is beginning to affect some parts of this reef, although the recovery time of the reef is unknown at present. Also, other parts of the reef elsewhere in the island, whilst not visited by significant numbers of tourist, might also be under stress from over-fishing and fish bombing. Thus, subject to obtaining future funding, we would hope to continue monitoring tourism's effects on the reef over time, to conduct re-studies, and examine other aspects of the island environment.

Discussion and Conclusions

In Gili Trawangan the development of small-scale backpacker tourism since the 1980s has been virtually unplanned with a gradual move toward more permanent accommodation, bigger restaurants and the island's first hotel. The number of tourists staying on Gili Trawangan increased significantly between March 1996 and August 1997 by around 30 per cent with up to 600 beds becoming available, and there was also an increase in day trippers, adding perhaps another 100 tourists per day in peak season.

The impact of the rapid growth of tourism on this small island's environment is beginning to be noticeable, both to islanders and increasingly the tourists. On land, some backpackers appeared aware of the immediate problems of litter and garbage disposal, the contentious issue of further large-scale development and the serious implications for limited water supplies. In terms of the marine environment, our coral survey indicates that the reef flat in the study area is beginning to show signs of damage, especially in the inner reef area where the snorkellers enter the water. In addition, growing tourist numbers generate increasing demand for large fish such as shark, barracuda, snapper and grouper and few large predators were seen on the reef. However, this may be due to other factors unconnected to tourism such as the possibility of over-fishing by Lombok fishing boats attempting to meet a growing domestic demand to feed the rising population.

What is unknown at present is the physical 'carrying capacity' of Gili Trawangan, and in particular the main coral reef. This issue requires further research as the resort changes over time. However, the continuing economic crisis in Indonesia and the terrorist bombings of 2002 and 2005 form the back-drop to this question. Therefore, the scale and future development of tourism in Gili Trawangan is itself highly dependent upon what now happens to Indonesia and whether or not the Jakarta government can restore stability and re-attract international tourists.

Concerning the implications of the rapid growth of tourism for other small tropical islands, Gili Trawangan raises certain issues. First, although it appears at first glance that tourism *per se* has directly led to increasing pressure on the island's terrestrial environment, exemplified by its increasing garbage problem, this should be seen within the wider context of rapid, albeit uneven, economic development in an LDC. Although the island's present type of international tourism is still small-scale – mainly backpackers – there is a question whether it is any less damaging for the island's environment than conventional mass tourism that could be concentrated into a resort enclave. Rodenburg (1980: 192) argues that tourism planners' notion of 'containment' was explicit in the design of Bali's Nusa Dua resort where tourists could be isolated 'like any other industrial effluent'. This referred to tourism's social and cultural impact, but a case can also be made on environmental grounds where some of the external costs of the damage could be captured within the prices charged. Our preliminary study, particularly of water use and sewage, suggests that present tourist levels may be sufficient for the island's systems to cope with, but that any increase in either the number of tourists staying or a change in the type of tourist who may demand more fresh water could pose serious problems for the island's environment. Nevertheless, compared with other possible economic activities, tourism may be the least bad option, that is, making the best of difficult choices facing a poor and relatively remote region.

Secondly, local participation could be encouraged in the management of the island's environment, as it can be argued that at present it is not being managed at all. Gili Trawangan faces increasing pressure from un-planned, rapidly growing tourism that appears to be linked to increasing damage to parts of the coral reef. If the reef continues to be damaged and goes beyond the coral's ability to recover, then tourists may go elsewhere to snorkel and dive. Without the attraction of the reef, Gili Trawangan is just another small tropical island amongst many in Southeast Asia. Further, if the fringing reef becomes badly damaged, its ability to protect the island's beaches will be affected, and these may be eroded away as happened in Candidasa, Bali (Knight et al., 1997). Although Indonesia has many environmental protection laws and presidential directives on the statute books it has problems with implementation, staffing and training (Whitten et al., 1996). The encouragement of community-based management, especially of the reef resource, might help reduce or minimize the damage. Given Indonesia's present economic situation this might require external funding and training of local wardens in international best practice. Recently this has begun in neighbouring Bali with the conservation organization WWF working with park rangers, marine police and local people to attempt to minimize reef damage (Bryan, 2002).

Concerning the possibility of seeking official marine park designation, it is unclear if this would be effective for Gili Trawangan, given the abuses common in such reserves such as fishing in protected areas in Indonesia and elsewhere. Rather, we would suggest that more local control and meaningful community-based participation by islanders would be more effective and equitable. It is possible that tourists wishing to dive and snorkel might be willing to pay a small fee of (say) $5 to support reef conservation around the island. Findings of Arin and Kramer (2002) from several Philippine dive sites suggest that tourists might be happier to pay if a local NGO was involved in the fee collection.

Thirdly, better information is needed to educate the backpackers especially about the fragility of coral, the particular problems of island environments (such as water scarcity) and to encourage recycling of plastic bottles and other waste.[12] Day trippers could also be encouraged to take their litter away, and their boats forbidden to land to the north. If the day-trip boats landed at the harbour, islanders could ferry the day trippers by *cidomo* the short distance to the snorkelling area, both saving further boat damage and generating some small income. It is recognized that this might be hard to implement given that day-trip boats originate from the large Senggigi resort on Lombok, and many boats are owned by large hotel groups with powerful influence. Again this illustrates how environmental issues are connected to the local political economy of who owns what in LDCs (Hampton, 2002; Mowforth and Munt, 2003; Scheyvens, 2002b).

Finally, the case study indicates that more data are required, particularly further detailed surveys of the reef flat, the mangroves and the beach (Suharsono, 1994). The assistance of divers could be sought to build up more detailed knowledge of the reefs around the island and how they may be changing. Techniques such as using video transects (Tratalos and Austin, 2001) and close participant underwater observation (Zakai and Chadwick-Furman, 2002) could provide further data both concerning reef damage and snorkeller/diver behaviour.

For many Gili Trawangan islanders tourism has generated significant economic opportunities as an alternative to fishing, harvesting seaweed or coconuts. However, our study suggests that the rapid and unplanned growth of tourism, albeit still mostly directed at the small-scale servicing of backpackers, is beginning to put increasing pressure upon the island's environment, both terrestrial and marine. Metaphorically speaking: is the 'beach party' over for Gili Trawangan? At present, it seems that the 'hosts' are beginning to be aware of the negative effects of having so many 'guests' in their small island.[13] In the medium term, all else being equal, and assuming that international tourism to Indonesia begins to recover, it may be that Gili Trawangan is rapidly approaching its limits, its 'critical level' (Dixon et al., 1993) and that further tourism expansion may result in more serious and possibly irreversible environmental impacts. If, and when, that happens the tourists will then move on to somewhere new, whereas the islanders will not, in the main, have that option. The challenge for small tropical islands like Gili Trawangan is how much tourism, even at this small-scale, is enough? In essence, the fundamental question remains whether or not even this small level of international tourism is ultimately sustainable for the island.

Given the drive for income-generating activities in this poor region in a country itself struggling with its most severe economic crisis and social unrest for thirty years, it is possible that the richness and beauty of the island's environment may be the loser. In cash terms, backpacker tourism can generate a useful income for poorer families compared with traditional activities. For example in Malaysia, average incomes of chalet operators in the Perhentian islands are over US$400 per month compared with under US$130 per month earned by local fishermen (Hamzah, 1995).

If Gili Trawangan is viewed through western eyes, then allowing the virtually un-checked growth of tourism, with its resultant environmental damage, appears to be somewhat myopic and short-termist. However, if seen through the eyes of a Gili Trawangan islander perhaps facing real hardship and uncertainty, then a western frame of reference becomes at least problematic.

Authors' Note

Thanks are due to Pak Andi; Judith Lim; and Wiendu Nuryanti, David Saunders and Hernowo Muliawan at Stuppa Research Associates, Yogyakarta. We also thank Tim

Forsyth, Stephen Royle and Olivier Thebaud for their critical comments on earlier versions of this chapter. However, the usual disclaimers apply.

Notes

1 Small islands are defined here as having under 1.5 million population following the upper limit suggested by the Commonwealth Secretariat (1997).

2 15 to 20 new bungalows were built in or around the main village in 1996. They were concrete breeze block construction unlike the older huts built of traditional materials such as wood and bamboo.

3 Due to the crisis the Indonesian rupiah became highly volatile thus rupiah:US dollar exchange rates varied widely from the fieldwork period in March 1996 at around 2,000 to 3,000 to the dollar, to the August 1997 visit at around 4,000, before averaging over 10,000 rupiah to the dollar.

4 Several backpackers complained about using saline water for washing (especially getting soap to lather) and tea often 'tasted salty'. The cost of transporting water across the island to many losmen and restaurants means that brackish water is used for tea. However, despite some complaints, most backpackers appeared unconcerned, illustrating the minimal requirements of this type of tourism. It is unlikely that many upmarket tourists would tolerate this and would demand 'normal' water for ablutions and hot drinks.

5 It was rumoured that the regency government planned a golf course for Gili Trawangan (cited in McCarthy, 1994 and also in two Lonely Planet guidebooks: Turner et al, 1995; Lyon and Wheeler, 1997). Since island water supplies barely meet present demand, this appears ill-judged, but in the context of an LDC with other examples of inappropriate planning permissions being granted, it seemed feasible. However, nothing has been heard of this rumour recently.

6 In 1997 we observed a man sorting through the garbage for drink cans. We were told that the cans could be sold in Lombok and then recycled.

7 This assumes a consumption of at least one (1.5 litre) bottle of water each day per tourist. Given local high humidity and temperature (around 33 degrees Centigrade in August) this appears reasonable. In addition the authors regularly drank this amount of water each day, plus soft drinks and tea.

8 It is possible that the numbers of beach parties being held every few days in high season may contribute to further mangrove destruction, as some parties advertised bonfires as part of the entertainment. The spread of beach parties across Asia by youth tourism, previously not a noticeable feature on Gili Trawangan, lies outside this chapter but would be worth tracing from its origins in Thailand's traditional full moon parties.

9 Litter is an increasing problem in Southeast Asia, especially plastic. A partial explanation is that food wrappings from markets and food stalls formerly consisted of biodegradable material such as banana leaves. Once the food was consumed, discarded wrapping would be eaten by animals or would biodegrade. However, most items are now wrapped in plastic. We observed that wrappings still tend to be thrown onto the ground near food stalls but being plastic do not degrade.

10 One author also visited Indonesia in late March 1998. Further information was gathered from personal observations and discussions with local tourism industry sources and Indonesian tourism academics.

11 Unlike other harbours there are no known sewage outflows, fresh water streams or soil run-off that might also affect the growth of coral.

12 It is encouraging that special text boxes containing environmental advice on responsible diving on coral reefs have now appeared in Lonely Planet and other guide books to the region.

13 Mowforth and Munt (2003) comment that the terms 'hosts' and 'guests' as commonly used in the literature are problematic and may disguise the unequal power relations within LDC tourism.

16 Current Issues in Southeast Asian Tourism

Michael Hitchcock, Victor King and Michael Parnwell

There has been an upsurge in publications on tourism in the Southeast Asian region since the appearance of our book on the subject in 1993. In order truly to capture the spirit of what has been happening one would need a literature review of all the disciplines of social science and the humanities that have been exploring the subject in the manner undertaken by King for anthropology in Chapter 2. Logical though this might appear to be, it would be a daunting task given the size of some of the disciplines concerned even though some of them, notably geography and economics, have their own journals dedicated to tourism. Interestingly, anthropology still does not have its own tourism journal despite the fact that as early as 1988 Jafari and Aaser were able to report that the number of anthropology doctoral dissertations on tourism was second only to those in economics in a continuously increasing trend within the social sciences in the 1970s and 1980s. Despite the lack of a dedicated journal it is still just about possible, albeit not an easy task, for a scholar to undertake a literature review on the anthropology of tourism in Southeast Asia (as King has done in Chapter 2), partly because the anthropologists working on this region tend to be networked with one another, and have an on-going interest in regional studies and are contributing to regional journals.

For geography and sociology the issue is a little different, not least because the members of these two disciplines with a strong regional orientation often get caught up in the orbit of the anthropologists and indeed appear in literature reviews that should be strictly anthropological, though it makes little sense to maintain such boundaries when scholars have something to say to one another. The risk for these disciplinary members is that they may be marginalized within their own disciplines (this is far less the case in anthropology) where, generally speaking, more credit is given to research contributing to broader theoretical developments than to regional expertise. Similar observations can be made with regard to economics, but with even greater emphasis, and perhaps it is not surprising that in this volume there is not one contribution by an economist as compared with the three who contributed to our collection in 1993: pressure to get publications accepted in mainstream disciplinary journals has clearly taken its toll.

At first glance it would appear that the 1993 volume was more broadly based in disciplinary terms than the current one, having included papers by two historians, one political scientist and one practitioner in addition to the anthropologists, sociologists, geographers and economists. To a certain extent this is true since the current volume is heavily biased in favour of anthropology, geography and sociology, but closer examination reveals a more interesting story that reflects subtle changes going on in both the way tourism is studied on the one hand and how regional studies are researched on the other. The first and perhaps most obvious point to make is that it is less easy to detect the disciplinary boundaries in this volume than in the previous one, not least because there appears to be more common ground this time round.

The second but far less evident point is that another discipline has in recent years become deeply interested in the subject of tourism both generally and in Southeast Asia in particular. The discipline concerned is language and literature, with its related interests in the media, and, though still underrepresented in this volume given its rapid development, there is at least one contributor from this background. Darma Putra has analysed contemporary Balinese short stories and novels, which often feature tourist characters and reveal some of the anxieties experienced by host communities. A third and related point concerns where the members of these different disciplines engaged in tourism research are located in the early twenty-first century. By and large, for example, the anthropologists who contributed to the 1993 volume were in anthropology departments, but since then there has been a radical change. In the current volume three of the anthropologists teach and research in schools of management, business or related areas, easily outnumbering contributors from anthropology departments. Interestingly, in a parallel development two of the contributors on the environment in Southeast Asia originate in schools of management, though the authors concerned did not begin their research on tourism with these contexts.

A fourth point arising from this is how the map of regional studies has altered in the intervening years, particularly in Europe. In the 1993 volume, four of the contributors were employed by the Centre for South-East Asian Studies at Hull University, which now exists in name only, its last remaining staff having transferred to Leeds University between 2003 and 2005. In the new volume six of the contributors, all of them with strong regional interests, are working in what can broadly be called the management field, as compared with two working in regional studies centres. The fact that management takes regional studies increasingly seriously is evidenced not just by the work on tourism represented in this volume but also by the growth of publications in other management fields. If management schools are prepared to accept and support research centres based on tourism, it is conceivable that this interest could eventually spread to Asian Studies.

Despite these changes and shifts in emphasis, there is a great deal of continuity between the two publications, not just in contributors, but also in further explorations of the same topics. Of the seventeen original contributors, six have written for this new volume, including of course the three editors. Interestingly, many of the new contributors have chosen to revisit issues raised in the original volume and these include: minorities in national parks; sex tourism; souvenirs and handicrafts; ecotourism and sustainability. Although the volume remains biased towards the Malay–Indonesian world, especially the latter in terms of coverage, Vietnam and Laos are included this time, whereas they only appeared in general papers in the previous volume. Significantly, the link between colonialism and tourism, which was solely seen in terms of European imperialism in the earlier volume, is broadened to include a consideration of Japanese colonialism in the new volume.

This brings us to another emerging theme that we have already touched on which Yamashita addresses in his chapter: the increasing importance of intra-Asian tourism. In our view, this will become a major preoccupation in tourism research in Southeast Asia in the next decade. Yamashita, for example, in examining Japanese perspectives on and encounters with Southeast Asia, demonstrates the diversity of Japanese touristic encounters with the region, as well as the perceptions of 'nostalgia' and 'healing' which Japanese hold and which are different from Western notions. Yuk Wah Chan's chapter also reveals the different perceptions which Chinese tourists and Vietnamese hosts have of each other and their respective countries in the context of cross-border tourism in northern Vietnam. We must, therefore, beware of placing too much emphasis on Western preoccupations about tourism, on the 'external tourist gaze', and on the character of cross-cultural encounters in Western–Asian contexts, and issue a word of warning. In spite of our realization of the importance of Asian tourism in Asia, both between and within Asian countries, with a few exceptions, our volume still does not reflect this importance. We attempted to secure other contributions on intra-Asian and domestic tourism, and to commission chapters written by local scholars about their own domestic industry, but, for various reasons, we were not successful. However, our recent involvement in organizing a conference on the theme of 'Tourism in Asia' in Leeds suggests that we shall be able to begin to address the intra-Asian dimension much more successfully in future publications.

Another comment is also necessary on intra-Asian tourist encounters. We suggest that there is a need to relate this issue much more closely to the emerging work that is being undertaken on social class in Asia, and specifically on the development of an affluent middle class in the region which has the time and the resources to travel and participate in cross-national networks of information. It is increasingly this category of people which is setting the agenda for the development of particular tourist sites and becoming involved in discourses about tourism activities. Debates within local civil society, among local intellectuals, artists, government representatives, professionals, businesspeople and NGO activists about such issues as sustainability (see Parnwell's chapter, for example), and the relationships between local or national identities, and the future direction of tourism development are becoming increasingly important. The theme of a 'multitude of voices' is also addressed in King's chapter on the importance of agency, and identifying those who play key roles in the development and representation of particular sites. Debates about particular locations and their trajectories also tend to intensify during moments of crisis, such as a terrorist atrocity (see the chapter by Darma Putra and Hitchcock on Bali) or a natural disaster and these debates increasingly take place on the internet, a medium which has profoundly influenced and complicated our perceptions of tourism in Southeast Asia and which deserves much more attention in future research.

Our volume has also revealed a paradox in the study of tourism in Southeast Asia. A primary theme which runs through the volume is the progressive differentiation and diversification of tourism, and that, in spite of globalization and increased international communication and interaction, tourism sites and representations retain and indeed, develop distinctively local flavours, as we have seen in Adams's chapter on the hybridization of handicrafts for the tourist market. One aspect of this diversification is that the concept of tourism as a leisure activity becomes ever more complex as it shades into such other activities as 'lifestyle migration' and longer term sojourns (see Yamashita's chapter). What also strikes us is the unpredictable directions in which tourism develops in response to the interaction of different agents and to such events as terrorism and natural disasters. However, in spite of this diversity and variation in Southeast Asian tourism in both time and space, we continue to rely on a rather restricted set of studies; it is an issue which the late David Wilson in 1993 drew attention to so incisively. We have noted that there has been an upsurge of studies on tourism in Southeast Asia during the past decade or so since the publication of our 1993 volume, yet we still base a considerable amount of our thinking and teaching on a small number of classic studies. The work of Picard on Bali and Cohen on Thailand, for example, have seemed to have attained paradigmatic status in the field. But we need to enlarge the scope and quantity of our research to many more tourist sites in the Southeast Asian region. It is to this end that we have not only revisited

312

Southeast Asian tourism, but hopefully, through the combined studies of some of the original contributors to our 1993 volume and of those who have added their perspectives to the current volume, also extended its range.

Finally, our volume ends on a much more optimistic note than was evident from our contributors in 1993 who were very much concerned about the negative social, cultural and environmental impacts of over-rapid and poorly regulated tourism development. While these impacts are still in evidence today, there is much more discussion in the present volume of reactions to the pernicious effects of tourism, be that in the form of heritage protection and management, conscientization and participatory planning, grassroots development and pro-poor tourism, co-management, and corporate social responsibility. Academic analysis and exposure, such as was contained in our 1993 volume, helps raise awareness of pressing impacts and issues, and leads eventually to change in policy, planning and management responses. Our current volume draws attention to some of the challenges to be faced in the coming years, not least from the massive diversification of Southeast Asian tourism (especially the boom in domestic tourism) and associated patterns of tourist behaviour. In order to rise to the academic challenge that such changes will create, and as we discussed in our Introduction, we need much more sophisticated, flexible, holistic and comparative sets of conceptual tools, and much fuller and more nuanced data.

Bibliography

Abrami, R. M., 2003, 'Vietnam in 2002: On the Road to Recovery', *Asian Survey*, 43, 1, 91–100.

Acciaioli, G., 1985, 'Culture as Art: From Practice to Spectacle in Indonesia', *Canberra Anthropology*, 8, 1 and 2, 148–174.

Adams, Kathleen M., 1984, 'Come to Tana Toraja, "Land of the Heavenly Kings": Travel Agents as Brokers in Ethnicity', *Annals of Tourism Research*, 2, 469–485.

—— 1993a, 'Club Dead, Not Club Med: Staging Death in Contemporary Tana Toraja (Indonesia)', *Southeast Asian Journal of Social Science*, 21, 62–72.

—— 1993b, 'Theologians, Tourists and Thieves: The Torajan Effigy of the Dead in Modernizing Indonesia', *The Kyoto Journal*, 22, 38–45.

—— 1995, 'Making-up the Toraja? The Appropriation of Tourism, Anthropology, and Museums for Politics in Upland Sulawesi, (Indonesia)', *Ethnology*, 34, 143–153.

—— 1997a, 'Touting Touristic "Primadonas": Tourism, Ethnicity and National Integration in Sulawesi, Indonesia', in Michel Picard and Robert Wood, eds, *Tourism, Ethnicity and the State in Asian and Pacific Societies*, Honolulu: University of Hawai'i Press, 155–180.

—— 1997b, 'Ethnic Tourism and the Re-negotiation of Tradition in Tana Toraja (Sulawesi, Indonesia)', *Ethnology*, 37, 309–320.

—— 1998a, 'More Than an Ethnic Marker: Toraja Art as Identity Negotiator', *American Ethnologist*, 25, 3, 327–351.

—— 1998b, 'Domestic Tourism and Nation-Building in South Sulawesi', *Indonesia and the Malay World*, 26, 75, 77–96.

—— 2001, 'Danger Zone Tourism: Prospects and Problems for Tourism in Tumultuous Times', in Peggy Teo, T. C. Chang and K. C. Ho, eds, *Interconnected Worlds: Tourism in Southeast Asia*, London: Pergamon, 265–281.

—— 2003, 'The Politics of Heritage in Tana Toraja, Indonesia: Interplaying the Local and the Global', *Indonesia and the Malay World*, 31, 89, 91–107 (special issue on 'Tourism and Heritage in South-East Asia', edited by Michael Hitchcock and Victor T. King).

—— 2004, 'Locating Global Legacies in Tana Toraja Indonesia', *Current Issues in Tourism*, 7, 4 and 5, 433–435.

—— 2005, 'Locating Global Legacies in Tana Toraja, Indonesia', in David Harrison and Michael Hitchcock, eds, *The Politics of World Heritage: Negotiating Tourism and Conservation,* Buffalo: Channel View, 153–156.

—— 2006, Art in Politics: Re-crafting Identities, Tourism, and Power in Tana Toraja, Indonesia, Honolulu: University of Hawai'i Press.

Aditjondro, G., 1995, *Bali, Jakarta's Colony: Social and Ecological Impacts of Jakarta-Based Conglomerates in Bali's Tourism Industry*, Working Paper, Murdoch University, Perth.

Allan, J., 2005, *Bali Blues*, Denpasar: Makara Media.

Allcock, A., 2004, *National Tourism Strategy for Lao PDR: 2005 to 2015* (Final Draft), National Tourism Authority of Lao PDR: Vientiane.

Allen, P. and C. Palermo, 2004, 'If *Ajeg* is the Answer, then what is the Question?: New Identity Discourses in Bali', Paper presented to the 15th Biennial Conference of the Asian Studies Association of Australia in Canberra, 29 June–2 July 2004.

—— 2005, '*Ajeg Bali*: Multiple Meanings, Diverse Agendas', *Indonesia and the Malay World*, 33/97, 239–255.

Allerton, Catherine, 2003, 'Authentic Housing, Authentic Culture? Transforming a Village into a "Tourist Site" in Manggarai, Eastern Indonesia', *Indonesia and the Malay World*, 31, 119–128 (special issue on 'Tourism and Heritage in South-East Asia', edited by Michael Hitchcock and Victor T. King).

Bibliography

Alneng, Victor, 2002, '"What the Fuck is a Vietnam?": Touristic Phantasms and the Popcolonization of (the) Vietnam (War)', *Critique of Anthropology*, 22, 4, 461–489.

Amster, Matthew H., 2004, 'The "Many Mouths" of Community: Gossip and Social Interaction among the Kelabit of Borneo', *Asian Anthropology*, 3, 97–127.

Anderson, Benedict, 1983, *Imagined Communities: Reflections on the Origin and Spread of Nationalism*, London: Verso.

—— 1991, *Imagined Communities. Reflections on the Origin and Spread of Nationalism*, London, New York: Verso, revised and expanded edition, originally published in 1983.

Anggraeni, D., 2003, *Who Did This to Our Bali?*, Brian Hill, Victoria: Indra Publishing.

Appadurai, Arjun, 1996, *Modernity at Large: Cultural Dimensions of Globalization,* Minneapolis: University of Minnesota Press.

Ardika, I. W. and Darma Putra, eds., 2004, *Politik Kebudayaan dan Identitas Etnik*, Denpasar: Fakultas Sastra Universitas Udayana dan Balimangsi Press.

Ari Dwipayana, A. A. G. N, 2005, *GloBALIsm: Pergulatan Politik Representasi atas Bali*, Denpasar: Uluangkep.

Arin, T. and R. Kramer, 2002, 'Divers' Willingness to Pay to Visit Marine Sanctuaries: An Exploratory Study', *Ocean and Coastal Management*, 45, 171–183.

Ariyama, Teruo, 2002, *Kaigai kankôryokô no tanjô* (The Birth of International Tourism in Japan), Tokyo: Yoshikawakôbunkan.

Aronsson, Lars, 2000, *The Development of Sustainable Tourism*, London: Cassell.

Ashley, Caroline, 2000, 'The Impacts of Tourism on Rural Livelihoods: Namibia's experience', Working Paper 128, London: Overseas Development Institute.

———— 2005, 'The Indian Ocean Tsunami and Tourism', ODI Opinions, No. 3 (www.odi.org.uk/publications/opinions).

Asian Development Bank, 1999a, *Social Sector Profiles: Lao PDR: Strategic Forward Look*, Manila: Asian Development Bank, January.

—— 1999b, Regional Technical Assistance 5893: Mekong/Lancang River Tourism Infrastructure Development Project.

—— 2002a, *Building on Success: A Strategic Framework for the Next Ten Years of the Greater Mekong Subregion Economic Cooperation Program*, Manila: Asian Development Bank.

—— 2002b, Report and Recommendation of the President to the Board of Directors on Proposed Loans to the Kingdom of Cambodia, Lao People's Democratic Republic, and Socialist Republic of Viet Nam for the Greater Mekong Subregion: Mekong Tourism Development Project, Manila: Asian Development Bank.

—— 2005, *The Greater Mekong Subregion Tourism Sector Strategy*, Manila: Asian Development Bank.

Atkinson, Adrian, 1991, *Principles of Political Ecology*, London: Belhaven.

Australian Tourism Export Council, 2003, 'SARS Tourism Downturn Exceeds Terrorism Impacts', Australian Tourism Export Council, 25 June 2003, (www.atec.net.au/MediaReleaseSARS_Tourism_Downturn_Exceeds_Terrorism_Impacts.htm).

Ayres, Robert, 1998, *Turning Point: End of the Growing Paradigm*, London: Earthscan.

Bachrach, Peter and Morton S. Baratz, 1963, 'Decisions and Non-Decisions: An Analytical Framework', *American Political Science Review*, (September), 632–642.

Backhaus, Norman, 2003, '"Non-place Jungle": the Construction of Authenticity in National Parks of Malaysia', *Indonesia and the Malay World*, 31, 151–60 (special issue on 'Tourism and Heritage in South-East Asia', edited by Michael Hitchcock and Victor T. King).

Bagus, I. G. N., 1999, 'Keresahan dan Gejolak Sepuluh Tahun Terakhir di Bali. Beberapa Catatan tentang Perubahan Sosial di Era "Glokalisasi"', in H. Chambert-Loir and H. M. Ambary, eds, *Panggung Sejarah. Persembahan kepada Prof. Dr. Denys Lombard*, Jakarta, EFEO/PPAN/Yayasan Obor Indonesia, 609–627.

Bakker, F. L., 1993, *The Struggle of the Hindu Balinese Intellectuals. Developments in Modern Hindu Thinking in Independent Indonesia*, Amsterdam, VU University Press.

Bali Post.

Bali Update, www.balidiscovery.com.

Bappeda, 2004, *Data Bali Membangun 2003*, Denpasar: Pemerintah Provinsi Bali.

Barry, Kathleen, 1996, *Vietnam's Women in Transition*, Basingstoke, Hampshire: Macmillan.

Barth, Fredrik, 1969, 'Introduction', in Fredrik Barth, ed., *Ethnic Groups and Boundaries: The Social Organisation of Difference*, Bergen and Oslo: Norwegian University Press and London: George Allen and Unwin, 9–38.

Bateson, G. and M. Mead, 1942, *Balinese Character: A Photographic Analysis*, New York: New York Academy of Sciences.

Bauer, Thomas and Bob McKercher, eds, 2003, *Sex and Tourism: Journeys of Romance, Love, and Lust*, London: The Haworth Hospitality Press.

Bawa, W., 2004, 'Apa yang dimaksud dengan Ajeg Bali?', in I. W. Cika dkk., eds, *Garitan Budaya Nusantara Dalam Perspektif Kebinekaan*, Kuta: Larasan, 251–258.

Bayly, Susan, 2004, 'Vietnamese Intellectuals in Revolutionary and Postcolonial Times', *Critique of Anthropology*, 24, 3, 320–344.

BBC Online, 2000, 'Moluccas Christians Bombed', Internet site, BBC News, Asia–Pacific. news.bbc. co.uk/hi/english/world/asia_pacific/newsid_1057000/1057465.stm, 7 December 2000.

—— 2001, 'Analysis: Indonesia's Problems', Internet site, BBC News, Asia–Pacific news.bbc.co.uk/hi/english/world/asia-pacific/newsid_1357000/1357539.stm, 29 May 2001.

Ben-Amos, Paula, 1977, 'Pidgin Languages and Tourist Arts', *Studies in the Anthropology of Visual Communication*, 4, 128–140.

Bergmann, Jorg R., 1993, *Discreet Indiscretion: The Social Organization of Gossip*, New York: Aldine De Gruyter.

Berkers, F., 2004, 'Rethinking Community-Based Conservation', *Conservation Biology*, 18, 3, 621–630.

Berno, Tracy and Kelly Bricker, 2001, 'Sustainable Tourism Development: The Long Road from Theory to Practice', *International Journal of Economic Development*, 3, 3, 1–18.

Bhabha, Homi K., ed., 1994, *Location of Culture*, New York: Routledge.

Bhopal, M. and Michael Hitchcock, eds, 2002, *ASEAN Management in Crisis*, London: Frank Cass.

Bianchi, Raoul V., 2002, 'Toward a New Political Economy of Global Tourism', in Richard Sharpley and David J. Teller, eds., *Tourism and Development: Concepts and Issues*, Buffalo: Channel View, 265–299.

Biles, Annabel, Kate Lloyd and William Logan, 1999, 'Romancing Vietnam: The Formation and Function of Tourist Images of Vietnam', in Jill Forshee, ed., *Converging Interests: Traders, Travelers and Tourists in Southeast Asia*, Berkeley: University of California Press, 207–234.

Bird, Bella, 1989, *Langkawi: from Mahsuri to Mahathir: Tourism for Whom?* Kuala Lumpur: Institute for Social Analysis.

Bird, G. W., 1897, *Wanderings in Burma*, Bournemouth: F. J. Bright and Son/London: Simkin, Marshall, Hamilton, Kent and Co.

Blamey, R. K., 2001, 'Principles of Ecotourism', in D. B. Weaver, ed., *The Encyclopaedia of Ecotourism*, Wallingford: CAB International, Chapter 1, 5–22.

Boissevain, J., 1974, *Friends of Friends: Networks, Manipulators and Coalitions*, Oxford: Basil Blackwell.

Boon, James A., 1977, *The Anthropological Romance of Bali 1597–1972: Dynamic Perspectives in Marriage and Caste, Politics and Religion*, Cambridge: Cambridge University Press.

Booth, Anne, 1990, 'The Tourism Boom in Indonesia', *Bulletin of Indonesian Economic Studies*, 26, 3, 45–73.

Borchers, H., 2004, *Jurassic Wilderness: Ecotourism as a Conservation Strategy in Komodo National Park, Indonesia*, Stuttgart: Ibidem.

Borrini-Feyerabend, G., M. T. Farvar, J. C. Nguinguiri and V. A. Ndangang, 2000, 'Co-Management of Natural Resources: Organising, Negotiating and Learning-by-Doing', GTZ and IUCN, Heidelberg: Kasparek Verlag.

Bourdieu, Pierre, 1977, *Outline of A Theory of Practice*, Cambridge: Cambridge University Press.

—— 1984, *Distinction: A Social Critique of the Judgment of Taste* (translated by Richard Nice), Cambridge, Massachusetts: Harvard University Press.

Bowman, G., 1989, 'Fucking Tourists: Sexual Relations and Tourism in Jerusalem's Old City', *Critique of Anthropology*, 9, 2, 73–93.

—— 1996, 'Passion, Power and Politics in a Palestinian Tourist Market', in Tom Selwyn, ed., *The Tourist Image: Myth and Myth Making in Tourism*, Chichester: Wiley, 83–103.

BPS: Biro Pusat Statistik, 2005, 'Hotel Nights by Indonesian and Foreign Visitors', Jakarta: Biro Pusat Statistik, www.bps.go.id, accessed 15 December 2005.

Bramwell, Bill, 1998, 'Selecting Policy Instruments for Sustainable Tourism', in William Theobald, ed. *Global Tourism*, 2nd edition, Boston: Butterworth-Heinemann, 361–379.

Brandon, K., 1996, *Ecotourism and Conservation: A Review of Key Issues*, Washington: The World Bank.

Brandon, K. and M. Wells, 1992, 'Planning for People and Parks: Design Dilemmas', *World Development*, 20, 4, 557–570.

Bras, C. H., 2000, 'Lombok and the Art of Guiding: The Social Construction of a Tourist Destination in Indonesia', Unpublished Ph.D. Thesis, Department of Leisure Studies, Tilburg University.

Bras, Karin, 2000, *Image-Building and Guiding on Lombok: the Social Construction of a Tourist Destination*, Amsterdam: K. Bras.

Bras, Karin and Heidi Dahles, 1998, 'Women Entrepreneurs and Beach Tourism in Sanur, Bali: Gender, Employment Opportunities, and Government Policy', *Pacific Tourism Review*, 1, 243–256.

Breckenridge, Carol, ed., 1994, *Consuming Modernity: Public Culture in a South Asian World,* Minneapolis: University of Minnesota Press.

Briguglio, L., 1995, 'Small States and their Economic Vulnerabilities', *World Development*, 23, 1615–1632.

Britton, S., 1991, 'Tourism, Capital and Place: Towards a Critical Geography of Tourism', *Environment and Planning D: Society and Space*, 9, 451–478.

Brown, K., W. N. Adger, E. Tompkins, P. Bacon, D. Shim and K. Young, 2001, 'Trade-off Analysis for Marine Protected Area Management', *Ecological Economics*, 37, 417–434.

Brown, L., 2000, *Sex Slaves: The Trafficking of Women in Asia*, Virago: London.

Brown, R. and O. Junek, 2004, 'LDCs and Global Tourism Effects of Disastrous Effects', *ASEAN Journal on Hospitality and Tourism*, 3, 1, 41–50.

Bruner, Edward M., 1991, 'Transformation of Self in Tourism', *Annals of Tourism Research*, 18, 238–250.

—— 1995, 'The Ethnographer/Tourist in Indonesia', in Marie-Francoise Lanfant, John B. Allcock and Edward M. Bruner, eds, *International Tourism: Identity and Change*, London: Sage Publications (Sage Studies in International Sociology 47), 224–241.

Bryan, H., 2002, 'Bali's Ruthless Fishermen', Internet site, BBC News, Asia–Pacific news.bbc.co.uk/hi/english/world/asia-pacific/newsid_2052000/2052233.stm, 19 June 2002.

Bryant, Raymond L., 1992, 'Political Ecology: An Emerging Research Agenda in Third World Studies', *Political Geography*, 11, 12–36.

Bryant, Raymond L. and Sinéad Bailey, 1997, *Third World Political Ecology*, London: Routledge.

Brysk, Alison, ed., 2002, *Globalization and Human Rights*, London: University of California Press.

Burns, Peter M., 1999, *An Introduction to Tourism and Anthropology*, London: Routledge.

Butler, R., 1980, 'The Concept of a Tourist Area Cycle of Evolution: Implications for Management of Resources', *Canadian Geographer,* 24, 5–12.

Campbell, John, 1964, *Honour, Family and Patronage*, Oxford: Clarendon Press.

Campbell, L. M., 2002, 'Conservation Narratives in Costa Rica: Conflict and Co-Existence', *Development and Change*, 33, 29–56.

Carslake, John, 1995, 'Tourism, Culture and the Iban', in Victor T. King, ed, *Tourism in Borneo: Issues and Perspectives*, Williamsburg: Borneo Research Council Proceedings Series, 67–90.

Cartier, Carolyn, 1996, 'Conserving the Built Environment and Generating Heritage Tourism in Peninsular Malaysia', *Tourism Recreation Research*, 21, 45–53.

—— 1997, 'The Dead, Place/Space and Social Activism: Constructing the Nationscape in Historic Melaka', *Environment and Planning D: Society and Space*, 15, 555–586.

—— 1998, 'Megadevelopment in Malaysia: From Heritage Landscape to 'Leisurescapes' in Melaka's Tourism Sector', *Singapore Journal of Tropical Geography*, 19, 151–176.

—— 2001, 'Imaging Melaka's Global Heritage', in Peggy Teo, T. C. Chang and K. C. Ho, eds, *Interconnected Worlds: Tourism in Southeast Asia*, Oxford: Elsevier Science, Pergamon, 193–212.

Cater, Erlet, 1994, 'Introduction', in E. Cater and G. Lowman, eds, *Ecotourism: A Sustainable Option?*, Chichester: John Wiley and Sons, 3–19.

—— 1999, *Tourism and Sustainability in the Yunnan Great Rivers ICDP, China*, Reading: University of Reading.

Causey, Andrew, 1999, 'Making a Man *Malu*: Western Tourists and Toba Bataks in the Souvenir Marketplace', in Jill Forshee, Christina Fink and Sandra Cate, eds, *Converging Interests: Traders, Travelers, and Tourists in Southeast Asia*, Berkeley: University of California at Berkeley, Center for Southeast Asian Studies, Monograph No. 36, 279–291.

—— 2003, *Hard Bargaining in Sumatra: Western Travelers and Toba Bataks in the Marketplace of Souvenirs*, Honolulu: University of Hawai'i Press.

—— 2005, 'Go Back to the Bataks, It's Safe There', paper presented at the International Studies Association, March 5, Honolulu, Hawai'i.

CGIAR: Consultative Group on International Agriculture Research, 2005, 'Adaptive Collaborative Management (ACM) in Tropical Forests', accessed via website of CGIAR/CIFOR (Center for International Forestry Research), August 23 2005.

Chang, T. C., 1997, 'From "Instant Asia" to "Multi-faceted Jewel": Urban Imaging Strategies and Tourism Development in Singapore', *Urban Geography*, 18, 542–562.

—— 2004, 'Tourism in a "Borderless" World: The Singapore Experience', Monograph No. 73, May, Honolulu: East–West Center.

Chazée, L., 2002, *The Peoples of Laos: Rural and Ethnic Diversities,* Bangkok: White Lotus Press.

Chibnik, Michael, 2003, *Crafting Tradition: The Making and Marketing of Oaxacan Wood Carvings*, Austin: University of Texas Press.

China Daily, various issues.

Chon, K. S. (Kaye), ed., 2000, *Tourism in Southeast Asia: A New Direction*, New York, London, Oxford: The Haworth Hospitality Press.

Chong, Vun Then, 1993, 'Ecotourism: Sabah's Niche in the Worldwide Travel and Leisure Market', Berita IDS, 8, 5, 3–5.

Chou, Cynthia and Vincent Houben, eds, 2006, *Southeast Asian Studies: Debates and New Directions*, Leiden: International Institute for Asian Studies and Singapore: Institute of Southeast Asian Studies.

Christensen, J. and S. Royle, 2002, 'Integrated Impact Appraisal: Lessons from the Faroe Islands', Paper read at the Islands of the World VII Conference, University of Prince Edward Island, Canada, 26–30 June 2002.

Clarke, Jackie, 1997, 'A Framework of Approaches to Sustainable Tourism', *Journal of Sustainable Tourism*, 5, 3, 224–233.

Clifford, James, 1988, *The Predicament of Culture: Twentieth-Century Ethnography, Literature, and Art*, Cambridge and London: Harvard University Press.

—— 1997, *Routes: Travel and Translation in the Late Twentieth Century*, Cambridge and London: Harvard University Press.

Cochrane, Janet, 1993a, 'Tourism and Conservation in Indonesia and Malaysia', in Michael Hitchcock, Victor T. King and Michael J. G. Parnwell, eds, *Tourism in South-East Asia*, London: Routledge, 317–326.

—— 1993b, 'Recommendations and Guidelines for Sustainable Marine Tourism in Indonesia', Jakarta: World Wide Fund for Nature, June, 32 pp.

—— 1996a, 'Reconciling Tourism and Conservation: A Small-scale Approach in the Bada Valley, Sulawesi', in W. Nuryanti, ed, *Tourism and Heritage Management,* Yogyakarta: Gadjah Mada University Press, 482–501.

—— 1996b, 'The Sustainability of Ecotourism in Indonesia: Fact and Fiction', in Michael J. G. Parnwell and Raymond L. Bryant, eds, *Environmental Change in South-East Asia: People, Politics and Sustainable Development*, London: Routledge, 237–259.

Cochrane, Janet and R. Tapper, 2006, 'Tourism's Contribution to World Heritage Site Management', in A. Leask, ed., *Managing World Heritage Sites*, London: Elsevier Press, 97–109.

Cockburn, Andrew, 2003, '21st Century Slaves', *National Geographic*, September, 2–29.

Cohen, Erik, 1971, 'Arab Boys and Tourist Girls in a Mixed Jewish–Arab Community', *International Journal of Comparative Sociology*, 12, 4, 217–233.

—— 1973, 'Nomads from Affluence: Notes on the Phenomenon of Drifter Tourism', *International Journal of Comparative Sociology,* 14, 1–2, 89–103.

—— 1974, 'Who is a Tourist? A Conceptual Clarification', *Sociological Review*, 22, 527–555.

—— ed., 1979b, 'Rethinking the Sociology of Tourism', *Annals of Tourism Research*, 6, 17–194.

—— 1979a/2001a, 'The Impact of Tourism on the Hill Tribes of Northern Thailand', in Erik Cohen, *Thai Tourism: Hill Tribes, Islands and Open-ended Prostitution*, Bangkok: White Lotus, 113–144 (reprint from *Internationales Asienforum*, 1979, 10, 5–38).

—— 1979c, 'A Phenomenology of Tourist Types', *Sociology*, 13, 179–201.

—— 1982a, 'Thai Girls and Farang Men: The Edge of Ambiguity', *Annals of Tourism Research*, 9, 3, 403–428.

—— 1982b, 'Marginal Paradises: Bungalow Tourism on the Islands of Southern Thailand', *Annals of Tourism Research,* 9, 189–228.

—— 1982c/2001a, 'Jungle Guides in Northern Thailand: The Dynamics of a Marginal Occupational Role', in Erik Cohen, *Thai Tourism: Hill Tribes, Islands and Open-ended Prostitution,* Bangkok: White Lotus, 87–112 (reprint from *Sociological Review*, 1982, 30, 234–266).

—— 1983a, 'The Dynamics of Commercialized Arts: The Meo and Yeo of Northern Thailand', *Journal of the National Research Council of Thailand*, 15, 1, 1–34.

—— 1983b/2001a, 'Hill Tribe Tourism', in Erik Cohen, *Thai Tourism: Hill Tribes, Islands and Open-ended Prostitution*, Bangkok: White Lotus, 67–86 (reprint from J. McKinnon and W. Bhruksasri, eds, *Highlanders of Thailand*, Kuala Lumpur: Oxford University Press, 1983, 307–325).

—— 1984a, 'The Dropout Expatriates: A Study of Marginal *Farangs* in Bangkok', *Urban Anthropology*, 13, 91–114.

—— 1984b, 'The Sociology of Tourism: Approaches, Issues and Findings', *Annual Review of Sociology*, 10, 373–392.

—— 1985a, 'Tourism as Play', *Religion*, 15, 291–304.

—— 1985b, 'The Tourist Guide: The Origins, Structure and Dynamics of a Role', *Annals of Tourism Research*, 12, 1, 5–29.

—— 1986, 'Lovelorn Farangs: The Correspondence Between Foreign Men and Thai Girls', *Anthropological Quarterly*, 59, 3, 115–127.

—— 1988a, 'Authenticity and Commoditization in Tourism', *Annals of Tourism Research*, 15, 371–386.

—— 1988b, 'Traditions in the Qualitative Sociology of Tourism', *Annals of Tourism Research*, 15, 29–46.

319

—— 1989/2001a, '"Primitive and Remote": Hill Tribe Trekking in Thailand', in Erik Cohen, *Thai Tourism: Hill Tribes, Islands and Open-ended Prostitution*, Bangkok: White Lotus, 31–66 (reprint from *Annals of Tourism Research*, 1989, 16, 30–61).

—— 1992/2001a, 'The Growing Gap: Hill Tribe Image and Reality', in Erik Cohen, *Thai Tourism: Hill Tribes, Islands and Open-ended Prostitution*, Bangkok: White Lotus, 145–148 (reprint from *Pacific Viewpoint*, 1992, 33, 165–169).

—— 1993a/2001a, 'Open-ended Prostitution as a Skillful Game of Luck: Opportunity, Risk, and Security among Tourist-oriented Prostitutes in a Bangkok *Soi*', in Erik Cohen, *Thai Tourism: Hill Tribes, Islands and Open-ended Prostitution*, Bangkok: White Lotus, 269–291 (reprint from Michael Hitchcock, Victor T. King and Michael J. G Parnwell, eds, *Tourism in South-East Asia*, London: Routledge, 1993, 155–178).

—— 1993, 'The Heterogeneization of a Tourist Art', *Annals of Tourism Research*, 20, 1, 138–163.

—— 1993c, 'The Study of Touristic Images of Native People: Mitigating the Stereotype of a Stereotype', in D. G. Pearce and B. W. Butler, eds, *Tourism Research*, London: Routledge, 36–69.

—— 1996, 'Touting Tourists in Thailand: Tourist Oriented Crime and Social Structure', in Abraham Pizam and Yoel Mansfield, eds, *Tourism, Crime, and International Security Issues*, New York: Wiley, 77–90.

—— 2000, *The Commercialized Crafts of Thailand: Hill Tribes and Lowland Villages*, Honolulu: University of Hawai'i Press.

—— 2001a, *Thai Tourism: Hill Tribes, Islands and Open-ended Prostitution*, Bangkok: White Lotus Press, Studies in Contemporary Thailand No 4, second edition.

—— 2001b, 'Thai Tourism: Trends and Transformations', in Erik Cohen, *Thai Tourism: Hill Tribes, Islands and Open-ended Prostitution*, Bangkok: White Lotus Press, Studies in Contemporary Thailand No 4, 2nd edition, 1–28.

—— 2001c, 'Thailand in "Touristic Transtion"', in Peggy Teo, T. C. Chang and K. C. Ho, eds, *Interconnected Worlds: Tourism in Southeast Asia*, Oxford: Elsevier Science, Pergamon, 155–175.

—— 2003, 'Transnational Marriage in Thailand', in Thomas Bauer and Bob McKercher, eds, 2003, *Sex and Tourism: Journeys of Romance, Love, and Lust*, New York: Haworth Press, 57–84.

—— 2004, 'Backpacking: Diversity and Change', in G. Richards and J. Wilson, eds, *The Global Nomad: Backpacker Travel in Theory and Practice*, Buffalo: Channel View, 43–59.

Cohen, Erik and Robert L. Cooper, 1987, 'Language and Tourism', *Annals of Tourism Research*, 13, 533–563.

Cole, Stroma, 2003, 'Appropriated Meanings: Megaliths and Tourism in Eastern Indonesia', *Indonesia and the Malay World*, 31, 140–150 (special issue on 'Tourism and Heritage in South-East Asia', edited by Michael Hitchcock and Victor T. King).

Commonwealth Secretariat, 1997, *A Future for Small States: Overcoming Vulnerability*, London: Commonwealth Secretariat.

Connor, L. and A. Vickers, 2003, 'Crisis, Citizenship, and Cosmopolitanism: Living in a Local and Global Risk Society in Bali', *Indonesia*, 75, 153–180.

Conway, T., C. Moser, A. Norton and J. Farrington, 2002, 'Rights and Livelihoods Approaches: Exploring Policy Dimensions', *Natural Resources Perspectives*, 78, May, London: Overseas Development Institute.

Cooper, M., 2000, 'Tourism in Vietnam: Doi Moi and the Realities of Tourism in the 1990s', in C. Michael Hall and Stephen Page, eds, *Tourism in South and Southeast Asia: Issues and Cases*, Oxford: Butterworth-Heinemann, 167–177.

Couteau, J., 1999, 'Bali et l'islam: 1. Rencontre historique', *Archipel*, 58, 159–188.

—— 2000, 'Bali et l'islam: 2. Coexistence et perspectives contemporaines', *Archipel*, 60, 45–64.

—— 2002, 'Bali: crise en paradis', *Archipel*, 64, 231–254.

—— 2003, 'After the Kuta Bombing: In Search of the Balinese "Soul"', *Antropologi Indonesia*, 27/70, 41–59.

Covarrubias, Miguel, 1937, *Island of Bali*, New York: A. A. Knopf.

Crick, Malcolm, 1989, 'Representations of International Tourism in the Social Sciences: Sun, Sex, Sights, Savings and Servility', *Annual Review of Anthropology*, 18, 307–344.

—— 1992, 'Life in the Informal Sector: Street Guides in Kandy, Sri Lanka', in D. Harrison, ed., *Tourism and the Less Developed Countries*, London: Belhaven Press, 135–147.

—— 1995, 'The Anthropologist as Tourist: An Identity in Question', in Marie-Francoise Lanfant, John B. Allcock and Edward M. Bruner, eds, *International Tourism: Identity and Change*, London: Sage Publications, Sage Studies in International Sociology 47, 205–223.

Crossette, Barbara, 1999, *The Great Hill Stations of Asia*, New York: Basic Books.

Crush, J. and P. Wellings, 1983, 'The Southern Africa Pleasure Periphery, 1966–1983', *Journal of Modern African Studies*, 21, 4, 673–698.

Crystal, Eric, 1989/1977, 'Tourism in Toraja (Sulawesi, Indonesia)', in Valene L. Smith, ed., *Hosts and Guests: The Anthropology of Tourism*, Philadelphia: University of Pennsylvania Press, 139–168 (second revised and expanded edition; first edition, 1977).

—— 1994, 'Rape of the Ancestors: Discovery, Display and Destruction of the Ancestral Statuary of Tana Toraja', in Paul Michael Taylor, ed., *Fragile Traditions: Indonesian Art in Jeopardy*, Honolulu: University of Hawai'i Press, 29–41.

Cukier, Judith, 2002, 'Tourism Employment Issues in Developing Countries: Examples from Indonesia', in Richard Sharpley and David J. Teller, eds, *Tourism and Development: Concepts and Issues*, Buffalo: Channel View, 165–201.

Dachanee Emphandhu and Surachet Chettamart, n.d., 'Thailand's Experience in Protected Area Management', conservation.forest.ku.ac.th/ecotourdb/cgi-bin/ARTICLE_pdf/thailand_experience.pdf.

Dahles, Heidi, 1996, 'Hello Mister!: De rol van informele gidsen in Yogyakarta, Indonesië', *Derde Wereld*, 15, 1, 34–48.

—— 1997, 'The New Gigolo: Globalization, Tourism and Changing Gender Identities', *Focaal: Tijdschrift voor Antropologie*, Special Issue: Globalization/Localization: Paradoxes of Cultural Identity, 30/31, 121–138.

—— 1998a, 'Of Birds and Fish: Street Guides, Tourists and Sexual Encounters in Yogyakarta, Indonesia', in M. Oppermann, ed., *Sex Tourism and Prostitution*, New York: Cognizant Communication Corporation, 31–41.

—— 1998b, 'Tourism, Government Policy, and Petty Entrepreneurs in Indonesia', *South East Asia Research*, 6, 1, 73–89.

—— 1999, 'Tourism and Small Entrepreneurs in Developing Countries: A Theoretical Perspective', in Heidi Dahles and Karin Bras, eds, *Tourism and Small Entrepreneurs: Development, National Policy and Entrepreneurial Culture: Indonesian Cases*, New York: Cognizant Communication Corporation, 1–19.

—— 2001, *Tourism, Heritage and National Culture in Java: Dilemmas of a Local Community*, Richmond: Curzon Press.

—— 2002, 'Gigolos and Rastamen: Tourism, Sex and Changing Gender Identities', in M. B. Swain and J. H. Momsen, eds, *Gender/Tourism/Fun(?)*, New York: Cognizant Communication Corporation, 180–194.

—— 2002, 'The Politics of Tour Guiding: Image Management in Indonesia', *Annals of Tourism Research*, 29: 783–800.

Dahles, Heidi and Karin Bras, 1999a, 'Entrepreneurs in Romance: Tourism in Indonesia', *Annals of Tourism Research*, 26, 2, 267–293.

—— eds, 1999b, *Tourism and Small Entrepreneurs: Development, National Policy and Entrepreneurial Culture: Indonesian Cases*, An edition in the series 'Tourism Dynamics', edited by Valene L. Smith and Paul F. Wilkinson, New York: Cognizant Communication Corporation.

Dahles, Heidi and E. Zwart, 2003, 'Tourism and Silk Trade in Post Civil War Cambodia', *Pacific Tourism Review*, 7, 3/4, 143–157.

Dann, Graham and Erik Cohen, 1991, 'Sociology and Tourism', *Annals of Tourism Research*, 18, 155–169.

Darling, D., 2003, 'Unity in Uniformity: Tendencies toward Militarism in Balinese Ritual Life', in T. A. Reuter, ed., *Inequality, Crisis and Social Change in Indonesia: The Muted Worlds of Bali*, London and New York: RoutledgeCurzon, 196–202.

Darma Putra, I Nyoman, 2004a, 'Bali Pasca-Bom: Konflik, kekerasan, dan rekonstruksi identitas budaya seputar 'Ajeg Bali'', in I. W. Cika dkk, eds, *Garitan Budaya Nusantara Dalam Perspektif Kebinekaan*, Kuta: Larasan, 206–232.

—— ed., 2004b, *Bali. Menuju Jagadhita: Aneka Perspektif*, Denpasar: Pustaka Bali Post.

Darma Putra, I Nyoman and Michael Hitchcock, 2005, '*Pura Besakih*: A World Heritage Site Contested', *Indonesia and the Malay World*, 33, 96, 225–237.

Davis, D. and C. Tisdell, 1995, 'Recreational Scuba-Diving and Carrying Capacity in Marine Protected Areas', *Ocean and Coastal Management*, 26, 1, 19–40.

De Albuquerque, K. and J. McElroy, 1992, 'Caribbean Small Island Tourism Styles and Sustainable Strategies', *Environmental Management*, 16, 5, 619–632.

De Kadt, Emanuel, ed., 1979, *Tourism: Passport to Development?*, New York: Oxford University Press.

De Lacy, Terry, Marion Battig, Stewart Moore and Steve Noakes, 2002, 'Public/Private Partnerships for Sustainable Tourism: Delivering a Sustainability Strategy for Tourism Destinations', APEC Tourism Working Group.

Dearden, Philip, 1996, 'Trekking in Northern Thailand: Impact Distribution and Evolution over Time', in Michael J. G. Parnwell, ed, *Uneven Development in Thailand*, Aldershot: Avebury, 204–225.

Dearden, Philip and Sylvia Harron, 1994, 'Alternative Tourism and Adaptive Change: Insights from Northern Thailand', *Annals of Tourism Research*, 21, 81–102.

DepHut, 1996, *Laporan Tahunan 1995/96, Taman Nasional Bromo–Tengger–Semeru, Buku I (Annual Report, Bromo Tengger Semeru)*, Malang, Indonesia, Departemen Kehutanan, Direktorat Jenderal PHPA.

—— 2005, *Bromo Visitor Figures*, Bromo Tengger Semeru National Park Head Office, Malang, Indonesia.

DfID, 1999a, *Tourism and Poverty Elimination: Untapped Potential*, London: Department for International Development.

—— 1999b, *Sustainable Tourism and Poverty Elimination Study*, London: Department for International Development.

Dhume, S., 2002, 'Jurassic Showdown', *Far Eastern Economic Review*, 16 March, 50–52.

Directorat Perlindungan dan Pembinaan Peninggalan Sejarah dan Purbakala, 1993, *Undang-Undang Republik Indonesia No. 5, Tahun 1992, Tentang Benda Cagar Budaya*, Jakarta.

Dixon, Chris, 2000, 'State Versus Capital: The Regulation of the Vietnamese Foreign Sector', *Singapore Journal of Tropical Geography*, 21, 3, 279–94.

Dixon, Chris and Andrea Kilgour, 2002, 'State, Capital, and Resistance to Globalization in the Vietnamese Transitional Economy', *Environment and Planning A*, 34, 4, 599–618.

Dixon, J., L. Scura and T. van't Hof, 1993, 'Meeting Ecological and Economic Goals: Marine Parks in the Caribbean', *Ambio*, 22, 2–3, 117–125.

Dodds, Rachel and Marion Joppe, 2005, 'CSR in the Tourism Industry? The Status of and Potential for Certification, Codes of Conduct and Guidelines', Study prepared for the CSR Practice, Foreign Investment Advisory Service, Investment Climate Department, International Finance Corporation, Washington DC.

Douglas, Ngaire and Norman Douglas, 2000, 'Tourism in South and Southeast Asia: Historical Dimensions', in C. Michael Hall and Stephen Page, eds, *Tourism in South and Southeast Asia: Issues and Cases*, Oxford, Butterworth-Heinemann, 29–44.

Dowling, Ross K., 2000, 'Ecotourism in Southeast Asia: A Golden Opportunity for Local Communities', in K. S. Chon, ed., *Tourism in Southeast Asia: A New Direction*, New York, Haworth, 1–20.

Eades, J. S., 2003, 'Translator's Introduction', in Shinji Yamashita, *Bali and Beyond: Explorations in the Anthropology of Tourism*, New York, Oxford: Berghahn Books, xiii–xix.

Echtner, Charlotte M. and Tazim B. Jamal, 1997, 'The Disciplinary Dilemma of Tourism Studies', *Annals of Tourism Research*, 24, 868–883.

The Economist, 1998 and 1999.

Economist Intelligence Unit, 1997, *Vietnam: Country Report,* 1st quarter, London: EIU Ltd.

—— 1996, *Country Profile, Indochina: Vietnam, Cambodia and Laos*, London: EIU Ltd.

Economy and Environment Program for South East Asia and the World Wide Fund for Nature (EEPSEA–WWF), 1998, 'The Indonesian Fires and Haze of 1997: The Economic Toll', Dated 29 May, Internet edition, www.idrc.org.sg/eepsea.fire.htm.

Edgel, D. L., 1990, *International Tourism Policy*, New York: Van Nostrand Reinhold.

Edgell, David Sr., 1999, *Tourism Policy: The Next Millennium*, Champaign, Il.: Sagamore Publishing Co.

Elkington, John and Julia Hailes, 1992, *Holidays that Don't Cost the Earth*, London: V. Gollancz.

Elliott, James, 1983, 'Politics, Power, and Tourism in Thailand', *Annals of Tourism Research*, 10, 377–393.

Elliot-White, Martin and R. Alison Lewis, 2004, *Tourism and Development*, London: Routledge.

Ellis, E., 2002, 'Bombing was Good: Bali Academic', *The Australian*, 22 October 2002.

England, V., 2001, 'The Trouble with Bali', *South China Moring Post*, 12 July 2001.

Enloe, Cynthia, 1989, *Bananas, Beaches and Bases: Making Feminist Sense of International Politics*, Berkely: University of California Press.

Enterprise Development Consultants Co. Ltd. and International Labour Office, ILO Bangkok Area Office and East Asia Multidisciplinary Advisory Team (ILO/EASMAT), 2002, *Study on Generating Employment through Micro and Small Enterprise and Cooperative Development in Lao PDR,* International Labour Organisation, Regional Office for Asia and the Pacific. (www.ilo.org/public/english/region/asro/bangkok/ability Accessed 3rd March 2006).

Environment North and Associated Consultants, 2001, *Komodo National Park Tourism Strategy*, North Cairns: Environment North.

Erawan, I Nyoman, 2003, 'Recovery Pembangunan Bali Pasca Bom Bali', in IGB Sudhyatmaka Sugeriwa, ed., *Bom Bali*, Denpasar: Biro Humas dan Protokol Setda Propinsi Bali, 264–267.

Erb, Maribeth, 1998, 'Tourism Space in Manggarai, Western Flores, Indonesia: The House as a Contested Space', *Singapore Journal of Tropical Geography*, 19, 177–192.

—— 2000, 'Understanding Tourists: Interpretations from Indonesia', *Annals of Tourism Research*, 27, 709–736.

—— 2001, 'Le Tourisme et la Quête de la Culture à Manggarai', *Antropologie et Sociétés*, 25, 93–108 (special issue on 'Tourisme et Sociétés Locales en Asie Orientale', edited by Jean Michaud and Michel Picard), Kuta: Larasan.

—— 2003, '"Uniting the Bodies and Cleansing the Village": Conflicts over Local Heritage in a Globalizing World', *Indonesia and the Malay World*, 31, 129–139 (special issue on 'Tourism and Heritage in South-East Asia', edited by Michael Hitchcock and Victor T. King).

Eriksen, T. H., 1991, 'The Cultural Contexts of Ethnic Differences', *Man*, 26, 1, 127–144.

Errington, Shelly, 1994, 'What Became of Authentic Primitive Art?', *Cultural Anthropology*, 9, 201–226.

—— 1998, *The Death of Authentic Primitive Art and Other Tales of Progress*, Berkeley: University of California Press.

Escobar, Arturo, 1998, 'Whose Knowledge, Whose Nature? Biodiversity Conservation and the Political Ecology of Social Movements', *Journal of Political Ecology*, 5, 53–82.

Evans, Grant, 1993, 'A Global Village? Anthropology in the Future', in Grant Evans, ed., *Asia's Cultural Mosaic: An Anthropological Introductio*n, Singapore: Prentice Hall, Simon and Schuster, 367–384.

—— 1999, *Laos: Culture and Society*, Chiang Mai, Thailand: Silkworm Books.

Evans, Grant, Christopher Hutton and Kuah Khun Eng, eds., 2000, *Where China Meets Southeast Asia: Social and Cultural Change in the Border Regions,* Singapore: Institute of Southeast Asian Studies.

Fabian, Johannes, 1983, *Time and the Other: How Anthropology Makes its Object,* New York: Columbia University Press.

Fallon, F., 2001, 'Conflict, Power and Tourism on Lombok', *Current Issues in Tourism,* 4, 6, 481–502.

FAO: Food and Agriculture Organization of the United Nations, 1982, *National Conservation Plan for Indonesia, Introduction, Evaluation Methods and Overview of National Nature Richness,* Field Report of UNDP/FAO National Park Deveopment Project INS/78/061, Bogor: April 1982.

Farrell, Bryan H. and Louise Twining-Ward, 2004, 'Reconceptualizing Tourism', *Annals of Tourism Research,* 31, 2, 274–295.

Farrer, James, 2002, '"Idle Talk": Neighborhood Gossip as a Medium of Social Communication in Reform Era Shanghai', in Thomas Gold, *et al.*, eds, *Social Connections in China: Institutions, Culture, and the Changing Nature of Guanxi,* New York: Cambridge University Press, 205–218.

Faulkner, B. and R. Russell, 1997, 'Chaos and Complexity in Tourism: In Search of a New Perspective', *Pacific Tourism Review,* 1, 93–102.

Fauzi, Y. E., 2001, 'Effort to Involve Community Falls Flat at Gunung Halimun', *Jakarta Post,* 16th January 2001.

Featherstone, Mike, Scott Lash and Roland Robertson, eds, 1995, *Global Modernities,* London: Sage Publications.

FEER, 2004, 'Coming Out, Cashing In: Why Gay Rights Make Economic Sense', Special Report. *Far Eastern Economic Review,* 28 October 2004.

Fennell, David A. and Kevin Ebert, 2004, 'Tourism and the Precautionary Principle', *Journal of Sustainable Tourism,* 12, 6, 461–479.

Fidler, David P., 2004, *SARS and the Globalization of Disease,* New York, Palgrave.

Firth, Raymond, 1967, *Tikopia Ritual and Belief,* London: George Allen and Unwin Ltd.

Forshee, Jill, 1999, 'Introduction: Converging Interests: Traders, Travelers and Tourists in Southeast Asia', in Jill Forshee, Christina Fink and Sandra Cate, eds, *Converging Interests: Traders, Travelers, and Tourists in Southeast Asia,* Berkeley, University of California: Center for Southeast Asian Studies, Monograph No 26, 1–19.

—— 2001, *Between the Folds: Stories of Cloth, Lives, and Travels from Sumba,* Honolulu: University of Hawai'i Press.

—— 2002, 'Tracing Troubled Times: Objects of Value and Narratives of Loss from Sumba and Timor Islands', *Indonesia,* 74, 65–77.

Forshee, Jill, Christina Fink and Sandra Cate, eds, 1999, *Converging Interests: Traders, Travelers, and Tourists in Southeast Asia,* Berkeley: University of California, Center for Southeast Asian Studies, Monograph No. 26.

France, Lesley, ed., 1997, *The Earthscan Reader in Sustainable Tourism,* London: Earthscan.

Francillon, Gerard, 1979, *Bali: Tourism, Culture, Environment,* Paris: UNESCO.

—— 1989, 'The Dilemma of Tourism in Bali', in W. Beller, P. d'Ayala and P. Hein, eds, *Sustainable Development and Environmental Management of Small Islands,* Paris: UNESCO, 267–272.

Friedman, Jonathan, 1994, 'The Political Economy of Elegance: An African Cult of Beauty', in J. Friedman, ed. *Consumption and Identity,* London: Harwood Academic Press, 167–187.

—— 2002, 'From Roots to Routes: Tropes for Trippers', *Anthropological Theory,* 2, 1, 21–36.

Furnivall, J. S., 1968, *Colonial Policy and Practice,* Cambridge: Cambridge University Press.

Gainsborough, M., 2002, 'Beneath the Veneer of Reform: The Politics of Economic Liberalisation in Vietnam', *Communist and Post-Communist Studies,* 35, 3, 353–68.

Gammeltoft, Tine, 2001, 'Faithful, Heroic, Resourceful: Changing Images of Women in Vietnam', in John Kleinen, ed., *Vietnamese Society in Transition: The Daily Politics of Reform and Change,* Amsterdam: Het Spinhuis, 265–280.

Ganster, Paul and David Lorey, eds, 2005, *Borders and Border Politics in a Globalizing World*, Lanham, MD: SR Books.

García Canclini Néstor, 2001, *Consumers and Citizens: Globalization and Multicultural Conflicts*, Minneapolis: University of Minnesota Press.

Gates, C. L., 1996, 'Economic Reform and Openness in Vietnam: Micro-economic Response and Transformation', *ASEAN Economic Bulletin*, 13, 2, 212–28.

Geertz, Clifford, 1963a, *Peddlers and Princes: Social Development and Economic Change in Two Indonesian Towns*, Chicago: University of Chicago Press.

—— 1963b, *Old Societies and New States: The Quest for Modernity in Asia*, Glencoe: Free Press.

Gellner, E., 1983, *Nations and Nationalism*, Ithaca: Cornell University Press.

Ghimire, K. B., 2001, *The Native Tourist: Mass Tourism Within Developing Countries*, London: Earthscan.

Giddens, Anthony, 1991, *The Consequences of Modernity*, Stanford: Stanford University Press; Cambridge: Polity Press.

Glassman, Ronald, 2000, *Caring Capitalism: A New Middle Class Base for the Welfare State*, New York: St Martin's Press.

Gluckman, Max, 1963, 'Gossip and Scandal', *Current Anthropology*, 4, 3, 307–316.

GMS Business Forum and Directory, 2006, 'Lao PDR: Main Investment Opportunities', www.gmsbizforum.com/index.php?option=com_content&task=view&id=40&Itemid=34 (Accessed 4th March)

Go, F. and C. Jenkins, eds, 1997, *Tourism and Economic Development in Asia and Australasia*, London and Washington: Cassell.

Goodwin, H. J., 1998, *Sustainable Tourism and Poverty Elimination*, Background Paper for Workshop on 'Sustainable Tourism and Poverty Elimination', Prepared for the 1999 Session of the Commission on Sustainable Development.

Goodwin, H. J., I. J. Kent, K. T. Parker and M. J. Walpole, 1997, *Tourism, Conservation & Sustainable Development: Volume III, Komodo National Park, Indonesia*, UK: Department for International Development.

Gossling, S., 2002, 'Human-Environmental Relations with Tourism', *Annals of Tourism Research*, 29, 2, 539–556.

Gossling, S., Hansson C. Borgstrom, O. Hortsmeier and S. Saggel, 2002, 'Ecological Footprint Analysis as a Tool to Assess Tourism Sustainability', *Ecological Economics*, 43, 199–211.

Government of Australia, 1995, *National Backpacker Tourism Strategy*, Canberra: Australian Government Publishing Service, Internet edition, tourism.gov.au/publications/backpackers.

Graburn, Nelson, ed., 1976, *Ethnic and Tourist Arts: Cultural Expressions from the Fourth World*, Berkeley: University of California Press.

—— 1983a, 'The Anthropology of Tourism', *Annals of Tourism Research*, 10, 9–33.

—— 1983b, 'Tourism and Prostitution', *Annals of Tourism Research*, 10, 3, 437–442.

—— 1987, 'The Evolution of Tourist Arts', *Annals of Tourism Research*, 11, 3, 393–420.

—— 1989/1977, 'Tourism: the Sacred Journey', in Valene L. Smith, ed., *Hosts and Guests: the Anthropology of Tourism*, Philadelphia: University of Pennsylvania Press, 21–36 (second revised and expanded edition, 1989; first edition, 1977).

—— 1997, 'Tourism and Cultural Development in East Asia and Oceania', in Shinji Yamashita, Kadir H. Din and J. S. Eades, eds, *Tourism and Cultural Development in Asia and Oceania*, Bangi: Universiti Kebangsaan Malaysia Press, 194–213.

Greenberg, James B. and Thomas K. Park, 1994, 'Political Ecology', *Journal of Political Ecology*, 1, 1–12.

Greenlees, Donald, 2005, 'The Subtle Power of Chinese Tourists', *International Herald Tribune*, 6 October, 2005.

Greenwood, Davydd, J., 1989/1977, 'Culture by the Pound: An Anthropological Perspective on Tourism as Cultural Commoditization', in Valene L. Smith, ed., *Hosts and Guests: the Anthropology of Tourism*, Philadelphia: University of Pennsylvania Press, 171–185 (second revised and expanded edition, 1989; first edition, 1977).

Guermonprez, J.-F., 2001, 'La religion balinaise dans le miroir de l'hindouisme', *Bulletin de l'École française d'Extrême-Orient*, 88, 271–293.

Gunder Frank, A., 1971, *Capitalism and Underdevelopment in Latin America*, Harmondsworth: Penguin.

Günther, A., 1998, 'Sex Tourism Without Sex Tourists', in M. Oppermann, ed., *Sex Tourism and Prostitution: Aspects of Leisure, Recreation, and Work*, New York: Cognizant Communication Corporation, 71–80.

Hadmoko, D., 1998, 'Editorial', *Travel Indonesia*, (March issue), Jakarta: P. T. Traviaduta.

Hall, C. Michael, 1992, 'Sex Tourism in South-East Asia', in David Harrison, ed., *Tourism in Less Developed Countries*, New York, Halsted Press, 64–74.

—— 1994, 'Gender and Economic Interests in Tourism Prostitution: The Nature, Development and Implications of Sex Tourism in South-east Asia', in V. Kinnaird and D. Hall, eds, *Tourism: A Gender Analysis*, New York: Wiley, 142–163.

—— 1996, 'Gender and Economic Interests in Tourism Prostitution', in Y. Apostolopoulos, S. Leivadi and A. Yiannakis, eds, *The Sociology of Tourism*, London: Routledge, 265–280.

—— 1997a, *Tourism in the Pacific Rim: Developments, Impacts and Markets*, South Melbourne: Addison, Wesley Longman, 2nd edition.

—— 1997b, *Tourism in the Pacific: Issues and Cases*, London: International Thomson Business Publishing.

—— 2000, 'Tourism in Indonesia: The End of the New Order', in Hall, C. Michael and Stephen Page, eds, *Tourism in South and Southeast Asia: Issues and Cases,* Oxford: Butterworth-Heinemann, 157–166.

—— 2000, 'Tourism in Cambodia, Laos and Myanmar: From Terrorism to Tourism?', in C. Michael Hall and Stephen Page, eds, *Tourism in South and South East Asia: Issues and Cases*, Butterworth-Heinemann, Oxford, 178–194.

—— 2003, 'Institutional Arrangements for Ecotourism Policy', in D. A. Fennell and R. K. Dowling, eds, *Ecotourism: Policy and Strategy Issues*, Wallingford: CABI Publishing, 21–38.

Hall, C. Michael and Alan A. Lew, eds, 1998, *Sustainable Tourism: A Geographical Perspective*, Harlow: Addison Wesley Longman.

Hall, C. Michael, and Alfred L. Oehlers, 2000, 'Tourism and Politics in South and Southeast Asian Tourism,' in C. Michael Hall and Stephen Page, eds, *Tourism in South and Southeast Asia: Issues and Cases*, Oxford, Butterworth Heinemann, 77–93.

Hall, C. Michael and V. O'Sullivan, 1996, 'Tourism, Political Stability and Violence', in A. Pizam and Y. Mansfield, eds, *Tourism, Crime and International Security Issues*, Chichester: John Wiley, 105–121.

Hall, C. Michael and Stephen Page, eds, 2000a, *Tourism in South and Southeast Asia: Issues and Cases*, Oxford: Butterworth Heinemann.

—— eds, 2000b, 'Conclusion: Prospects for Tourism in Southeast and South Asia in the New Millennium', in C. Michael Hall and Stephen Page, eds, *Tourism in Southeast and South Asia: Issues and Cases*, Oxford: Butterworth-Heinemann, 286–290.

Hall, C. Michael, D. J. Timothy and D. T. Duval, eds, 2003, *Safety and Security in Tourism: Relationships, Management and Marketing*, New York: The Haworth Press.

Hamilton-Merritt, J., 1999, *Tragic Mountains: The Hmong, the Americans, and the Secret Wars for Laos, 1942–1992*, Bloomington: Indiana University Press.

Hampton, Mark, 1998, 'Backpacker Tourism and Economic Development', *Annals of Tourism Research*, 25, 3, 639–660.

—— 2003, 'Entry Points for Local Tourism in Developing Countries: Evidence from Yogyakarta, Indonesia', *Geografiska Annaler B: Human Geography*, 85, 2, 85–101.

—— 2005, 'Heritage, Local Communities and Economic Development', *Annals of Tourism Research,* 32, 3, 735–759.

Hamzah, A., 1995, 'The Changing Tourist Motivation and its Implications on the Sustainability of Small-Scale Tourism Development in Malaysia', paper read at the World Conference on Sustainable Tourism, Lanzarote, Spain, 24–29 April.

Hamzah, A., Z. Khalifah, N. Dahlan and A. Kechik, 2003, 'Planning for Ecotourism in Protected Areas of Malaysia: Some Reflections on Current Approaches', paper presented to the IMT–GT International Conference on Ecotourism: Issues and Challenges, 12–14 October, Universiti Utara Malaysia.

Handelman, Don, 1973, 'Gossip in Encounters: The Transmission of Information in a Bounded Social Setting', *Man,* 8, 2, 210–227.

Handler, Richard, 2000, 'Anthropology of Authenticity', in N. J. Smelser and P. B. Baltes, eds, *International Encyclopedia of the Social and Behavioural Sciences,* Oxford: Pergamon, 963–67.

Handoyo, J., 2002, 'Pascatragedi Bom Bali, garap pasar domestik secara terpadu', *Kompas,* 23 October 2002 (Article on the effect of the Bali Bomb on the tourism industry).

Hanna, Willard A., 1972, 'Bali in the Seventies: Part I: Cultural Tourism', *American Universities Field Staff Reports,* Southeast Asia, 20/2, 1–7.

—— 1976, *Bali Profile: People, Events, Circumstances (1901–1976),* New York: American Universities Field Staff.

Hanson, J., 1998, 'Child Prostitution in Southeast Asia: White Slavery Revisited?' in M. Oppermann, ed., *Sex Tourism and Prostitution: Aspects of Leisure, Recreation, and Work,* New York: Cognizant Communication Corporation, 51–59.

Harkin, Michael, 1995, 'Modernist Anthropology and Tourism of the Authentic', *Annals of Tourism Research,* 22, 650–670.

Harrell-Bond, B., 1978, 'A Window on the Outside World: Tourism and Development in the Gambia', *American Universities Field Staff Reports,* 19, New Hampshire: Hanover.

Harris, Rob, Tony Griffin and Peter Williams, 2002, *Sustainable Tourism: A Global Perspective,* Oxford: Butterworth-Heinemann.

Harrison, David, 2001, 'Tourism and Less Developed Countries: Key Issues', in David Harrison, ed., *Tourism and the Less Developed World: Issues and Case Studies,* Wallingford, U. K. and N. Y.: CAB International, 23–46.

—— 2003, 'Themes in Pacific Island Tourism', in David Harrison, ed., *Pacific Island Tourism,* New York: Cognizant Communication Corporation, 1–23.

—— 2005, 'Introduction: Contested Narratives in the Domain of World Heritage', in David Harrison and Michael Hitchcock, eds, *The Politics of World Heritage: Negotiating Tourism and Conservation,* Buffalo: Channel View, 1–10.

Harrison, David and Michael Hitchcock, eds, 2005, *The Politics of World Heritage,* Buffalo: Channel View.

Harrison, David and Stephen Schipani, 2007, 'Lao Tourism and Poverty Alleviation: Community-Based Tourism and the Private Sector', *Current Issues in Tourism,* 10, 2-3, 194–230.

Hartono, T., 2005, 'Community-Based Ecotourism: The Case of Halimun National Park, West Java', in J. Damanik, H. A. Kusworo and D. T. Raharjana, eds, *Poverty Alleviation through Tourism,* Yogyakarta: Kepel Press, 77–86.

Hawkins, J. and C. Roberts, 1993, 'Effects of Recreational Scuba Diving on Coral Reefs: Trampling on Reef-Flat Communities', *Journal of Applied Ecology,* 30, 25–30.

—— 1994, 'The Growth of Coastal Tourism in the Red Sea: Present and Future Effects on Coral Reefs', *Ambio,* 23, 8, 503–508.

Hefner, R. W., 1994, 'Reimagined Community: A Social History of Muslim Education in Pasuruan, East Java', in C. F. Keyes, L. Kendall and H. Hardacre, eds, *Asian Visions of Authority: Religion and the Modern States of East and Southeast Asia,* Honolulu: University of Hawai'i Press, 75–95.

Henderson, Joan C., 1999, 'Southeast Asian Tourism and the Financial Crisis: Indonesia and Thailand Compared', *Annals of Tourism Research*, 2, 4, 294–303.

—— 2001, 'Regionalisation and Tourism: The Indonesia–Malaysia–Singapore Growth Triangle,' *Current Issues in Tourism*, 4, 2–4, 78–93.

—— 2003, 'The Politics of Tourism in Myanmar,' *Current Issues in Tourism*, 6, 2, 97–118.

Henderson, Joan C. and Alex Ng, 2004, 'Responding to Crisis: Severe Acute Respiratory Syndrome (SARS) and Hotels in Singapore', *International Journal of Tourism Research*, 6, 411–419.

Hendry, J., 2000, *The Orient Strikes Back*, Oxford: Berg.

Herold, E., R. Garcia and T. DeMoya, 2001, 'Female Tourists and Beach Boys: Romance or Sex Tourism?', *Annals of Tourism Research*, 28, 4, 978–997.

Heyman, Josiah and Hilary Cunningham, 2004, 'Introduction: Mobilities and Enclosures at Borders', *Identities*, 11, 3, 289–302.

Hill, H., 2000, 'Indonesia: The Sudden and Strange Death of an Asian Tiger', *Oxford Development Studies*, 28, 2, 117–139.

Hill, Lewis and Michael Hitchcock, 1996, 'Anthropology', in Mohammed Halib and Tim Huxley, eds, *An Introduction to Southeast Asian Studies*, London and New York: I. B. Tauris Publishers, 11–45.

Hitchcock, Michael, 1993, 'Dragon Tourism in Komodo, Eastern Indonesia', in Michael Hitchcock, Victor T. King and Michael J. G. Parnwell, eds, *Tourism in Southeast Asia*, London: Routledge, 303–316.

—— 1997, 'Indonesia in Miniature', in Michael Hitchcock and Victor T. King, eds, *Images of Malay–Indonesian Identity*, Kuala Lumpur: Oxford University Press, 227–235.

—— 1999, 'Tourism and Ethnicity: Situational Perspectives', *International Journal of Tourism Research*, 1, 17–32.

—— 2000, 'Ethnicity and Tourism Entrepreneurship in Java and Bali', *Current Issues in Tourism*, 3, 204–225.

—— 2001, 'Tourism and Total Crisis in Indonesia: The Case of Bali', *Asia Pacific Business Review*, 8, 2, 101–120.

—— 2005, 'Afterword', in David Harrison and Michael Hitchcock, eds, *The Politics of World Heritage: Negotiating Tourism and Conservation,* Buffalo: Channel View, 181–186.

—— 2003, 'Souvenirs, Intangible and Tangible Authenticity', unpublished conference paper, 4 November 2003, Havana, Cuba.

—— 2003c, 'Concluding Remarks', in *Indonesia and the Malay World*. Vol. 31, No. 89: 161–164.

Hitchcock, Michael and Sian Jay, 1998, 'Eco-tourism and Environmental Change in Indonesia, Malaysia and Thailand', in Victor T. King, ed., *Environmental Challenges in South-East Asia*, Richmond: Curzon and Copenhagen: NIAS, 305–316.

Hitchcock, Michael and Victor T. King, eds, 2003a, 'Tourism and Heritage in South-East Asia', Special Issue of *Indonesia and the Malay World*, 31.

—— 2003b, 'Discourses with the Past: Tourism and Heritage in South-East Asia', *Indonesia and the Malay World*, 31, 3–15 (special issue on 'Tourism and Heritage in South-East Asia', edited by Michael Hitchcock and Victor T. King).

Hitchcock, Michael, Victor T. King and Michael J. G. Parnwell, eds, 1993, *Tourism in South-East Asia*, London: Routledge.

Hitchcock, Michael and Lucy Norris, 1995, *Bali. The Imaginary Museum: The Photographs of Walter Spies and Beryl de Zoete*, Kuala Lumpur: Oxford University Press.

Hitchcock, Michael and Wiendu Nuryanti, eds, 2000, *Building on Batik: the Globalisation of a Craft Community*, Aldershot: Ashgate.

Hitchcock, Michael and I Nyoman Darma Putra, 2005, 'The Bali Bombings: Tourism Crisis Management and Conflict Avoidance', *Current Issues in Tourism*, 8, 1, 62–76.

—— 2007, *Tourism Development and Terrorism in Bali*, Aldershot: Ashgate-Gower.

Bibliography

Hitchcock, Michael and Ken Teague, 2000, *Souvenirs: The Material Culture of Tourism*, Aldershot: Ashgate.

Hobart, Angela, Urs Ramseyer and Albert Leemann, 2001, *The People of Bali*, Oxford: Blackwell, The Peoples of South-East Asia and the Pacific, paperback, first published in 1996.

Hobsbawm, Eric and Terance Ranger, eds, 1983, *The Invention of Tradition*, Cambridge: Cambridge University Press.

Holden, Andrew, 2000, *Environment and Tourism*, London: Routledge; Introductions to the Environment Series.

Holden, A. and M. Ewen, 2004, 'Issues of Natural Resource Usage, Social Well-Being and Tourism in the Annapurna Area of Nepal', ASEAN Journal on Hospitality and Tourism 3, 1, 51–63.

Holdiman, T., 1985, 'Indonesian Adventure . . . Rituals and Culture in Tanah Toraja', *Sunset* (May), 80–81.

Holloway, J. Christopher, 1983, 'The Guided Tour: A Sociological Approach', *Annals of Tourism Research*, 10, 377–402.

Holtorf, Cornelius, 2001, 'Is the Past a Non-Renewable Resource?', in R. Layton, P. Stone and J. Thomas, eds, *Destruction and Conservation of Cultural Property*, London: Routledge, 286–297.

Holtorf, Cornelius and T. Schadla-Hall, 1999, 'Age as Artifact: On Archaeological Authenticity', *European Journal of Archaeology*, 2, 229–47.

Hong, Evelyne, 1985, *See the Third World While it Lasts*, Penang: Consumer Association Penang.

Hottola, Petri, 1999, 'The Intercultural Body: Western Women, Culture Confusion and Control of Space in the South Asian Travel Scene', unpublished dissertation, University of Joensuu (Finland).

Houellebecq, M., 2002, *Platform*, London: Heinemann.

Howe, Leo, 2001, *Hinduism and Hierarchy in Bali*, Oxford: James Currey.

—— 2005, *The Changing World of Bali: Religion, Society and Tourism*, London and New York: Routledge-Curzon.

Hu, Ching-Fang, 2005, 'Review of *The Asian Mystique: Dragon Ladies, Geisha Girls, & Our Fantasies of the Exotic Orient*', *Far Eastern Economic Review*, July, 67–68.

Hughes-Freeland, Felicia, 1993, 'Packaging Dreams: Javanese Perceptions of Tourism and Performance', in Michael Hitchcock, Victor T. King and Michael J. G. Parnwell, eds, *Tourism in South-East Asia*, London: Routledge, 138–154.

Hutajulu, Rithaony, 1995, 'Tourism's Impact on Toba Batak Ceremony', *Bijdragen tot de Taal-, Land – en Volkenkunde*, 151, 639–655.

I. C. G., 2003, *The Perils of Private Security in Indonesia: Guards and Militias on Bali and Lombok*, Jakarta and Brussels: International Crisis Group.

IBRD/IDA, 1974, *Bali Tourism Project: Appraisal Report*, Washington: Tourism Projects Department.

Ikeda, Mitsuho, 1997, 'Kosutarika no eko-tsûrizumu' (Ecotourism in Costa Rica), in Shinji Yamashita, ed., *Idô no minzokushi* (Ethnography of Transnational Migration), Tokyo: Iwanami Shoten, 61–93.

Ingold, Tim, 2000, *The Perception of the Environment: Essays on Livelihood, Dwelling and Skill*, London: Routledge.

Ioannides, D., Y. Apostolopoulos and S. Sonmez, eds, 2001, *Mediterranean Islands and Sustainable Tourism Development*, London: Continuum.

IRIP News Service, 1996, 'Beaches and Broken Homes', Internet extract on Indonesia Daily News, www.uni-stuttgart.de/indonesia/news.

Iwata, Keiji, 1975, *Nihonbunka no furusato* (The homeland of the Japanese culture), Tokyo: Kadokawa Shoten.

Jafari, J. and D. Aaser, 1988, 'Tourism as a Subject of Doctoral Dissertations', *Annals of Tourism Research*, 15, 407–429.

The Jakarta Post.

Jamal, T. B. and D. Getz, 1995, 'Collaboration Theory and Community Tourism Planning', *Annals of Tourism Research*, 22, 1, 186–204.

Jamieson, Neil, 1993, *Understanding Vietnam*, Berkeley: University of California Press.

Janamijaya, I. G., I. N. Wiratmaja and I. W. G. Suacana, eds, 2003, *Eksistensi Desa Pakraman di Bali*, Denpasar: Yayasan Tri Hita Karana Bali.

Jarvie, J., R. Kanaan, M. Malley, T. Roule and J. Thomson, 2003, *Conflict Timber: Dimensions of the Problem in Asia and Africa*, report for USAID by Associates in Rural Development, Inc, cited in INCL 6–29a, 21 July 2003.

Jenkins, Gwynn, 2003, 'Contested Spaces: Heritage and Identity Reconstructions: An Enquiry into Conservation Strategies within a Developing Asian City: George Town, Penang, Malaysia', Unpublished PhD Thesis, University of Hull.

Jenkins, Gwynn and Victor T. King, 2003, 'Heritage and Development in a Malaysian City: George Town Under Threat?', *Indonesia and the Malay World*, 31, 44–57 (special issue on 'Tourism and Heritage in South-East Asia', edited by Michael Hitchcock and Victor T. King).

Jepson, P., 1997, *Birding Indonesia*, Singapore: Periplus Editions.

Jerndal, Randi and Jonathan Rigg, 1999, 'From Buffer State to Crossroads State', in G. Evans, ed., *Laos: Culture and Society*, Silkworm Books: Chang Mai, Thailand, 35–60.

Jessop, B., 1995, 'The Regulation Approach, Governance and Post-Fordism: Alternative Perspectives on Economic and Political Change?', *Economy and Society*, 24, 3, 307–333.

Johnson, Mark, 2001, 'Renovating Hue (Vietnam): Authenticating Destruction, Reconstructing Authenticity', in R. Layton, P. Stone and J. Thomas, eds, *Destruction and Conservation of Cultural Property*, London: Routledge, 75–92.

Johnson, Michael, 1996, 'Violence Against Women in the Family: The United States and Vietnam', in Kathleen Barry, ed., *Vietnam's Women in Transition*, Basingstoke, Hampshire: Macmillan, 287–296.

Joy, R., 1997, *Development of Ecotourism Enterprises in Gunung Halimun National Park, West Java, Indonesia*, in RECOFTC, *Ecotourism for Forest Conservation and Community Development*, Proceedings of International Seminar on Ecotourism for Forest Conservation and Community Development, Chiang Mai, 28–31 January 1997, 220–226.

Kadir H. Din, 1982, 'Tourism in Malaysia: Competing Needs in a Plural Society', *Annals of Tourism Research*, 9, 453–480.

—— 1986, 'Differential Ethnic Involvement in the Penang Tourist Industry: Some Policy Implications', *Akademika*, 29, 3–20.

—— 1988, 'Social and Cultural Impacts of Tourism', *Annals of Tourism Research*, 15, 563–566.

—— 1989, 'Islam and Tourism: Patterns, Issues and Options', *Annals of Tourism Research*, 16, 542–563.

—— 1993, 'Dialogue with the Hosts: An Educational Strategy Towards Sustainable Tourism', in Michael Hitchcock, Victor T. King, and Michael J. G. Parnwell, eds. *Tourism in South-East Asia*, London, Routledge, 327–336.

—— 1997, 'Tourism and Cultural Development in Malaysia: Issues for a New Agenda', in Shinji Yamashita, Kadir H. Din and J. S. Eades, eds, *Tourism and Cultural Development in Asia and Oceania*, Bangi: Universiti Kebangsaan Malaysia Press, 104–118.

Kagami, Haruya, 1997, 'Tourism and National Culture: Indonesian Policies on Cultural Heritage and its Utilization in Tourism', in Yamashita et al., ed., *Tourism and Cultural Development in Asia and Oceania*, Kebangsan, Malaysia, Penerbit Universiti: 61–82.

Kahn, Joel S., 1997, 'Culturalizing Malaysia: Globalism, Tourism, Heritage, and the City in Georgetown', in Michel Picard and Robert E. Wood, eds, *Tourism, Ethnicity, and the State in Asian and Pacific Societies*, Honolulu: University of Hawai'i Press, 99–127.

—— 1998, 'Southeast Asian Identities: Introduction', in Joel S. Kahn, ed., *Southeast Asian Identities: Culture and the Politics of Representation in Indonesia, Malaysia, Singapore, and Thailand*, Singapore and London: Institute of Southeast Asian Studies, 1–27.

—— 2001, 'Anthropology and Modernity', *Current Anthropology*, 42, 5, 651–664.

Kamsma, T. and K. Bras, 1999, 'Gili Trawangan: Local Enterprise in Tourism Under Pressure', in H. Dahles and K. Bras, eds, *Tourism and Small Entrepreneurs: Development, National Policy and Entrepreneurial Culture: Indonesian Cases,* New York: Cognizant Communcations, 67–78.

Kaosa-ard, M., D. Bezic and S. White, 2001, 'Domestic Tourism in Thailand: Supply and Demand', in K. Ghimire, ed., *The Native Tourist*, London: Earthscan Publications, 109–141.

Karch, C. A. and G. H. S. Dann, 1981, 'Close Encounters of the Third World', *Human Relations,* 4, 249–268.

Kawamura, Minato, 1993, 'Taishû orientarizumu to Ajia ninshiki (Popular Orientalism and Japanese perception of Asia)', *Iwanamikôza kindai nihon to shokuminchi* (Iwanami series of modern Japan and colonies), 7, 107–136. Tokyo: Iwanami Shoten.

King, Victor T., 1993, 'Tourism and Culture in Malaysia', in Michael Hitchcock, Victor T. King and Michael J. G. Parnwell, eds, *Tourism in South-East Asia*, London: Routledge, 99–116.

—— 1999, *Anthropology and Development in South-East Asia: Theory and Practice*, Kuala Lumpur: Oxford University Press.

—— 2005, 'Defining Southeast Asia and the Crisis in Area Studies: Personal Reflections on a Region', Lund University: Centre for East and South-East Asian Studies, Working Papers in Contemporary Asian Studies, 13.

—— ed., 1995, *Tourism in Borneo: Issues and Perspectives,* Williamsburg: Borneo Research Council Proceedings Series.

King, Victor T. and William D. Wilder, 2003, *The Modern Anthropology of South-East Asia*, London and New York: Routledge.

Kinnard, V. and D. Hall, 1994, *Tourism: A Gender Analysis*, New York and Chichester: Wiley.

Kleiber, D. and M. Wilke, 1995, *Aids, Sex und Tourismus. Ergebnisse einer Befragung deutscher Urlauber und Sextouristen*, Baden-Baden: Nomos-Verlagsgesellschaft.

Kleinen, John, ed., 2001, *Vietnamese Society in Transition: The Daily Politics of Reform and Change*, Amsterdam: Het Spinhuis Publishers.

Knight, D., B. Mitchell and G. Wall, 1997, 'Bali: Sustainable Development, Tourism and Coastal Management', *Ambio*, 26, 2, 90–96.

Koeman, Annalisa and Nguyen Van Lam, 1999, 'The Economics of Protected Areas and the Role of Ecotourism in their Management: The Case of Vietnam', Paper presented to the Second Regional Forum for Southeast Asia of the IUCN World Commission for Protected Areas, Lakse, lao PDR, 6–11 December 1999.

Kokudokôtsûshô (Ministry of Land and Communication) ed., 2005, *Heisei 17 nenban kankô hakusho* (Tourism white paper 2005), Tokyo: National Publishing Bureau.

Kolko, G., 1997, *Vietnam: Anatomy of a Peace*, London and New York: Routledge.

Kompas, 2006, 'Pariwisata Bali Sekarat! (Bali's Tourism in Agony)', Wednesday, 11 January, 34–35.

Kontogeorgopolos, Nick, 2003a, 'Towards a Southeast Asian Model of Resort-Based "Mass Ecotourism": Evidence from Phuket, Thailand and Bali, Indonesia', *ASEAN Journal on Hospitality and Tourism*, 2, 1, 1–16.

——, 2003b, 'Keeping up with the Joneses: Tourists, Travelers, and the Quest for Cultural Authenticity in Southern Thailand', *Tourist Studies*, 3, 171–203.

—— 2004, 'Ecotourism and Mass Tourism in Southern Thailand: Spatial Interdependence, Structural Connections, and Staged Authenitcity', *GeoJournal*, 61, 1–11.

—— 2005, 'Community-Based Ecotourism in Phuket and Ao Phangnga, Thailand: Partial Victories and Bittersweet Remedies', *Journal of Sustainable Tourism*, 13, 1, 4–23.

Kratoska, Paul H., Remco Raben and Henk Schulte Nordholt, eds, 2005, *Locating Southeast Asia: Geographies of Knowledge and Politics of Space*, National University of Singapore: Singapore University Press and Athens: Ohio University Press, Research in International Studies, Southeast Asia Series No. 111.

Krause, Gregor, 1922, *Insel Bali*, Hagen i. W.: Folkwang Verlag GMBH.

—— 1988, *Bali 1912*, Wellington: January Books.

Kruhse-Mount Burton, S., 1995, 'Sex Tourism and Traditional Australian Male Identity', in M. F. Lanfant, J. B. Allock and E. M. Bruner, eds, *International Tourism: Identity and Change*, London: Sage, 192–204.

Kua, Juliana and Tom Baum, 2004, 'Perspective in the Development of Low-Cost Airlines in South-East Asia', *Current Issues in Tourism*, 7, 3, 262–276.

Kurus, Bilson, 1998, 'Migrant Labour Flows in the East ASEAN', *Borneo Review*, 9, 2, 156–184.

Kusaka, Yôko, 2000, *Taniya no shakaigaku* (Sociology of Taniya), Tokyo: Mekon.

Lacan, Jacques, 1977, *Écrits: A Selection*, (translated by Alan Sheridan), London: Tavistock.

Lanfant, Marie-Francoise, 1995a, 'Introduction', in Marie-Francoise Lanfant, John B. Allcock and Edward M. Bruner, eds, *International Tourism: Identity and Change*, London: Sage Publications, Sage Studies in International Sociology 47, 1–23.

—— 1995b, 'International Tourism, Internationalization and the Challenge to Identity', in Marie-Francoise Lanfant, John B. Allcock and Edward M. Bruner, eds, *International Tourism: Identity and Change*, London: Sage Publications, Sage Studies in International Sociology 47, 24–43.

Lao National Tourism Administration, 2006, *2005 Statistical Report on Tourism in Laos*, NTAL, Statistics, Planning and Co-operation Division: Vientiane.

Lao People's Democratic Republic, 1990, *National Plan for the Development of Tourism in the Lao People's Democratic Republic*, United Nations Development Programme: Vientiane.

—— 2003, *National Growth and Poverty Eradication Strategy*, Lao PDR: Vientiane.

—— 2004, *Law on the Promotion of Foreign Investment*, National Assembly, No.11/NA, 22nd October.

Lao People's Democratic Republic, United Nations Development Programme and the World Tourism Organisation, 1998, *National Tourism Development Plan for Lao PDR*, Vientiane.

Laske, Tomke and Stefan Herold, 2005, 'An Observation Station for Culture and Tourism in Vietnam: A Forum for World Heritage and Public Participation', in David Harrison and Michael Hitchcock, eds, *The Politics of World Heritage: Negotiating Tourism and Conservation*, Buffalo: Channel View, 119–131.

Lasswell, Harold, 1936, *Politics: Who Gets What, When and How*, New York: McGraw-Hill.

Law, Lisa, 2000, *Sex Work in Southeast Asia: The Place of Desire in a Time of Aids*, London: Select Books.

Le, Ba Thao, 1997, *Vietnam: The Country and its Geographical Regions*, Hanoi: The Gioi Publishers.

Le, Thi Guy, 1996, 'Domestic Violence in Vietnam and Efforts to Curb it', in Kathleeen Barry, ed., *Vietnam's Women in Transition*, Basingstoke, Hampshire: Macmillan, 263–74.

Lea, John, 1988, *Tourism and Development in the Third World*, London and New York: Routledge.

Lee, W., 1991, 'Prostitution and Tourism in South-East Asia', in N. Redclift and M. T. Sinclair, eds, *Working Women: International Perspectives on Gender and Labour Ideology*, London and New York: Routledge, 79–103.

Leheny, David, 1995, 'A Political Economy of Asian Sex Tourism', *Annals of Tourism Research*, 22, 2, 367–384.

Leifer, M. and J. Phipps, 1991, *Vietnam and Doi Moi: Domestic and International Dimensions of Reform*, London: Royal Institute of International Affairs.

Leiman, R., 2002, 'The Conservancy's Response to 'Jurassic Showdown'', *Far Eastern Economic Review*, May 16, online, available at:

www.komodonationalpark.org/downloads/dhume2002.pdf (accessed 26 June 2002).

Leong Wai-Teng, Laurence, 1989, 'Culture and the State: Manufacturing Traditions for Tourism', *Critical Studies in Mass Communication*, 6, 355–375.

—— 1997, 'Commodifying Ethnicity: State and Ethnic Tourism in Singapore', in Michel Picard and Robert E. Wood, eds, *Tourism, Ethnicity, and the State in Asian and Pacific Societies*, Honolulu: University of Hawai'i Press, 71–98.

Lett, James, 1989, 'Epilogue' (to 'Touristic Studies in Anthropological Perspective' by Theron Nuñez), in Valene L. Smith, ed., *Hosts and Guests: The Anthropology of Tourism*, Philadelphia: University of Pennsylvania Press, 275–279 (second revised and expanded edition).

Levine, J. J., 1998, 'Untapped Potential', *Vietnam Business Journal*, January–February, 1–5.

Lew, Alan A., 1999, 'Tourism and the Southeast Asia Crises of 1997 and 1998: A View from Singapore', *Current Issues in Tourism*, 2, 4, 304–315.

Liddle, M. and A. Kay, 1989, 'Impact of Human Trampling in Different Zones of a Coral Reef Flat', *Environmental Management*, 4, 509–520.

Lim, Ai Lee, 1998, 'Council Should be More Strict with PDC', *The Star*, Malaysia: Northern Edition, 6, 6.

Lim, Lin Lean, ed., 1998, *The Sex Sector: The Economic and Social Bases of Prostitution in Southeast Asia*, Geneva: ILO.

Lloyd, K., 2003, 'Contesting Control in Transitional Vietnam: The Development and Regulation of Traveller Cafes in Hanoi and Ho Chi Minh City', *Tourism Geographies*, 5, 3, 350–366.

—— 2004, 'Tourism and Transitional Geographies: Mismatched Expectations of Tourism Investment in Vietnam', *Asia Pacific Viewpoint*, 45, 2, 197–215.

Logan, William, 2002, 'Introduction', in William S. Logan, ed., *The Disappearing 'Asian' City: Protecting Asia's Urban Heritage in a Globalizing World*, New York: Oxford University Press, xii–xxi.

Loker-Murphy, L., and P. Pearce, 1995, 'Young Budget Travelers: Backpackers in Australia', *Annals of Tourism Research*, 22, 4, 819–843.

Luong, Hy V., ed., 2003a, *Postwar Vietnam: Dynamics of a Transforming Society*, Singapore: Institute of Southeast Asian Studies.

—— 2003b, 'Gender Relations: Ideologies, Kinship Practices, and Political Economy', in Hy V. Luong, ed., *Postwar Vietnam: Dynamics of a Transforming Society*, Singapore: Institute of Southeast Asian Studies; Lanham, Maryland: Rowman and Littlefield, 201–223.

Lyon, J., and T. Wheeler, 1997, *Bali and Lombok: A Travel Survival Kit,* (6th Edition), Hawthorne, Victoria: Lonely Planet Publications.

Lyttleton, C. and A. Allcock, 2002, *Tourism as a Tool for Development: UNESCO-Lao National Tourism Authority Nam Ha Ecotourism Project – External Review July 6–18, 2002,* Vientiane: NTAL and UNESCO.

Mabbett, H., 1987, *In Praise of Kuta: From Slave Port to Fishing Village to the Most Popular Resort in Bali*, Wellington: January Books.

MacCannell, Dean, 1973, 'Staged Authenticity: Arrangements of Social Space in Tourist Settings', *American Journal of Sociology*, 79, 589–603.

—— 1984, 'Reconstructed Ethnicity: Tourism and Cultural Identity in Third World Communities', *Annals of Tourism Research*, 11, 375–391.

—— 1992. *Empty Meeting Grounds: The Tourist Papers*, London: Routledge.

—— 1999, *The Tourist: A New Theory of the Leisure Class*, New York: Schocken Books.

—— 2001, 'Tourist Agency', *Tourist Studies*, 1, 1, 23–37.

MacDougall, J. M., 2003, 'From *puik* (silencing) to *politik*: Transformations in Political Action and Cultural Exclusion from the Late–1990's', *Antropologi Indonesia*, 27, 70, 60–76.

Mackie, V., 1992, 'Japan and South-East Asia: The International Division of Labour and Leisure', in D. Harrison, ed., *Tourism and the Less Developed Countries*, London: Belhaven Press, 75–84.

MacLellan, L. R., P. U. C. Dieke and B. K. Thapa, 2000, 'Mountain Tourism and Public Policy in Nepal', in P. M. Godde, M. F. Price and F. M. Zimmerman, eds, *Tourism and Development in Mountain Regions*, Wallingford and New York: CABI Publishing, 173–198.

MacRae, G., 1997, 'Economy, Ritual and History in a Balinese Tourist Town', unpublished PhD thesis, University of Auckland.

—— 2003, 'The Value of Land in Bali: Land Tenure, Land Reform and Commodification', in T. A. Reuter, ed., *Inequality, Crisis and Social Change in Indonesia: The Muted Worlds of Bali*, London and New York: RoutledgeCurzon, 143–165.

Maoz, Darya, 2006, 'The Mutual Gaze', *Annals of Tourism Research*, 33, 221–239.

Marcus, George E. and Fred R. Myers, eds, 1995, *The Traffic in Culture: Refiguring Art and Anthropology,* Berkeley: University of California Press.

Markandya, A., S. Pedroso and T. Taylor, 2005, 'Tourism and Sustainable Development: Lessons from Recent World Bank Experience', Chapter 8 in A. Lanza, A. Markandya and F. Pigliaru, eds, *The Economics of Tourism and Sustainable Development,* Cheltenham: Edward Elgar.

Martana, S. P., 2003, 'Bali after the Blast: Reorientation in Development Priorities', *Asean Journal of Hospitality and Tourism,* 2, 1, 47–60.

Mason, Peter, Peter Grobowski and Wei Du, 2005, 'Severe Acute Respiratory Syndrome, Tourism and the Media', *International Journal of Tourism Research,* 7, 11–21.

Matsuda, Misa, 1989, 'Japanese Tourists and Indonesia: Images of Self and Other in the Age of *kokusaika* (Internationalization)', MA Thesis, Asian Studies, Australian National University.

Matsui, Yayori, 1993, *Ajia no kankôkaihatsu to nihon* (Asian Tourist Development and Japan), Tokyo: Shinkansha.

McCarthy, J., 1994, *Are Sweet Dreams made of This? Tourism in Bali and Eastern Indonesia,* Melbourne: IRIP.

McCool, S., 1994, 'Planning for Sustainable Nature Dependent Tourism Development: The Limits of Acceptable Change System', *Tourism Recreation Research,* 19, 2, 51–55.

McElroy, J., 2002, 'Tourism Development in Small Islands across the World', paper read at the Islands of the World VII Conference, University of Prince Edward Island, Canada, 26–30 June 2002.

McGregor, Andrew, 2000, 'Dynamic Texts and Tourist Gaze: Death, Bones and Buffalo', *Annals of Tourism Research,* 27, 27–50.

McKean, Philip Frick, 1973, 'Cultural Involution: Tourists, Balinese, and the Process of Modernization in Anthropological Perspective', unpublished PhD dissertation, Brown University, University Microfilms.

—— 1976, 'Tourism, Culture Change and Culture Conservation in Bali', in David J. Banks, ed., *World Anthropology: Changing Identities in Modern Southeast Asia,* The Hague, Paris: Mouton, 237–247.

—— 1977a, 'From Purity to Pollution? A Symbolic Form in Transition', in A. Becker and A. Yengoyan, eds, *The Imagination of Reality: Symbol Systems in Southeast Asia,* Tucson: University of Arizona Press, 293–302.

—— 1989/1977b, 'Towards a Theoretical Analysis of Tourism: Economic Dualism and Cultural Involution in Bali', in Valene L. Smith, ed., *Hosts and Guests: The Anthropology of Tourism,* Philadelphia: University of Pennsylvania Press, 119–138 (revised and expanded second edition 1989; first edition 1977).

McKercher, Bob, 1999, 'A Chaos Approach to Tourism Management', *Tourism Management,* 20, 425–34.

McKercher, Bob and Kaye Chon, 2004, 'The Over-Reaction to SARS and the Collapse of Asian Tourism', *Annals of Tourism Research,* 31, 3, 716–719.

Meijer, Martha, ed., 2001, *Dealing with Human Rights: Asian and Western Views on the Value of Human Rights,* Oxford: Greber Publications.

Meisch, L. A., 1995, 'Gringas and Otavalenos: Changing Tourist Relations', *Annals of Tourism Research,* 22, 2, 441–462.

Merry, Sally Engle, 1984, 'Rethinking Gossip and Scandal', in Donald Black, ed., *Toward a General Theory of Social Control* (vol. 1), London: Academic Press, 271–301.

Meyer, C. A., 1997, 'Public-Nonprofit Partnerships and North–South Green Finance', *Journal of Environment and Development,* 6, 2, 123–146.

Meyer, W., 1988, *Beyond the Mask,* Verlag breitench: Saarbucken and Fort Lauderdale.

Michaud, Jean, 1995, 'Questions about Fieldwork Methodology', *Annals of Tourism Research,* 22, 681–687.

Michaud, Jean and Michel Picard, eds, 2001, 'Tourisme et Societes Locales en Asie Orientale', *Anthropologie et Societes,* 25, 1–166, special issue.

Miller, Daniel, ed., 1995, *Worlds Apart: Modernity Through the Prism of the Local,* New York: Routledge.

Mings, R. C. and S. Chulikpongse, 1994, 'Tourism in Far Southern Thailand: A Geographical Perspective', *Tourism Recreation Research,* 19, 1, 25–31.

Mingsarn Kaosa-ard, 1999, 'Development and Management of Tourism Products: The Thai Experience', *Chiang Mai University Journal,* 1, 3, 289–301.

Ministry of Forestry, 2001, *Draft: National Forest Statement; Through Multi-Stakeholder Participation,* Jakarta: Ministry of Forestry.

Mok, Connie and Terry Lam, 2000, 'Vietnam's Tourism Identity: Its Potential and Challenges, in K. C. Chon, ed., *Tourism in Southeast Asia,* New York, Haworth, 157–164.

Momsen, J., 1994, 'Tourism, Gender, and the Development of the Caribbean', in V. Kinnaird and D. Hall, eds, *Tourism: A Gender Analysis,* New York and Chichester: Wiley, 106–120.

Moon, O., 1997, 'Tourism and Cultural Development: Japanese and Korean Contexts', in S. Yamashita, Kadir H. Din and J. S. Eades, eds, *Tourism and Cultural Development in Asia and Oceania,* Bangi: Penerbit Universiti Kebangsaan Malaysia, 178–193.

Moor, K., 2003, 'Murder in Bali', *Herald Sun,* 2 October 2003.

Mowforth, Martin and Ian Munt, 1998, *Tourism and Sustainability,* London and New York: Routledge.

—— 2003, *Tourism and Sustainability: Development and New Tourism in the Third World,* (Second edition), London: Routledge.

Muller, K., 1992, *Underwater Indonesia: A Guide to the World's Greatest Diving,* Hong Kong: Periplus.

Murdoch, Lindsay, 2006, 'Bashir Clear on Bali Blasts as Attack Fears Grow', *The Age,* Australia, December 22.

Musa, Ghazali, 2003, 'Sipadan: An Over-Exploited Scuba Diving Paradise', in Garrod Briar and Julie C. Wilson, eds, *Marine Ecotourism,* Sydney, Channel View, 122–137.

Muzaini, Hamzah, 2006, 'Backpacking Southeast Asia: Strategies of "Looking Local"', *Annals of Tourism Research,* 33, 144–161.

Nash, Dennison, 1981, 'Tourism as an Anthropological Subject', *Current Anthropology,* 22, 461–468.

—— 1984, 'The Ritualization of Tourism: Comment on Graburn's *The Anthropology of Tourism*', *Annals of Tourism Research,* 11, 503–522.

—— 1989/1977, 'Tourism as a Form of Imperialism', in Valene L. Smith, ed., *Hosts and Guests: The Anthropology of Tourism,* Philadelphia: University of Pennsylvania Press, 37–52 (second revised and expanded edition, 1989; first edition, 1977).

—— 1996, 'On Anthropologists and Tourists', *Annals of Tourism Research,* 23, 691–694.

Nash, Dennison and Valene L. Smith, 1991, 'Anthropology and Tourism', *Annals of Tourism Research,* 18, 12–25.

National Tourism Authority of Lao PDR, undated, *The Official Lao PDR Tourism Guide Book,* NTAL: Vientiane.

—— 2003, *2003 Statistical Report on Tourism in Laos,* NTAL, Statistics, Planning and Co-operation Division: Vientiane.

—— 2004, *2004 Statistical Report on Tourism in Laos,* NTAL, Statistics, Planning and Co-operation Division: Vientiane.

—— 2005, *National Ecotourism Strategy and Action Plan: 2004–2010,* NTAL: Vientiane.

Nederveen Pieterse, Jan, 1993, *Globalization as Hybridization,* Working Paper No. 152, The Hague: Institute of Social Studies.

—— 2003, *Globalization and Culture: Global Mélange,* Lanham, Maryland: Rowman and Littlefield.

Ness, Sally Ann, 2003, *Where Asia Smiles: An Ethnography of Philippine Tourism,* Philadelphia: University of Pennsylvania Press.

—— 2005, 'Tourism-Terrorism: The Landscaping of Consumption and the Darker Side of Place', *American Ethnologist,* 32, 1, 118–140.

Nguyen Nhu Binh and M. Brennan, 2000, 'Vietnamese Tourism: The Challenges Ahead', unpublished paper, 1–19.

Nguyen, Khac Vien, 1993, *Vietnam: A Long History*, Hanoi: The Gioi Publishers.

Noronha, Raymond, 1973, *A Report on the Proposed Tourism Project, Bali*, Washington: IBRD.

Nuñez, Theron, 1989/1977, 'Touristic Studies in Anthropological Perspective', in Valene L. Smith, ed., *Hosts and Guests: The Anthropology of Tourism*, Philadelphia: University of Pennsylvania Press, 265–274 (second revised and expanded edition, 1989; first edition, 1977).

Oakes, Tim, 1999, 'Bathing in the Far Village: Globalization, Transnational Capital, and the Cultural Politics of Modernity in China', *Positions: East Asia Cultures Critique*, 7, 2, 307–342.

O'Harrow, Stephen, 1995, 'Vietnamese Women and Confucianism: Creating Spaces from Patriarchy', in Wazir Jahan Karim, ed., *'Male' and 'Female' in Developing Southeast Asia*, Oxford: Berg, 161–180.

O'Malley, J., 1988, 'Sex Tourism and Women's Status in Thailand', *Loisir et Société*, 11, 1, 99–114.

Ong, Aiwah, 1985, 'Industrialisation and Prostitution in Southeast Asia', *Southeast Asia Chronicle*, 96, 2–6.

Ono, Mayumi, 2005, 'Young Japanese Settlers in Thailand: The Pursuit of Comfort and Alternative Lifestyle', Working Paper 4, The Institute of Contemporary Japanese Studies, Waseda University.

Ooi, Can-Seng, 2001, 'Dialogic Heritage: Time, Space and Visions of the National Museum of Singapore', in Peggy Teo, T. C. Chang and K. C. Ho, eds, *Interconnected Worlds: Tourism in Southeast Asia*, Oxford: Elsevier Science, Pergamon, 176–192.

—— 2002a, 'Contrasting Strategies: Tourism in Denmark and Singapore', *Annals of Tourism Research*, 29, 689–707.

—— 2002b, *Cultural Tourism, Tourism Cultures: The Business of Mediating Experiences in Copenhagen and Singapore*, Copenhagen: Copenhagen Business School.

—— 2003, 'Identities, Museums, and Tourism in Singapore: Think Regionally, Act Locally', *Indonesia and the Malay World*, 31, 80–90 (special issue on 'Tourism and Heritage in South-East Asia', edited by Michael Hitchcock and Victor T. King).

Oppermann, Martin, 1992, 'Intranational Tourist Flows in Malaysia', *Annals of Tourism Research*, 19, 482–500.

—— 1998, 'Introduction', in M. Oppermann, ed., *Sex Tourism and Prostitution: Aspects of Leisure, Recreation and Work*, New York: Cognizant Communication Corporation, 1–19.

Orams, M. B., 2001, 'Types of Ecotourism', in D. Weaver, ed., *The Encyclopedia of Ecotourism*, Wallingford and New York: CAB International, Chapter 2, 23–36.

Organisation for Economic Cooperation and Development (OECD), 1967, *Tourism Development and Economic Growth*, Paris: OECD.

Pagdin, C., 1989, 'Assessing Tourism Impacts in the Third World: A Nepal Case Study', *Progress in Planning*, 44, 3, 185–226.

Page, S., 1995, *Urban Tourism*, London: Routledge.

Pakkawadee Panusittikorn and Tony Prato, n.d., 'Conservation of Protected Areas in Thailand: The Case of Khao Yai National Park', *The George Wright Forum*, 18, 2, 66–76 (www.georgewright.org/182panusitt.pdf).

Parameshwar-Gaonkar, Dilip, ed., 1999, *Alternative Modernities*, Durham: Duke University Press.

Parenti, Michael, 1977, *Democracy for the Few*, New York: St. Martin's Press.

Parnwell, Michael J. G., 1993, 'Environmental Issues and Tourism in Thailand', in Michael Hitchcock, Victor T. King and Michael J. G. Parnwell, eds, *Tourism in South-East Asia*, London: Routledge, 286–303.

—— 1998, 'Tourism, Globalisation and Critical Security in Myanmar and Thailand', in Peggy Teo and T. C. Chang, eds, *Singapore Journal of Tropical Geography*, special issue on Tourism in Southeast Asia, 19, 212–231.

PATA, 2003, 'Bali Recovery Task Force', Bangkok: Pacific Asia Travel Association, patanet.org/archives, accessed 21 December 2005.

—— 2006, *Our Quest for Sustainable Tourism Partners*, Bangkok: Pacific Asia Travel Association.

Pattullo, P., 1996, *Last Resorts: The Cost of Tourism in the Caribbean*, London: Cassell.

PBS News Hour, 2005, 'The Wave that Shook the World', March 29 2005.

—— 2005, February 21 2005.

PCLCP (People's Committee of Lao Cai Province), 1999, *Systems of Documents on Priority Investment in Lao Cai Province*, Lao Cai: People's Committee of Lao Cai.

Pearce, P., 1990, *The Backpacker Phenomenon: Preliminary Answers to Basic Questions*, Townsville: James Cook University of North Queensland.

Peleggi, Maurizio, 1996, 'National Heritage and Global Tourism', *Annals of Tourism Research*, 23, 432–448.

Pelton, R. Y., 1999, *Come Back Alive*, New York: Broadway Books.

Pelton, R. Y, C. Aral and W. Dulles, 1998, *Fielding's The World's Most Dangerous Places*, Redondo Beach, California: Fielding World Wide, Inc.

Pemberton, John, 1994, *On the Subject of 'Java'*, Ithaca, New York and London: Cornell University Press.

Penang Tourism Action Council, 2005, www.tourismpenang.gov.my.

Perkins, Harvey and David Thorns, 2001, 'Gazing or Performing: Reflections on Urry's Tourist Gaze in the Context of Contemporary Experience in the Antipodes', *International Sociology*, 16, 2, 185–204.

Persoon, Gerard and Henry Heuveling van Beek, 1998, 'Uninvited Guests: Tourists and Environment on Siberut', in Victor T. King, ed., *Environmental Challenges in South-East Asia*, Richmond: Curzon and Copenhagen: NIAS, 317–341.

Pettus, Ashley, 2003, *Between Sacrifice and Desire: National Identity and the Governing of Femininity in Vietnam*, New York: Routledge.

Phan, Thi Vang and Pham Thu Thuy, 2003, 'Let's Talk About Love: Depictions of Love and Marriage in Contemporary Vietnamese Short Fiction', in Lisa B. W. Drummond and Mandy Thomas, eds, *Consuming Urban Culture in Contemporary Vietnam*, London and New York: RoutledgeCurzon, 202–218.

Philip, Janette and David Mercer, 1999, 'Commodification of Buddhism in Contemporary Burma', *Annals of Tourism Research*, 26, 21–54.

Phillips, Ruth and Christopher B. Steiner, 1999, *Unpacking Culture: Art and Commodity in Colonial and Postcolonial Worlds*, Berkeley: University of California Press.

Phong Dang and Melanie Beresford, 1998, *Authority Relations and Economic Decision-Making in Vietnam: An Historical Perspective*, Copenhagen: NIAS Publications.

PHPA: Direktorat Jendral Perlindungan Hutan dan Pelestarian Alam, 1992, *Kumpulan Peraturan tentang Punguton dan Iuran Bidang Pariwisata Alam serta Pungutan Masuk Kawasan Pariwisata Alam* (regulations on fees for entry to national parks), Jakarta: Ministry of Forestry.

Picard, Michel, 1987, 'Du 'Tourisme Culturel' à la 'Culture Touristique'', *Problems of Tourism*, 10, 38–52.

—— 1990a, '"Cultural Tourism" in Bali: Cultural Performances as Tourist Attraction', *Indonesia*, 49, 37–74.

—— 1990b, '*Kebalian Orang Bali*: Tourism and the Uses of "Balinese Culture" in New Order Indonesia', *Review of Indonesian and Malaysian Affairs*, 24, 1–38.

—— 1993, '"Cultural Tourism" in Bali: National Integration and Regional Differentiation', in Michael Hitchcock, Victor T. King and Michael J. G. Parnwell, eds, *Tourism in South-East Asia*, London: Routledge, 71–98.

—— 1995, 'Cultural Heritage and Tourist Capital: Cultural Tourism in Bali', in Marie-Francoise Lanfant, John B. Allcock and Edward M. Bruner, eds, *International Tourism. Identity and Change*, London: Sage Publications, Sage Studies in International Sociology 47, 44–66.

—— 1996, *Bali: Cultural Tourism and Touristic Culture* (translated by D. Darling), Singapore: Archipelago Press.

—— 1997, 'Cultural Tourism, Nation-Building, and Regional Culture: The Making of a Balinese Identity', in Michel Picard and Robert E. Wood, eds, *Tourism, Ethnicity, and the State in Asian and Pacific Societies*, Honolulu: University of Hawai'i Press, 181–214.

—— 1999, 'Making Sense of Modernity in Colonial Bali: The Polemic between Bali Adnjana and Surya Kanta (1920s)', *Dinamika Kebudayaan*, 1, 3, 73–91.

—— 2000, 'Agama, Adat, Budaya: The Dialogic Construction of Kebalian', *Dialog*, 1, 1, 85–124.

—— 2003, 'Touristification and Balinization in a Time of *Reformasi*', *Indonesia and the Malay World*, 31, 108–118 (special issue on 'Tourism and Heritage in South-East Asia', edited by Michael Hitchcock and Victor T. King).

—— 2004, 'What's in a Name? *Agama Hindu Bali* in the Making', in M. Ramstedt, ed., *Hinduism in Modern Indonesia. A Minority Religion Between Local, National, and Global Interests*, London and New York: RoutledgeCurzon, 56–75.

—— 2005, '*Otonomi Daerah* in Bali: The Call for Special Autonomy Status in the Name of *Kebalian*', in M. Erb, P. Sulistiyanto and C. Faucher, eds, *Regionalism in Post-Suharto Indonesia*, London and New York: RoutledgeCurzon, 111–124.

Picard, Michel and Jean Michaud, 2001, 'Presentation: Tourisme et Societes Locales', in Jean Michaud and Michel Picard, eds, *Anthropologie et Societes*, special issue on 'Tourisme et Societes Locales en Asie Orientale', Université Laval, Quebec, 25, 5–13.

Picard, Michel and Robert E. Wood, eds, 1997a, *Tourism, Ethnicity and the State in Asian and Pacific Societies*, Honolulu: University of Hawai'i Press.

—— 1997b, 'Preface', in Michel Picard and Robert E. Wood, eds, *Tourism, Ethnicity, and the State in Asian and Pacific Societies*, Honolulu: University of Hawai'i Press, vii–xi.

Pitana, I. G., 2004, 'Memperjuangkan Otonomi Daerah: Mencegah sandyakalaning pariwisata Bali', in I. N. Darma Putra, ed., *Bali. Menuju Jagaditha: Aneka Perspektif*, Denpasar: Pustaka Bali Post, 1–19.

Pizam, A. and Mansfield, Y., 1996, 'Introduction', in A. Pizam and Y. Mansfield, eds, *Tourism, Crime and International Security Issues*, Chichester: John Wiley and Sons, 1–17.

PKA (Direktorat Jenderal Perlindungan dan Konservasi Alam) and TNC (The Nature Conservancy) (translation in full), 2000a, *25 Year Master Plan for Management Komodo National Park, Book 1: Management Plan*, Jakarta: Direktorat Perlindungan dan Konservasi Alam.

—— 2000b, *25 Year Master Plan for Management Komodo National Park, Book 2: Data and Analysis*, Jakarta: Direktorat Perlindungan dan Konservasi Alam.

Poon, A., 1993, *Tourism Technology and Competitive Strategies*, Oxford: CAB International.

Pottier, Johan, 2003, 'Negotiating Local Knowledge', in Johan Pottier, Alan Bickers and Paul Sillitoe, eds, *Negotiating Local Knowledge: Power and Identity in Development*, London: Pluto Press.

Prasso, Sheridan, 2005, *The Asian Mystique: Dragon Ladies, Geisha Girls, and Our Fantasies of the Exotic Orient*, New York: Public Affairs Press.

Prescott, Elizabeth, 2003, 'SARS: A Warning', *Survival*, 45, 3, 207–226.

Prideaux, Bruce, 1999, 'Tourism Perspectives of the Asian Financial Crisis: Lessons for the Future', *Current Issues in Tourism*, 2, 4, 279–293.

Pruitt, D., 1993, '"Foreign Mind": Tourism, Identity and Development in Jamaica', unpublished PhD thesis, University of California, Berkeley.

Pruitt, D. and S. LaFont, 1995, '"For Love and Money": Romance Tourism in Jamaica', *Annals of Tourism Research*, 22, 2, 422–440.

Purnomo, A. and R. Lee, 2004, 'The Winds of Change: Recent Progress Towards Conserving Indonesian Biodiversity', *INCL*, 8, 3, January.

Puska, Susan M., 2005, 'SARS 2003–2004: Case Study in Crisis Management', in Andrew Scobell and Larry M. Wortzel, eds, *Chinese National Security Decision-making Under Stress*, Carlisle, Pennsylvania: U. S. Army War College, 85–134.

Putra, I Nyoman Darma and Michael Hitchcock, 2005, 'Pura Besakih: World Heritage Site Contested', *Indonesia and the Malay World*, 33, 96, 225–237.

Putra, I Nyoman Darma and W. Supartha, eds., 2001, *K. Nadha, Sang Perintis*, Denpasar: Pustaka Bali Post.

Rabasa, A. M., 2003, *Political Islam in Southeast Asia: Moderates, Radicals and Terrorists*, Oxford: Oxford University Press for the International Institute for Strategic Studies.

Raditya, 2004, 'Ajeg Bali atau Ajeg Hindu', *Raditya*, 89, December 2004.

Rajasuriya, A., M. Ranjith and M. Ohman, 1995, 'Coral Reefs of Sri Lanka: Human Disturbance and Management Issues', *Ambio*, 24, 7–8, 428–437.

Ramseyer, U., 2001, 'Prologue: Tears in Paradise', in U. Ramseyer and I G. R. Panji Tisna, eds, *Bali: Living in Two Worlds: A Critical Self-Portrait*, Basel: Museum der Kulturen and Verlag Schwabe and Co. AG, 9–14.

Rao, N. and K. Suresh, 2001, 'Domestic Tourism in India', in K. Ghimire, ed., *The Native Tourist*, London: Earthscan Publications, 198–228.

Rapoport, Amos, 1984, 'Culture and Urban Order', in John Agnew, John Mercer and David Sopher, eds, *The City in Cultural Context*, Boston: Allen and Unwin, 50–75.

Ratter, B., 1997, 'Resource Management Changes in the Caribbean: The Eco-Eco Approach', in B. Ratter and W-D. Sahr, eds, *Land, Sea and Human Effort in the Caribbean*, Proceedings of the 28th International Geographical Congress Symposium. Hamburg: Institute of Geography, University of Hamburg.

Raz, Aviad E., 1999, *Riding the Black Ship: Japan and Tokyo Disneyland*, Cambridge: Harvard University Asia Center.

Reid, Anthony, 1988, *Southeast Asia in the Age of Commerce 1450–1680: Volume One: The Lands Below the Winds*, New Haven: Yale University Press.

—— 1993, 'Introduction: A Time and a Place', in Anthony Reid, ed., *Southeast Asia in the Early Modern Era: Trade, Power and Belief*, Ithaca: Cornell University Press, 1–19.

—— 1994, 'Early Southeast Asian Categorization of Europeans', in Stuart B. Schwartz, ed., *Implicit Understandings: Observing, Reporting, and Reflecting on the Encounter between Europeans and Other Peoples in the Early Modern Era*, Cambridge: Cambridge University Press, 268–294.

Reisinger, Yvette and Carol J. Steiner, 2006, 'Reconceptualizing Object Authenticity', *Annals of Tourism Research*, 33, 65–86.

REST, 2003, *Community-Based Tourism: The Sustainability Challenge*, Responsible Ecological Social Tours Project, Thailand.

Rex, J., 1986, *Race and Ethnicity*, Milton Keynes: Open University Press.

Richter, Linda K., 1989, *The Politics of Tourism in Asia*, Honolulu, University of Hawai'i Press.

—— 1992, 'Political Instability and Tourism in the Third World', in David Harrison, ed., *Tourism in the Less Developed Countries*, New York: Halsted Press, 35–46.

—— 1993, 'Tourism Policy-Making in South-East Asia', in Michael Hitchcock, Victor T. King and Michael J. G. Parnwell, eds, *Tourism in South-East Asia,* London: Routledge, 179–199.

—— 1999, 'After Political Turmoil: The Lessons of Rebuilding Tourism in Three Asian Countries,' *Journal of Travel Research*, 38, August, 41–45.

—— 2001, 'Where Asia Wore A Smile: Lessons of Philippine Tourism Development', in Valene L. Smith and Maryann Brent, eds, *Hosts and Guests Revisited: Tourism Issues of the 21st Century*, New York: Cognizant Publications, 283–297.

—— 2003, 'International Tourism and Its Global Health Consequences', *Journal of Travel Research*, 41, 4, 340–347.

—— 2004, 'Not Home Alone: International Issues Surrounding the Travelling Child', *Tourism Recreation Research*, 29, 1, 27–35.

—— 2005, 'Not a Minor Problem: Developing Travel Policy for the Welfare of Children,' *Tourism Analysis,* 10, 1, 27–36.

—— 1980, 'The Political Uses of Tourism: A Philippine Case Study', *Journal of Developing Areas*, 14, 234–257.

Richter, Linda K. and William L. Waugh, 1986, 'Terrorism and Tourism as Logical Companions', *Tourism Management*, 7, 4, 230–238.

—— 1991, 'Terrorism and Tourism as Logical Companions', in S. Medlik, ed., *Managing Tourism*, Oxford: Butterworth-Heinemann, 318–327.

Richter, Linda K. and William L. Richter, 1985, 'Policy Choices in South Asian Tourism', *Annals of Tourism Research*, 12, 2, 201–217.

Richter, William L. and Linda K. Richter, 2003, 'Human Trafficking, Globalization and Ethics', *PA Times*, 26, 2, February, 4.

Riedel, J. and W. S. Turley, 1999, *The Politics and Economics of Transition to an Open Market Economy in Vietnam*, Technical Papers No. 152, Paris: OECD Development Centre.

Riley, P., 1988, 'Road Culture of International Long-Term Budget Travellers', *Annals of Tourism Research*, 15, 313–328.

Robertson, A. F., 1984, *People and the State: An Anthropology of Planned Development*, Cambridge: Cambridge University Press.

Robertson, Roland, 1994, *Globalization: Social Theory and Global Culture*, 3rd edition, London: Sage.

—— 1995, 'Glocalization: Time-Space and Homogeneity-Heterogeneity', in M. Featherstone et al., eds, *Global Modernities*, London: Sage Publications, 25–44.

Robinson, G. B., 1995, *The Dark Side of Paradise: Political Violence in Bali*, Ithaca: Cornell University Press.

Robson, J. H. M., 1911 and 1923, 'Hints for Motorists', in Cuthbert Woodville Harrison, ed., *An Illustrated Guide to the Federated Malay States*, London: The Malay States Information Agency.

Rodenburg, E., 1980, 'The Effects of Scale in Economic Development: Tourism in Bali', *Annals of Tourism Research*, 7, 2, 177–196.

Roebuck, J. and P. McNamara, 1973, 'Ficheras and Free-Lancers: Prostitution in a Mexican Border City', *Archives of Sexual Behaviour*, 2, 3, 231–244.

Rogers, C., 1988, 'Damage to Coral Reefs in Virgin Islands National Park and Biosphere Reserve from Recreational Activities', *Proceedings of the Sixth International Coral Reef Symposium*, Townsville, Australia, 2, 405–410.

Rosaldo, Renato, 1989, *Culture and Truth: The Remaking of Social Analysis*, Boston: Beacon Press.

Ross, W., 2003, 'Sustainable Tourism in Thailand: Can Ecotourism Protect the Natural and Cultural Environments?', Second Meeting of the Academic Forum for Sustainable Development, 17–19 September 2003, Fremantle, Western Australia.

Royle, S. A., 2001, *A Geography of Islands: Small Island Insularity*, London: Routledge.

Ruitenbeek, J. and C. Cartier, 2001, *Komodo National Park, Indonesia: Economic Issues, Analyses and Prescriptions*, Washington, D. C.: International Finance Corporation.

Said, Edward, 1978, *Orientalism*, Harmondsworth: Penguin.

—— 1993, *Culture and Imperialism*, New York: Alfred Knopf.

Salazar, Noel B., 2005, 'Tourism and Glocalization: "Local" Tour Guiding', *Annals of Tourism Research*, 32, 628–646.

Samudra, Imam, 2004, *Aku Melawan Teroris* (I Oppose Terorism), Solo: Jazera.

Santikarma, D., 2001, 'The Power of "Balinese Culture"', in U. Ramseyer and I G. R. Panji Tisna, eds, *Bali: Living in Two Worlds: A Critical Self-Portrait*, Basel: Museum der Kulturen and Verlag Schwabe and Co. AG, 27–35.

—— 2003a, 'The Model Militia: A New Security Force in Bali is Cloaked in Tradition', *Inside Indonesia*, 73, 14–16.

—— 2003b, 'Bali Erect', *Latitudes*, 34, 12–17.

—— 2003c, '*Ajeg* Bali: Dari gadis cilik ke Made Schwarzenegger', *Kompas*, 7 December 2003.

Sarad, 2002a, 'Bali Bom Bening', *Sarad*, 32, November 2002.

—— 2002b, 'Ketika Bali Tanpa Toris', *Sarad*, 33, December 2002.

—— 2003a, 'Bukan Salah Krama Tamiu Datang', *Sarad*, 34, January 2003.

—— 2003b, 'Payung baru desa adat', *Sarad*, 36, March 2003.

—— 2003c, 'Setahun Bom Bali', *Sarad*, 42, October 2003.

—— 2003d, 'Titah Latah Ajeg Bali', *Sarad*, 43, November 2003.

—— 2003e, 'Sudahi Kelahi Sesami Bali', *Sarad*, 44, December 2003.

—— 2005a, 'Tanda-Tanda Zaman Kehancuran', *Sarad*, 60, April 2005.

—— 2005b, 'Musuh Bersama Bali', *Sarad*, 61, May 2005.

Sarsorn, Nuan, 1997, 'Tourism and Cultural Development in Thailand', in Shinji Yamashita, Kadir H. Din and J. S. Eades, eds, *Tourism and Cultural Development in Asia and Oceania*, Kebangsan, Malaysia: Penerbit Universiti, 48–60.

Sato, Machiko, 2001, *Farewell to Nippon: Japanese Lifestyle Migrants in Australia,* Melbourne: Trans Pacific Press.

Satria Naradha, A. B. G., ed., 2004, *Ajeg Bali. Sebuah Cita-cita*, Denpasar: Pustaka Bali Post.

Saunders, Graham, 1993, 'Early Travelers in Borneo', in Michael Hitchcock, Victor T. King, and Michael J. G. Parnwell, eds. *Tourism in South-East Asia*, London, Routledge, 271–285.

SCETO, 1971, *Bali Tourism Study: Report to the Government of Indonesia*, Paris: UNDP/IBRD.

Schalken, W., 1999, 'Where are the Wild Ones? The Involvement of Indigenous Communities in Tourism in Namibia', *Cultural Survival Quarterly*, Summer, 40–42.

Scheyvens, R., 1999, 'Ecotourism and the Empowerment of Local Communities', *Tourism Management*, 20, 245–249

—— 2002a, 'Backpacker Tourism and Third World Development', *Annals of Tourism Research,* 29, 1, 144–164.

—— 2002b, *Tourism for Development: Empowering Communities,* London, Prentice Hall.

Schipani, S., 2002, *Ecotourism Status Report: Lao PDR*, Vientiane: SNV Lao PDR.

—— 2005, 'The Nam Ha Ecoguide Service in Luang Namtha: Organizational Structure and Direct Financial Benefits Generated by Community-based Tours in Luang Namtha, Lao PDR', Bangkok, UNESCO.

Schipani, Steven and Guy Marris, n.d., 'Monitoring Community Based Ecotourism in the Lao PDR: The UNESCO-NTA Lao Nam He Ecotourism Project Monitoring Protocol', UNESCO-National Tourism Authority of Lao PDR Nam Ha Ecotourism Project.

Scholte, Jan Aart, 1997, 'Identifying Indonesia', in Michael Hitchcock and Victor T. King, eds, *Images of Malay–Indonesian Identity*, Kuala Lumpur: Oxford University Press, 21–44.

Scholtes, P. R., 1998, 'Business Services and Institutional Support for Industrial Development in Vietnam', *ASEAN Economic Bulletin*, 15, 2, 184–205.

Schuerkens, Ulrike, 2003, 'The Sociological and Anthropological Study of Globalization and Localization', *Current Sociology*, 51, 3/4, Monograph 1, 2, 209–222.

Schulte Nordholt, H., 1994, 'The Making of Traditional Bali: Colonial Ethnography and Bureaucratic Reproduction', *History and Anthropology,* 8, 1–4, 89–127.

—— 2005, 'Bali: An Open Fortress'. Unpublished paper.

Seaton, A. N., 1999, 'War and Thanatourism: Waterloo 1815–1914', *Annals of Tourism Research*, 26, 1, 130–158.

Sekimoto, Teruo, 2003, 'Batik as a Commodity and a Cultural Object', in Shinji Yamashita and J. S. Eades, eds, *Globalization in Southeast Asia: Local, National and Transnational Perspectives*, New York and Oxford: Bergham Books, 111–125.

Selwyn, Tom, 1993, 'Peter Pan in South-East Asia: Views from the Brochures', in Michael Hitchcock, Victor T. King and Michael J. G. Parnwell, eds, *Tourism in South-East Asia*, London: Routledge, 117–137.

—— 1996, 'Introduction', in Tom Selwyn, ed., *The Tourist Image: Myths and Myth Making in Tourism*, Chichester: Wiley.

Setia, P., 1993, *Kebangkitan Hindu Menyongsong Abad ke–21*, Jakarta: Pustaka Manikgeni.

—— 2002, *Mendebat Bali: Catatan Perjalanan Budaya Bali Hingga Bom Kuta*, Denpasar: Pustaka Manikgeni.

Sharpley, Richard and David J. Telfer, eds, 2002, *Tourism and Development: Concepts and Issues*, Buffalo: Channel View.

Shaw, B. and G. Shaw, 1999, '"Sun, Sand and Sales": Enclave Tourism and Local Entrepreneurship in Indonesia', *Current Issues in Tourism*, 2, 1, 68–81.

Shaw, G. and A. M. Williams, 1994, *Critical Issues in Tourism: A Geographical Perspective*, Oxford: Blackwell.

Sheehan, N., 1992, *Two Cities: Hanoi and Saigon*, London: Jonathan Cape.

Shepherd, Noah, 2002a, 'How Ecotourism Can Go Wrong: The Cases of Sea Canoe and Siam Safari, Thailand', *Current Issues in Tourism*, 5, 3–4, 309–318.

Shepherd, Robert, 2002b, '"A Green and Sumptuous Garden": Authenticity, Hybridity and the Bali Tourism Project', *South East Asia Research*, 10, 63–97.

Shevan-Keller, S., 1995, 'The Jewish Pilgrimage and the Purchase of a Souvenir in Israel', in Marie-Francoise Lanfant, John B. Allcock and Edward Bruner, eds, *International Tourism: Identity and Change*, London: Sage Publications, Sage Studies in International Sociology 47, 143–158.

Shimizu, Hajime, 2005, 'Southeast Asia as a Regional Concept in Modern Japan', in Paul H. Kratoska, Remco Raben and Henk Schulte Nordholt, eds., *Locating Southeast Asia: Geographies of Knowledge and Politics of Space*, Singapore: Singapore University Press, 82–112.

Shimokawa, Yûji, ed., 2001, *Shin-sukininachatta Bankoku* (I Fall in Love with Bangkok), (New Edition), Tokyo: Futabasha.

Shimomura, Akio, 2002, 'Shakai-shisutemu toshiteno ekotûrizumu ni mukete' (Toward Ecotourism as a Social System), *Kagaku* (Science Journal), Tokyo: Iwanami Shoten, 72–7, 711–713.

Shirakawa, Tôko, 2002, *Kekkon sitakutemo dekinai otoko, Kekkon dekitemo shinai onna* (Men unable to marry despite their desire, women who won't marry even though they are able to), Tokyo: Sunmark Publishing.

Shute, Nancy, 2005, 'Of Birds and Men', *U. S. News and World Report*, April 4, 40–47.

Simamora, Adianto P. and Bambang Nurbianto, 2003, 'S. Sulawesi Now Shifts Priority to Local Tourists', *The Jakarta Post*, March 2 2003, www.kabar-irian.com/pipermail/kabar-indonesia/2003-March/000259. html (accessed June 20, 2003).

Singh, Amrik, 2000, 'Growth and Development of the Cruise Line Industry in Southeast Asia', in K. C. Chon, ed., *Tourism in South East Asia*, New York: Haworth, 139–155.

Smillie, Ian, 1997, 'NGOs and Development Assistance: A Change in Mind-Set?', *Third World Quarterly*, 18, 3, 563–577.

Smith, Valene L., ed., 1989a/1977, *Hosts and Guests: The Anthropology of Tourism*, Philadelphia: University of Pennsylvania Press (second revised and expanded edition, 1989; first edition, 1977).

—— 1989b, 'Introduction', in Valene L. Smith, ed., *Hosts and Guests: The Anthropology of Tourism*, Philadelphia: University of Pennsylvania Press, 1–17 (second revised and expanded edition, 1989; first edition, 1977).

—— 1989c, 'Preface', in Valene L. Smith, ed., *Hosts and Guests: The Anthropology of Tourism*, Philadelphia: University of Pennsylvania Press, 1–17 (revised edition; first edition, 1977).

—— 2005, 'Tourism and Terrorism: The New War', in Julio Aramberri and Richard Butler, eds, *Tourism Development: Issues for a Vulnerable Industry*, London: Channel View, 275–293.

SNV, 2006, *SNV: Lao PDR*, www.snv.org.la (accessed 2nd January 2006).

Sofield, Trevor H. B., 2000, 'Rethinking and Reconceptualizing Social and Cultural Issues in Southeast and South Asian Tourism Development', in C. Michael Hall and Stephen Page, eds, *Tourism in Southeast and South Asia: Issues and Cases*, Oxford: Butterworth-Heinemann, 45–57.

—— 2001, 'Globalization, Tourism and Culture in Southeast Asia', in Peggy Teo, T. C. Chang and K. C. Ho, eds, *Interconnected Worlds: Tourism in Southeast Asia*, Oxford: Elsevier Science, Pergamon, 103–120.

—— 2003, *Empowerment for Sustainable Tourism Development*, London: Pergamon.

Bibliography

Sofield, Trevor H. B. and F. M. S. Li, 2003, 'Processes in Formulating an Ecotourism Policy for Nature Reserves in Yunnan Province, China', in D. A. Fennell and R. K. Dowling, eds, *Ecotourism Policy and Planning*, Oxford: Cromwell Press, 141–167.

Son, Johanna, 1995, 'Changing Attitudes Key to Ending Child Sex Trade', *Street Children: Asia and the Pacific*, InterPress Service, 23 January 1995, pangaea.org/street_children/asia/asiasex.htm (visited August 2005).

Sontag, Susan, 1973, *On Photography*, New York: A Delta Book.

Specter, Michael, 2005, 'Nature's Bioterrorist', *The New Yorker*, February 28, 50–61.

Spergel, B., 2001, *Raising Revenues for Protected Areas: A Menu of Options*, Washington: World Wildlife Fund.

Spillane, J., 1987, *Pariwisata Indonesia – Sejarah dan Prospeknya*, Yogyakarta: Kanisius.

Spreithofer, Guenter, 1998, 'Backpacking Tourism in South-East Asia', *Annals of Tourism Research*, 25, 979–983.

Stanley, N., 1998, *Being Ourselves for You: The Global Display of Cultures*, London: Middlesex University Press.

Staudt, Kathleen and David Spencer, eds, 1998, *The U. S.–Mexico Border: Transcending Divisions, Contesting Identities*, Boulder: Lynnne Rienner.

Steiner, Christopher B., 1994, *African Art in Transit*, New York: Cambridge University Press.

Stewart, Pamela and Andrew Strathern, 2004, *Witchcraft, Sorcery, Rumours and Gossip*, Cambridge: Cambridge University Press.

Stewart, Susan, 1993, *On Longing: Narratives of the Miniature, the Gigantic, the Souvenir, the Collection*, Durham: Duke University Press.

Stockwell, A. J., 1993, 'Early Tourism in Malaya', in Michael Hitchcock, Victor T. King and Michael J. G. Parnwell, eds, *Tourism in South-East Asia*, London: Routledge, 258–270.

Stonich, Susan C., 1998, 'Political Ecology of Tourism', *Annals of Tourism Research*, 25, 1, 25–54.

Suardika, I Wayan, 1996a, 'Megikat Gigolo lewat Anak', *Nusa Tenggara Minggu*, February 25 1996.

—— 1996b, 'Wanita Bule di Sarang Gigolo', *Nusa Tenggara Minggu*, February 25 1996.

Suasta, P., 2001, 'Between Holy Waters and Highways', in U. Ramseyer and I G. R. Panji Tisna, eds, *Bali: Living in Two Worlds: A Critical Self-Portrait*, Basel: Museum der Kulturen and Verlag Schwabe and Co. AG, 37–44.

Suasta, P. and L. H. Connor, 1999, 'Democratic Mobilization and Political Authoritarianism: Tourism Development in Bali', in R. Rubenstein and L. H. Connor, eds, *Staying Local in the Global Village: Bali in the Twentieth Century*, Honolulu: University of Hawai'i Press, 91–122.

Sudhyatmaka Sugriwa, I. B. G., ed., 2003, *Bom Bali*, Denpasar: Biro Humas dan Protokol Setda Propinsi Bali.

Sugimoto, Yoshio, 1993, *Nihonjin wo yameru hôhô* (The way to stop the Japanese), Tokyo: Chikuma Shobô.

Suharsono, 1994, 'The Status of Coral Reef Resource Systems and Current Research Needs in Indonesia', in J. Munro and P. Munro, eds, *The Management of Coral Reef Systems*, Metro Manila, Philippines: International Center for Living Aquatic Resources Management, ICLAM Conference Proceedings 44.

Sujaya, I. M., 2004, *Sepotong Nurani Kuta: Catatan seputar sikap warga Kuta dalam tragedi 12 Oktober 2002*, Kuta: Lembaga Pemberdayaan Masyarakat Kelurahan Kuta.

Sulistyo, H., ed., 2002, *Bom Bali: Buku putih tidak resmi investigasi teror bom Bali*, Jakarta: Pencil, 324.

Supartha, I. W., ed., 1998, *Baliku Tersayang: Baliku Malang*, Denpasar: Bali Post.

Surpha, W., 2002, *Seputar Desa Pakraman dan Adat Bali*, Denpasar: Bali Post.

Suryawan, I. N., 2004, '"Ajeg Bali" dan Lahirnya "Jago-jago" Kebudayaan', *Kompas*, 07 January 2004.

—— 2005, *Bali: Narasi Dalam Kuasa: Politik dan Kekerasan di Bali*, Yogyakarta: Ombak.

Sutherland, A., 1986, *Caye Caulker, Economic Success in a Belizean Fishing Village*, Boulder: Westview Press.

Szerszynski, Bronislaw and John Urry, 2006, 'Visuality, Mobility and the Cosmopolitan: Inhabiting the World from Afar', *The British Journal of Sociology,* 57, 1, 113–131.

Takekoshi, Yosaburô, 1942 (1910), *Nangokuki* (On the Southern Countries), Tokyo: Nihonhyôronsha.

Tan Chee-Beng, Sidney C. H. Cheung and Yang Hui, eds, 2001, *Tourism, Anthropology and China*, Bangkok: White Lotus Press, Studies in Asian Tourism No 1.

Tạp chí Du lịch (*Vietnam Tourism Review*), Institute of Tourism Development Research – Vietnam National Administration for Tourism (VNAT), Hanoi: various issues.

Tashiro, A., 2001, 'Heritage Conservation and Local Inhabitants: A Case Study of the Angkor Heritage Site' (in Japanese), *Renaissance Culturelle du Cambodge*, 18, 219–255.

Taylor, Paul Michael, ed., 1994, *Fragile Traditions: Indonesian Art in Jeopardy*, Honolulu: University of Hawai'i Press.

TDRI, 1995, *Green Finance: A Case Study of Khao Yai*, Bangkok: Thailand Development Research Institute and Harvard Institute.

Telfer, David, 2002, 'Tourism and Regional Development Issues', in R. Sharpley and D. J. Telfer, eds. *Tourism and Development: Concepts and Issues*, Buffalo: Channel View, 112–148.

Templer, R., 1998, *Shadows and Wind: A View of Modern Vietnam*, London: Abacus.

Teo, Peggy, 2003, 'The Limits of Imagineering: A Case Study of Penang', *International Journal of Urban and Regional Research*, 27, 3, 545–563.

Teo, Peggy and T. C. Chang, eds, 1998, 'Tourism in Southeast Asia', *Singapore Journal of Tropical Geography*, special issue, 19, 119–237.

Teo, Peggy, T. C. Chang and K. C. Ho, eds, 2001a, 'Preface', in Peggy Teo, T. C. Chang and K. C. Ho, eds, *Interconnected Worlds: Tourism in Southeast Asia*, Oxford: Elsevier Science, Pergamon, vi–ix.

—— 2001b, 'Introduction', *Interconnected Worlds: Tourism in Southeast Asia*, Oxford: Elsevier Science, Pergamon, v–vi.

—— 2001c, *Interconnected Worlds: Tourism in Southeast Asia*, London, Pergamon.

Teo, Peggy and Shirlena Huang, 1995, 'Tourism and Heritage Conservation in Singapore', *Annals of Tourism Research*, 22, 589–615.

Teo, Peggy and Sandra Leong, 2006, 'A Postcolonial Analysis of Backpacking', *Annals of Tourism Research*, 33, 109–131.

Teo, Peggy and Lim Hiong Li, 2003, 'Global and Local Interactions in Tourism', *Annals of Tourism Research*, 30, 287–306.

Teo, Peggy and Brenda S. A. Yeoh, 1997, 'Remaking Local Heritage for Tourism', *Annals of Tourism Research*, 24, 192–213.

Terborgh, J. and C. A. Peres, 2002, 'The Problem of People in Parks', in J. Terborgh, C. van Schaik, L. Davenport and M. Rao, eds, *Making Parks Work: Strategies for Preserving Tropical Nature*, Washington: Island Press, 307–319.

Theis, J., and H. Grady, 1991, *Participatory Rapid Appraisal for Community Development*, London: IIED.

Tilley, Christopher, 1997, 'Performing Culture in the Global Village', *Critique of Anthropology.* 17, 1, 67–89.

Tilmant, J. and G. Schmal, 1981, 'A Comparative Analysis of Coral Damage on Recreationally Used Reefs within Biscayne National Park, Florida', *Proceedings of the Fourth International Coral Reef Symposium*, University of the Philippines, 1, 187–92.

Timothy, Dallen J., 1998, 'Cooperative Tourism Planning in a Developing Destination', *Journal of Sustainable Tourism*, 6, 1, 52–68.

—— 2000, 'Tourism Planning in South East Asia: Bringing Down Borders Through Cooperation', in K. C. Chon, ed., *Tourism in Southeast Asia*, New York, Haworth, 1–38.

—— 2002, 'Tourism and Community Development Issues', R. Sharpley and D. J. Telfen, eds, *Tourism and Development: Concepts and Issues*, Buffalo, Channel View, 149–164.

—— 2003, 'Supranationalist Alliances and Tourism: Insights from ASEAN and SAARC', *Current Issues in Tourism*, 6, 3, 250–266.

Timothy, Dallen J. and Geoffrey Wall, 1997, 'Selling to Tourists: Indonesian Street Vendors', *Annals of Tourism Research*, 24, 322–340.

Titib, M., ed., 2005, *Dialog Ajeg Bali*, Surabaya: Paramita.

TNC (The Nature Conservancy), PHKA (Direktorat Jenderal Perlindungan Hutan dan Konservasi Alam) and Putri Naga Komodo, 2002, *Komodo National Park Collaborative Management Initiative: Smart Partnership for Conservation*, Online.

Tomlinson, John, 1999, *Globalization and Culture*, Chicago: University of Chicago Press.

Tổng cục Du lịch Viet Nam, 1997, *He Thong Cac Van Ban Hien Hanh ve Quan ly Du lich* (The System of Operative Legal Texts in the Administration of Tourism), Ha Noi: Nha Xuat ban Chinh tri Quoc gia (National Political Publishing House).

Tosun, C., 2000, 'Limits to Community Participation in the Tourism Development Process in Developing Countries', *Tourism Management*, 21, 613–633.

Tourism Indonesia, 2002, 'Foreign Tourist Arrivals Up', Tourism Indonesia Internet site, www.tourismindonesia.com/index_news.html, news item dated 2 February 2002.

Tourism Malaysia, 2005, www.mocat.gov.my.

Tourism Resource Consultants, 1999, *Report on the Pacific Ecotourism Workshop*, Taveuni, Fiji Islands, 28–31 July 1998, Tourism Resource Consultants: Wellington.

TourismConcern, 2000, 'Fair Trade in Tourism', Bulletin 2: Corporate Social Responsibility, London: TourismConcern (www.tourismconcern.org.uk/downloads/pdfs/corp-soc-responsibility.pdf).

Toyota, Mika, 1996, 'The Effects of Tourism Development on an Akha Community: A Chiang Rai Village Case Study', in Michael J. G. Parnwell, ed., *Uneven Development in Thailand*, Aldershot: Avebury, 226–240.

Tran Van Dan, 1999, '39 năm Du lịch Việt Nam' (39 years of tourism in Vietnam), *Tap chi Du lich*, July, 7, 34.

Tratalos, J. and T. Austin, 2001, 'Impacts of Recreational SCUBA Diving on Coral Communities of the Caribbean Island of Grand Cayman', *Biological Conservation*, 102, 67–75.

The Travel Industry Yearbook, 2001, *The Big Picture, 2001*, Spencertown, New York: Travel Industry Publishing Co.

Tribe, John, 1997, 'The Indiscipline of Tourism', *Annals of Tourism Research*, 24, 638–657.

Truong, Thanh-Dam, 1983, 'The Dynamics of Sex-Tourism: The Case of Southeast Asia', *Development and Change*, 14, 4, 533–553.

—— 1990, *Sex, Money and Morality: Prostitution and Tourism in South-East Asia*, Zed Books: London.

Turner, L. and J. Ash, 1975, *The Golden Hordes: International Tourism and the Pleasure Periphery*, London: Constable.

Turner, P., B. Delahunty, P. Greenway, J. Lyon, C. McAsey and D. Willett, 1995, *Indonesia: A Travel Survival Kit*, (4th Edition), Hawthorne, Victoria: Lonely Planet Publications.

Turner, Patricia, 1993, *I Heard It on the Grapevine: Rumor in African-American Culture*, Berkeley: University of California Press.

U. S. Department of State, 2004, 'Background Note: Cambodia', October. www.state.gov/r/pa/ei/bgn/2732.htm.

—— 2004, 'Background Note: Laos', October. www.state.gov/r/pa/ei/bgn/2770.htm.

UNDP (United Nations Development Programme), 2005, *Human Development Report 2005*, UNDP/Oxford University Press: Oxford.

UNDP (United Nations Development Programme)/World Bank, 2003, *Bali, Beyond the Tragedy: Impact and Challenges for Tourism-led Development in Indonesia*, Jakarta, UNDP/USAID/The World Bank.

UNEP (United Nations Environment Programme), 2001, 'Ecotourism and Sustainability', *Industry and Environment*, 24, 3–4, Nairobi: United Nations Environment Programme.

—— 2005, *After the Tsunami: Rapid Environmental Assessment*, (www.unep.org/tsunami/tsunami_rpt.aspf) accessed 24 June 2005.

UNESCO, 2004, *The National Tourim Authority of Lao PDR-UNESCO Nam Ha Ecotourism Project, Phase II*, Bangkok: UNESCO.

Urry, John, 1990, *The Tourist Gaze: Leisure and Travel in Contemporary Societies*, London: Sage.

—— 1993, 'The Tourist Gaze "Revisited"', *The American Behavioural Scientist*, 36, 2, 172–186.

—— 1995, *Consuming Places*, London: Routledge.

Van Broeck, A., 2002, 'The (Missing) Gender Dimension: A Review of Tourism Literature on Latin America and the Caribbean', in H. Dahles and L. Keune, eds, *Tourism Development and Local Participation: Latin American and Caribbean Cases*, New York: Cognizant Communication Corporation, Chapter 9.

Van Schaardenburgh, A. M., 2002, 'Locals and Foreigners: Tourism Development, Ethnicity, and Small-Scale Entrepreneurship in Chauita, Costa Rica', in H. Dahles and L. Keune, eds, *Tourism Development and Local Participation: Latin American and Caribbean Cases*, New York: Cognizant Communication Corporation, Chapter 5.

Vann, Elizabeth F., 2006, 'The Limits of Authenticity in Vietnamese Consumer Markets', *American Anthropologist*, 108, 2, 286–296.

Vatikiotis, M., 1993, *Indonesian Politics Under Suharto: Order, Development and Pressure for Change*, London: Routledge.

Vickers, Adrian H., 1987, 'Hinduism and Islam in Indonesia: Bali and the Pasisir World', *Indonesia*, 44, 31–58.

—— 1989, *Bali: A Paradise Created*, California: Periplus Editions Inc.

—— 2002, 'Bali Merdeka? Internal Migration, Tourism and Hindu Revivalism', in M. Sakai, ed., *Beyond Jakarta: Regional Autonomy and Local Society in Indonesia*, Adelaide: Crawford House, 80–101.

—— 2003, 'Being Modern in Bali after Suharto', in T. A. Reuter, ed., *Inequality, Crisis and Social Change in Indonesia: The Muted Worlds of Bali*, London and New York: RoutledgeCurzon, 17–29.

Vietnam Investment Review (VIR), Ministry of Planning and Investment and Vietnam Investment Review Ltd, Hanoi, various issues.

Vogt, J., 1976, 'Wandering: Youth and Travel Behaviour', *Annals of Tourism Research*, 4, 2, 74–105.

Volkman, Toby Alice, 1984, 'Great Performances: Toraja Cultural Identity in the 1970s', *American Ethnologist*, 11, 152–169.

—— 1985, *Feasts of Honor: Ritual and Change in the Toraja Highlands*, Urbana and Chicago: University of Illinois Press.

—— 1987, 'Mortuary Tourism in Tana Toraja', in Rita Kipp and Susan Rodgers, eds, *Indonesian Religions in Transition*, Tucson: University of Arizona Press, 161–167.

—— 1990, 'Visions and Revisions: Toraja Culture and the Tourist Gaze', *American Ethnologist*, 17, 91–110.

Wagner, Ulla, 1977, 'Out of Time and Place: Mass Tourism and Charter Trips', *Ethnos*, 42, 38–52.

Wagner, Ulla and B. Yamba, 1986, 'Going North and Getting Attached: The Cases of Gambians', *Ethnos*, 51, 3–45.

Walker, Andrew, 1999, *The Legend of the Golden Boat: Regulation, Trade and Traders in the Borderlands of Laos, Thailand, China and Burma*, Richmond, Surrey: Curzon Press.

Wall, Geoffrey, 1996a, 'One Name: Two Destinations: Planned and Unplanned Coastal Resorts in Indonesia', in L. Harrison and W. Husbands, eds, *Practicing Responsible Tourism*, Chichester: Wiley, 41–57.

—— 1996b, 'Perspectives on Tourism in Selected Balinese Villages', *Annals of Tourism Research*, 23, 123–137.

—— 2001, 'Conclusion: Southeast Asian Tourism Connections: Status, Challenges and Opportunities', in Peggy Teo, T. C. Chang and K. C. Ho, eds, *Interconnected Worlds: Tourism in Southeast Asia*, Oxford: Elsevier Science, Pergamon, 312–324.

Wall, Geoffrey and Heather Black, 2004, 'Global Heritage and Local Problems: Some Examples from Indonesia', *Current Issues in Tourism*, 7, 4 and 5, 436–439.

Walle, Alf H., 1997, 'Quantitative Versus Qualitative Tourism Research', *Annals of Tourism Research*, 24, 524–536.

Wallerstein, Immanuel, 1976, *The Modern World System: Capitalist Agriculture and the Origins of the European World Economy in the Sixteenth Century*, New York: Academic Press.

—— 1979, *The Capitalist World Economy*, Cambridge: Cambridge University Press.

Walpole, M. J. and H. J. Goodwin, 2000, 'Local Economic Impacts of Dragon Tourism in Indonesia', *Annals of Tourism Research*, 27, 3, 559–576.

—— 2001, 'Local Attitudes Towards Conservation and Tourism Around Komodo National Park', *Environmental Conservation*, 28, 2, 160–166.

Walpole, M. J., H. J. Goodwin and K. G. R. Ward, 2001, 'Pricing Policy for Tourism in Protected Areas: Lessons from Komodo National Park, Indonesia', *Conservation Biology*, 15, 1, 218–227.

Wang, Ning, 1999, 'Rethinking Authenticity in Tourism Experience', *Annals of Tourism Research*, 26, 349–370.

Wanhill, Stephen, 1998, 'The Role of Government Incentives', in William Theobald, ed., *Global Tourism*, 2nd edition, Boston: Butterworth-Heinemann, 339–360.

Warna, W. dkk., 1990, *Kamus Bali-Indonesia*, Denpasar: Dinas Pendidikan Dasar Propinsi Dati I Bali.

Warner, R., 1997, *Shooting at the Moon: Story of America's Clandestine War in Laos*, Vermont: Steerforth Press.

Warren, C., 1990, *The Bureaucratisation of Local Government in Indonesia: The Impact of the Village Government Law (UU N°5 1979) in Bali*, Clayton, Monash University, Working Paper 66.

—— 1993, Adat *and* Dinas: *Balinese Communities in the Indonesian State*, Kuala Lumpur: Oxford University Press.

—— 1998, 'Symbols and Displacement: The Emergence of Environmental Activism on Bali', in A. Kalland and G. Persoon, eds, *Environmental Movements in Asia*, Richmond, Surrey: Curzon Press, 179–204.

—— 2000, '*Adat* and the Discourses of Modernity in Bali', in A. Vickers and I. N. Darma Putra, eds, *To Change Bali: Essays in Honor of I Gusti Ngurah Bagus*, Denpasar: Bali Post, in association with the Institute of Social Change and Critical Inquiry, University of Wollongong, 1–14.

—— 2004, '"Adat" in Balinese Discourse and Practice: Locating Citizenship and the Commonwealth', unpublished paper presented to the Workshop on Adat Revivalism in Indonesia's Democratic Transition, organised by Asia Research Institute, National University of Singapore, on 26–27 March 2004, at the Nongsa Point Marina, Batam, Indonesia.

Watson, G. Llewellyn and Joseph P. Kopachevsky, 1994, 'Interpretations of Tourism as Commodity', *Annals of Tourism Research*, 21, 643–660.

Weaver, David B., 1990, 'Grand Cayman Island and the Resort Cycle Model', *Journal of Travel Research*, 2, 2, 4–15.

—— 2002, 'Asian Ecotourism: Patterns and Themes', *Tourism Geographies*, 4, 153–172.

—— 2006, *Sustainable Tourism: Theory and Practice*, Oxford: Elsevier Butterworth-Heinemann.

Wedakarna, A. A. N. A., 2002, 'Mempertanyakan aksi "Bali For The World"', *Bali Post*, 22 December 2002.

WES: World Ecotourism Summit, 2002, 'Quebec Declaration on Ecotourism'.

Westerhausen, K., 2002, *Beyond the Beach: An Ethnography of Modern Travellers in Asia*, White Lotus: Bangkok.

Wheeller, B., 1994, 'Eco-tourism: A Ruse by any Other Name', in C. Cooper and A. Lockwood, eds, *Progress in Tourism and Hospitality Management,* Volume 6, Chichester: John Wiley, 3–11.

White, Luise, 2000, *Speaking with Vampires: Rumor and History in Colonial Africa,* Berkeley: University of California Press.

Whitten, T., M. Mustafa and G. Henderson, 1987, *The Ecology of Sulawesi,* Yogyakarta: Gadjah Mada University Press.

Whitten, T., Soeriatmadja and S. Afiff, 1996, *The Ecology of Java and Bali: Volume II,* The Ecology of Indonesia Series, Hong Kong: Periplus.

Widnyani, I. N. and I. K. Widia, 2003, *Ajeg Bali. Pecalang dan Pendidikan Budi Pekerti,* Surabaya: SIC.

Wiendu Nuryanti, 1996, 'Heritage and Postmodern Tourism', *Annals of Tourism Research*, 23, 249–260.

—— 1998, 'Tourism and Regional Imbalances: The Case of Java', *Indonesia and the Malay World*, 26, 136–144.

Wijaya, I. N., 2004, 'Melawan Ajeg Bali: Antara Eksklusivitas dan Komersialisasi', *Tantular. Jurnal Ilmu Sejarah*, 2, 158–178.

Wilkinson, P., 1989, 'Strategies for Tourism in Island Microstates', *Annals of Tourism Research*, 16, 153–177.

Wilkinson, Paul F. and Wiwik Pratiwi, 1995, 'Gender and Tourism in an Indonesian Village', *Annals of Tourism Research*, 22, 283–299.

Williams, China, et al., 2004, *Southeast Asia on a Shoestring*, 12th edition, Oakland: Lonely Planet.

Williams, M. C., 1992, *Vietnam at the Crossroads,* London: Pinter Publishers.

Wilshusen, P. R., S. R. Brechin, C. L. Fortwangler and P. C. West, 2002, 'Reinventing a Square Wheel: Critique of a Resurgent "Protection Paradigm" in International Biodiversity Conservation', *Society and Natural Resources*, 15, 17–40.

Wilson, David, 1993, 'Time and Tides in the Anthropology of Tourism', in Michael Hitchcock, Victor T. King and Michael J. G. Parnwell, eds, *Tourism in South-East As*ia, London: Routledge, 32–47.

—— 1997, 'Paradoxes of Tourism in Goa', *Annals of Tourism Research*, 24, 1, 52–75.

Wilson, Thomas and Hastings Donnan, eds, 1994, *Border Approaches: Anthropological Perspectives on Frontiers,* Lanham: University Press of America.

—— eds, 1998, *Border Identities: Nation and State at International Frontiers,* Cambridge: Cambridge University Press.

—— 1999, *Borders: Frontiers of Identity, Nation and State*, New York: Berg.

Winter, Tim, 2003, 'Tomb Raiding Angkor: A Clash of Cultures', *Indonesia and the Malay World*, 31, 58–68 (special issue on 'Tourism and Heritage in South-East Asia', edited by Michael Hitchcock and Victor T. King).

—— 2004, 'Landscape, Memory and Heritage', *Current Issues in Tourism*, 7, 4, 330–345.

Wockner, Cindy, 2006a, 'Bali Bomb Code', *The Daily Telegraph*, 26 April, 2006.

—— 2006b, 'How Bali Bombers Planned Mission', *The Advertiser*, 29 April 2006.

Wolf, Y., 1993, 'The World of the Kuta Cowboy: A Growing Subculture of Sex, Drugs and Alcohol is Evident Among Male Youth in the Tourist areas of Bali and Lombok as they Seek an Alternative to Poverty', *Inside Indonesia*, June 1993, 15–17.

Wolters, O. W., 1999, *History, Culture and Region in Southeast Asian Perspectives*, Ithaca, New York: Cornell University, Southeast Asia Publications, Studies on Southeast Asia 26, revised edition in cooperation with the Institute of Southeast Asian Studies, Singapore, originally published by ISEAS, Singapore, 1982.

Wong, P. P., 2001, 'Small-Scale Tourism and Local Community Development: The Case of the Gili Islands, Lombok, Indonesia', Proceedings of the WTO/UNEP Asia-Pacific Seminar on Island Tourism in Asia and the Pacific. World Tourism Organization: Madrid.

Wood, Megan Apler and Thaïs Leray, 2005, 'Corporate Responsibility and the Tourism Sector in Cambodia', Washington D. C.: Foreign Investment Advisory Service, International Finance Corporation.

Wood, Robert E., 1979, 'Tourism and Underdevelopment in Southeast Asia', *Journal of Contemporary Asia*, 9, 274–287.

—— 1984, 'Ethnic Tourism, the State, and Cultural Change in South-East Asia', *Annals of Tourism Research*, 11, 353–374.

—— 1993, 'Tourism, Culture and the Sociology of Development', in Michael Hitchcock, Victor T. King and Michael J. G. Parnwell, eds, *Tourism in South-East Asia*, London: Routledge, 48–70.

—— 1997, 'Tourism and the State: Ethnic Options and "Constructions of Otherness"', in Robert E. Wood and Michel Picard, eds, *Tourism, Ethnicity and the State in Asian and Pacific Societies*, Honolulu: University of Hawai'i Press, 1–34.

—— 1980, 'International Tourism and Cultural Change in Southeast Asia', *Economic Development and Cultural Change*, 28, 3, 561–581.

Worah, S., 2002, 'The Challenge of Community-Based Protected Area Management', *Parks*, 12, 2, 80–90.

Worden, Nigel, 2003, 'National Identity and Heritage Tourism in Melaka', *Indonesia and the Malay World*, 31, 31–43 (special issue on 'Tourism and Heritage in South-East Asia', edited by Michael Hitchcock and Victor T. King).

World Bank, 2005, *Country Assistance Strategy for the Lao People's Democratic Republic (PDR). Report No. 31758 LA*, Southeast Asia Country Unit: East Asia and Pacific Region, 10 March.

World Commission on Environment and Development, 1987, *Our Common Future*, Oxford: Oxford University Press.

World Health Organisation, 2003, 'World Health Organisation Issues Emergency Travel Advisory', 15 March 2003, www.who.int/crs/sars/archive/2003_03_15/en/ (accessed 24 June 2005).

World Land Trust, 1997, 'Tourism: The Industry Without Chimneys', *World Land Trust News*, 7.

WTO, 1996, *Compendium of Tourism Statistics: 1990–1994*, Madrid: World Tourism Organisation.

—— 1998, *Guide for Local Authorities on Developing Sustainable Tourism*, Madrid: UN World Tourism Organization.

—— 1999a, *Compendium of Tourism Statistics: 1993–1996*, Madrid: World Tourism Organisation.

—— 1999b, *Tourism: 2020 Vision*, Madrid: World Tourism Organisation.

—— 2001, *Compendium of Tourism Statistics: 2001 Edition*, Madrid: World Tourism Organisation.

—— 2002, *Compendium of Tourism Statistics: 2002 Edition,* Madrid: World Tourism Organisation.

—— 2005a, *Compendium of Tourism Statistics: Data 1999–2003: 2005 Edition,* Madrid: World Tourism Organisation.

—— 2005b, *Tourism Highlights, 2005*, www.world-tourism.org/facts/menu.html.

—— 2005c, 'A New Horizon for Bali's Tourism', United Nations World Tourism Organisation press release on crisis management and repositioning seminar held in Bali, 10–11 December 2005.

—— 2006, *Yearbook of Tourism Statistics*, Madrid: United Nations World Tourism Organization.

WTO News, 2004, Quarter 4, Issue No. 4, 7.

World Travel and Tourism Council, 2005a, 'Southeast Asia: The 2005 Travel and Tourism Economic Research', www.wttc.org/2005tsa/pdf/1. Southeast%20Asia.pdf (accessed on 24 June 2005).

—— 2005b, *World Travel and Tourism: Sowing the Seeds of Growth: The 2005 Travel and Tourism Economic Research*, London: World Travel and Tourism Council.

Wu, A., 1998, 'Taiwanese Cultural Identity: Tourism and Museum Perspectives', Unpublished MA Thesis, University of North London.

WWF, 2000, *Tourism Certification: An Analysis of Green Globe 21 and Other Tourism Certification Programmes*, Surrey: World Wildlife Fund UK.

Xie Guangmao, 2000, 'Women and Social Change along the Vietnam–Guangxi Border', in Grant Evans, Chris Hutton and Kuah Khun Eng, eds, *Where China Meets Southeast Asia: Social and Cultural Change in the Border Regions,* Singapore: Institute of Southeast Asian Studies, 312–327.

Yahya, Faizal, 2003, 'Tourism Flows Between India and Singapore', *International Journal of Tourism Research*, 5, 347–67.

Yamashita, Shinji, 1994, 'Manipulating Ethnic Tradition: The Funeral Ceremony, Tourism, and Television among the Toraja of Sulawesi', *Indonesia,* 58, 69–82.

―― 1997, 'Manipulating Ethnic Tradition: The Funeral Ceremony, Tourism, and Television among the Toraja of Sulawesi, Indonesia', in Shinji Yamashita, Kadir H. Din and J. S Eades, eds, *Tourism and Cultural Development in Asia and Oceania*, Bangi: Universiti Kebangsaan Malaysia Press, 83–103.

―― 2003a, *Bali and Beyond: Explorations in the Anthropology of Tourism*, translated with an introduction by J. S. Eades, New York and Oxford: Berghahn Books.

―― 2003b, 'Introduction: "Glocalizing" Southeast Asia', in Shinji Yamashita and J. S. Eades, eds, *Globalization in Southeast Asia: Local, National and Transnational Perspectives*, New York and Oxford: Berghann Books, 1–17.

―― 2004, 'Constructing Selves and Others in Japanese Anthropology: The Case of Micronesia and Southeast Asia', in Shinji Yamashita, J. Bosco and J. S. Eades, eds., *The Making of Anthropologies in East and Southeast Asia,* New York and Oxford: Berghahn Books, 90–113.

―― forthcoming, 'Global Touristscapes in a Rainforest: Ecotourism in Sabah, Malaysia', in William C. Gartner and Cathy H. C. Hsu, eds, *Handbook of Tourism Research*, Binghamton, New York: The Haworth Press.

Yamashita, Shinji, Kadir H. Din and J. S. Eades, eds, 1997, *Tourism and Cultural Development in Asia and Oceania*, Bangi: Penerbit Universiti Kebangsaan Malaysia.

Yamashita, Shinji, J. S. Eades and Kadir H. Din, 1997, 'Introduction: Tourism and Cultural Development in Asia and Oceania', in Shinji Yamashita, Kadir H. Din and J. S. Eades, eds, *Tourism and Cultural Development in Asia and Oceania*, Bangi: Penerbit Universiti Kebangsaan Malaysia, 13–31.

Yamashita, Shinji and Mayumi Ono, 2006, '"Long-Stay" Tourism and International Retirement Migration: A Japanese Perspective', paper presented at the workshop on 'pensioners on the move', 5–7 January 2006, Singapore.

Yeoh, Brenda S. A., Tan Ern Ser, Jennifer Wang and Theresa Wong, 2001, 'Tourism in Singapore: An Overview of Policies and Issues', in Tan Ern Ser, Brenda S. A. Yeoh and Jennifer Wong, eds, *Tourism Management and Policy: Perspectives from Singapore*, Singapore: World Scientific.

Yeoh, Brenda S. A., and Lily Kong, 1995, *Portraits of Place, History, Community and Identity in Singapore*, Singapore: Times Editions.

Zakai, D. and N. Chadwick-Furman, 2002, 'Impacts of Intensive Recreational Diving on Reef Corals at Eilat, Northern Red Sea', *Biological Conservation*, 105, 179–187.

Zeppel, Heather, 1995, 'Getting to Know the Iban: The Tourist Experience of Visiting an Iban Longhouse in Sarawak', in Victor T. King, ed., *Tourism in Borneo: Issues and Perspectives*, Williamsburg: Borneo Research Council Proceedings Series, 59–66.

―― 1997, 'Meeting "Wild People": Iban Culture and Longhouse Tourism in Sarawak', in Shinji Yamashita, Kadir H. Din and J. S. Eades, eds, 1997, *Tourism and Cultural Development in Asia and Oceania*, Bangi: Penerbit Universiti Kebangsaan Malaysia, 119–140.

Zoete, B. de and W. Spies, 1938, *Dance and Drama in Bali*, London: Faber and Faber.

Index

357